THE SAFE CITY

The European Institute for Comparative Urban Research, EURICUR, was founded in 1988 and has its seat with Erasmus University Rotterdam. EURICUR is the heart and pulse of an extensive network of European cities and universities. EURICUR's principal objective is to stimulate fundamental international comparative research into matters that are of interest to cities. To that end, EURICUR coordinates, initiates and carries out studies of subjects of strategic value for urban management today and in the future. Through its network EURICUR has privileged access to crucial information regarding urban development in Europe and North America and to key persons at all levels, working in different public and private organizations active in metropolitan areas. EURICUR closely cooperates with the Eurocities Association, representing more than 100 large European cities.

As a scientific institution, one of EURICUR's core activities is to respond to the increasing need for information that broadens and deepens the insight into the complex process of urban development, among others by disseminating the results of its investigations by international book publications. These publications are especially valuable for city governments, supranational, national and regional authorities, chambers of commerce, real estate developers and investors, academics and students, and others with an interest in urban affairs.

EURICUR website: http://www.euricur.nl

This book is one of a series to be published by Ashgate under the auspices of EURICUR, the European Institute for Comparative Urban Research, Erasmus University Rotterdam. Titles in the series are:

National Urban Policies in the European Union
Leo van den Berg, Erik Braun and Jan van der Meer

The European High-Speed Train and Urban Development
Leo van den Berg and Peter M.J. Pol

Growth Clusters in European Metropolitan Cities
Leo van den Berg, Erik Braun and Willem van Winden

Information and Communications Technology as Potential Catalyst for Sustainable Urban Development
Leo van den Berg and Willem van Winden

Sports and City Marketing in European Cities
Leo van den Berg, Erik Braun and Alexander H.J. Otgaar

Social Challenges and Organising Capacity in Cities
Leo van den Berg, Jan van der Meer and Peter M.J. Pol

City and Enterprise
Leo van den Berg, Erik Braun and Alexander H.J. Otgaar

The Student City
Leo van den Berg and Antonio P. Russo

European Cities in the Knowledge Economy
Leo van den Berg, Peter M.J. Pol, Willem van Winden and Paulus Woets

The Safe City
Safety and Urban Development in European Cities

LEO VAN DEN BERG
PETER M.J. POL
GIULIANO MINGARDO
CAROLIEN J.M. SPELLER

Euricur
EUROPEAN INSTITUTE FOR COMPARATIVE URBAN RESEARCH

European Institute for Comparative Urban Research
Erasmus University Rotterdam
The Netherlands
www.euricur.nl

Routledge
Taylor & Francis Group
LONDON AND NEW YORK

First published 2006 by Ashgate Publishing

Reissued 2019 by Routledge
2 Park Square, Milton Park, Abingdon, Oxon, OX14 4RN
52 Vanderbilt Avenue, New York, NY 10017

Routledge is an imprint of the Taylor & Francis Group, an informa business

Publisher's Note
The publisher has gone to great lengths to ensure the quality of this reprint but points out that some imperfections in the original copies may be apparent.

A Library of Congress record exists under LC control number:

ISBN 13: 978-0-8153-9820-2 (hbk)
ISBN 13: 978-1-138-35752-5 (pbk)
ISBN 13: 978-0-429-06062-5 (ebk)

Contents

List of Figures

List of Tables

Preface

Safety has become a topical subject for many European cities. Numerous local authorities are investing in the attractiveness of urban areas hoping to attract new inhabitants and economic activities. Closely related to this attractiveness is the perceived safety. It appears that fear of crime can have a large impact on location decisions of urban actors. When, for instance, people perceive urban areas as unsafe and decide to out-migrate or not to locate there, there can be serious economic consequences for those areas.

For the City of Rotterdam safety is also a topical subject. It was the most important issue during the local election campaigns in 2002 and since then security has become the most important policy topic. Furthermore, Rotterdam installed a dedicated alderman for safety, an administration office for safety and has introduced a Safety Index to enable the progress of the local policies to be monitored. In addition, it was the mayor of Rotterdam who initiated this comparative urban study on safety, in which 11 European cities are involved.

The comparative study is embedded within the European URBACT SecurCity network. SecurCity officially began in February 2004. The SecurCity network concentrates on the improvement and effectiveness of policies and actions to combat (perceived) insecurity in the participant cities. SecurCity addresses one of the main areas of intervention of URBAN: the improvement of safety and the quality of life (see http://www.urbact.org).

We should like to express our very special thanks to the key initiators of this study: Mr I.W. Opstelten (Mayor of Rotterdam), Chris de Lange, Murat Altunbas, Cleo Pouw and Hugo van der Leek (all from the Development Corporation Rotterdam). Their support has greatly contributed to this study. Furthermore, we would like to thank our contact persons from the participating cities. Their help and input has been of great value in preparing and organizing our visits to the cities. And, perhaps most importantly, it was very pleasant to work with them. Therefore, many thanks to Marc Smits, Tom Meeuws (Antwerp), Ann Fehilly, Phil Walker (Glasgow), Hans Metzemakers (The Hague), Ulla Korhonen-Wälmä (Helsinki), Roel Kraaij (Heerlen), Keith Lawrence (Leeds), Angelo Pansini (Bari), Kevin Mitchell, Mark Kenwood (Birmingham), Michael Kneisel, Janine Tavangarian (Gera) and Alena Šindlerová (Prague).

Also, we should like to thank all the people we interviewed in the 11 cities who were willing to dedicate some of their precious time to our study. They were our main source of information and new insights. Of course, the authors take full responsibility for the content of this study.

Rotterdam, June 2005

Chapter 1

Introduction

In the 1970s and 1980s many cities in Europe experienced a severe crisis. Their population decreased and their economic base weakened. Families left the centres of larger cities for suburban dwellings or smaller communities. Increasing congestion and inner city deterioration made cities a less attractive place. The growing mobility of citizens – thanks to increased car ownership and improved public transport – allowed people to live further away from their work, in larger houses. The centres of many European cities became less attractive, the quality of housing deteriorated, and low-skilled immigrants moved in. Shopping functions suffered from the loss of purchasing power in the city and faced heavy competition from new suburban shopping malls. For Western Europe, many observed a turning point in this downward spiral by the end of the 1980s (van den Berg, 1987; Cheshire and Hay, 1989). Population decline came to an end in several European cities; several cities managed to transform their industrial base and developed new economic growth sectors (van den Berg et al., 2001); this trend was confirmed in the 1990s, when a number of European cities experienced a remarkable revival. In time, this 'turning point' coincided with the start of a set of developments that is commonly described under the heading of 'the information revolution'. This refers to economic, societal and institutional changes that are driven and/or strongly supported by innovations in information and communication technologies (ICTs), and their widespread adoption by companies and citizens (Castells, 1996).

Many cities have benefited from the information revolution because they offer favourable conditions for networks of complex exchange and transactions. In the information age, face-to-face contact appears to be very important as a source of information and in the exchange of tacit knowledge (Leonard-Barton, 1982; Malmberg et al., 1996). Dense cities with good connections enhance the possibility of such contacts. Consequently, the information revolution is associated with the emergence of new location factors (van den Berg, 1987; Mitchell, 1999). Cities need to be pleasant and easily accessible in order to attract (or retain) transient companies and highly-skilled workers. Soft location factors have become important. In particular, the quality of the urban living and working environment is gaining ground as a condition for economic success.

Cities of a certain minimum size that have been able to offer high quality of life as well as excellent connections have been able to benefit most. They manage to attract the demanding well-educated workforce, and are able to attract more visitors as well. The global cities in particular have proved very successful; they have a number of mutually reinforcing resources. In sum, the information revolution made agglomeration economies more important. The welfare development of many cities appears, however, to be threatened by increasing feelings of insecurity. 'From being a relatively safe space, the city has – especially over the past 100 years – become associated more with danger than with safety. The density of cities tends to intensify such dangers as civil unrest, crime and contaminated air and water' (Ellin, 2001, p. 869).

In general, urban safety is a very basic precondition for urban economic and social development. Or, to put it negatively, insecurity, caused by whatever factors, seriously hampers it. 'Further, the fear of crime, which received scant attention until the 1980s, is now recognised as a more widespread problem than crime itself (Hale, 1996, quoted in Bannister and Fyfe, 2001, p. 807). Increasingly, the perceived safety of a place is becoming a factor in choice of location for companies and citizens. In many cities neighbourhoods with high crime rates face a downward spiral as companies and citizens tend to abandon these areas. 'Together, crime and the fear of crime have been seen to blight urban life, attacking the economic, social and political fabric of cities. Seemingly, crime and the fear of crime have drained cities of their vital essence: the celebration of difference' (Bannister and Fyfe, 2001, p. 807). 'The fear factor has certainly grown in recent decades if measured by locked car and house doors, security systems, the popularity of gated communities, the purchasing of hand-guns and the increasing surveillance of public spaces, not to mention the unending reports of danger emitted by the mass media' (Ellin, 2001, p. 872).

In this international investigation, we discuss how actual and perceived safety have evolved within the last decade. In this respect, we shall try to infer some safety trends in the participating cities and to find out whether the actual and perceived safety are related to each other. The perceived safety might also be influenced by other factors, such as media covering and the quality of the built environment. We also want to study such influencing factors. Moreover, in this research, we shall try to discover the role (perceived) safety plays in urban development. We should like to know whether (perceived) insecurity could hinder a sound development of urban areas. In addition, we want to see how local authorities react to (perceived) insecurity. What kind of policies are being developed and carried out and what are the results of these policies? Do local actors have (sufficient) influence on insecurity? It can be assumed that they are dependent on other actors, such as the national government. We want to find out who the relevant actors are, what their contributions are and how they cooperate. Furthermore, we should like to find out *best practices* in tackling insecurity.

1.1 Methodology and Research Questions

Our central research question is:

> What is the role of security in urban development in the twenty-first century and what are the local policy implications?

From this, we derived the following sub-questions:

1 Can statistics reveal a (significant) change of urban safety and/or urban attractiveness? Have cities become less safe (and attractive) during the last decades in the perception of citizens? With respect to the urban region involved which endogenous and exogenous factors influence (the changed perception of) urban safety? What factors seem to have the largest influence on safety perceptions?
2 What are the economic, social and spatial consequences of the changed perception of urban safety and attractiveness? How can the changed spatial behaviour affect economic development of different types of urban regions?
3 What do local authorities do to increase the safety and attractiveness within urban areas? What can be learned from successful safety projects in cities?

To be more concise on the issue, we built up a theoretical framework in which we link safety with urban development (see Figure 1.1). This SAP model is elaborated in this chapter and will be applied to the case studies. SAP is the acronym for **S**afety perception, urban **A**ttractiveness and Spatial behaviour and **P**olicy reactions. These three factors influence each other and have impact on urban development. By studying these three elements we can get a good insight into the role of security in urban development and into the local policy implications. 'Sap' also means a vital juice circulating in plants, implying vigour or vitality. With the help of this theoretical model and the empirical application we hope to contribute to more knowledge on the vitality of urban regions.

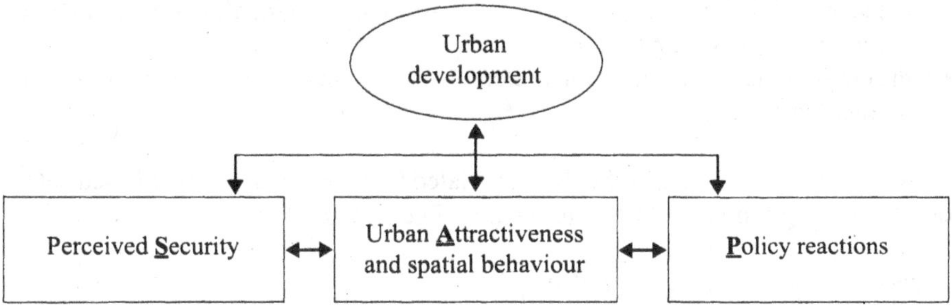

Figure 1.1 The SAP model and the structure of the chapters of this book

This research aims to contribute to the knowledge exchange among cities on the role of security in urban development. By participating as a case study in this project, cities could share experiences and learn from one another. We carried out 11 case studies: Rotterdam, Antwerp, Glasgow, The Hague, Helsinki, Heerlen, Leeds, Bari, Birmingham, Gera and Prague. The case study of Rotterdam is larger and more detailed than the others as the project started with this city and they are the leading partner in the network. Due to time constraints, the remaining case studies are less detailed. Nevertheless, all case studies cover the above-mentioned topics of perceived security, urban attractiveness and spatial behaviour and policy reactions.

This research project is part of a European exchange network programme, SecurCity (URBACT).[1] Within this programme several workshops have been held on urban safety topics. These workshops supported this research programme, because there was a clear intended synergy between the contents of the workshop and the research project. The political attention for urban safety is high in all these European cities. This was for these cities a reason to participate in the exchange network and the related research project. Moreover, this high political attention showed that these cities were interesting to analyse, because apparently it is a relevant topical issue for them, with potential consequences on the urban growth possibilities. In each city we held eight to 22 semi-structured field interviews with key persons involved in urban safety and safety policies. Moreover, we analysed relevant (policy) documents from the cities involved. The draft case studies were sent to the discussion partners, who sent back their remarks to the authors.

1.2 Themes of the Case Studies

For our case studies, we chose – together with representatives of each participating city – a policy programme or project that aims to improve (the perception of) urban safety. Prerequisites for these programmes or projects were:

- the project or programme was related to one of the themes mentioned below;
- the programme or project had a sufficient critical size;
- the scope of the programme or project was quite substantial: that is, it included several policy fields and actors;
- the programme or project should preferably have an innovative approach or include innovative aspects.

We focused on three specific themes related to urban security: area-based safety problems; drugs and insecurity; and youth crime and insecurity.

Theme 1 Area-based Safety Problems

It appears that many cities develop policies focused on specific areas with safety problems. These could be central or deprived areas. By developing tailor-made safety policies, the specific problems of these areas can be tackled in a better way. We tried to identify the actual safety problems and the perceived safety in those specific areas. Moreover, we wanted to discuss the possible social, spatial and economic consequences of changing safety situations in those areas. Finally, we wanted to find out what kind of specific area-based policies are being set up and to discuss some 'best practices'. Cases with area-based safety problems in this study are Rotterdam, Antwerp, Glasgow, The Hague, and Helsinki.

Figure 1.2 The case studies involved in this comparative research

Theme 2 Drugs and Insecurity

For many cities the production, trade and use of drugs are important sources of safety problems. They can generate a relatively high level of nuisance for local residents, who might decide, as a consequence, to move to other areas. Therefore, this safety problem can have direct social, spatial and economic consequences. For the cases within this theme, Leeds and Heerlen, we wanted to find out the actual and perceived safety problems related to drugs. We also wanted to study the related consequences and the developed safety policies to reduce the problem. For this topic, too, we will discuss some best practices.

Theme 3 Youth Crime and Insecurity

In some cities, fear of crime is particularly influenced by youth behaviour. It can be a source of nuisance, diminishing the perceived attractiveness of urban neighbourhoods. In other cities, the situation might be worse; relatively much (petty) crime committed by youth can take place. This can be the reason for a considerable amount of policy attention by local authorities, because relatively innocent petty crime might ultimately lead to serious crime if insufficient measures are being taken. Moreover, perceived unsafe situations caused by youth behaviour might also lead to changing the behaviour of inhabitants and companies, possibly resulting in declining neighbourhoods. For these cases we will study the actual and perceived safety situations, possible consequences for local urban developments, developed policies and best practices. Cases for the topic 'youth crime and insecurity' are Bari, Birmingham, Gera and Prague.

1.3 Structure

The book will be structured as follows. Chapter 2 will evaluate existing theories on safety and urban development. Besides, the framework of analysis for all case studies will be introduced. Chapters 3 to 13 describe the separate case studies. As mentioned before, there is an emphasis on the case of Rotterdam. Therefore, Chapter 3 will be more extensive than the other case studies. Each case study is structured according to the framework of analysis, meaning that all three pillars of the SAP model (see Figure 1.1) are covered. Finally, the synthesis of Chapter 14 evaluates and draws conclusions about the safety problems and policy measures undertaken by four different types of cities.

Note

1 All cities mentioned are member of the URBACT-SecurCity network, with the exception of the city of Antwerp.

Chapter 2

Security and Urban Development

2.1 Introduction

In this chapter, we present some theoretical considerations concerning safety and urban development. Moreover, we present and discuss the framework of analysis for the case studies. In Section 2.2 we discuss the meaning of urban safety and security. Section 2.3 discusses the actual and perceived security and causes of insecurity. In Section 2.4 we go into the changing perception of urban safety and attractiveness and the factors that influence the perceived insecurity. Moreover, this section discusses the spatial behaviour of urban actors as a consequence of a changing perception. In Section 2.5, we go into policy reactions of local public and private actors. Section 2.6 concludes this theoretical chapter.

2.2 Urban Safety and Security

The notion 'security' is broader than 'safety'. Safety concerns particularly physical protection (for example, against robberies, violence and traffic accidents). Security also concerns more intangible threats, such as terrorist attacks, natural disasters and war. To both notions, safety and security, the essence is the lack of the opposite situation: feeling unsafe and insecurity. Security is the quest for a situation or moment in which something undesirable does not exist or does not occur (Crawford, 2002, p. 7). Safety is the condition of being safe from risk or danger; the quality or state of not presenting or involving risk or danger. Security, however, means more; it is guarding or guaranteeing freedom from danger or anxiety. Besides, 'fear of crime can be defined as the wide range of emotional and practical responses to crime and disorder made by individuals and communities' (Pain, 2001, p. 901). However, this difference exists only in the English language and most of the policy documents used in this comparative study do not acknowledge this linguistic distinction. Therefore, we will use safety and security as synonyms in this document.

Security can be predominantly related to a spatial entity, such as a nation or an urban region that wants to protect its citizens against all kinds of possible risks and threats. There are quite a number of risks and threats in an urban environment, varying in nature and impact. They vary from violence, physical threats and street robbery, via drugs nuisance, nuisance from prostitution and human traffic, corruption, unsafe traffic situations and environmental problems to terrorist attacks (see Figure 2.1). In

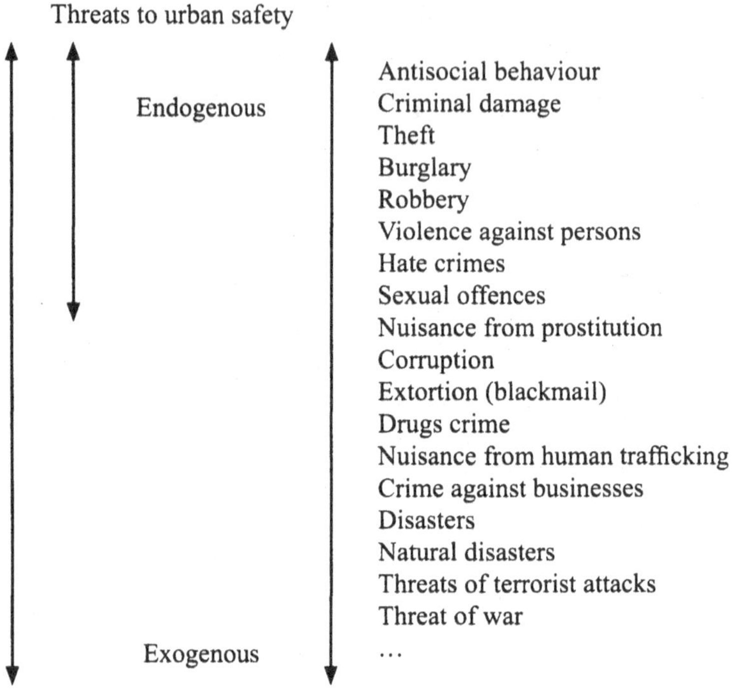

Figure 2.1 Possible threats to the safety of an urban environment

this research, we categorize the factors influencing urban safety in a range between two extremes. On one side we consider endogenous factors – those factors that can be influenced by measures taken by local authorities. On the other side there are exogenous factors – factors that cannot be influenced by measures taken by local authorities.

The meaning of 'security' varies according to different disciplines. The term 'security' operates at both a macro and micro level, relating to mass threats of warfare and political terrorism as well as to small-scale, localized disorders, antisocial behaviour and affronts to quality of life (Crawford, 2002, p. 6). In the current research we directly link 'security' with 'quality of the urban living and residential working environment'. When choosing a location or transport mode, with a growing welfare level, the demands of urban actors for quality of life rise because a secure environment contributes to a better quality of life.

According to Maslow's pyramid, security comes after physiological needs such as food and drink as the most fundamental need of human beings (Maslow, 1943) (see Figure 2.2). When someone's primary needs are not satisfied, they will demand all that person's attention, while the other needs play a minor role at that moment (Verhage and Cunningham, 1984, p. 110). When physiological needs are satisfied,

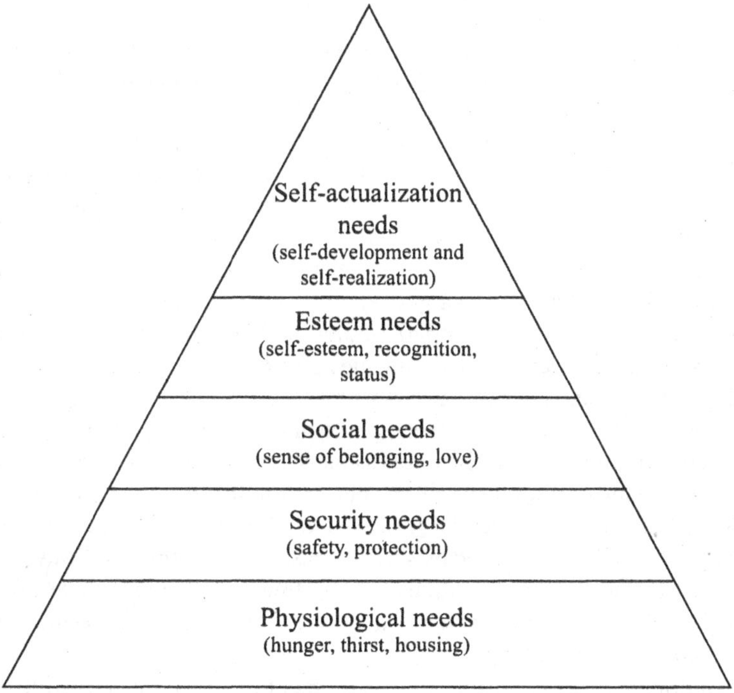

Figure 2.2 Maslow's hierarchy of human needs

Source: Kotler, 1984, p. 138.

but not those of security, the latter will assume priority. The actor involved will try to improve their security situation, but this is not always possible on the short term. When security is no longer guaranteed in urban districts, people who can afford to move will leave those areas. It is therefore logical that urban policy-makers want to change such situations because, in the long term, urban insecurity might imply that particularly middle and high-income groups leave certain urban areas and that those areas end up in downward patterns.

2.3 Perceived Security and the Causes of Insecurity

2.3.1 Perception of Urban Security

There is a long tradition of fighting fear of crime, from the urban walls in pre-modern cities to gentrified enclaves in modern cities. The construction of walls around the pre-modern city was partly motivated by fears for the physical safety of the inhabitants, but it was also about protecting the profitability of economic activity within the city (Bannister and Fyfe, 2001, p. 810). Hausmann's rebuilding of Paris in the mid-nineteenth century was unequivocally a political project designed to reduce the threat posed by 'dangerous classes' (Ellin, 1997, p. 18). Nowadays, a multitude of actions are undertaken to improve the perception of urban security. Christopherson (1994) highlights, for instance, the ways in which the abilities to maintain property values in gentrified enclaves of inner cities and profits in the malls, restaurants and cultural centres of downtown are inevitably bound up with questions of security. One of the questions related to gentrified enclaves is whether those enclaves increase or reduce fear of crime. Ellin (1996, p. 153) argued that though gates, policing and surveillance systems, defensive architecture, and neo-traditional urbanism do contribute towards giving people a greater sense of security, they also contribute to accentuating fear by increasing paranoia and distrust among people.

Nowadays we are aware of the importance of having plenty of openness in urban environments in order to stimulate cities as places of diversity, because this diversity can boost economic development. For a sound economic development of cities their openness appears to be an essential feature. This openness, or freedom of the urban actors, can however be threatened by safety measures. According to Crawford (2002, p. 6) security occupies a tense relationship with freedom; there is a trade-off between the two, such that more freedom demands less security and more security demands less freedom.

Is insecurity in cities increasing, or is the perception of security changing? In 2001, in The Netherlands, the large majority of the population (70 per cent) felt safe, 25 per cent sometimes felt unsafe and 5 per cent often felt unsafe (Sociaal en Cultureel Planbureau, 2002). These percentages have been quite stable in the last decade. According to Vanderveen (2001), there is, however, an increasing 'riskism' because, among other things, there is so much (media) attention on insecurity. She wants to express with this notion that people want to *exclude* risks; they are no longer willing to face any risks. If there is a risk, people want to directly involve institutions such as the government. They are, however, disappointed in the government, because in many urban regions the police and the judicial system seem to be incapable of fighting the increasing amount of crime.

Fear is also determined in relation to an individual's ability to exercise control over his or her own life and the behaviour and activities of others. People are fearful because of their inability (on their own or with the assistance of others) to prevent or to cope with the consequences of victimization (Bannister and Fyfe, 2001, p. 809). If the police are less able to clear up crimes it is, on the one hand, more attractive for criminals to commit crimes and, on the other hand, people might become more fearful of becoming a victim of crime.

2.3.2 Factors Influencing Perceived Insecurity

Perceived insecurity is influenced by many factors. It is not only objective safety (or simply, the crime rate) that determines people's perception of safety: factors like the quality of the built environment, the balance of the socioeconomic growth or disasters may have in impact as well. As previously stated, the factors influencing safety perceptions can be categorized between two poles: those that can be influenced by local authorities (endogenous factors) and those that cannot be influenced by local authorities (exogenous factors) (see Figure 2.1). The division between these two categories is continuous, meaning that exogenous factors can be partly endogenous as well. In what follows the most striking factors threatening perceptions of urban safety will be described.

Actual crime

As stated, the most obvious cause of perceived insecurity is the occurrence of actual crime. The idea of higher population shares being afraid of crime in case of higher crime rates might be plausible. Thus a high frequency of, *inter alia*, theft, burglary, robbery and violence against persons will normally lead to relatively much fear of crime. On the contrary, however, the occurrence of relatively little crime does not mean that there is a relatively low fear of crime. Because there are many other causes of fear of crime, like those we will discuss within this section, there might be urban areas with relatively low in actual crime rates but simultaneously facing relatively high fear of crime.

Poor quality of the built environment

In the current information era, and with the relatively high welfare of people, urban actors set great store by a high quality of built environment. Normally, people will perceive urban districts with a relatively bad quality of public spaces and houses as less safe than those with relatively good quality. The key for understanding fear of crime lies not in direct experiences of crime, or with control *per se*, but rather in how people experience and interpret urban space. Fear is embedded in the physical and social characteristics of place and the familiarity of that space to the individual (Bannister and Fyfe, 2001, p. 809). Decisive factors in this respect are the quality of the public space, the presence of attractive amenities and facilities and the quality of the houses. Regarding the last-mentioned, the *broken-windows* theory (Wilson and Kelling, 1982) suggests, among other things, that community order, disorder and crime are connected in a 'kind of developmental sequence', such that relatively small acts of incivility (for example, broken windows) progressively lead to other, potentially larger ones, including criminal behaviour. An example used is the experiment of abandoned automobiles left on the streets of the Bronx in New York and Palo Alto, California, where both were plundered and destroyed following initial acts of theft and vandalism (Schneider and Kitchen, 1992, p. 117).

An example of the influence of the quality of the houses is the decision of the borough board of the Rotterdam suburb Hoogvliet to destroy one-quarter of its housing stock, in order to rebuild a district that is expected to be perceived as more secure. Part of the housing stock was considered to be unattractive (predominantly four-storey 'galleried flats'). The average time that apartments stood empty was two years. Only those people who could not afford anything else rented these flats. This resulted in a too large concentration of low-income groups (van den Berg et al., 2003,

p. 25). With the renewed housing stock, Rotterdam Hoogvliet hopes to attract more affluent people.

People might perceive buildings with a 'human scale' as more secure than those lacking this feature. After the terrorist attacks on New York of 9 September 2001, some urban actors wanted to avoid living, working or staying in high-rise buildings, in particular those buildings that are for some reason conspicuous, situated for instance near famous landmarks. On the other hand, apartments in high-rise buildings in particular are often better protected against all kinds of threat than 'normal houses' are, because of, amongst other things, underground parking, a 24-hour door service and closed-circuit television camera systems. That is one reason why such apartments are in high demand among the security-conscious rich. A year after 9/11, in spite of sombre predictions, high-rises were still firmly in fashion in cities such as New York and London.[1]

Familiarity with urban districts influences the safety perception of urban actors. Some actors seldom visit certain areas, but they might hear or read about incidents in those areas. From that limited information, they may think that those areas are unsafe (or are 'no-go areas'), though this does not have to be the perception of people who visit those places frequently. Thus the mental map of places may differ according to familiarity with those places. Examples of such areas are the Bronx in New York and the Bijlmer in Amsterdam.

As a reaction to perceived lack of safety, there might be a tendency to build gated communities. High-income earners in particular might be inclined to protect their living environment from the surroundings. The phenomenon of gated communities (which can be found in the USA particularly) can be seen as an example of private security operation, in the sense that people use their purchasing power to opt into a security system that is designed to keep others out, or at the very least to screen them carefully (Schneider and Kitchen, 2002, p. 275). As a result, complete housing districts can become private areas, forbidden to outsiders. This might be counterproductive for the attractiveness and living conditions of an urban area.

Socioeconomic structure

The socioeconomic structure (income differences, number of low-skilled inhabitants, unemployment rates) has an impact on safety perception. Urban actors might perceive districts with many inhabitants earning relatively low incomes as less safe compared to districts with inhabitants earning relatively high incomes. This might be an important reason for suburban districts with a domination of higher income groups not to provide houses for low-income groups. In addition, people with a rising income set greater store on urban attractiveness and safety and will pay more for security measures.

In an information economy there is a close relationship between the composition of the population and the regional-economic structure. In general, the more knowledge-intensive the local economic activities are, the higher the average education level of the population will be. On the other hand, cities with predominantly industrial activities will have a relatively low average education level. In addition, it can be stated that the more vital a local economy is, the lower the local unemployment will be and the more successful a local economy is, the larger its attraction for (potential) inhabitants (well-educated as well as poorly-educated). Furthermore, within a region with a relatively weak economic structure, people might feel less comfortable because of bad economic perspectives. Consequently, in such a region the fear of crime might be higher than, *ceteris paribus*, in a strong economic region because people often engage in criminal behaviour if they do not have legal alternatives, such as education and regular employment.

According to Ehrlich (1973), there is a strong positive relation between income inequality and crimes against property. The larger the income inequality, the more crime against property will take place. Consequently, in urban districts with relatively large income differences there is a greater chance of crime against property. We assume that the larger the welfare differences, the bigger the demand for measures to reduce fear of crime, such as building gentrified enclaves, will be.

Threats and risks related to welfare differences are relevant for varying spatial scale levels: at district level and urban level as well as national and international level. At district level, relatively large welfare differences might lead to many burglaries. At urban level, they might lead to relocation of inhabitants and companies, but also to riots. At national and international level, they might lead to migration flows. At international level, large welfare differences might lead to tensions bewteen countries which could culminate in war or terrorist attacks.

The occurrence of a dual society with increasing differences between the 'haves' and the 'have-nots' can thus lead to more crime. A policy implication is that reducing income differences at several spatial levels will lead to a reduction of crime and thus a possible improvement of the perceived urban security.

Disasters

In recent years, several large-scale disasters have occurred in Europe with large social-economic consequences. Examples are the fireworks-storage explosion in the Dutch city of Enschede and the fires in the tunnel of Mont Blanc between France to Italy. As a result, there is an increasing awareness that it is important to prevent the occurrence of such serious disasters.

With latent disasters, there can be a clear relationship between economic activities and possible risks (as with the storage of fireworks or chemicals). In other cases there can be a direct relationship between the built environment and possible risks to the society (for instance, with tunnels or rail infrastructure). The presence of a large airport or seaport in an urban region will increase the chances of disasters occurring. Moreover, the larger the population density in an urban area, the larger the effect of disasters can be. When there are serious disasters, emergency services can often only try to prevent the extension of the effects of disasters. That means that in such situations a certain number of fatalities cannot be avoided.

It is thus important to consider the risks of disasters in an early stage. For large infrastructure projects already in the development stage it is essential to try to reduce chances or the effects of disasters. Another implication of the growing awareness is that certain economic activities (like fireworks factories and storage) will no longer be allowed in built-up areas. Rules and legislation have become stricter in this field. This means either the restriction of residential development (for instance in port and industrial areas), or the restriction of industrial development (in the vicinity of residential areas). It can thus be expected that the growing awareness of the risks of disasters – because of increasing scarcity of good sites and stricter security requirements – will increase the costs of economic activities and infrastructure projects.

Immigration without integration In the last decade the number of immigrants from developing to developed countries has increased sharply. Immigrants tend to settle predominantly in urban regions. Because of language and other integration problems this might generate tensions with the local population. The larger the influx of foreigners in urban areas, the bigger the integration problems might become.

Because of their often relatively weak socioeconomic position, immigrants tend to locate and concentrate in urban areas with the lowest housing prices. These areas are normally the least attractive places within urban regions. In districts with relatively many inhabitants with a foreign background people might feel less safe, because of communication problems (foreigners unable to speak the local language), unemployment (and consequently low incomes) or other integration problems.

According to Engbersen (1997), exclusion from the formal society can take place in four domains: labour, state care and state access, family and spatial planning. Regarding labour, there are long-time unemployed people who have very little prospect of a normally paid job. They are decribed as the *outsider class*, a group of citizens outside the formal employment structure. Regarding state care, there are citizens who receive little or no (financial) support from the government and regarding state access, there are citizens who have no legal status in a country.[2] The domain family refers to having limited supporting social networks and the domain spatial planning refers to concentrations of vulnerable population groups in certain neighbourhoods. People acting in the informal world (criminals) can have a strong negative influence on the security perception of urban actors.

Also, Oude Engberink (2001) argues that in The Netherlands in government debates and scientific circles three dimensions in the relationship between ethnic minorities and crime have been intensively discussed in the 1990s continuing up to the present:

- petty crime by certain groups of youngsters of ethnic origin and their troubled relationship with the forces of law and order and society in general, in the context of urban safety;
- serious, organized crime in drug trafficking, involving the criminal activities of foreign groups and their possible infiltration into parts of the bureaucratic system and the real-estate market;
- and, more recently, the organized trafficking of illegal immigrants and the trade in foreign women for prostitution.

Discussions about the impact of immigration on the security of a city are often troubled by taboos. It can be argued, however, that immigrants often have a relatively weak position in the labour market, caused by lack of linguistic skills and lack of education and/or degrees. Without a regular job, immigrants can be inclined to find other (informal) ways to raise money, which can sometimes lead to committing crimes.

There is an increasing awareness of the importance of good integration into local society, parallel with an increasing awareness of the structural character of the immigration flows in cities in the western hemisphere. Much attention will have to be paid to education and integration of immigrants to prevent them from operating in informal activities.

Terrorist attacks

The strong link between urban security and urban development has never been as clear as in the city of New York. There, the terrorist attacks of 9 September 2001 undermined the very basic feelings of safety. The events were a catalyst for the USA to build a large global coalition to fight terrorism. But there is an urban dimension to this as well. Many cities all over the globe have become aware of their immense vulnerability. They have started a process of rethinking the importance of safety and seeking appropriate answers to cope with new threats.

What will the longer run impacts of events like 9/11 and Madrid train bombings of 11 March 2004 be? Companies might realize that it is unwise to concentrate many (human) resources in one spot. Deconcentration may be a longer-run response. If true, the question will be whether deconcentration will take place on the metropolitan level (from inner cities to suburbs) or on the urban system level (from major cities to smaller cities).

According to Savitch and Ardashev (2001), cities have become the central venues for terror. Terrorism can come in many forms: bombing raids, biochemical attacks, plane hijacking, etc. A vulnerability analysis is advisable for this aspect: what are the most likely targets, and what means do terrorists have to achieve their goals? Not only has terrorism taken on a global cast with international linkages, it is also apparent that cities have become the stage on which this tragic drama is played. There are many reasons why this has occurred:

1 the *assets* of cities make them *rich targets*. Densely packed and heterogeneous with a great mix of industrial and commercial infrastructure, cities are the wellsprings of prosperity and economic growth (Prud'homme, 1994; Savitch, 1996);
2 cities have become 'nodes' for a *vast international network of communications*. Economic complexity and global interdependence have converted cities into powerful command centres, directing billions of dollars in investment, managing millions of people and controlling thousands of worksites around the globe (Friedman and Wolff, 1982; Meyer, 1986). This may be an considerable sign of power, but it is also a very visible sign of vulnerability. A well-placed explosion can produce enormous reverberations and paralyse a city;
3 cities have considerable *symbolic value*. They are not only dense agglomerations of people and buildings, but guardians of national prestige and assets. They hold the tangible symbols of military, political and financial power on a national scale.

The seriousness of terrorist attacks such as 9/11 and the bombings in the Madrid trains will determine the length of the period in which investors and tourists change their location behaviour (because of fear). Crucial questions in this respect are how much trust actors have in the security of certain urban areas and, how much can this trust be damaged by (fear of) terrorist attacks?

Natural disasters

A last important factor for insecurity is the possible occurrence of natural disasters. Examples are flooding, earthquakes, hurricanes and the eruption of volcanoes. It is clear that within some urban regions the fear of specific natural disasters is much higher than in other regions. The specific geographical situation largely determines whether a particular urban region is sensitive to natural disasters. Moreover, whether an urban region will be able to take sufficient measures to limit damages after the actual occurrence of disasters depends particularly on the prosperity of that region. In addition, the higher the probability of the occurrence of a natural disaster, the more such measures will be legitimated. When, for instance, the flooding of a river is not very probable, a city will be less inclined to take measures to prevent such a disaster.

2.4 Urban Attractiveness and Spatial Behaviour

2.4.1 Introduction

We assume that perceived safety influences spatial behaviour (location and transport behaviour) of citizens, companies, business visitors and tourists.[3] When people perceive cities as becoming less safe the urban attractiveness will inevitably decrease, despite eventual high investments in public areas and architecture. We discern two types of behavioural responses: short term (travel decisions) and long term (location decisions). In the short term, problems tourist and/or business visitors may decide not to visit certain urban areas (for example, Jerusalem or New York) because of perceived safety. In the long term, because of increasing fear for crime, urban actors may choose not to live or work within densely populated urban areas. The simple model can be applied on different spatial scales: the neighbourhood, metropolitan, or city system level.

Van den Berg (1987) argues that the spatial behaviour of urban actors is determined by their drive to maximize welfare. Location preferences of residents are influenced by the accessibility of three welfare potentials: 1) urban attractiveness, influenced by the perceived urban security; 2) availability and diversity of jobs and the ensuing income differences; and 3) the supply of such facilities as shops, schools, health care, culture and leisure activities. All inhabitants have their own location preferences, which influence their behaviour. One resident may prefer to live close to cultural facilities in an inner city, while another attaches more value to living in the country, enjoying the open space. The attractiveness of a location is determined by the extent to which the supply of welfare meets the demand.

The location pattern of economic activities influences location choices of inhabitants. Traditionally, it is the location of companies that determines employees' location choices. They want to live not too far from their work location. Schafer and Victor (1997, quoted in Pol, 2002) have developed the hypothesis that the typical travel-time budget stretches to one and a half hours per person per day in a wide variety of economic, social and geographic settings. With increasing welfare, people have increasing demands regarding the quality of their living environment. Since the 1960s particularly, with the rapid growth of car ownership and the extension of the highway network, people have become able live at increasing distances from urban centres of economic activities. This is particularly true for people with relatively high incomes and high education levels. It is expected that those areas that can supply a high quality of the living environment, and thus attract highly-educated inhabitants, also have enhanced chances to attract knowledge-intensive activities. In this respect also *security* can play an important role, as a high perceived social security improves the perceived quality of life in an area. Those regions that can supply a relatively secure environment will, *ceteris paribus*, attract highly-educated people and, indirectly, knowledge-intensive activities.

2.4.2 Disentanglement of Safety Perception into Three Domains

Safety problems can be disentangled into three domains (see Figure 2.3): to live and work, to visit and to move. These domains can sometimes mutually overlap; for analytical purposes it might, however, be advisable to use this distinction to study how people perceive safety in these domains, how they react to that and what specific policy reactions can be related to these domains.

To live and work

People might, for instance, judge lack of safety as a factor in the decision not *to live* in a specific area, because of the possible risks to their children. For that reason they may choose to live outside that urban area and accept relatively long daily travel times between home and work. To get a very good job in that same area might however be considered as less problematic, because they only have to be there during the daytime and they do not have to bring their children there. But if they do not definitely have to go in that specific area, people will avoid it. For instance, for (business) tourist purposes they will choose another destination that is perceived to be more safe.

When an urban area is perceived by many actors as being unsafe, it might attract only specific groups of people, such as students and immigrants, who can only afford low-rent houses. This can have a large impact on the number of business companies in that area: because of relatively low spending power all kinds of commercial facilities will close and service companies may move away because they cannot find adequate personnel there. For an urban government this can be a legitimate reason for taking specific measures to upgrade that area in order to attract other residents and business companies again (like in the already mentioned case of Rotterdam-Hoogvliet).

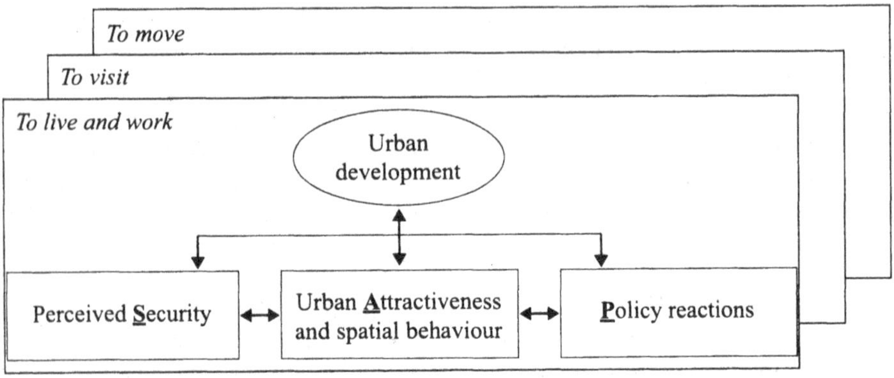

Figure 2.3 Safety perception can be disentangled into three domains

To move
Transport safety is both about the perceived safety within public transport systems and about traffic safety. Firstly, people might feel unsafe in public transport modes or at stations during some parts of the day or on certain tracks. They may therefore prefer individual transport (often the car). If the public transport system is (perceived to be) unsafe, this greatly reduces the internal accessibility, particularly in cities with high levels of congestion. Unsafe transport systems entail high social costs in terms of under-utilization of costly infrastructure. Secondly, when traffic systems are not safe, the urban attractiveness may decrease. This might be the case in urban areas in which the police are not able (any longer) to check and sanction obedience to traffic rules. For instance, when car drivers do not obey traffic rules (they exceed speed limits or neglect traffic lights), not only pedestrians and cyclists, but also other car drivers may react by wantng to avoid those urban areas.

To visit
Some urban areas have a specific meaning for cities, like the historical inner city or the central-station area. For urban governments it might be of the essence that such places are perceived to be safe, because they have an important symbolic value and/or determine the status or image of the urban region. It is indeed in these areas where most tourists and shoppers can be expected. If people perceive the inner city as relatively safe, more tourists, residents, companies and visitors might be attracted, not only in the inner city, but in the whole urban area. Cities therefore often focus their policy reactions on those places.

2.4.3 Value of Buildings and Insecurity

We expected that there might be a certain relationship between the perception of security in areas and the value of buildings. Moreover, we assumed that this relationship would be much stronger in living areas than in working areas. Thus, perceived lack of safety will probably, *ceteris paribus*, lead to stronger price decreases for residential buildings than for office buildings. This can be explained by several factors. Firstly, residents are normally confronted with unsafe environments for longer than office workers; the former for 16 hours to 24 hours a day, the latter typically not more than about eight hours a day (and only on working days). Secondly, office workers are normally more able to distance themselves from their environment than residents. Thirdly, people sometimes feel unsafe during evening and night hours, at which they are normally not at the office and often at home. Fourthly, parents do not want to present their children with unsafe situations; families thus often chose to live in relatively safe areas. Relatively safe areas located within commuting distance of important economic centres are thus often in high demand and have relatively high house prices, while relatively unsafe areas have relatively low house prices.

As already stated, there might be a relationship between perceived safety and attracting companies in the longer term. If residents move *en masse* out of a region because of safety reasons, in the next stage economic activities might follow. The first to be expected to leave in this respect are commercial activities within neighbourhoods perceived as relatively unsafe. Among the consequences will be decreasing values of both houses and commercial buildings.

Value of houses by using hedonic pricing

In this research we are interested in how urban security and attractiveness influence the location behaviour of residents. We can obtain an indication of the security and attractiveness of an urban district by the land and housing prices. This in turn will be translated in the willingness of urban developers to develop new houses, buildings for economic activities and amenities. Current and (potential) future residents will make their housing decisions according to the elements that influence the urban attractiveness, amongst other things. We have assumed that these elements are the quality of the houses, the quality of the public space, and the perception of safety.[4] We can obtain an insight into the value of houses by using *hedonic pricing*. Hedonic pricing means that a dwelling is composed of a bundle of individual components (the elements of which determine urban attractiveness), each of which has an implicit price (O'Sullivan, 2000, p. 368).

Quality of public space

The demand for housing and its price are higher in districts with a relatively high quality of public space. House owners are thus interested in a high quality of public space. This might be an important reason for the government to stimulate house ownership in urban neighbourhoods with relatively many rental houses. In the long term, this might lead to a better quality and maintenance of the public space.

Quality of the houses

(Potential) residents will judge the suitability of a house to move to according to a number of aspects, such as size, location, age and interior features. This assessment will be influenced by the *neighbourhood effect*: positive changes in the exterior appearance of one house cause *spillover benefits* (increases in market value) for surrounding houses. Consequently, house owners do have an interest in the maintenance activities of their neighbours. In contrast, when residents do not sufficiently care about the quality of their houses – for instance, when they only rent their house, and they are not interested in consolidating or increasing its value – a neighbourhood might deteriorate, with a negative impact on house prices.

Sometimes, particularly in slum neighbourhoods, there are property exploiters ('slum landlords') who buy houses at relatively low prices and let out those houses for relatively high prices (considering the quality of the houses) to inhabitants who cannot afford or do not have access to regular houses. These slum landlords who want to buy houses at relatively low prices are, in contrast with most house owners, interested in there being a relatively low quality of public space, because that would imply that they can buy more houses for relatively low prices, thus increasing their production capacity. It is in the direct interest of urban governments that want to increase the attractiveness of urban areas to fight these slum landlords.

The perception of safety

O'Sullivan (2000, p. 229) argues that the prices of housing and land are higher in communities with lower crime rates. Thus also the extent of security perception forms a component of the price of a house. This is indicated in Figure 2.4: P_N shows an urban situation in which there is hardly any crime. Here, house prices are relatively high in the city centre, and they become substantially lower, when the distance to the city centre increases. P_Y is a price function in a situation with relatively much crime. The result is low housing prices in the city centre and relatively high prices in the safer suburbs. In this situation, prices in the periphery are similar to those in the city centre. P_S shows an intermediary situation.

Thus, the higher the crime rates and/or the more people perceive an urban area as being unsafe, the lower the demand for houses will be in that district. One of the consequences of unsafe areas will be that high-income households will move to other districts, since they have higher ambition levels concerning urban attractiveness and safety, and they can afford to move sooner to other (more expensive) safer places. The result will be that land and house prices in the unsafe district will decrease. One of the questions in this respect is: what are the costs for society of decreasing land and house prices in certain urban areas?

The more successful safety policies are in an urban district, the safer the area will become: housing prices will rise and more (private) actors will be attracted to invest in housing in that area. Consequently, several developments might support each other; a Myrdalian cumulative causation process might occur (Myrdal, 1957). Positive upward patterns might be induced, generating *gentrification* effects within urban districts.

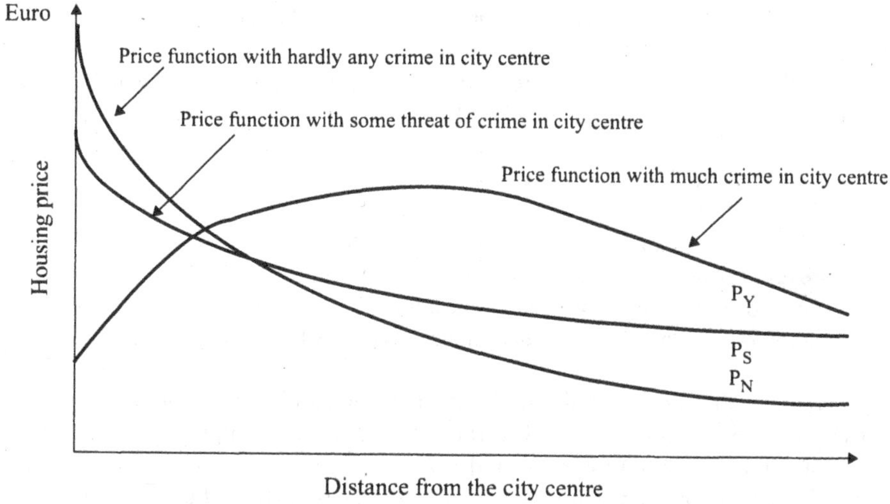

Figure 2.4 The relationship between crime in a city and housing prices

Source: O'Sullivan, 2000, p. 229.

2.5 Policy Reactions: Security Policies

2.5.1 The Interests of the Urban Government

In many cities since the 1980s there has been a noticeable trend for more organizations get involved in safety policies: this is called the *multi-agency approach*. Before that period it was more or less the exclusive domain of the judiciary and the police. Urban governments have become increasingly involved in developing policies to improve the security perception of their inhabitants. Moreover, they increasingly have to cooperate with many other actors such as inhabitants, urban planners and private developers to be effective in this field.

Normally, an urban government wants to enhance well-being within its jurisdiction. It can do so by influencing the spatial distribution, quality and quantity of the location factors. It lays down certain ambitions regarding the housing, service and economic potential of its region. The priorities set by the authorities evolve over time and with the economic conditions, and can change with the coming to office of a new (elected) government.

How the government behaves is determined by the discrepancies between the levels of the welfare potential it considers desirable and those it perceives in reality. The government will try to reduce these discrepancies, attaching different weights to different welfare elements. It may do so by adjusting the quantity and the quality of the welfare elements in question. Thus, if there is a low quality built environment, the government can stimulate the building of new houses, and/or make public spaces such as parks and streets more attractive. In addition, the government can try to make the different welfare elements more accessible by the construction of transport infrastructure or by influencing the use made of the infrastructure.

For local governments there are a number of possible motives for developing policies to improve the feelings of security and to reduce crime levels:

- to strengthen the local economy;
- to attract middle- and higher-income groups;
- to induce gentrification trends in an urban district;
- to prevent turmoil/disruption in the local community;
- to show commitment to the local community;
- to win elections and/or consolidate their power position.

Governmental bodies are limited by their responsibilities, financial means and capacity of their administration. Governments will always, implicitly or explicitly, make a trade-off between the costs and benefits of safety measures. Not all safety measures will pay off sufficiently to compensate the high costs of undertaking them. With regard to fighting local crime, O'Sullivan (2000, p. 665) discusses optimum crime levels: those situations in which the marginal prevention costs equal the marginal victim costs. According to Becker (1968, quoted in van Velthoven, 1994) the government should develop such policies by balancing the chances of getting caught and punishments in such a way that the societal welfare loss caused by criminality and by fighting criminality is as small as possible.

2.5.2 Repressive, Preventive, Reactive and Proactive Security Policies

Urban as well as national security policies can be positioned in a diagram with repressive and preventive policies on the vertical axis and reactive and proactive policies on the horizontal axis (see Figure 2.5). Repressive policies are aimed at suppressing actual crime and preventive policies at averting criminal activities. Reactive policies are those activities which react to occurring incidents. These policies have, by definition, only a short- or middle-term time horizon. Proactive policies are about strategically anticipating changes. With proactive policies cities try to fight causes of insecurity structurally.

Reactive-repressive policy is particularly about reducing crime by actions of the police and justice. When there is (too) much actual crime within urban areas, these actors are expected to react by arresting people who are committing crimes. Whether this will take place or not depends particularly on the capacity and the priorities of the police. Table 2.1 shows the differences in capacities of police forces in several European countries. Prison capacity can also be enlarged so that more punishments can be actually carried out. The USA is an example of a country in which policies are particularly reactive-repressive (Body-Gendrot, 2001, p. 921).

Reactive-preventive policies are aimed at preventing the occurrence of crime, and have a short-term or middle-term effect. Examples are the use of closed-circuit television (CCTV)-systems to prevent small-scale criminal acts and frightening potential criminals

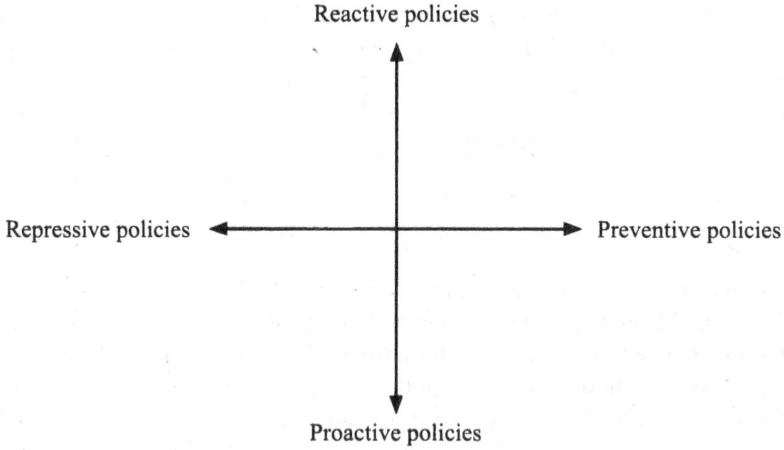

Figure 2.5 Distinction of security policies

Table 2.1 Size of police force related to number of inhabitants

	Per 100,000 inhabitants	Year of measurement
Italy	531	1998
Spain	452	2000
Greece	422	2000
France	410	2000
Belgium	406	2000
Austria	360	1999
Ireland	348	2000
USA	344	1998
England and Wales	333	2000
Sweden	319	1999
Germany	305	1999
The Netherlands	270	2001
Denmark	270	1999
Finland	202	1999

Source: 'Juridische infrastructuur in internationaal perspectief', in Ministerie van Justitie (2002), *Criminaliteitsbeheersing, Investeren in een zichtbare overheid.*

off by enlarging punishments. Organized crime can be prevented via air- and seaport checks (for instance, container scanning), intelligence actions and by information exchange between security organizations involved. An example of a country in which reactive-preventive policies are dominant is France (Body-Gendrot, 2001, p. 921). Much can also be learned in this respect from examples of the USA (see Box 2.1).

Box 2.1 Improving safety perception in urban districts in the USA

To improve the safety perception and attractiveness of urban districts some lessons can be learned from experiences in cities in the United States. Philadelphia and New York are examples of cities that improved the situation in an effective and decisive way. Key notions in their approach are *a sense of community*, *a clean city*, *investing in public space* and *zero tolerance.*

A sense of community. Backward neighbourhoods, which are perceived as insecure, often lack social structures. Moreover, they normally have an unbalanced socioeconomic structure. The disappearance of a sense of community is considered a core problem. In Philadelphia, therefore, the basis of the approach is to help building new communities. The notion *community* is, however, interpreted in a relatively broad way. Not only the inhabitants but also professionals working in a district, police officers and street cleaners form part of a community. Community Partnership Programs are set up to stimulate cooperation in order to increase the living conditions of neighbourhoods. Moreover, communities are supposed to have their own responsibilities for improving and maintaining the perceived attractiveness and security. On the one hand citizens may expect that the government will undertake the correct action, but on the other the government may also expect that citizens contribute to improving the living conditions of neighbourhoods. The latter is considered to be a fundamental element. It appears that in European countries in particular, citizens expect that the government will solve all problems to do with living conditions. This is however impossible; it will be crucial to convince each community member that they have their own responsibilities in this matter.

A clean city. Citizens feel safer in clean districts, and in clean districts there are fewer misdemeanours (cf. the *broken-windows* theory). Where small offences are tolerated, larger violations will inevitably follow, which can lead to increasing insecurity feelings, to inhabitants and companies leaving the area, and ultimately to economic, social and physical disintegration of a neighbourhood. In the American cities mentioned, 'clean' means 'very clean', thus there are no gradations of cleanness, as is often the case in European cities.

Investing in public space and facilities. Generally speaking, people feel safer when the quality of the built environment is a relatively high and neighbourhoods attract more inhabitants when there are good facilities and when they are clean.

Upward socioeconomic patterns can be expected in those neighbourhoods that meet these basic conditions. In Philadelphia and New York, special tax measures have been taken to stimulate companies to invest in backward neighbourhoods (*empowerment zones* and *keystone opportunity zones*). The aim of these measures is to restore the attractiveness of old vacant district centres for shops and offices. Moreover, rich inhabitants are invited to subsidize parks and squares. Specific public-private partnerships have been set up to fulfil this aim. For instance, private actors helped to invest in the NY Central Park to raise its quality and attractiveness. In addition, in these American cities, safety and functionality is considered more important for the use of parks and squares than their appearance.

Zero tolerance. To fight crime and misdemeanours, there is a person-related approach. Persons rather than areas (hot-spots) are central. A proper information supply is crucial in this respect. More knowledge about the facts and history of suspected wrong-doers has become available by connecting information on crime and misdemeanours (COMSTAD in NY). There are *community courts* in urban districts that penalize minor misdemeanours within a very short time period. Suspects have to appear in the community court within 24 hours and within 48 hours they have to work very visibly in their own neighbourhood as recompense to the community. Furthermore, the police work in a more efficient way, after decoupling police and administrative tasks. There was also considerable pressure on the judiciary to operate in a more effective way. This has led to reorganizations and more efficiency, with almost the same capacity. Moreover, there is a *three-strikes doctrine*: criminals receive a very long imprisonment after being sentenced three times (lifelong: in practice 15 years). To increase safety even more, within public-transport vehicles there are armed undercover police officers with the authority to arrest, rather than unarmed supervisors.

Source: Kragten and Stekelenburg, 2003.

Proactive-repressive policies are aimed at activities to fight actual crime structurally. They have a repressive character, but also a relatively long time horizon. An example is hot-spot policies in which, for the longer term, repressive policies are focused on specific areas at risk. Another example is forced psychiatric hospitalization. By proactively putting persons with psychiatric problems within closed hospitals, cities might contribute to reducing actual crime within a longer time period.

Proactive-preventive policies are aimed at preventing the occurrence of crime and risks in the longer term. The probability of actually-occurring threats and crimes can be reduced by, for instance, investing in the quality of the built environment and the socioeconomic structure. Better-educated inhabitants and new economic activities can be attracted, and informal activities can be forced back by investing in the built environment. Inhabitants' chances of getting regular jobs will increase by improving education in a region. In general, when a regional economy is doing well, informal activities can be reduced more easily.

Safety policies thus can be distinguished in four categories, although it must be stressed that these categories are not exclusive: depending on the aims of the particularly policy, a measure can be both repressive and preventive or reactive and proactive. For example, CCTV-systems can be seen as preventive, because the presence of the cameras alone may already prevent criminal behaviour. At the same time, the CCTV-system can be seen as repressive, because it is being used to track down any perpetrators.

2.5.3 Analysis According to the Organizing Capacity Framework

We are predominantly interested in *urban* policy reactions. We will investigate the possibilities of urban actors to interfere in policy fields that are related to urban safety. Legal situations of cities differ as do the abilities of cities to counteract crime. They are particularly dependent on the (financial) opportunities created by national governments. The latter often determine, for instance, the immigration policy and the (financial and juridical) preconditions for operations by police and justice. Sometimes the national (and/or European) government initiates specific security policies, through which urban governments acquire more possibilities to take action.

In this research, we focus on the policy reactions at the urban level. We want to analyse urban policy reactions on urban insecurity (given the institutional frameworks) and discuss the performance of these policy reactions. To this end, we will use the theoretical framework of organizing capacity (van den Berg et al., 1997; van den Berg et al., 2003; see Figure 2.6).

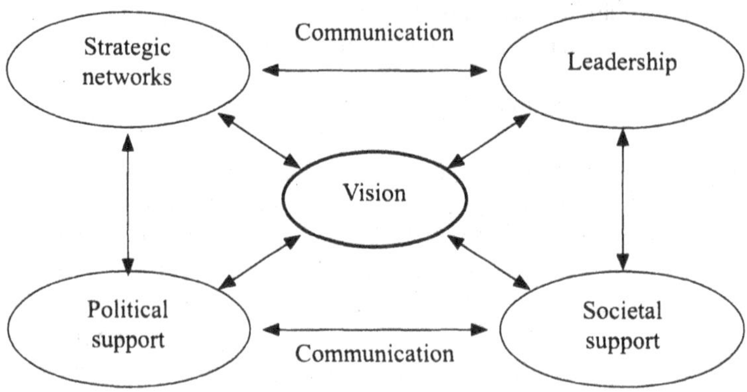

Figure 2.6 Tools for organizing capacity

Organizing capacity is understood here as the ability of those responsible for solving a problem to convene all concerned partners (public and private, internal and external), in order to jointly generate new ideas and formulate and implement a policy that responds to fundamental developments and creates conditions for sustainable economic growth. Organizing capacity refers to the entire process, from the identification of certain needs through the development of strategies and policy to the implementation of the policy and the monitoring of the results. Figure 2.6 is a schematic representation of the framework for the present research. It is based on the analytical framework of *metropolitan organizing capacity* as developed by van den Berg et al. (1997), originally for the purpose of evaluating the role of a city's organizing capacity with respect to metropolitan economic revitalization and infrastructure projects. Key tools for organizing capacity are vision, strategic networks, leadership, political support, societal support and communication.

Vision

A sound vision of the development of an urban region as well as plans to solve security problems should be able to gain broad support. To that end, such a vision will have to be sufficiently realistic and well-oriented to the opportunities and problems of the urban region. Also, it has to do justice to the interests and targets of all stakeholders in a balanced way. A sound vision forms the basis for formulating objectives and strategies. It can help to prevent inconsistencies, for new development strategies always need to be tested against the agreed vision. Therefore, the vision can, once accepted as the common reference framework, help to guide the relevant actors in their behaviour.

Strategic networks

Strategic networks can be conceived of as patterns of interaction between mutually dependent actors that evolve in response to policy problems or projects. A network consists of the total relations linking (public and private) organizations, such relations being marked by a degree of two-way dynamics (van den Berg et al., 1997, p. 11). Networks among and within organizations have to be identified. The aim is to find out who cooperates with whom in the development and implementation of security policies, and how and to what extent this cooperation takes place.

Leadership

Every organization, programme and project needs a leading actor to initiate, continue and complete it. The assumption is that the leadership of key actors contributes substantially to the successful design, development and implementation of projects. Leadership is a necessity, whether relying on specific competencies (the position in the administrative hierarchy, financial capabilities, specific know-how or other powers) or on the charisma of public or private individuals who successfully 'drive' the project forward (van den Berg et al., 1997, p. 12).

Political support Political support is a prerequisite for organizing capacity, since political relations and financial preconditions are decisive for the opportunities to initiate and implement new security policies (van den Berg et al., 1997). Security policy frequently depends on the political will to tackle safety problems. Politicians are, therefore, often key actors when new security programmes are to be introduced.

Societal support
No matter how valuable a project might be for sustainable metropolitan development, lack of support from those directly involved (the 'clients' or 'customers') or interested (local population, business society, interest groups) may curtail the chances of successful implementation (van den Berg et al., 1997, p. 13). Societal support for measures to overcome security problems depends on the active involvement of citizens/target groups.

Communication
With the help of good communication between all relevant actors a broadly supported vision for the perceived security problems can be developed. Furthermore, communication is needed to bring the message of the vision and related policies to the networks involved, the (potential) leaders, the politicians and society, including the very important target groups of the security policy. Much of the communication will proceed through the regular media channels (newspapers, regional/local radio/TV and the Internet). Excessive media attention on occasional disturbances and instances of pointless violence can build up strong incidental support for the solution of certain security problems, but 'regular' measures of safety policy, which draw less publicity could also benefit from some more positive attention.

Security as integrating concept
Within the framework of this research, we expect that security will increasingly become an integrating concept for urban governance. In many cities it seems that the demand for more security receives high priority. Indeed, because of crimes and threats of terrorist attacks and large-scale disasters, the locational attractiveness of urban regions is at stake. When security receives the highest priority, this might imply that administrative structures are adapted particularly to security policies. This can be done by setting up specific cooperations between actors involved in security policies or, for instance, by setting up specific local organizations to deal with local security problems. In the latter case, divisional administrative structures might have to be changed.

2.6 Synthesis

Figure 2.7 shows the extended version of our theoretical SAP model on the role of security in urban development. In this figure, the three basic elements of safety perception, urban attractiveness and spatial behaviour and policy reaction are further elaborated. Conclusions of this elaboration are given below.

2.6.1 Changing Security Perception

- During the 1990s there was a revival of large cities. Many cities have benefited from the information revolution, because they offer favourable conditions for networks

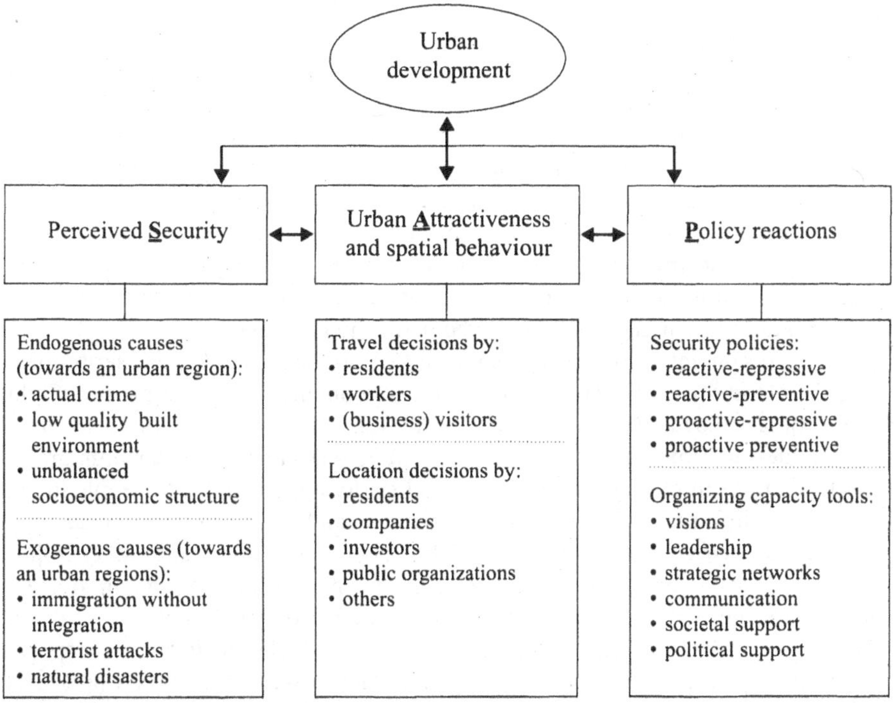

Figure 2.7 The SAP model – extended version

of complex exchange and transactions. In the current knowledge economy one of the most important location factors in attracting inhabitants as well as companies is an attractive living environment. One of the essential aspects that makes a living environment attractive is that it is perceived as being relatively safe.

- Security is the most fundamental human need, after physical needs such as food, drink and housing. There is a long tradition of fighting feelings of insecurity in urban areas. Risks and dangers of cities are related to the openness of urban regions. However, this open character is also essential for the diversity of cities to stimulate economic development. Preserving this openness should be an important starting point for simultaneous improvement of security and the economic potentials of cities.
- There seems to be a shift in the nature of the perception of insecurity. People increasingly want to exclude the possibility of being confronted with any risks in society ('riskism'). If there is a risk, people want to involve governmental institutions directly. They are, however, disappointed in the government, because in many urban areas the police and the judicial system do not seem to be capable of fighting the increasing number of crimes.

Causes of perceived insecurity

- The perception of security in an urban region is influenced by several different factors. The most striking factors influencing safety perceptions are actual crime rates, quality of the built environment, socioeconomic structure, disasters, immigration without integration, terrorist attacks and natural disasters.
- How people experience and interpret the built environment has a large impact on their security perception. Investing in the quality of the built environment is an important instrument for local governments. By meeting in a sufficient way the locational needs of the current and future inhabitants, local authorities can contribute substantially to an improved perception of safety.
- The socioeconomic structure of a region influences the probability and seriousness of threats and crimes. The weaker a local economy, the more people might become excluded. Exclusion from the regular society may imply that these actors develop informal activities. This will be particularly true for immigrants who are not sufficiently integrated. To make a living, unemployed people might engage in informal activities. Those activities can be a threat to urban security and attractiveness. The most important link between economy and safety is thus probably via the formal job market. We expect that the smaller the unemployment rates are, the better the safety perception will be. It is thus not only a direct economic interest for a city to stimulate the number of jobs, but it can also improve the safety perception, which indirectly stimulates economic growth. For a local authority it is thus important to know whether the local population sufficiently meets the needs of the job market. If this is not the case, it is in the direct interest of the local authority to, for instance, ameliorate education and/or integration programmes.
- There is a growing awareness regarding the risks of large-scale disasters. This has resulted in among other things stricter rules and legislation regarding the location of hazardous economic activities. The risks of most new large infrastructure projects are increasingly considered during the development stage. The growing awareness of disaster risks leads to higher costs of infrastructure projects and fewer possibilities for locating economic and residential functions.
- In general, the larger the welfare differences, the bigger the demand for improving security. This is true for different spatial scale levels. At neighbourhood level, large welfare differences can lead to burglaries and robbery. High-income groups will react by taking more security measures. At global level, relatively high welfare differences can lead to more migration flows and migration without sufficient integration in local societies will also increase fear of crime and will normally lead to local policy reactions, varying from immigration stops to integration policies.
- The 9/11 and Madrid train attacks made clear that cities are attractive targets for terrorists. Urban areas do indeed often form a concentration of richness, are nodes of crucial though vulnerable international communication networks and can be of important symbolic value as signs of military, political and financial power. The

variety of possible terrorist threats is in principle unlimited. Attacks can never be fully prevented and can undermine trust in the locational attractiveness of an urban region.

- The probability of the occurrence of natural disasters depends on the specific geographical situation of cities. The higher the probability of such disasters, the more prevention policies and policies to limit possible damage are legitimated. However, whether they will be able to take sufficient measures depends on the prosperity of the regions involved.
- The impact of fear of crime depends on the domains in which urban actors are operating. The acceptance of the probability of crime is, for instance, lower for residential domains than for working areas. We expect that in inner cities, residential areas and transport systems particularly, a secure environment will become a decisive factor to attracting and retaining urban actors, and therefore to stimulating urban growth and renewal.

2.6.2 Urban Attractiveness and Spatial Behaviour

- The safety perception can change the spatial behaviour of actors in an urban area. In the short term this can be a changed transportation, shopping or recreation behaviour. In the long term, actors might decide to move to another area. When an urban inhabitant has the perception that their environment is too insecure, and this actor has no possibility of increasing the safety in the area, they will move to another place. Normally, the only people who will remain in unsafe areas are those who cannot afford to move or those who are engaged in informal activities.
- We can expect that the larger the perceived insecurity in a central urban area, the more spatial deconcentration effects will take place. People will visit urban areas that are perceived to become less safe less often and/or might move to other areas.
- Companies can decide to move because of lack of safety, but they will also follow location behaviour of inhabitants. When certain population groups leave urban areas for safety reasons, companies might follow at a later stage. Major reasons for this might be a loss of clients and/or a lack of good labour force in the unsafe areas. To stimulate a sound local economic development, local decision-makers should thus have to take care of security in urban areas.
- An indication of the relative attractiveness of an urban district as a living area can be obtained via housing prices. It is assumed that the quality of houses, the quality of the public space and the perception of security are factored into these prices. The occurrence of much criminality in an inner city can imply that the value of houses (and to a lesser degree of offices) will reduce, and simultaneously those in suburbs will increase. Insecurity can thus, like inaccessibility, have a large impact on the value of land and real estate.

2.6.3 Policy Reactions by Public and Private Actors Involved

- Governments will always, implicitly or explicitly, make a trade-off between the costs and benefits of safety measures. When insecurity has a large impact on urban development potential, safety measures might generate relatively large benefits. In these cases, governments might be willing to take relatively expensive measures to improve urban security. The behaviour of local authorities can be strongly influenced by important signals from the local society and by changing political preferences.
- In this research we have tried to analyse what policies urban actors develop to improve the perceived security in urban areas. We wanted to find out what the focus is of these policies (repressive, preventive, reactive and/or proactive). Moreover, we have tried to analyse what such a focus might mean for urban development. We have assume that, to realize a relatively safe city in the long term, there has to be a certain balance between repressive, preventive and proactive policies.

Notes

1 See *Financial Times*, 9 November 2002, p. XXII (by Emma Tucker).

2 The number of illegal foreigners in the United States is estimated at 3 million, in Western Europe at 2.5 million and in The Netherlands at 60,000 (Engbersen, 1997, pp. 9 and 13).

3 Behavioural responses to insecurity depend on: 1) the type of threat – hijacked airplanes evoke different response than robberies; 2) the repetition of the action (the impact of a single murder are much less severe than that of repeated murders); and 3) the trust of the general public in prevention measures.

4 Here we abstract from the availability and diversity of jobs, the supply of facilities, the accessibility and demand-supply relationships in the housing market.

Chapter 3

The Case of Rotterdam

3.1 Introduction

Rotterdam is under the spell of safety. To enhance the feeling of safety and security in the city seems to be the main concern of every policy effort. Rotterdam is going all out to chart the security risks, and to design and carry out plans to reduce them. As far as security is concerned, Rottwrdam even seems to have become exemplary for other European cities. That the city is indeed a pioneer of safety policy may be concluded from the following evidence:

- the numerous *policy initiatives* taken in Rotterdam to make the city safer;
- the *pressure exerted on the national government* to amend laws and regulations (for instance, privacy rules) to permit the effective execution of its own security policy, and to make more funds available for strengthening the weak links in the security chain of police, justice and care institutions. A result of this pressure is, amongst other things, the proposed amendment for the obligation to work if not participating in education and an increase in the age for compulsory education to 23;
- the *efforts to push safety policy to the very limits of legislation*. Examples are preventive body search, the prohibition to enter certain areas for some people and taking persistent offenders to court for several crimes at the same time;
- the *great interest shown by other cities* in the policy initiatives taken in Rotterdam.

This case report examines the role of safety and security in urban development and the policy consequences. Section 3.2 provides a brief profile of the urban region of Rotterdam. Next, in Section 3.3, we will concentrate on the perception of social security in urban districts, in particular in the neighbourhood Spangen in the district of Delfshaven (see Figure 3.2). Disasters and terrorist threats will be touched upon occasionally. Section 3.4 goes into the relation between urban attractiveness and spatial behaviour. Next, Section 3.5 describes the policy responses within the urban region of Rotterdam. Finally, the synthesis in Section 3.6 presents the conclusions and recommendations of the case study. In this case study information from two time periods has been used: 2003 and 2005. Therefore, where necessary, we have inserted short updates of the most apparent changes.

Figure 3.1 Geographical position of the city of Rotterdam in Europe

3.2 Profile of Rotterdam

3.2.1 Situation in the Randstad conurbation

Rotterdam is located in the Rhine Delta, on Europe's busiest river and in open connection with the world's busiest sea. The Rotterdam region counts nearly 1.2 million inhabitants and is situated less than 30 km from the regions of The Hague (700,000 people), Delft/Westland (250,000) and the '*Drecht*' cities (Dordrecht region, 210,000). The Rotterdam region is part of the Randstad conurbation, along with the city regions of Amsterdam, The Hague, Utrecht and some smaller urban regions in between. The *Randstad* (including the 'Green Heart') covers about one quarter of the Dutch territory and houses about two-fifths (6 million) of the Dutch population.

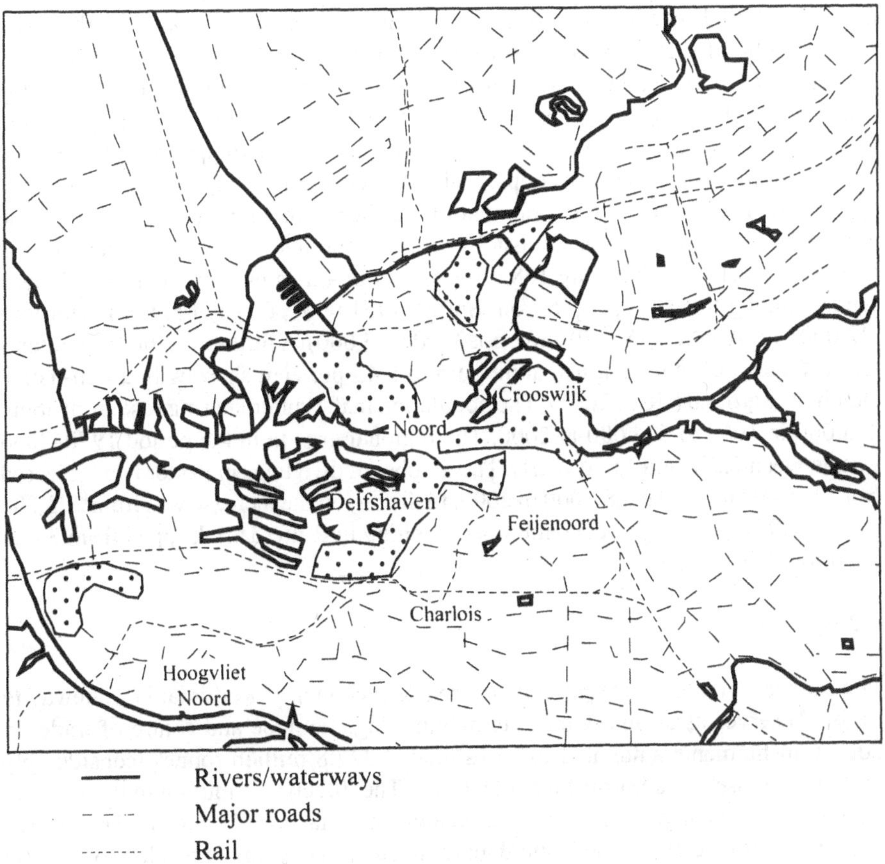

Figure 3.2 Schematic map of the city of Rotterdam

Lacking a formal status, it extends across three of the 12 provinces and covers a large number of independent municipalities.

As well as being one of the world's largest seaports, Rotterdam has a small regional airport (mainly used by business flights) and is a prominent transport and distribution hub for rail, road and water traffic. Rotterdam Central Station will be connected to the high-speed rail link Amsterdam-Schiphol-Brussels-Paris/London in 2007.

3.2.2 Demography

Rotterdam, the second city of The Netherlands, has 595,000 inhabitants (2001). Since the end of the nineteenth century, when shipbuilding, dock work, petrochemical industry, wholesale trade, etc. were flourishing, Rotterdam's population had grown fast to a peak of 740,000 residents by 1965. From the 1970s on, increased prosperity and shifting housing preferences, smaller households and a national housing policy favouring spatial deconcentration caused a net population drop of some 175,000 in 20 years. The highly selective suburbanization process, together with the effects of the energy crises of 1973 and 1978, resulted in serious social-economic problems in the early 1980s. Drastic policy changes at the national and local level (allotting housing schemes to big cities and not just to selected suburbs; state participation in large-scale urban revitalization schemes), coupled with new economic chances for cities, helped to turn the tide. Since 1985 the population has been growing again and at the time of writing stands at 595,000. Almost 32 per cent (190,000) of the inhabitants belong to ethnic minorities. There are 168 different nationalities in Rotterdam. The largest groups among them are people from Surinam (51,000), Turkey (41,000), Morocco (32,000), the Antilles (18,000) and Cape Verde (15,000). A further 110,000 inhabitants are foreigners of other origins, adding up to a 45 per cent share with a non-native Dutch background (COS, 2005). The population in the suburban ring rose from about 275,000 in 1960 to 574,000 in 2000. The regional growth in the period 1970–2000 was between 2,000 and 3,000 yearly. The number of dwellings in Rotterdam increased from 201,000 in 1960 to 284,000 in 2000. In the region the increase was from 273,000 to 522,000. The average occupation per dwelling in Rotterdam dropped from 3.6 in 1960 to 2.1 in 2000.

3.2.3 Economy

The seaport complex is the pillar of the regional economy. Rotterdam ('Gateway to Europe') serves as an important international logistic node and centre of trade. In 2003 transhipments amounted to an estimated 327.8 million tonnes, considerably more than those of its European competitors. The direct contribution to the national economy is estimated at nearly €6 billion annually (Havenbedrijf Rotterdam, 2004). Until well into the 1960s the Rotterdam (and Dutch) economy expanded so fast that 'guest labourers' (from Turkey and Morocco mainly) were attracted for those (simple and dirty) vacant jobs for which Dutch workers were hard to find. From the middle of the 1960s industrial development stagnated. Shipbuilding and ship repair ran into difficulties and new growth sectors were poorly represented in the city. As people became more aware of the environment, Rotterdam acquired a bad reputation as far as quality of the living environment was concerned. The vulnerable Rotterdam economy suffered heavily under the economic recession of the early 1980s. Unemployment in the city quickly rose to one fifth of the active population (about 60,000 people were looking for a job).

In the 1970s an extensive urban renewal programme, almost entirely publicly financed, was prepared and to a great extent carried out (predominantly rehabilitation of the social residential function) and, through investments in the port, Rotterdam managed to consolidate its position as a major port. From the mid-1980s on the economy started to grow again, helped by an energetic urban revitalization policy. Companies like Unilever, ING (banking and insurance), Stad Rotterdam (insurance), Robeco Group (investment company), Mees & Hope (banking), Nedlloyd (shipping) and Crédit Lyonnais (banking) invested in new offices in the city centre, often of striking architecture. The office space increased from 2.5 million m^2 in 1986 to 3.6 million in 1999 (COS, 2000). A new World Trade Centre was completed, as well as a casino, a new conference venue linked to the concert hall, exclusive high-rise apartment buildings, new shopping opportunities, etc. The large-scale revitalization scheme *Kop-van-Zuid*, connected with the city centre by an eye-catching 140-metre tall landmark bridge, provided space for city-centre expansion in former docklands. Here, too, public and private parties invested in offices, residential functions and leisure activities. The metamorphosis has given the city its modern identity and international character. In recent years the city has developed more and more explicitly into a city of art and culture. Its nomination as Cultural Capital of Europe (together with Porto) in 2001 acknowledges the ambition not only to be known as a port city but to change its image into that of a diversified, modern European city.

Since 1996, employment (especially in business and health services) has grown substantially, but the Rotterdam economy still lags behind that of other Dutch cities (like Amsterdam) and the national average. The officially registered unemployment figure decreased from 38,000 (17 per cent of the active population) in 1994 to 24,000 (6 per cent) in 2002 (COS, 2005). Comparable national figures are 8 per cent in 1994 and 3 per cent in 2000, which is less than half the Rotterdam percentages. According to municipal statistics the number of people looking for a job, including non-registered, amounts to 34,000 (16,000 more than the 'official' figure). Moreover, 44,000 persons were entitled to social allowances in 2003. The participation degree was 58 per cent in 2002 (working people as a percentage of the population between the ages of 15 and 65), which is rather low (COS, 2005).

Because the port and transport are not generating so many jobs anymore, the Rotterdam authorities try to support the diversification of the economy by stimulating some promising clusters, such as ICT, media, health care and tourism. Most policy attention is still focused, however, on port and port-related activities. Table 3.1 shows the recent employment structure of Rotterdam.

Under the economic recession of the early 1980s, unemployment in the city rose to one fifth of the active population, with ethnic minorities being most affected. The number of Turkish and Moroccan unemployed in particular rose sharply. When the city began to rehabilitate its economic structures in the mid-1980s it was once more the immigrants and other low-skilled groups who suffered. There ensued a distinct polarization between those participating in the new information society and those left behind, huddling together in the meaner city quarters. Socially vulnerable groups are old-age pensioners, one-parent families, long-term unemployed and households of foreign ethnic origin. In 2003, about 7 per cent of the Rotterdam population were dependent on some kind of social benefit. In 2000, the average disposable income was 10 per cent below the national average. However, compared to the situation in 1996, when the average disposable income was 20 per cent below the national average, this is a large improvement (COS, 2004). And along with unemployment and relative poverty have come the well-known big-city problems of exclusion, crime, alcohol and drugs abuse, etc.

Table 3.1 The employment structure of Rotterdam (2003)

Sector	Percentage employment
Industry	9
Construction industry	6
Wholesale, retail and repairs	13
Hotel and catering industry	3
Transport, storage and communication	12
Financial services	6
Commerical services	18
Public services	6
Education	8
Welfare and health	14
Other	5

Source: Gemeente Rotterdam (2004a).

3.2.4 Administrative Framework

Compared to most other European countries, municipalities in The Netherlands are strongly dependent for their financial means on general and specific payments from the state (more than four-fifths of the municipal income), but local authorities are quite free to formulate their own policies and spend their own budgets. Many policies are decentralized, which gives cities the opportunity to develop integrated strategies. The *Grotestedenbeleid* (GSB, Major-City Policy), initiated by the state in 1994, clusters and coordinates city-oriented grants, subsidies and city policies from nine ministries. The cities involved in the programme have to draw up an integrated social strategy that has to be approved by the state. On the strength of the implementation and evaluation of the strategy, contracts are signed between the local and national authorities.

In the 1980s discussions started (again) to reform the administrative organization by forming metropolitan authorities in the seven largest urban regions. However, in unofficial referenda held in Amsterdam and Rotterdam an overwhelming majority of citizens voted against that initiative. The national authorities withdrew their plans and what is left is a formalized regional cooperative body in which autonomous municipalities are committed to reach agreement about the planning and execution of a restricted number of regional, mainly space-related tasks.

3.2.5 Role of Districts

The two largest cities in The Netherlands are divided into *deelgemeenten* (sub-districts or districts). Districts have their own elected local governors, who concern themselves with affairs directly affecting the local citizens. A district has no complete package of public tasks, but the practice is for the municipality to consult the districts on all matters of local interest. District boards are responsible for local welfare policy and for the management rather than the realization of projects. Being well-informed of local needs in their limited jurisdiction, district boards can operate coherently and integrally. Financially they are dependent on the municipality, which allots them funds to implement policy measures in the fields of employment, district economy and safety and they are more or less free to decide how to spend their budget. The Amsterdam districts are more independent than the Rotterdam ones in that they can have their own departments carry out works. They can also decide to work together, for instance for the sake of scale economies.

3.3 The Perception of Security in Rotterdam

3.3.1 The Perception of Social Security

Since the end of the 1990s feelings of insecurity in the city appear to have been growing. This tendency has received quite a lot of attention in the media and, for the local elections of 2002 and the ensuing board programme, safety has been a central theme. In the spring of 2002 about one third of the electoral public voted for the political party (*Leefbaar Rotterdam* – Liveable Rotterdam) that had proclaimed safety its main election slogan.

In fact, however, insecurity had been increasing in The Netherlands for much longer. That can be illustrated with (objective) data about recorded crime and unsolved cases. Figure 3.3 shows that recorded crime in The Netherlands has grown almost tenfold since 1950. The number of unsolved felonies, on the other hand, has grown threefold, but remains still far behind the increase in recorded crime and in absolute figures has even slightly diminished since 1990 (Ministerie van Justitie, 2002, p. 7). Apparently, the steepest rise of crime occurred from the 1970s until the mid-1980s, the years when investment in crime control lagged behind (Ministerie van Justitie, 2002, p. 11).

Having systematically scanned 62 Rotterdam neighbourhoods, the City of Rotterdam came to the conclusion that five of them can be qualified as genuinely unsafe in 2003. Furthermore there were 11 problem neighbourhoods, 11 threatened ones, 11 districts calling for attention and 24 (reasonably) safe ones (Programmabureau Veilig, 2004). This is already an improvement compared to the situation a few years ago, when 13 neighbourhoods qualified as unsafe in 2001 (Gemeente Rotterdam, 2001a). However, at a time when the quality of living and housing is an increasingly decisive factor in cities' economic prospects, that conclusion appears to reflect a threat to the port city. Drugs nuisance, violence and trouble from young hooligans are considered prominent causes of insecurity.

In order to examine the trends in the development of objective and subjective safety, the Rotterdam has designed a Security Index. Although the Security Index seems to express a slow improvement of both actual and perceived safety, the safety situation is not (yet) satisfactory in all neighbourhoods. Another growing problem

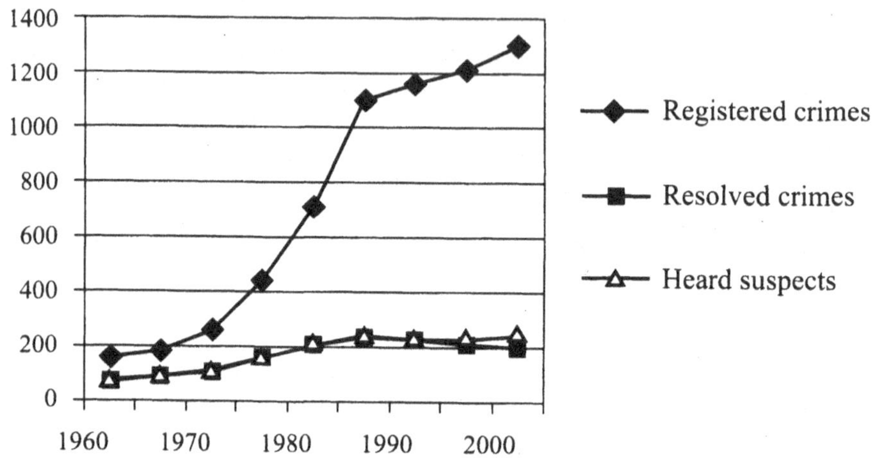

Figure 3.3 Volume of registered crime, resolved cases and heard suspects, The Netherlands, *1,000

Source: CBS (2001) *Politiestatistiek* in Ministerie van Justitie, 2002, p. 8.

regarding safety perceptions is that some people start to compare the current safety situation with a desired situation instead of with the situation of one or two years ago. They do not see what has been improved but only what remains to be improved. This is also called the '*theory*' *of rising expectations*.

Drugs and nuisance

There are in Rotterdam some 3,500 problematic drug addicts, of whom 700 cause serious nuisance. Since *crack* (boiled cocaine) became fashionable in the mid-1990s the drugs scene has become much harder and more aggressive. After the closure of 'platform zero', the shelter for drug addicts beside the Central Station, the drugs scene has fanned out across the Rotterdam districts, becoming notably troublesome in the district of *Spangen*. Several protest marches to the Town Hall were thereupon organized. In the summer of 1999 the Rotterdam Town Hall was besieged by residents, shopkeepers and the Junky Union, who considered that the drugs disturbances had risen to an unacceptable level and demanded prompt measures to reduce them. The Municipality thereupon initiated an comprehensive set of measures in the worst problem areas. One experiment carried out in Rotterdam to reduce drugs-related crime has been to provide a number of those most addicted with drugs under medical supervision.

The city attracted many young foreigners (in particular from Northern France, Belgium and Germany) intent on buying drugs. So-called drugs runners guided them to drugs premises, in Delfshaven in particular. By regular actions against these drugs runners on motorways and in international trains, the authorities hoped to reduce such activities, but the much-wanted separation between the local and international drugs markets seemed a mission impossible.

The streets in the districts where drugs were traded tended to show the all too common pattern of users gathering, cars coming and going, groups of dealers active in the streets, drug consumption and blowing in doorways, people relieving themselves in the street, persons ringing the wrong bells, prostitutes soliciting, car doors being slammed and other unpleasant noises, quarrelling and shouting, fights among users, fights among dealers and intimidation of residents (Littooij et al., 1998).

In 2001, the reported instances of drugs nuisance were almost entirely concentrated in the city centre (26 reports per 1,000 residents) and Delfshaven (12 reports per 1,000 residents). Moreover, inquiries revealed that in these very districts 32 per cent and 36 per cent of the residents respectively, saw drugs nuisance as a high-incidence problem, a substantially higher rate than in the other neighbourhoods.

It seems that the number of nuisance-causing drug addicts in Rotterdam and in the Delfshaven district as well has decreased over the period 2001–2004. Some of these people was taken into one of the five provided sections of care (forced admission, drug care by criminal law under pressure, imprisonment, care for the addicted prostitutes at the Keileweg and 'medical care'). But it is likely that some of the drug addicts have disappeared to other municipalities. The current result is that the problems around drug nuisance have diminished a great deal. This does not mean, however, that the problems are solved. Drug problems are still a topical issue in Rotterdam, but they have become controllable.

Violence

The most frequent form of violence in Rotterdam was street robbery, followed by assault, threat and public violence (Gemeente Rotterdam, 2001a). Like drugs nuisance, violence was concentrated in the city centre and Delfshaven. There were 7,400 people found guilty of violent misdemeanours in Rotterdam in 2001 (1.3 per cent of the population). Among them were relatively many persistent offenders. Violence is committed in homes as well as on the street.

As well as the entertainment circuit, public transport suffers from a high incidence of violence. The number of incidents reported to the RET (the Rotterdam public transport company) has risen fast in the past few years, the rate being 9,900 reports in 2003. The problems were especially grave on the city railway (metro), with violence and aggression being most reported to the RET (Programmabureau Veilig, 2004). So naturally the RET sets great store by efforts to improve safety in their vehicles. The target for 2006 (the end of the council programme) is a reduction of incidents of 10 per cent in relation to 2002 for all tram and metro lines and a reduction of 15 per cent for the most unsafe lines.

Youth and safety

Much criminal and violent behaviour occurs among teenagers. Youth violence comprises mostly vandalism, theft and violence, speeding on scooters, graffiti and the activities of young layabouts. Unless effectively taken in hand, petty crime often leads to the youngsters' increasing involvement in informal circuits.

With teenagers, a direct link can be made with education. A large proportion of the problem youngsters are, for a variety of reasons, seriously behind at school, the reasons for which include language problems, lack of (good) teachers, insufficient motivation, the attraction of the 'world of serious money' (think of drugs running) and family and school trouble. Owing to such factors and their frequent absence from school some of the young people lose their chances on the formal labour market and land in various informal networks.

3.3.2 The District of Delfshaven

The district of Delfshaven, situated in the western part of Rotterdam, has approximately 73,000 inhabitants. They are relatively young, with many children. The proportion of ethnic minorities is very high. Many newly established migrants from abroad have found shelter in this district: approximately 70 per cent of the population is foreign (COS, 2005). In the years 1999 and 2000 the district was considered unsafe by the Security Index, but by 2002 the situation had improved and this trend continued in 2003 (Programmabureau Veilig, 2004). Delfshaven was one of the first areas to implement the new security policy, with evident success. In addition, with the help of European subsidies (in the framework of the URBAN programme) Delfshaven has been able to invest generously in the attractiveness of its living environment.

The neighbourhood Spangen in Delfshaven is much troubled by dealing in and the consumption of drugs and the troubles exacerbated by the proximity of the Keileweg prostitution zone. It is estimated that approximately 500 persons are involved in the local drugs trade. Two-thirds of them come from outside the district. Delfshaven exerts a strong atttraction on dealers from outside because it is easily accessible and close to the city centre as well as to the prostitution precinct. The Keileweg has a very bad influence on the perception of security in Delfshaven. The drug dealers and consumers attracted by the prostitution zone cause nuisance in the neighbourhood. The problems are very difficult to keep in check. The proximity of the prostitution precinct is one explanation why in this part of the city a kind of underworld cluster has developed. To try and improve the situtation, the city decided to gradually close the zone down. Since 1 April 2005 the opening hours of the prostitution zone have been shortened: the zone now opens at 8 p.m. instead of 6 p.m. and closes at 2 a.m. instead of 6 a.m. The city is also planning to take action to eradicate the habit of drug use among prostitutes and place them under supervision. These measures are being criticized strongly, as citizens are not keen on accommodating (ex-)prostitues. Another point of discussion is whether or not such a zone should be recreated elsewhere or whether the municipality should refrain from financing such a provision altogether.

In 2002, 50 criminals in Delfshaven received a written injunction forbidding them to enter the district for six months, under threat of a summons. Twenty of them immediately left the neighbourhood. With the imposition of territorial exclusion on some residents of Delfshaven the City of Rotterdam wanted to test whether local government legislation could be used for the purpose. The Court judged (on 6 September 2002) that it was permissible, but required more careful preparation (one condition being better forewarning of the targetted individuals).

Many parts of Delfshaven are being firmly taken in hand. An example is the activity in the Schippersbuurt, where many houses are demolished and rebuilt and space has been set aside for the construction of new parks. Another example is a project started in Spangen-Below-the-Dyke, an area sorely tried by drugs-related trouble. The project will take many years, but seems to have a reasonable chance of success thanks to the sound political support from the aldermen involved. In this area some higher-class houses are being built to attract the higher-income groups.

Whenever neighbourhoods are taken in hand, much attention is given to education, since that aspect is considered of vital importance. There are certain streets in Delfshaven where Turkish and Moroccan are the only languages spoken. An appreciable portion of the population cannot speak Dutch, which renders integration with the indigenous population well-nigh impossible. For a structural solution of that problem, the education level has to be raised substantially in the entire city, since many immigrant families tend to move regularly from one neighbourhood to another.

Many physical and social problems can only be solved by a comprehensive approach, because their solution requires funds, new rules and regulations, coordination between departments and organizations, etc. Attempts to deal with entire streets at once are often frustrated because expropriation procedures cannot be applied or house owners obstruct the municipal policy or the means for renovation are inadequate. The Mathenesserstraat is a good illustration: one side of the street has been renovated, while the other is left to decay. With the €11 million now available to pull the 'rotten teeth', only part of the street can be dealt with.

3.3.3 The Security Index

The City of Rotterdam makes use of a Security Index to assess the security situation of Rotterdam's districts. The index combines objective data (tax returns and social-economic key figures) with subjective appreciation (surveys among 10,850 Rotterdam residents), weights being allotted to the various elements of the index. Such an index is inevitably arbitrary and the weights will always be susceptible to criticism. In popular perception, theft (shoplifting!) and drug nuisance tend to weigh heavier than, say, local loss of population and business or the number of local benefit drawers. To arrive at an acceptable overall judgement of the safety situation in districts, the composers of the index need to use their imagination and feeling for reality to estimate how serious certain transgressions are in the eyes of residents and companies.

With the help of the Security Index, the districts have been divided into five categories: 1) unsafe districts (scores < 3.9); 2) problem districts (3.9–5.0); 3) threatened districts (5.0–6.0); 4) districts requiring attention (6.0–7.1); and 5) safe districts (> 7.1) (Programmabureau Veilig, 2005). Early in 2001, 13 of the total of 62 districts, mostly in the Centre and in West and South Rotterdam, were labelled unsafe (Gemeente Rotterdam, 2001a). The present Board of Mayor and Aldermen

(2002–2006) have set as their target that by 2006 there will be no more unsafe districts. The five labelled as such must then have gone up two categories, while no others must be allowed to fall into the unsafe category.

Table 3.2 indicates the values of the Security Index for the entire city and for the 13 districts of Rotterdam. In 2004, only the city centre was qualified as unsafe. The district Delfshaven is still a problem area, but has made good progress since 2001. The aim of the City of Rotterdam is not to allow a decrease of the Security Index in a single neighbourhood.

3.3.4 Social-economic Structure

Table 3.3 shows that in 1996, Rotterdam had a substantially higher rate of the poorly-educated than other Randstad cities. The figure declined somewhat in 1999, but is still higher than elsewhere in the Randstad. The table does show a positive trend in a rising proportion of highly-educated and a decreasing rate of poorly-educated, but Rotterdam is still lagging persistently behind the other major cities. While evidently profiting from the overall rise of the proportion of higher-educated in The Netherlands, Rotterdam is on the other hand consolidating its arrears, and additional policy efforts are necessary to catch up.

Table 3.4 reveals that the average disposable household income is lowest in the two largest cities (Amsterdam and Rotterdam). Of the four major cities, Utrecht clearly boasts the highest average disposable household income. As Table 3.3 shows, this is also the city with by far the highest share of highly-educated people.

Table 3.5 shows that there is a large concentration of jobseekers in the district of Delfshaven. In that district, judged relatively unsafe by the Security Index (2001, 1.80), the unemployment rate is more than half as much again as the Rotterdam average. By contrast, in the district of Prins Alexander, which is judged to be relatively safe (2001, 3.71), the unemployment rate is just over half the Rotterdam average. Table 3.5 also shows that relatively unsafe districts are the very ones with the highest number of welfare-benefit claimants.

3.3.5 Quality of the Built Environment

Rotterdam has a poor image in terms of quality of the physical environment, in spite of the great improvements achieved since about 1985 by such striking projects as Kop van Zuid (Southern Headland), the development of the office boulevard along Weena and the Beurstraverse (Exchange concourse). Like many other great cities, Rotterdam is not attractive to the medium- and higher-income groups. Generous investment in suitable houses will hopefully enhance Rotterdam's attractiveness as a residence for the affluent.

Management and maintenance

To judge from demographic surveys, citizens often complain about what is popularly described as 'cleanliness and wholeness'. Some of our discussion partners believe,

Table 3.2 The Security Index for the districts of Rotterdam

Districts	1999	2000	2001	2002	2003	2004
City centre	2.7	2.8	2.1	2.3	3.0	3.6
Delfshaven	2.6	3.1	3.8	4.2	4.8	5.5
Overschie	6.6	6.6	6.9	7.0	7.9	8.6
Noord	5.2	5.5	5.2	4.8	5.8	5.9
Hillegersberg-Schiebroek	7.5	7.5	7.7	7.9	8.3	8.8
Kralingen-Crooswijk	5.4	5.3	5.0	5.2	5.4	6.1
Feijenoord	4.9	4.9	4.9	4.9	5.2	5.5
Ijsselmonde	6.7	6.6	6.2	6.2	6.6	7.1
Pernis	8.0	8.2	7.9	8.3	8.7	9.2
Prins Alexander	7.3	7.6	7.7	7.5	8.2	8.4
Charlois	4.6	4.7	4.7	4.7	5.1	5.5
Hoogvliet	6.8	7.1	6.7	6.6	7.3	7.2
Hoek van Holland	8.6	8.8	8.4	8.8	9.5	9.6
Rotterdam	5.5	5.6	5.6	5.6	6.2	6.6

Scores:

Unsafe	< 3.9
Problem	3.9–5.0
Threatened	5.0–6.0
Needs attention	6.0–7.1
Safe	> 7.1

Source: Programmabureau Veilig, 2005.

Table 3.3 Education level of the working population

	1996			2002		
City	Low	Middle	High	Low	Middle	High
Amsterdam	30.0	31.7	38.1	20.9	34.5	44.9
Rotterdam	40.4	34.5	25.1	34.0	35.8	30.6
The Hague	34.5	34.7	30.5	25.5	38.2	36.3
Utrecht	26.6	29.8	43.5	19.4	24.8	55.8

Source: CBS, 2005.

Table 3.4 Average disposable household income, 2000

	€
Amsterdam	22,300
Rotterdam	21,800
The Hague	23,200
Utrecht	24,300

Source: CBS, 2005

Table 3.5 Concentration index (CI) of unemployed jobseekers among the active population, 1996–2001, number of welfare-benefit claimants (BU) in 2001 as a percentage of the population of 15–64 and Security Index 2001 (VI)

	CI 1996	CI 2001	BU 2001	VI 2001
Charlois	113.3	126.6	15.9%	2.28
Delfshaven	154.0	141.0	16.3%	1.80
Kralingen/Crooswijk	106.4	98.8	13.1%	2.48
Prins Alexander	52.9	54.2	5.6%	3.71
Noord	114.9	112.2	11.5%	2.48
Feyenoord	138.7	147.4	14.8%	2.24
Rotterdam	24.3% (= 100)	12.3% (= 100)	11.5%	

Source: ISEO/CBS in Ecorys, 2002 and Gemeente Rotterdam, 2002a.

therefore, that the municipality should orient its actions more than before to being 'clean and whole'. Pollution and degradation have a direct influence on the safety perception of residents. Moreover, such regrettable developments are apt to invite petty crime ('broken-windows theory').[1] The present Board programme strives for 'level 3 cleanliness', but districts do not think this is ambitious enough; in their view a higher level ought to be aimed at, for the sake of a better living climate in districts and neighbourhoods (Kragten en Stekelenburg, 2003). By the end of 2003, the average score of cleanliness level was well above the required 3. In total 58 of the 2,207 measuring points throughout the city scored under 3, which is an improvement compared to the end of 2002 when 240 out of 2,400 measuring points scored under 3 (Gemeente Rotterdam, 2005).

Maintenance and management of public areas are often quoted as the City of Rotterdam's serious weaknesses. Much money has been channelled to projects which soon after completion fall into disrepair for lack of proper maintenance. The new quay along the Westersingel and the Schouwburgplein (Theatre Square) with their look of dilapidation are regrettable examples. An example of a successful project is the Beurstraverse, which is kept in good repair by private stakeholders under the supervision of developers. The area is indeed clean and perceived as quite safe. Admittedly, in such a closed-in precinct maintenance is relatively simple. The city is hardly in a position to control the management, a task better left to the neighbourhood level. The suggestion emerged from the discussions that the municipality would be well advised to have more of the execution of cleaning and maintenance work undertaken by private subcontractors. In that case, if the work is not completed to satisfaction, employees can be stimulated or dismissed, or the work can be given to another company. That might help to achieve the targets.

Commercial facilities and surrounding neighbourhoods

There is a growing belief that the principle of 'add-a-diamond' could help to make neighbourhoods physically more attractive. The idea is that attractive services 'planted' in a neighbourhood could have a positive effect on the whole community. A successful example is the upgrading of the services in the Witte de Withstraat, which has enhanced the wider area. Attractive commercial facilities could serve as 'diamonds-to-be-added-to'.

In some shopping precincts in Rotterdam shops stand vacant. The Vuurplaat in Kop-van-Zuid (a neighbourhood on the South Bank) is illustrative: owners are prepared to reduce the rent to find tenants for the shops, since empty shops stand out, diminishing the appeal of the entire shopping centre. Unoccupied premises are an invitation to vandalism and give visitors a feeling of insecurity, making them wary of shopping there. Such a shopping centre may be caught in a downward spiral. Our discussion partners have stressed how important active shopkeepers' associations – capable of guarding their interests and making sure their problems are effectively solved – are in such neighbourhoods.

There is no lack of occupancy near the Mathenesserplein in Delfshaven, even though the district scores rather poorly on the Security Index. Apparently, the shops attract enough custom for shopkeepers to accept the safety risks. The shops in the Mathenesserplein fulfil a central function for quite an extensive neighbourhood. Apart from some establishments of major chains (AH, Blokker and Trekpleister), very nearly all the shopkeepers in the Mathenesserplein are of foreign extraction. Apparently, in certain districts with a high proportion of non-native residents, small native shopkeepers tend to give way to foreign entrepreneurs, mostly Turkish and Chinese. The square is easily accessible and the physical environment has recently been upgraded.

A simple cost-benefit analysis can tell shopkeepers whether or not a location offers economic prospects in spite of its relatively insecure status. Shops need a strategic situation to generate sufficient revenues. On the cost side, enough money has to be invested in the quality of the public space to give customers a feeling of security. Safety measures such as the purchase of roller blinds and the hiring of security guards may be required. If the location's revenues are expected sufficiently to exceed the costs, including the price of security measures, shopkeepers may well decide to settle there. However, a cost-benefit analysis gives no insight into the effects on an entire neighbourhood. The impact of good shopping facilities may be such as to lift it into an upward spiral. Such *social* benefits should be included in the shopkeepers' assessment. The concurrence of private and public interests calls for a form of public-private cooperation. Public actors can encourage private investors to contribute to the upgrading of unpopulr neighbourhoods and private actors could, from social involvement and/or through stimuli, invest preferentially in problem neighbourhoods.

Slum landlords

The national government would like to see more private house-ownership in urban neighbourhoods, on the assumption that buyers of houses have a greater stake in a qualitative high-grade environment than tenants, and presumably would be more inclined to co-invest in it. Housing corporations are therefore stimulated to sell their properties to private persons, as indeed they are doing, but on condition that the houses in question must be resold exclusively to the corporation.

However, precisely in problem neighbourhoods private house-ownership seems to work adversely. Many of the premises in such neighbourhoods are in the hands of so-called slum landlords, owners who rent out (parts of) their houses at relatively high prices, without spending any money on them to keep them in good or even reasonable repair. Often their tenants are illegal immigrants who cannot obtain a dwelling otherwise. These slum landlords actually have an interest in a relatively poor living environment, where dwellings can be acquired relatively cheaply.

The problem of the slum landlords is a hard nut for the municipality to crack, because of the inflexible legislation. The municipality's actions used to be house-oriented rather than owner-oriented: it could not in one fell swoop take in hand a whole block of dwellings owned by a single landlord but must in principle deal with each suspected dwelling separately, irrespective of who owns it. Once the Building and Housing Inspection Department has established that the quality of the dwelling is unsatisfactory, the owner receives a written summons to improve it. As often as not, the municipality keeps running behind the facts, finding the house in question sold to somebody else so that proceedings have to be started anew. New legislation is being designed to hit the slum landlords financially. Taxation Law can be used to impose fines for the illegal collection of rentals and, by the so-called Victoria Act, premises can be boarded up on account of repeated nuisance. What sometimes happens is that the municipality or the housing corporations buy out the slum landlords for a relatively large sum, which the latter subsequently use to buy up other dwellings at housing auctions and exploit them in the same reprehensible manner. In that way, an undesirable system can survive for a long time. To dispossess and impose financial sanctions on the fraudulent owners would undoubtedly be a better way, affecting the slum landlords directly.

In the period 2002–2005 extra measures were implemented or experimented with in order to tackle the above-mentioned housing problems. It is now easier to take in hand a whole block of dwellings owned by one single landlord, on the condition that the landlord has open debts, for example with the treasury. In addition, the City Council began an experiment of repossessing houses of owners refusing to maintain their property. If the maintenance of a property is in the interest of public health, the City Council can try to repossess the house. Another new measure implemented are the 'preventive fines' for slum landlords. The amount of the fine is based on the expected annual profit of the rented rooms and is on average €300 per room. In the summer of 2004, the City Council proposed an experiment for introducing a housing permit in (parts of) the districts Charlois, Feijenoord and Delfshaven. New residents wanting to rent in these districts now need a housing permit. These properties these requests involve will be checked for income and overcrowding (Gemeente Rotterdam, 2004).

3.3.6 Disasters and Terrorist Threats

After the events in New York of 11 September 2001, in Madrid of 11 March 2003, and more locally on 2 November 2004 in Amsterdam (the murder of cineaste Theo van Gogh), people have increasingly become aware of the risk of terrorist attack. That is notably true of so-called symbol cities – cities that are symbols of Western society. The port of Rotterdam holds a prominent symbol status as a main European port and as the premier port in the world. Accordingly, *security* is a crucial factor for the port of Rotterdam. While in the 1970s and 1980s the impact on the environment took pride of place, *security* now dominates harbour policy. Both factors have a direct influence on the attractiveness of the Rotterdam region as a business location. When the port jeopardizes the quality of the living environment in the Rotterdam region, the attraction of medium- and higher-income groups and consequently of high-grade service companies becomes questionable. Likewise, real (or perceived) threats to security can harm the urban region's attractiveness to residents and business companies.

A *vulnerability* study has pointed out the 10 riskiest objects. The threats have been charted in the form of scenarios, and prevention and contingency policies developed. Since 9/11, more attention than before has been paid to industrial risks and their time-space dimensions: what will happen after a disaster has occurred in a certain area at a certain time? The number of scenarios is in principle unlimited. A few dominant scenarios have been elaborated and linked to certain generic measures that are necessary in the event of certain types of threat. For instance, if a terrorist action from the air is imminent, the air space should be sealed off instantly and the air defence activated. For many other threats such measures are evidently unnecessary. Clearly, to cope with disasters and terrorist threats, the actors need to be well informed. An inventory of threats, possibilities of defence, and what to do in the event of a disaster, is therefore of the essence.

3.4 Urban Attractiveness and Spatial Behaviour

The economic growth of the Rotterdam region lags behind that of competing urban regions, which makes it hard to overcome such serious problems as the relatively high rate of unemployment, the social segregation and the poor quality of the living environment. The urban region of Rotterdam shows a lack of equilibrium in several aspects: the economy is not sufficiently diversified; the demographic composition is lopsided and so is the housing supply; city and port are not developing harmoniously; and there is a discrepancy between the developments in the northern and southern parts of the urban region. All these discrepancies and disharmonies are slowing down regional economic growth. So, to inspire confidence and incite actors to settle and/or invest in the region, Rotterdam badly needs to stimulate new growth and find ways to restore the overall balance.

More particularly, Rotterdam needs to boost its attractiveness as a residence for the higher-income groups and the higher-educated population groups, an ambition that may well be frustrated by its prevailing image as an unsafe environment. Following that line of thought, we have tried to analyse how far (un-)safety scores are reflected in the price of houses, on the assumption that housing prices reflect the relative attractiveness of neighbourhoods as places of residence.

3.4.1 Relation between the Security Index and the Value of Houses

To find out how far a district's security is reflected in the price of houses, we have compared the values of the Security Index with the values of houses. Table 3.6 and Figure 3.4 show the results. Figure 3.4 reveals a close correlation between the two values. Lack of safety in a district seems indeed to be reflected in the price of property. High property prices occur in relatively safe districts, low ones in relatively unsafe ones. Hence, efforts to make the districts safer may boost the price of property, which in turn may stimulate local economic growth.

On the other hand, Figure 3.4 also displays a clear discrepancy between the price of houses in the City Triangle (the inner city) and the local security index. Evidently, dwellings in the city centre are much in demand, which is reflected in relatively high prices. The price of housing seems hardly to be affected by the serious lack of safety in the centre. Perhaps house-owners just take for granted that crime tends to abound in urban centres. The multitude of shops and places of entertainment in metropolitan cities draws the crowds and crowds inevitably comprise a proportion of undesirable individuals. The outcome confirms in part the expectation expressed in the theoretical Chapter 1, namely that the attractiveness of an urban centre, with its inherent advantages of multimodal accessibility and metropolitan facilities, is likely to push up property prices higher than in the suburbs. We have now shown that even in a somewhat unsafe situation property prices rise higher in the city centre than in the suburbs, though perhaps not quite to the level that could be feasible in a (perceptibly) safe city centre. Should the situation become really dangerous, the property prices in the city centre might well sink below the level of the outer areas, but at the moment there is no question of that in Rotterdam.

What does transpire, however, is that in suburbs like Zevenkamp, Hillegersberg and Terbregge the average rentals are superior to those in the centre. That can be ascribed in part to the composition of the housing stock in those suburbs, but also to

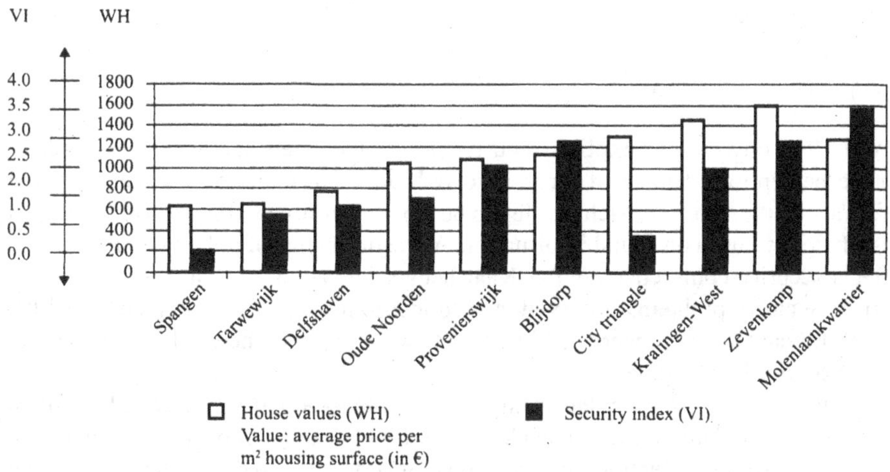

Figure 3.4 Security index and values of owner-occupier houses in selected Rotterdam districts, 1999

Sources: House values, COS, 2002; Security Index, Bestuursdienst, Gemeente Rotterdam, 2002.

the perceived local safety. The expectation is warranted, therefore, that the average inner-city rentals will rise with physical investments in the city, in particular in appealing houses and public spaces, and with improved safety.

Another fact that strikes the eye in Figure 3.4 is the situation of West Kralingen. The houses there are quite expensive in view of the poor security situation, a discrepancy that spells friction. House-owners naturally want the safety level of the district raised to prevent loss of value of their property. To keep the higher-income groups in the city and attract more of them, the city of Rotterdam will have to pay special attention to such discrepancies (neighbourhoods where the houses are expensive but the (perceived) lack of safety is worrying).

With respect to the rentals of offices in the city centre we expect a similar development to that of houses. At the time of writing office rentals in the centre and in the outer districts do not differ much. Early in 2003 the top rentals in the centre were €185 per m^2 and in the Brainpark, for instance, €175 per m^2 (DTZ, 2005). The expectation is that the office prices in the centre are most apt to rise as the centre becomes more attractive through physical investment in accessibility and quality of the living environment. Although the latest figures show a decline of offices prices (€193 in 2003 versus €185 in 2005), probably due to the economic recession of the past few years (DTZ, 2005). The advent of the high-speed train and the redevelopment of the station area will play a primary role in the increase in office prices in the city centre of Rotterdam. The boost of office prices hinges upon the area's social security for employees and visitors of the offices, the same condition on which the successful attraction of private investors to the city centre depends.

3.5 Policy Responses

3.5.1 Security Policy Intensified

From 1994 onward, an explicit security policy has been pursued in Rotterdam. In the perception of most of those involved, until 2001 that policy had achieved preciously little. The approach was felt to be too project-oriented and too reactive, and insufficiently based on sound information. A drastic change of policy was introduced after a security conference held at Kaatsheuvel in March 2001 in response to the serious security problems observed, and to increasing signals from society. All the key Rotterdam actors concerned with security were present. The outcome was a Five-Year Security Programme.

At the local elections in the spring of 2002 the local party Leefbaar Rotterdam (Liveable Rotterdam), under the leadership of Pim Fortuyn (who was assassinated in May 2002), won the elections after a campaign largely based on the theme 'improve urban security'. The newly-formed Board of Mayor and Aldermen adopted and intensified the security programme initiated by their predecessors. Even more than

Table 3.6 Values of houses and the security index in selected Rotterdam neigbhourhoods. The housing stock in Rotterdam on 1 January 2001 according to the property tax rate (WOZ-value) at reference dates 1 January 1995 and 1 January 1999. Selection: houses built before 1995. Value: average price per m² housing surface (in €)

	House values			Security index		
Neighbourhoods	1995	1999	2001 development	1995	1999	2001 development
Spangen	453	638	41%	0.50	1.33	166%
Tarwewijk	430	649	51%	1.37	1.59	16%
Delfshaven	536	773	44%	1.59	1.66	4%
Oude Noorden	661	1045	58%	1.76	1.93	10%
Provenierswijk	676	1075	59%	2.54	2.50	−2%
Blijdorp	757	1136	50%	3.15	3.27	4%
City triangle	938	1296	38%	1.00	0.86	−14%
Kralingen-West	893	1449	62%	2.45	2.29	−7%
Zevenkamp	1282	1591	24%	3.15	3.40	8%
Molenlaankwartier	830	1276	54%	3.88	4.06	5%

Note: Security Index scored: unsafe: < 1.6; problem: 1.6–2.2; threatened: 2.2–2.8; to be taken in hand: 2.8–3.4; safe: > 3.4.

Sources: COS; Security index: Bestuursdienst, Gemeente Rotterdam, 2002a.

before, security became the linch-pin of Rotterdam's policy. Funds and organizations had to be adjusted to fit an effective campaign against insecurity. The Board formulated as target for its own 'time in office' that there must be *no more unsafe neighbourhoods* in Rotterdam and that no neighbourhoods should be allowed to diminish in security. The targets were looked upon as highly ambitious by the discussion partners, who were of the opinion that some but certainly not all might be achieved. The closing down of the prostitution zone at the Keileweg, for example, is virtually a 'mission impossible'. Nor has a 25 per cent decrease in crime ever been known to occur in The Netherlands, though it has achieved in New York.

One feature of the new safety policy is the formulation of measurable *targets* combined with systematic monitoring. These targets were based on the outcomes of the measurement of the Security Index in 2001. Concrete performance agreements have been concluded with the municipal departments and districts for the implementation of the five-year programme. Performance agreements have also been concluded with welfare institutes and housing corporations (budget volume, actors involved). Moreover, police and justice have committed themselves to the municipal safety policy and are trying to realize certain proposed *targets*.

The main objective of the security programme is *to enhance security in the neighbourhoods and in the city as a whole*. To that end a more target-oriented approach to the problems than has ever been taken before is foreseen, based on sound information and effective collaboration of the key actors involved. The other themes chosen are, in order of importance, *housing*, *education and youth*, *the settling-in of immigrants* and finally *economic development*. For the 2002–2006 period, some €100 million have been set aside for the security policy, a reasonable amount in the eyes of the stakeholders. To make these financial means available, several urban development projects had to be cancelled and the municipal apparatus restructured.

The Rotterdam security policy is based on:

1 a city-wide *person-oriented* approach to drugs problems, violence and youth;
2 a *neighbourhood-oriented* approach, with a central role for the districts.

3.5.2 A City-wide Person-oriented Approach to Key Problems

Drugs and nuisance policy So far, the measures against drugs disturbances have been mostly reactive. They were introduced during times of serious trouble, after local residents had protested (as was the case, for example, in the Spangen district). For each drugs premise closed down, another one was opened elsewhere. One of the obstacles is the fragmentation of the communication about drugs problems which, therefore, failed to serve its purpose. Several agencies, such as the police, the Municipal Health-Care Department and the City Council were informed about some of the problems, but they lacked an overall view.

From 1998 onwards, some experience has been gained with the more comprehensive so-called *Alijda* approach. This is a joint action against drugs runners and drugs dealers, aimed at reducing the nuisance caused by drugs and crime in

Rotterdam. The underlying philosophy is to 'hit' drugs runners and dealers 'through their wallets', for instance by stopping or decreasing benefits, collecting tax debts and/or seizing goods. Police and justice agencies cooperate with the Tax Bureau, the Department of Social Affairs and Employment, the Immigration Authorities, and the Building and Housing Supervision Department. More than 1,200 persons are registered. Most of the persons known to the police as drugs runners are young men under 25 of Moroccan extraction. The result of the *Alijda* action was that 145 drugs runners were indeed apprehended, that is 41 per cent of the 350 repeat offenders, less than the 75 per cent the the approach had envisaged (Snippe et al., 2000). The results of the approach in the first two years justified its continuation in 2000 and 2003. Over the period 1998–2002 114 tax assessments were imposed for a total amount of €6 million, social allowances of 58 drug runners were ended and the persons involved were taken into a programme which has to lead to work and 216 houses creating a drugs nuisance were written to for backlog in maintenance (SIDV, 2004).

A major weapon in the fight against drugs nuisance is the boarding-up of premises by order of the mayor, a legal action possible since the amendment (Victoria) of 1997. The instrument has served to make it clear that the privacy of those causing nuisance is subordinate to the protection of the public domain and the privacy of the local residents (Littooij et al., 1998). Although this amendment increased the possibilities of tackling people causing a nuisance, it still seems to be difficult to address a small group of drug addicted who refuse care. These people cause severe nuisance for the local residents, but also are a serious threat for their own well-being.

In 2003, the police drew up a regional list of 700 persons (PGA-700) causing drug-related nuisance. This initiative was taken as a consequence of the person-oriented approach (PGA – *Persoonsgebonden Aanpak*) made by the police and their partners. The aim of the PGA-700 is to tackle the problems related to persons causing most nuisances and simultaneously avoiding care. This coordinated and on-going approach of the police increases the pressure on persons causing nuisance, which hopefully leads to more persons voluntarily checking in to care provisions. In 2003 the PGA-700 list consisted of 465 persons. With help of this list, 601 persons were brought to justice throughout the year 2003. The aim of arresting 700 dealers appeared to be unrealistic. The total number of arrests for dealing of hard drugs was 557 (Politie Rotterdam-Rijnmond, 2004).

The persons on the PGA-700 list are subdivided in four groups: nuisance-causing and care-avoiding drug addicts; criminal and nuisance-causing youths; persistent violent offenders; and criminal and/or nuisance-causing illegal persons. Files of each person on the list are maintained. When one large or several smaller offences are recorded, they can be addressed with either repressive measure or health care, or a combination of the two. In total, five different 'sections of care' are offered: forced admission (mental care forced by court); drug care by criminal law under pressure (*SOV drang*); imprisonment; care for drug-addicted prostitutes at the Keileweg; and 'medical care' (*bemoeizorg*) (Gemeente Rotterdam, 2004a).

The explicit aim of the Rotterdam drugs and nuisance policy is to come to grips with the consumption and dealing of drugs. The attack is not directed against the kind of organized drugs activity that does not cause much trouble, such as the sale of cocaine-filled small balloons from Hoogvliet controlled by Antilleans. The new anti-drugs strategy against drug-related nuisance can be characterized as repressive and comprehensive. Comprehensive, because information flows from several organizations are combined to produce a better insight into the problems and thus better prospects for well-directed actions are opened-up. Dossiers are being composed about the 700 most troublesome and care-refusing drug addicts, with a view to taking them off the streets and guiding them into a trajectory of criminal justice or aid (Priority 6 of the Board programme). The best way to achieve integration and cohesion is to appoint a single party – the city, the relief organizations, or the police – to pilot the policy. In order to combat so-called revolving-door criminals more effectively, penalties in the trajectory of criminal justice should be raised by combining offences.

A matter of some delicacy is how to aid drug addicts. The capacity to give shelter and support to troublesome drug addicts is limited. Moreover, in the current situation professional helpers are often not able to treat the worst problem cases (the drug addicts with psychological disturbances) optimally. Despite the attempts of some care institutions, the current situation does not provide the boundary conditions for dedicated care. The 'worst cases' are either not treated at all or they fall back on 'amateur' relief and shelter. The City Board's programme promises 'day and night shelters, (forced) clinical treatment and assistance in finding housing and work'. But while many repressive measures are related to concrete targets, the above-mentioned promises are not associated with target years or target figures.

The present strategy of tackling the most perilous areas first (the hot-spot approach, Priority 2 of the Board Programme) is in fact a strategy of dispersion. Its presumption is to reduce the overall nuisance in the entire city. The troubles in the hot-spots are many and manifold: drugs nuisance, degradation of the public space, violence in the streets and behind front doors, and troublesome teenagers.

There is a lot of unpleasantness in and around the Keileweg prostitution precinct. Addicted prostitutes work in this zone and this attracts a host of drug consumers and dealers. Since April 2003 only licensed prostitutes are allowed to work at the zone preventing new women from arriving. The intention is to close down the precinct by the end of 2005 (Priority 5 of the Board Programme), thus eliminating a centre of drugs-related problems and upgrading the surrounding neighbourhoods. For the prostitutes, special care programmes with permanent housing possibilities are being designed. This is a controversial measure, because residents in the vicinity of the proposed houses oppose it.

Suppression of violence

Measures to reduce violence are mainly repressive. To be able to act severely and effectively against recidivists a person-oriented approach (PGA) has been adopted in this respect as well. As stated, criminal and/or nuisance-causing illegal persons and persistent violent offenders are also included in the PGA-list.

Criminal and/or nuisance-causing illegal persons are considered to be people who stay in The Netherlands without legal permission and who have committed 10 or more offences. In Rotterdam 50 of these persons have been included in the PGA-700 list since January 2004. Offences are systematically filed by the police. Whenever possible they are taken into custody or even deported. The police's own immigration authorities cooperate with the Immigration and Naturalization Department, the Public Prosecution and the Programme Office Safety.

Persistent violent offenders are considered to be people who have more than 10 official reports regarding violence or people who have been convicted for violence by court three times in the previous five years. Again, personal files are recorded in order to increase the possibility of penalizing them. The police are targeted to hand over 500 suspects to the judiciary annually. In this respect, the police cooperate with Public Prosecution, Rehabilitation, and the Programme Office Safety. At the time of writing, the City of Rotterdam has initiated a research project about the offences and profiles of suspects in order to provide more finely-tuned care facilities.

There are plans to impose the duty to report any incidents on social agencies such as schools' sports clubs and municipal departments. The final goal – to instil acceptable behaviour – is clearly a long process. By explicitly tackling violence behind front doors as well as on the streets, the authorities hope to some degree to prevent excesses in the public domain.

Youth and safety

Youth is the fourth focus group of the PGA. To tackle youth crime (Priority 7 of the Board programme), repression and prevention go hand-in-hand. Education and schooling are the vehicles for both lines of action.

Repressive measures are predominantly person-oriented. For well-directed actions against persistently misbehaving young people, so-called 'lout lists' are composed. On the other hand, youth gangs are being approached as groups. Persons on the list are criminal and nuisance-causing people up to age of 23. These persons are visited at home by the police to talk about their (mis-)behaviour. The police also talk to their parents or guardians about their responsibilities. To tackle youth crime, the partners of the police are Public Prosecution, the Youth-care Office and the involved district. One of the existing bottlenecks in the approach towards young criminals is the Youth-care Office's waiting list.

Care institutions for young people are often not adequately equipped for those young persons with multiple problems. In order not to send them from one institution to another, the City of Rotterdam designed a balanced approach. All care institutions, organizations, projects and initiatives aimed at youth are joined together in DOSA, the District Organization Balanced Approach (*Deelgemeentelijke Organisatie Sluitende Aanpak*). The local DOSA director receives all indications of youngsters at risk in his or her district and applies this information to the care provisions involved. DOSA focuses on a broader group young people than PGA. In total, there are about 35,000 young people possibly causing nuisance or criminal behaviour in Rotterdam. Only part of this group is included in the PGA youth list (Gemeente Rotterdam, 2004b).

The situation in schools can be improved. The first thing to deal with is the language deficiency of infants. Many 4-year-olds of foreign extraction do not understand what their teachers try to tell them. Such children tend to lag behind in their education, with the sad consequence of frequent absenteeism and early school-leaving. One remedy is to teach them the Dutch language from the age of two. Moreover, the City Board believes that absence from school should be attacked more severely. Another suggestion is to invest in well-equipped youth clubs and sports centres where teenagers can enjoy themselves.

There is a shortage of good teachers in Rotterdam. To correct that situation, the City Board proposes to offer awards and attractive secondary work conditions to teachers prepared to work in one of the major cities. Another source of concern is the poor state of repair of many schools. Hopefully, additional investment will give schools a more central place in the neighbourhoods.

3.5.3 Neighbourhood Approach

While on the municipal level the accent is mainly on repression (notably with respect to drugs-related nuisance, violence and youth crime), the districts are expected to concern themselves first and foremost with preventive and proactive tasks, orchestrating the improvement of neighbourhood security. To that end they have been invited to draw up Neighbourhood Security Action Programme. On the basis of an analysis of the local security level and the living climate, such plans indicate what actions are most urgent and appropriate to raise the level of security in the neighbourhoods. The districts are expected to point out what has to be done in the way of supervision and enforcement, investment in the housing stock, management and maintenance of the public space, social infrastructure, the prevention of and fight against youth misconduct, violence and drugs-related nuisance. The districts are also supposed to make choices, set targets and priorities and decide what concrete measures are needed. To prevent criminal behaviour they might, for instance, suggest the establishment of more and better activity centres for the young. The scarcity of capable youth workers is then a frequent constraint.

Unfortunately, the Neighbourhood Security Action Programmes are often written under heavy time pressure at the expense of accuracy. In that respect, it is essential to agree about performance targets and to monitor the results carefully. Experiments were made with the formulation of performance agreements for a year, with sub-optimum results. One problem is that the activities of the organizations and persons involved are so specialized that their individual contributions to the solution of certain problems are hard to assess.

To finance their security policy the districts receive a 'security' budget from the City. Often, however, they find it hard to recruit the right kind of staff. Sometimes staff are hired from external companies for the performance of certain specialized tasks. For instance, the district of Alexander has enlisted the help of an external company to draw up a Neighbourhood Security Action Programme. In their role as directors, the districts control the investment and management performed by municipal departments in the neighbourhoods. To that end they are expected to establish performance agreements with the departments and to supervise their observation. The fact that many municipal departments are not area-oriented gives rise to friction.

For the most unsafe neighbourhoods an experiment with a new instrument has been decided on, namely, the appointment of so-called *city marines*, high-status personalities with a wide mandate. The underlying philosophy is that, since the worst problems occur in the neighbourhoods, it is there the best people need to be put to work.[2] In total, there are nine city marines, seven linked to a district and two linked to the themes youth and PGA. The city marines' task is to motivate the departments, district officials and other stakeholders to achieve the targets in the most efficient manner. They have to be actually on the spot, communicate with all those involved, signal problems and (persistently) call the responsible actors to account for any deficiencies. A difficulty is that the city marines do not in principle belong to any organization and hardly have any complementary funds or personnel at their disposal. So their effectiveness depends largely on their individual capacity and skill.

The appointment of the city marines must be seen as a temporary measure to enhance the effectiveness of the districts. In the long term, the districts should be structurally strengthened to consolidate that effectiveness. That means allocation of more means to the districts, appointment of more and better staff and reinforcement of the organization. To attract better people to the districts, the preconditions (responsibilities, work environment, salary and status) need enhancement as well. A circulation strategy could perhaps be drawn up, by which (outstanding) civil servants employed in central departments could be temporarily stationed at the districts.

After two years, positive comments about the role of the city marines in the local safety approach have been heard. In most cases, the *city marine* contributes positively to motivating local actors involved to prioritize certain problems and to cooperate. However, the outsider position of the *city marine* in the district may also cause authority problems. As stated before, the success of the city marines depends very much on the individual capacity and skills.

3.5.4 Old Problems, New Measures

The new and strict safety approach of the City of Rotterdam has led to several new instruments and approaches for tackling crime. Some examples are preventive frisking, area bans, VIP (very irritating policing), cutting back personal allowances, etc. Although sometimes quite effective, some of these instruments or approaches are highly controversial as well. The use of area bans, for example, was challenged in the courts several times and limitations have been set. Another example is the use of preventive frisking by the police in certain areas. This appears to be controversial as it is perceived as infringement of privacy by the population.

In tackling the safety problem in the urban area, the City of Rotterdam tests the limits of legislation. Sometimes this is controversial, but sometimes it is even used as an example for national policy or even legislation.

3.5.5 The District of Delfshaven

The main priorities of the urban security policy relate to youth, violence and drugs.

In the district of Delfshaven priorities are slightly different. Here, the number one priority is drugs. The dealing and trafficking of drugs is a long-standing problem in Delfshaven. Since the appointment of the Keileweg as a prostitution zone, these problems have increased, especially in the Spangen neighbourhood.

The District Council formulated three priorities in the District Security Action Programme: drugs, a clean and well-maintained built up area and youth. Fixed targets have been set to address these problems in the current policy period. As Delfshaven is regarded as one of the less safe districts, a *city marine* has been appointed in order to give additional attention to some issues and to bring all involved actors together. He also has additional financial means to invest in the main problems. In Delfshaven, the *city marine* has given priority to drugs-related problems and to physical renovations.

Over the period 1999–2004 positive results have been recorded. The Security Index shows that, although not all neighbourhoods meet the basic requirements yet, remarkable improvements have been made. This is especially true for the district of Delfshaven where the Security Index improved from a 2.6 (unsafe area) in 1999 to a 5.5 (problem area) in 2004.

3.5.6 Implementation of the Security Policy

The role of the City of Rotterdam

A central part in the security policy has been conferred on the Security Steering Group, formed by the 'triangle' of Mayor, Chief Public Prosecutor and Police Chief Superintendent of the Rotterdam Rijnmond region, and completed by the Alderman for Security and the Alderman for Neighbourhood Affairs. Other aldermen with related missions can be added if necessary. This group controls the Security Programming Office, a unit that enjoys a special status in relation to the Administrative Department, not being part of the hierarchy but coordinated with the Department. The office is charged with reporting on the development of security problems, helping districts to perform analyses on behalf of neighbourhood security plans, creating networks for the exchange of experiences and dispersing best practices.

As well as fulfilling a prominent role in the security policy and giving support to its various stakeholders, the City of Rotterdam is directly responsible for the administration of certain areas, one of which is the strategically important Keileweg zone.

The responsible alderman would prefer more central influence on spatial planning, for one thing in the interest of security and general urban appeal. To promote innovate ideas, a 'portfolio team' has been appointed – a team of young civil servants from the two departments most involved (dS+V and OBR), who are to give direct support to the alderman in developing his policy.

To carry out its security policy, the City of Rotterdam depends on national legislation and national allocation of funds and capacity. The City Board experiences its range of action as too constricted and is exerting pressure on The Hague to get it widened.

On behalf of the City Board and the 'Triangle', in October 2002 the mayor offered to the National Parliamentary Committees for Justice and Internal Affairs a list of suggestions for removing certain bottlenecks from national legislation, the so-called 10-point plan (www.rotterdam.nl). The first item on that list was 'adjustment of the privacy laws', to permit data from different agencies to be combined in one file, for the express purpose of getting to grips with troublesome addicts and fraudulent slum landlords. Another prominent item on the list is extension of the capacity of the police, the public prosecution, the courts and cell accommodation. In addition, wider opportunities were requested to place addicts in a care trajectory, if necessary forcibly, and to extend the provision of narcotics under medical supervision. Apart from that, the municipality strongly requested intensified supervision of foreigners.

The role of police and justice

Being regional rather than municipal agents, the police and justice agencies have to spread their human and financial resources across a larger territory than the City of Rotterdam. The Public Prosecutor's instructions come from The Hague. Nevertheless the two organizations have committed themselves to the City of Rotterdam's Five-Year Programme by adopting its priorities and targets, which represent a truly cultural conversion on the part of the police. That the Public Prosecutor no longer follows national priorities (such as the implementation of the 'Strip-'em-Bare' legislation) is regarded as a kind of velvet revolution. The police recently increased their capacity from 4,400 to over 5,100 personnel. As a result they can now proceed more effectively.

Justice agencies suffer from structural undercapacity. While not receiving a share of the additional funds (€100 million) set aside for improving security in Rotterdam, justice agencies are included in the national retrenchment moves. The Public Prosecutor, for example, has to economise a net sum of €17 million and at the same time achieve some concrete targets, such as the dispatch, in 2003, of 5,600 cases of violence. That number is based on experience and marked up by an 'inflation correction'. The 5,600 cases represent between 10 per cent and 25 per cent of the total number of instances of violent misdemeanour.

The conclusion from the discussions is that efficiency measures do actually improve the performance of the available capacity. Operations have already become visibly more target-oriented thanks to the change in attitude. There is a decided inclination to take the most urgent problems effectively in hand. However, to achieve good results overall and not only in the problem neighbourhoods, capacity expansion is inevitable.

The role of the districts

To implement the neighbourhood-oriented approach, the position of the districts should be reinforced. In concrete terms it means increasing the capacity and the allocated means. On the one hand, the districts are expected to call the departments to task for their failure to attain the agreed performances. On the other, the districts do not have a leg to stand on if – as sometimes happens – they are themselves slow in their commitment to the targets set. As stated, in the districts with the most urgent problems city marines have been appointed. They attract extra funding and try to influence the efficiency and effectiveness of the implementation of the local security policy by prioritizing certain issues and bringing involved actors together.

The role of the municipal departments

While on the one hand departments are forced to a drastic retrenchment (because their allotted funds are curtailed), on the other they are expected to achieve well-defined targets. Performance contracts are concluded for the accomplishment of safety targets with the Heads of Municipal Departments. It means that most municipal departments have to reconsider their priorities and to put greater weight on matters related to security. The shift of priorities often proves difficult because municipal departments are inherently inert. Often they have quite rigid budgets for separate purposes, which render amendment difficult. The problems are most pronounced in departments like Health and Social Affairs and Employment which have already had to economise stringently to deal with cuts imposed by the central government and the municipality.

A novelty is the Security Directorate, in which the municipal departments most involved in security are represented at the management level. The members meet regularly to discuss bottlenecks and best practices in security policy. The Directorate will be a worthy partner to the city marines. The Directorate can pass on information about difficulties observed to the marines, who can then submit them to the relevant departments to be remedied.

The mayor and aldermen have committed themselves to the achievement of some measurable objectives – such as the construction of 3,000 houses a year for the middle sector – which are to be translated into management contracts with the departments. The difficulty with the departments of dS+V and OBR is that they are not themselves the builders of the envisaged quantity of houses and other buildings, which the very achievement by which the mayor and aldermen would preferably judge their performance. To make the judgement possible, conversion rounds are in order, for which several starting points suggest themselves. For instance, within the term X, Department Y will make land available for 3,000 dwellings, or the department will offer help towards the accelerated or phased demolishing of existing buildings in the unsafe neighbourhoods, or a contribution will be made towards a safer environment of businesses, shopping streets and business parks.

In the end, the responsibility for achieving the targets lies with the Board of Mayor and Aldermen. The Board rather than the departments will answer politically for the non-achievement of certain objectives. Hopefully, however, the precise formulation of targets for the departments will inspire a culture of judgement ar the level of civil services. The relevant civil servants need to be stimulated more than before to accomplish certain targets without sheltering behind a curtain of procedure.

The role of the RET public transport company

The RET has made proactive efforts to improve safety in public transport. Prominent means are monitored entry systems and camera monitoring. The check on passengers on public transport, virtually abolished in the 1970s because it was deemed to be their own responsibility, now seems to be acceptable again. The fact is that quite a large proportion of passengers were riding without paying the fare and many of them were the kind of passenger who does not exactly contribute to a feeling of safety in trams, trains and buses. The situation is now being drastically changed: the ticket gates are coming back at light-railway stations, and guarded entries will be restored in all modes of public transport.

On the Caland Line of the city railway, turnstiles are being installed which can be worked by a chip card. The entrance check that has been re-installed on certain tram lines seems to function well: there is less fare-dodging and travel times have become shorter. The municipality of Rotterdam has made €3.8 million available to bring conductors back to all trams. In buses, a closed entrance regime has been in force for several years.

Camera supervision has been greatly extended and improved: more than 30 RET staff keep a watch on the images from 1,000 cameras at metro stations. In addition, cameras will be installed in trains and metro coaches. The intention is for the police to be permitted to use the camera pictures too. A glass-fibre network will enable policemen to watch a back-up of the video images.

The role of housing corporations

The city and the housing corporations are trying out schemes to buy up dwellings on the market, upgrade them and sell them at higher prices, accepting some financial loss. That is what happened for instance in the Millinx neighbourhood, where the city put up €14 million, and in Nieuw-Crooswijk, where housing corporations played a leading role in the redevelopment. One problem with neighbourhood upgrading is the length of time involved in the complete process. What with the tangle of red tape slowing down the proceedings, the renovation of a neighbourhood can easily take seven to eight years. Emergency legislation might help to speed things up.

Housing corporations have an important complementary part to play in the battle for security. They can, for instance, proceed against troublesome tenants by resorting to rent law, claiming those people spoil other tenants' enjoyment of their residence. If other residents have reported drugs-related nuisance to the police, the housing corporation has the right to evict the undesirable tenants or the corporations can go to court against troublemakers, as a clear signal that nuisance will not be tolerated.

The role of care institutions

Care institutions are involved in the care of people on the PGA-700 list, as many of these persons have mental health problems or need other kinds of help. For example for the 'ladies of the Keileweg', new care provisions are being designed which will provide them with permanent supervision. The philosophy is that some people in society are simply unable to look after themselves. Some people believe a proactive approach towards those people is required to structurally diminish the nuisance they cause. Offering them a safe place to live, structural health and mental care and, when possible, a supervised job would give them structure and might help reduce the nuisance they are causing.

Such care provisions are new and controversial as well: not all care institutions believe in the need for and the effectiveness of this approach.

Cooperation between police and care providers is believed to be a bottleneck in the implementation of the local safety policy. This is mainly related to the autonomy and the privacy of patients. Slowly, the awareness of the negative side-effects of too much autonomy for people who are believed to be unable to take care of themselves is growing. Solutions are believed to be found in a better cooperation and better tuning between (mental) care, police, judiciary, and the City Council. However, a mutual lack of trust and understanding seems to hinder this development.

Policy response to the danger of possible disasters and terrorist attacks

The International Maritime Organization (IMO) and the US Coast Guard have issued recommendations for improved security in seaports, recommendations that are likely to be introduced on the European level. Since 11 September the American authorities have tightened their conditions as to the checking of ships' cargoes from and to the USA. Several measures taken (such as intensive mutual collaboration of the organizations involved and the introduction of container scans) have gained the Rotterdam harbour the status of a Safe Port. The implication is that in America goods from Rotterdam are dispatched more speedily.

City and port are in close administrative cooperation to enhance *security* in the port. Some programmes against crime in the harbour were already in place even before security was given political priority. Since 1995, regional consultation on the fight against disasters has been a matter of course. To chart the threat of terrorism and other risks and take appropriate measures, the Port Security Development Group was founded, involving several public organizations such as the Health Department, the Harbour Authority, the police, the Public Prosecutor, the administrative department, the environmental department and the fire brigade. Since 11 September there has been increasing pressure to give due attention to the prevention of and dealing with disasters, explicitly inclusive of terrorist attacks. The cooperation among safety organizations was thereupon intensified through the Port Security Policy Board (PSPB). The Customs and the Sea-port Police are also involved in the approach to security in the port (see Box 3.1).

The security paradox

A triangular schematic of prevention-response-risk can be drawn up (see Figure 3.5). The risk is the product of the chance of a disaster and its effect. Both elements should be kept as small as possible. To minimize the chance of a disaster (prevention) is largely the task of the central security actor, namely, the fire brigade. Should anything untoward happen nonetheless, then the negative consequences should be kept at a minimum (response-activity). In the event of a disaster the public, the media and the politicians are apt to respond first and foremost to the effects (think of the many deaths in Kaprun and the devastating effects of the firework disaster in Enschede). It is for the authorities to inform the public of risks and to instruct them how to react when a disaster occurs. However, that task may clash with the interests of the local

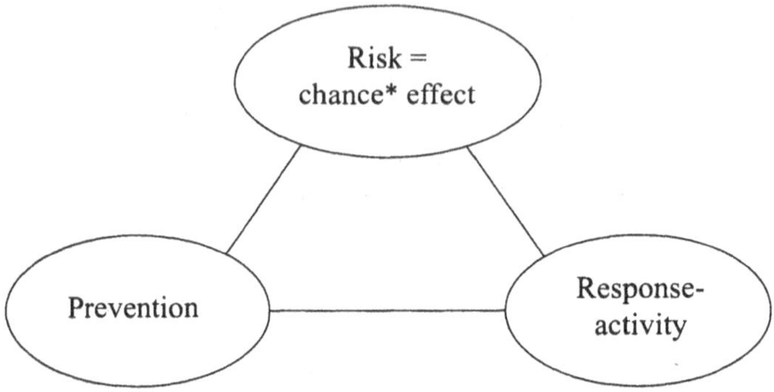

Figure 3.5 The triangular schematic of prevention-response-risk

government. If the authorities put too heavy an accent on potential dangers in the Rotterdam region, Rotterdam's status as a location and residence may be seriously harmed. As a result people and private enterprise might move out and/or decide not to settle here after all, a situation that has sometimes been called the security paradox. Attention to safety aspects should make a region more secure, but too much public stress on security control might produce the opposite effect, inspiring a perception of insecurity among the population.

At present, the fire brigade coordinates the input of all emergency services and the design of contingency plans. Increasingly, the need is felt for a multidisciplinary executive. The organizations involved should form a project team charged with the prevention of and fight against catastrophes and disasters. On the whole, prevention and proactiveness should be given a more prominent role.

New developments: better information on people at risk

In preventing the criminal behaviour of certain people, there is a growing need for the collecting and coordination of information. After an criminal incident it often appears that many people already had some information about the possible misfortune, but nobody was aware of the information held by other agencies or individuals. What is missing is someone with a 'helicopter view' and the responsibility overall care. A good example involves youth crime: schools might have some signs of truancy, the police could have a file showing some minor offences, a neighbour might be aware that the child is going through the trauma of its parents' divorce and a family doctor might even have a file containing information on mental problems. All these factors together could indicate a raised risk of serious problems. Providing information centres where all this information is collected is believed to be essential for early intervention. However, several bottlenecks still hinder the use of information systems effectively. Firstly, the privacy regulation and autonomy of the individual prevent institutions from cooperating. Secondly, the care provision agencies are not always fully equipped to provide extra care; capacity is low and waiting lists are long.

Box 3.1 Press Communiqué from the Municipal Harbour Authority of Rotterdam, 5 November 2002

On Monday 4 November 2002, the Mayor, Mr Opstelten, founded the Port Security Policy Board (PSPB). This is a purely harbour-oriented multidisciplinary group for security consultation. The object of the PSPB is to shape, adjust and evaluate the Rotterdam policy for security in the harbour. Besides, the Board is expected to promote collaboration among the various services and departments involved. Moreover the Board is to advise the Mayor on matters of legislation and on guidelines and recommendations towards a univocal Rotterdam safety policy.

The following officials sit on the PSPB:

- a member of the Board of Directors of the City of Rotterdam Harbour Authority;
- the Harbour Master, City of Rotterdam Harbour Authority;
- the Police Superintendent, Rotterdam-Rijnmond;
- the District Head, Seaport Police;
- the Regional Medical Official (Regional Assistance Department, Rotterdam-Rijnmond, medical assistance in case of accidents and disasters);
- the manager of DCMR;
- the Head of Public Order and Security of the Rotterdam Administrative Department of the City of Rotterdam;
- a representative of the Public Prosecutor;
- the head of the Tax Authority, Rotterdam Customs District.

The Commander of the Rotterdam Fire Brigade has been appointed chairman of the Port Security Policy Board.

3.6 Synthesis

This section recapitulates the most important conclusions of the Rotterdam case, focusing first of all, in subsection 3.6.1, on the perception of safety and the factors that affect that perception (see Figure 3.6). Subsection 3.6.2 deals with spatial behaviour inspired by changing urban attractiveness. Subsection 3.6.3 presents *best practices* and conclusions with respect to policy responses. Subsection 3.6.4 describes the organizing capacity of the City of Rotterdam regarding safety policies. Finally, subsection 3.6.5 formulates some recommendations.

3.6.1 Security Perception

Management and maintenance What Rotterdam citizens complain about most is the lack of a 'clean and well maintained built up area' ('*schoon en heel*') environment. Degeneration and pollution make residents feel insecure and give rise to much petty

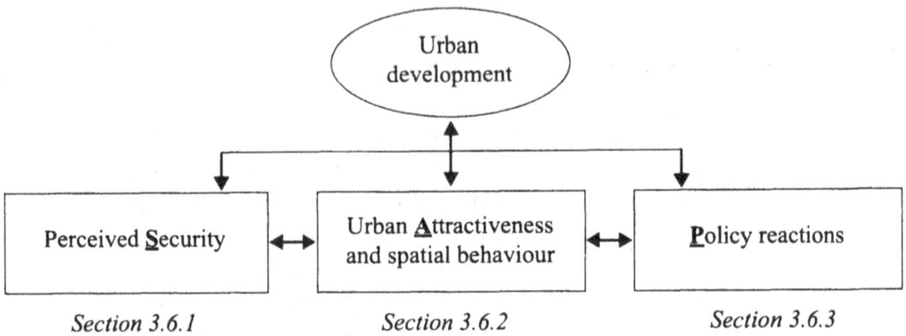

Figure 3.6 Structure of the conclusions

crime. Many judge the physical management and maintenance in the City of Rotterdam to be relatively weak. In spite of heavy investments in a variety of urban building projects, through poor management and sub-optimum repairs the municipality has failed to maintain an acceptable level of quality. To strive for an ambitious level of cleanness and wholeness might well raise the perceived safety level among residents and reduce petty crime.

'Diamonds' and spread effects
A stock of well-managed shops helps to make a neighbourhood attractive and can thus contribute to the overall feeling of security. A case in point is the *Witte de Withstraat*, where the establishment of several attractive commercial and cultural services has boosted both feelings of security and the attractiveness of the surrounding neighbourhood. The support of similar services in other problem neighbourhoods – adding a few 'diamonds' to the ordinary rocks – is highly recommended in order to proactively improve the perceived security.

Urban renewal
Efforts to make neighbourhoods more attractive physically are complicated by the time factor. For one thing, the procedure to acquire a property is a lengthy one and the city's budget for the purpose limited. Emergency legislation to circumvent the sluggish procedures seems warranted in the face of the threat that badly degenerated neighbourhoods constitute to the local perception of security. Ways and means should also be developed to take a firm stand against crooked house-owners, and to encourage private parties (for instance by tax exemptions) to participate in urban renewal projects.

3.6.2 Urban Attractiveness and Spatial Behaviour

Lack of security reduces Rotterdam's chances of attracting residents with medium and high incomes, the very categories so badly needed to enhance the city's attractiveness and competitive position in the present knowledge economy. Unsafe conditions are reflected to some degree in the relatively low prices of houses and offices. However, as we have shown, properties in the city centre are relatively expensive in spite of the perceived bad safety conditions there and the odds are that property prices as well as office rentals will rise even higher as safety improves. At the moment, prices in and outside the city centre are not widely different, but that situation is expected to change in the near future when the connection to the HST network is a fact. The city centre is likely to become a lot more attractive, provided sufficient money is invested in an attractive station area and inner city, and more particularly in overall feelings of security. Under such conditions private investors will probably be more inclined to invest in the city centre as well.

3.6.3 Policy Responses

Best practice 1: changed attitude under heavier pressure

Many years of mainly preventive policy measures without decisive and purposeful repression have fostered feelings of insecurity among the Rotterdam population. Its perception is that policy and justice had no proper response to the fast-rising aggression and felony, and consequently they had lost confidence in the ability of police and justice agencies to repress the negative forces and remedy the deteriorating situation.

Now that safety has been given pride of place in the new social and political climate, some change for the better can already be observed. Heavy pressure on the authorities has achieved a striking turnaround. Municipal bodies as well as police and justice agencies now seem firmly committed to taking safety problems jointly and decisively in hand. The first concern is now the effective solution of urgent problems. Corporate or individual property owners who are called upon to solve certain problems are from that moment on categorized as 'problem owners', who can no longer take shelter behind arguments like 'We lack the money or the capacity', or 'It is not our problem'. Nor can 'partitions' between the intervening organizations still hold up policy implementation, since those involved will join forces where necessary and desirable.

Moreover, safety policy has become innovative. New measures have been invented, experiments carried out and pressure exerted on the national government to grant extensive competencies. The introduction of 'area prohibitions' and 'preventive body-searching' are good illustrations.

Best practice 2: setting priorities and targets

The 'Rotterdam approach' has been summarized in five principles. Firstly, the choice of some well-defined policy priorities. In the recent past, the multitude of initiatives on urban projects made it very hard for the municipality to make a choice. Lately the municipality has opted for a safety policy that is person- as well as area-oriented. Secondly, to focus on implementation rather than on planning. Thirdly, to orient the policy to objectives, that is to say set targets for which the managers can be called to account. Fourthly, to have the municipality recognized as a reliable partner, committed to keep their promises. And fifthly, to give the citizen a prominent place in policy-making: the policy must be carried out for and with the Rotterdam people.

In May 2005, results of the new safety approach were published. Regarding the Security Index, there was a modest improvement. On a scale of 1 to 10, the safety situation improved from 5.5 to 6.6. Within some districts there were larger positive changes and in others larger negative changes. The safety situation in Delfshaven has improved the most. These results were calculated over a five-year period. In the first few years little progression, and in some districts even deterioration, were recorded. Only now can significant results be seen. This shows that it is difficult to score on safety policies in the short term. What has gone wrong during several decades cannot be changed overnight. However, the largest short-term benefit of the new urban safety policies is considered to be the relatively large commitment and sense of urgency of so many actors to tackle the problems in a more effective way.

Best practice 3: appointment of city marines

A prominent aspect of the safety policy is the *multi-agency approach*. Relatively many organizations are involved to help bring about a feeling of safety among urban actors. Pressure brought to bear on the organization's attitudes and a well-defined set of targets should bring about better mutual cooperation, and are indeed doing so. So-called city marines have an important role in that set-up: their task is to signal local bottlenecks. Their 'bell ringing' will hopefully be a powerful instrument towards achieving the targets and enhancing perceived security. As flexible links, city marines can stimulate actors to realize targets without adding to the bureaucracy (since no new administrative layer or agency is inserted). They have to be highly qualified persons whose help is enlisted to lubricate the bureaucracy. City marines seem to be a good experiment opening up good prospects towards the ambitious targets set by the Board. And after two years of implementation the involved actors seem to be positive about the contribution of the city marine to the developments of local safety. Three aspects of city marines appear to have been decisive in the success: they have been given authority (they are appointed by the City Council and have direct links with directors and management of services and institutions); they have an adequate budget to work with; and they have an independent position within the district.

3.6.4 Organizing Capacity with Regard to the Rotterdam Safety Policy

The present Rotterdam safety policy was initiated and the underlying *vision* developed by the Board of Mayor and Aldermen of the period 1998–2002. However, its implementation has gained momentum under the Board which took office after the local elections in the spring of 2002.

The City of Rotterdam (with the mayor as protagonist) clearly plays the leading role in implementing its new safety policy. To achieve the aims of the new policy, there are additional means available. Moreover, there is support of a clear administrative leadership helped by a competent organization to carry out the safety policy. The City is trying to get all the actors in line and to stimulate effective strategic partnerships. The univocal political results of the local elections of 2002 (with safety as a dominant theme) supported that line of action. Many actors were showing a firm commitment to the new safety policy and there was quite good political and social support for drastic measures to enhance the perception of safety. Illustratively, the regionally-organized police and justice agencies fully subscribed to the importance of the new policy. For the City of Rotterdam the effective enlistment of the districts and municipal departments, in particular in the proactive medium-term safety policy, was of the essence. By dint of setting them concrete targets it hoped that within its term of office valuable and measurable concrete steps to that effect could be taken.

The districts are important as directors of neighbourhood safety policy. However, they are also considered a weak link in policy implementation because of their permanent lack of resources. The city marines are intended to give support to the districts, but for the latter's longer-term effective operation more structural measures concerning personnel, organization and financial resources are imperative. Perhaps it would be a good plan to have (high-grade) municipal officers circulating among the districts.

Communication is a vital aspect of the present safety policy, especially as regards: 1) information and involvement of the population; 2) stimulating the actors involved (police, justice agencies, districts, departments, educational and care institutions); and 3) exerting pressure on the national government for more policy freedom. The so-called Security Index is an important instrument of communication, and it is hoped it can help identify bottlenecks in good time, give orientation to the policy and demonstrate that the policy produces results. A word of warning is warranted about the paradox associated with communication. Too much attention on safety measures could be harmful to the city's image as a residence, in that it might give some (potential) residents the impression of a highly unsafe city, while in fact the opposite is being aimed for.

3.6.5 Recommendations

Bottlenecks with the judiciary and care agencies

The actors involved, even the regionally organized justice agencies, seem wholeheartedly to support the policy choices made. Nevertheless, a serious bottleneck threatens in that very area. Because of lack of financial and human resources the courts are unable to deal with all the cases presented. By setting priorities they can take in hand the most serious cases, but a portion of criminal activity goes unpunished. Some improvement is expected through efficiency measures, but not enough. A solution is also needed for the lack of capacity in the aid to drug addicts, in particular those with psychological disturbances. In that connection as well, concrete targets should be set.

In addition, as it is believed that more structural care and supervision for a small group of persistent (often addicted) offenders is essential, a more proactive role by care agencies is required. To support the care agencies in this responsibility, the basic (spatial) infrastructure of a city needs to be adapted to this demand by the municipal (and national) government.

Investing more in education, integration and living climate

At the moment, safety policy is mostly repressive and there are many who argue that this is a good thing, since preventive measures are useless without a well-functioning repressive apparatus. Others, however, are concerned that too little attention is given to policy elements such as education and integration; they feel that neglect in those areas could in the long term prove lethal to a sound social-economic urban development. Therefore, the next course must be a sound comprehensive preventative and proactive policy. A reinforced social cohesion counts as a crucial condition for safety and since education and integration are indispensable to social cohesion, their promotion is in the long run also crucial for safety. Consequently, failure to invest properly in education and integration may in the long run produce a strongly segregated urban community.

Apart from all that, the city, together with private partners, must invest generously and proactively in the quality of the living and location environment as an essential condition for attracting medium- and high-income groups to the city. Though it will be important to build more high-quality houses in the short term, it will be crucial to think twice about the real needs of inhabitants. This should be done not only by planners and architects but also by safety and quality experts and predominantly by (potential) users of new buildings and houses. Public actors can encourage private investors to contribute to the upgrading of deprived neighbourhoods and private actors could, either through social involvement and/or stimuli, invest preferentially in problem neighbourhoods. And finally, there must be continuous efforts to maintain a high level of 'cleanliness and wholeness' throughout the city, since to many residents cleanness and wholeness are the prominent aspects of a safe environment. The relation between the safety perception and the occurrence of petty crime appears to be so obvious that the target 'clean and whole' deserves the highest policy priority.

Anchoring the safety concept within the Rotterdam region

At the time of writing, the main concern of public organizations in the Rotterdam region is safety. The new municipal policy and its organizational implementation are strongly oriented to the improvement of safety. Many new policy measures are viewed through the prism of safety. A great variety of policy efforts, ranging from the enlistment of police and justice agencies to schools and neighbourhood renewal, are intended to enhance the feeling of security within Rotterdam. Such efforts are inspiring new cross-over partnerships. For instance, the directors of the municipal departments are regularly in consultation about their contributions to the safety policy and city marines are put to work as valuable links between districts, municipality and departments to guard and stimulate the progress of the safety policy. Moreover, the city is trying to anchor the new working methods by codifying tacit knowledge on it and emphasizing the importance of implementing the new working methods among all involved actors.

Safety has always been a municipal concern, but it is now considered the number one urban theme. To guarantee an urban environment perceived as safe for a long time to come, the safety concept will have to be anchored within the urban organizations involved. It means that safety should be a permanent item on the agendas of all urban organizations concerned (such as the RET and the Harbour Authority) as well as the municipal departments (such as dS+V and OBR). Moreover, the Safety Programme Office, which at present serves as an active stimulator for all stakeholders, could be given a firm position within the urban structure.

In 2006, the current safety policy of the City of Rotterdam will elapse. Currently, new policy will have to be designed. As the positive results booked in safety are still fragile, a continued political attention is required. In the coming period the measures and methods used to improve safety will have to be consolidated.

Notes

1 See Chapter 1 for an explanation of the broken-windows theory.
2 See 'Eindrapport van de Taakgroep Sociale Infrastructuur' (Final Report of the Working Group on Social Infrastructure), March 2002.

Chapter 4

The Case of Antwerp

4.1 Introduction

In this case study, we focus on the social security in the city of Antwerp. First, Section 4.2 gives a concise profile of this urban region. In Section 4.3, we deal with possible causes of feelings OF insecurity within the city of Antwerp. Next, in Section 4.4, we will go into the related spatial behaviour of local inhabitants. We focus thereby on the developments within 'underprivileged neighbourhoods'. Section 4.5 goes into policy reactions regarding urban unsafety. In this section we will give specific attention to four *best practices*. Finally, Section 4.6 presents conclusions and some recommendations.

4.2 Profile of Antwerp[1]

4.2.1 Demography

In 2005 the city of Antwerp counted 457,000 inhabitants. The 'functional' Antwerp city region (based on commuter relations) houses over 1.1 million, a little more than the nearly one million accommodated in the administrative region of Antwerp. In the early 1970s the area which is now the city of Antwerp counted 550,000 inhabitants, which implies a reduction of 100,000. However, in the last decade of the twentieth century the decline slowed down considerably and since 2001 the population volume seems to be increasing slightly (DSPA, 2005). So far, there have not been any signs of the new metropolitan growth ('reurbanization') that seems to have been instigated in several European central towns through a renewed interest in urban living, an urban policy that tries to restore the appeal of city life and considerable natural growth among citizens of foreign extraction. Within the Antwerp region, it is the more 'rural' municipalities in the second ring east of the town, far from the harbour industry in the west, that show clear growth tendencies. The urbanization features of the first ring around the city are very similar to those of the central city itself.

The impression is that single persons (46 per cent of all households), ethnic minorities (over 11 per cent), senior citizens (one-fifth are older than 65), lower-income groups and social benefit recipients dominate the urban population in 2004 (DSPA, 2005). That is confirmed by the lagging growth of purchasing power within Antwerp and the fact that the average income of the Antwerp population is 11 percentage points below the Belgian average.

Figure 4.1 Geographical position of the city of Antwerp in Europe

4.2.2 Economy and Employment

The multimodal transport junction Antwerp is prominently situated within the European core triangle made up by the Paris, London and Randstad regions. It is also well positioned in relation to the Ruhr Area. As a European port, Antwerp comes second (after Rotterdam) in terms of tonnage, with general cargo and containers as its strongest points. Data from the 1993–1996 period shoed that the Antwerp regional economy was doing well. In growth of turnover (over 11 per cent) and value added (nearly 9 per cent), Antwerp ranks above Flanders. Remarkably, in those respects the city seems to score even better than its suburban municipalities. More recent figures confirm a continuation of this trend: the gross value added increased over the period 1998–2002 with 17 per cent (Belgostat, 2005). The growth figures for investments are more reason for concern: Antwerp is clearly trailing behind the Flemish average (3.9 versus 5.8 per cent). 'Lack of space and lack of public funds to attract business companies are apparently driving investors away from the cities towards regional urban areas (Stad Antwerpen, 2000, p. 25). Figures from the National Bank reveal that there is a sharp contrast between the positive growth of value-added in the city of Antwerp during the 1990–1996 period and the decline in employment (–6.2 per cent) and investments (–22.4 per cent). The National Bank concludes that though the suburban municipalities have managed to compensate for the drop in employment and investment, the region of Antwerp still trails behind the average Flemish growth. In the following period (1998–2002) investments in Antwerp showed an increase of approximately 10 per cent although the last year investments appeared to be declining again (Belgostat, 2005).

Table 4.1 Data of metropolitan profile of Antwerp

Characteristic	Antwerp
Population of the district of Antwerp (2004)	162,000
Population of the city (2004)	455,000
Population of the urban region (2000)	1,161,000
Growth of the urban population (city, %) (1991–2003)	–3.2
Share of the population of foreign extraction (district, %) (2003)	18
Share of the population of foreign extraction (city, %) (2003)	11
Proportion of population of working age in employment (district, %) (1999)	59
Unemployment rates (city, %) (2000)	11
Proportion of employment in industry (city, %) (1997)	24.9
Proportion of employment in services (city, %)(1997)	71.1
Number of administrative tiers (including state and boroughs)	5
Borough Boards	No

Source: DSPA, 2005 and van den Berg et al., 1998.

Antwerp functions as employment centre for the region. Two thirds of the people who work in Antwerp live outside the city. The employment ratio is 100, which means that in quantity, local employment equals the potential active population. However, the position as employment centre is in jeopardy. Since 1985 Antwerp has suffered a net loss of 2000 jobs, while 30,000 new jobs have on balance been created in the region. The loss of jobs in industry could not be fully compensated by the growth in services. In the port in particular, many jobs were lost: compared to 1985, the number of jobs dropped by one fifth. On the other hand, the port achieves strong turnovers and much value added. In fact, the creation of jobs can no longer keep pace with the generation of prosperity. Industrial towns like Antwerp are in particular confronted with that divergence, 'the more so as the local industry is slow to renovate and assume its proper place in the new economy' (Stad Antwerpen, 2000, p. 15). The loss of jobs in industry resulted in high unemployment figures (14 per cent in 2002) which could not be compensated by new jobs in service industries. A qualitative mismatch between supply and demand of labour has emerged.

The Antwerp economy is dominated by a few large companies. The enlarged scale of the production structure makes the city sensitive to the decisions of those companies, decisions that are often made outside Antwerp (and even outside Belgium). The formation of European and global conglomerates of internationally-operating companies has rendered many European cities, including Antwerp, more dependent on decisions made abroad. Most of the large companies are found in manufacturing industry, which accounts for about one quarter of total employment. Within industry, metal works and chemical companies are dominant (together accounting for three-fifths of total industrial employment).

The tertiary sector is good for three-quarters of all jobs, the greatest numbers being found in transport and storage (one quarter), business and financial services (one third) and trade (one quarter). Compared to other large Western European towns, the share of industry in local employment is high.

Employment is growing fastest in business services (20 per cent between 1993 and 1998), waste processing (16 per cent), and public government (12 per cent). In business services, part of the growth is due to making up for lost time. The strongest clusters within the Antwerp economy are still transport and distribution and the port-related industrial cluster. The diamond trade is traditionally a strong element of Antwerp's export trade. There appear to be promising prospects for cluster development in environmental technology, telematics and tourism. The growth of tourism is reflected in, among other things, the progress of hotels and catering, accounting for nearly 5 per cent of all employment. Compared to dominant industrial sectors such as chemicals (almost 6 per cent) and metal industry (8.4 per cent), the hotels and catering branch (at any rate in terms of employment) constitutes an economic sector to reckon with.

The port of Antwerp is still the motor of the economy but no longer the most prominent generator of jobs. Antwerp has made the switch to a modern service economy, but as such is still trailing behind its direct surroundings. One negative effect of the growing service sector is the lack of jobs for low-skilled or unskilled workers and the ensuing persistent unemployment. Like other labour markets, that of Antwerp is characterized by the spatial paradox of great demand for labour side-by-side with considerable unemployment. With seven jobseekers to each vacancy, entrepreneurs are still complaining that they cannot find suitable workers. In 2004, 11 per cent of workers in the city of Antwerp were out of work. In the suburban municipalities the percentage was a mere 5 per cent, which brings regional unemployment to some 8 per cent.

Obstacles to further economic development are the lack of space for new activity, the greatly increased traffic congestion, and the poor cooperation with the suburbs in the functional Antwerp region. Yet another bottleneck is the weak financial position of the city, which prevents large-scale public investment in traffic infrastructure or development of the waterfront, for which there is a considerable need and good opportunities available.

4.2.3 The Central Station Area: An Economic Chance

Thanks to financial support from the federal government, one important project has been taken in hand, namely the construction of a tunnel for the Paris-Brussels-Amsterdam HST section, in which Antwerp Central Station is to be a stopping place. That opens prospects of revitalization for the station area. However, this is mainly a concern for Antwerp itself, possibly supported by Flanders in the matter of infrastructure. The response to that opportunity seems to have become decisive for the successful revitalization of the backward neighbourhoods of Northeast Antwerp, Borgerhout and the *Eilandje* (small island). Indeed, these neighbourhoods could profit in particular from the quality impetus of the HST. An important condition for success is good internal access to the station. An early solution on that score is not in sight (van den Berg and Pol, 1999). Such an involved intra-urban project requires a comprehensive approach in which the various functions (living, working, transportation, hotels and catering, leisure, culture, meeting) can be balanced for mutual reinforcement. The combined strength and knowledge of all the public and private parties involved can create an added value that could never be achieved by any one of the parties on their own. In view of the social problems, the challenge is to seize this opportunity, which is not likely to be repeated in the coming years. It is a matter of profiting from the momentum, if necessary by resorting to creative financing methods (van den Berg and Pol, 1999).

4.2.4 Administration[2]

The administrative situation of the municipalities in Belgium has changed somewhat during the last few decades because of the federalization process of the country. This means that competencies were redistributed, with a diminution at the national (this is federal) level and an enlargement for the regional level. Because the regional level contains the specific territorial competencies, most of the municipal control and the urban policies are linked to this level.

The provinces are also an intermediate level between the national and the local authorities. However, their function towards the largest cities, of which Antwerp, is rather limited. They control a number of activities of the municipalities and may report deficiencies to the governor and the (regional) minister. Quite often their impact is limited to giving a helping hand and to the controlling functions mentioned above. During previous years the role of the provinces was discussed quite seriously. A few years ago the idea existed that this intermediate level was no longer needed. In the end, however, the existence of the provinces was confirmed, although a new delimitation of their competencies was needed. To date only the Flemish government has succeeded in the formulation of these new functions (CBO, 1997).

The financial situation of the municipalities is more or less in equilibrium, although the largest cities especially have some serious difficulties. This results from debts from earlier times and the repayment of the loans from these periods. The debt crisis was so heavy that the higher authorities interfered. In Wallonia especially, a large part of the debts were changed from the municipal to the higher authorities. In Flanders, this movement was much more limited, which means that Antwerp still has to pay back about 7 billion francs a year until several years into the twenty-first century. The Flemish Commission for the Organization of Domestic Administration (CBO, 1997) regards this as one of the main problems for the development and implementation of the right policies by the local government, at least if no significant help is given at the higher level.

The joining of seven suburbs with Antwerp in 1983 (which more than doubled its territory) has not improved the cooperation with the regional municipalities that were not included in the merger. Rather, intra-regional competition has sharpened, for one thing making the problem of scarce business sites harder to solve. For another, the present regional distribution of municipal revenues and expenses is unacceptable to Antwerp. There is a painful lack of balance between the rich suburbs which draw upon the relatively poor Antwerp for services, beset as it is with social, accessibility and environmental problems.

In 2003, the City of Antwerp faced a severe political-administrative crisis, because of an accusation of misuse of public funds. The end result of the crisis was the departure of several local politicians and high-ranking civil officers. Consequently, the administrative system was temporarily functioned less well.

4.3 The Perception of Security in Antwerp

During the last 10 years there has been a more or less continuous increase of crime rates in Antwerp. In 2001 and 2002, there were the first stagnations of crime rates for a decade. In 2001 there was only a small increase of 0.19 per cent in criminal activities in relation to the year 2000 (Scoyer, 2002), and in 2002 an even smaller increase of 0.1 per cent. IN previous years there had been increases of 3 per cent, 4 per cent, 5 per cent and even of 10 per cent (van Baelen, 2002). After 2002, the crime rates even seemed to be falling: in 2002 the crime rate was 53,000, 12 per cent lower than the previous year (Lokale Politie Antwerpen, 2004). In 2001, the crimes with the largest share were thefts from/out of cars (23 per cent), normal thefts (13 per cent), pickpocketing (8 per cent), vandalism (8 per cent), burglary of houses (7 per cent) and violence (7 per cent) (Scoyer, 2002).

Crime rates cannot always be fully trusted, however. When there is much attention on a certain problem the number of notifications can increase substantially. In 2002 for instance, the number of sexual offences were 30 per cent higher in relation to 2001 (van Baelen, 2002). Representatives of the police think that this is predominantly due to the fact that it has become easier to report them to the police, including incidents that took place several years ago.

The perception of security among residents is relatively low. Almost 18 per cent of the population in 2002 stated they always or often felt unsafe (CDO and HABE, 2004). Compared to other cities in the region, this is the highest share. Over the period

1998–2002, this share has been fluctuating (see Table 4.2). Compared to 1998, the share has been rising, but over the last period a small decrease could be noticed.

Table 4.2 Population share in Antwerp always or often feeling unsafe, %

	1998	2000	20002
Antwerp	16.5	17.9	17.7

Source: CDO and HABE, 2004.

The biggest complaints of the local inhabitants seem not related to crime rates but to nuisance and pollution. Residents and local policy-makers identify the main problem as one of 'social disorganization', caused by the impoverishment of communication and mutual contact, combined with a lack of clear norms and values for appropriate behaviour, a negative image of the neighbourhood and, last but not least, a lack of perspective for economically and culturally deprived groups (van den Broeck, 2002, p. 176).

The 457,000 inhabitants of Antwerp include many different nationalities. Within some districts groups of different nationalities do not live very well together. This is also quite difficult, for there are about 150 different nationalities living in an area of about 5 km^2. The Jewish (about 20,000 inhabitants) and the Moroccan communities (12,000 inhabitants) are relatively large (DSPA, 2005). Both groups are poorly integrated into urban social structures. In general, the latter group generates more security problems than the former (for instance petty crime). Integration policies are consequently more focused on the Moroccan than on the Jewish community.

After the signing up of the Schengen Treaty, many immigrants from Eastern European countries entered Antwerp. Some of them, in particularly Albanian and Russian people, were highly involved in illegal activities (Danneels and Tuerlinckx, 2002). They thereby also contributed to greater feelings of insecurity among the Antwerp population. With the further enlargement of the European Union more problems with illegal immigrants are expected.

4.4 Urban Attractiveness and Spatial Behaviour: Underprivileged Neighbourhoods[3]

As in many other Western European cities, suburbanization processes took place in Antwerp during the 1960s and 1970s. People who could afford it left central urban areas and moved to greener areas where they could find more space and better housing. They left behind people who were not able (or willing) to move to suburban locations. New inhabitants in the old central urban areas were often immigrants and people with relatively low income and education.

The selective emigration process resulted in a fall of the population figure. The selectivity implied the growth of the share of the poorer groups. The general structure of the urban region consists in a relatively poorer centre and relative rich suburbs and residential areas at the outskirts of the FUR (de Brabander, 1998). The suburbanization was not limited to the population, however. As elsewhere, industrial estates around the centre attracted new and expansive existing companies. Moreover the distribution of population as well as the rise in mobility resulted in an extra impulse to the spatial distribution of commercial activities, not least by the creation of new shopping centres (de Brabander et al., 1996).

In 1987 the City of Antwerp commissioned the University of Antwerp to carry out a preliminary inquiry into the phenomenon of 'deprivation'. The specific situation and the social-economic profile of the socially underprivileged neighbourhoods have been charted in the 'Atlas of Deprivation'. The outcome was that there are 25 poor neighbourhoods to be found in the ancient city quarters along the quays, stretching from the Zuid to the St Andries Quarter and on to the Eilandje. Stuivenberg and the ancient part of Borgerhout also count as poor neighbourhoods, as are, in the northern part of Antwerp, the environment of the Dam down to the Merksem Docks (van Hove, 1987).

Other inquiries into Antwerp's underprivileged neighbourhoods were undertaken in 1994 by the RISO (Lescrauwaet) and in 1996 by the Catholic University of Leuven (Kesteloot, 1996). Here we find that underprivileged neighbourhoods are defined as:

> those urban neighbourhoods that are often marked by external decay due to the convergence of economic depression, loss of employ, departure of tradesmen and the outflow of the more affluent citizens. The process is often attended by loss of social tissue, cultural experience and solidarity. Especially the simultaneous occurrence of certain factors causes a kind of social, economic, cultural and architectural tension that causes a neighbourhood to come under the definition of deprivation. (Stad en OCMW Antwerpen, 1999, p. 7)

All these neighbourhoods house a high concentration of lower income groups who are incapable of investing in their environment and thus find their neighbourhood gradually falling into decay. This group comprises unemployed people, persons who are entitled to a disablement benefit and people who exist on a minimum wage or a small pension. In addition, there are those who are at a disadvantage in any case, namely, low-skilled or unskilled labourers and migrants. And finally, single individuals who have to survive without the support of a sound social structure. Deprived neighbourhoods are marked by poor housing, empty buildings, inadequate social services and a relatively poor-quality living environment. It appears that the combination and concentration of problems in certain neighbourhoods causes (feelings of) insecurity. In addition, the ongoing discussion on insecurity, for example in the media, reinforces the image of unsafe neighbourhoods (van den Broeck, p. 173). In particular, the original inhabitants who still live in those neighbourhoods feel unsafe. They often barely communicate with new (immigrant) inhabitants, so no mutual understandings will arise.

4.5 Policy Reactions

In this section, we will consider the policy reactions in the city of Antwerp to the increased perceived insecurity. Firstly, some taboos which possibly hinder an effective approach are considered. Then we will consider the problem of the relatively large number of projects in the field of urban security developed at different involved government levels. Subsequently, we will go into two specific projects: the approach of the drug problem and line-spotting in public transport. Then, we consider two problems at the level of the city of Antwerp: the fragmented security policy within the City of Antwerp and the image problem of the Antwerp police. In this case study information from two moments in time has been used: 2003 and 2005. Within this time period there have been some striking changes regarding safety policies. Therefore, where necessary we have inserted short updates of the most apparent changes. We end this section with two *best practices*: the BIN networks (a kind of neighbourhood watch) and a comprehensive policy on prostitution.

4.5.1 Taboos

In Antwerp, developing specific policies for problem neighbourhoods is difficult for two reasons. Firstly, some issues are not debatable, because of taboos. It is, for instance, hardly possible to discuss the role of foreign people in urban development. Moreover, it is not possible to talk about problem districts; they are euphemistically indicated as 'districts needing attention' or 'underprivileged neighbourhoods'. Consequently, it has been very difficult to develop specific policies on such topics. And because of the highly diversified political constitution of the City of Antwerp (the *Cordon Sanitair:* the coalition in which all local political parties except the *Vlaams Blok* (Flemish Bloc, currently Flemish Interest) are participating), no real, fundamental, decisions can be made.

It seems that since 2003 some taboos have been broken down. Issues like camera monitoring of public spaces, relocalizing of provisions for drug addicts, and the possibility of penalizing people for minor offences more easily are now open for discussion. In some cases new measures have been taken. For example, thanks to adjusted (national) legislation it is now possible to penalize nuisance and petty crime with help of Municipal Administrative Sanctions (*Gemeentelijke Administratieve Sancties*) without interference of the Public Prosecutor. This is an extra tool for the police and the municipality to deal with nuisance and petty crime and to indirectly improve safety perceptions.

4.5.2 'Plethora' of Projects

One of the complaints concerning urban safety policies is a lack of transparency and participation of the population. Security policies are particularly top-down, without tailor-made solutions for specific problem neighbourhoods. Problems of transparency and participation are furthermore related to the 'plethora' of projects and initiatives which have been launched by different authorities. Each project and agency has its own objectives, timing and financing and often originates from different policy levels (van den Broeck, 2002, pp. 183–4).

Five governmental levels are involved in safety policies: the European Commission, the federal government, the Flemish region, the province of Antwerp and the City of Antwerp (see Table 4.3). Each level has its own responsibilities concerning safety topics: the European Commission on migration policies, human trafficking, organized crime, amongst other things; the federal government on large cities policy, prostitution, police and drugs; the Flemish government on well-being, youth, drugs and victim assistance; the province of Antwerp on disasters and violence within families and the City of Antwerp on nuisance and youth. The different government levels also set up their own programmes to finance projects that contribute to a better security perception.

Table 4.3 Responsibilities and policy programmes of the five involved governmental levels

Governmental level	Responsibilities	Policy programmes
European Union	Migration policies Human trafficking Organized crime	Urban I and II, Objective II
Belgian government	Large-city policies Prostitution Police and drugs	Security contracts
Flemish region	Well-being Youth Drugs Victim assistance	Social Impulse Fund
Province of Antwerp	Disasters Violence within families	
City of Antwerp	Nuisance and youth	

The European Union also subsidises with its Urban-I and -II and Objective-II programmes projects in backward neighbourhoods. They have their own objectives and timing and their own evaluation requirements. The Objective-II programme supports projects that contribute to the transition to a new urban-economic structure. The URBAN programmes were launched to relieve some of the most acute problems in urban areas related to a lack of economic prospects, low incomes and mostly unfavourable living conditions.

Since 1993, the federal government of Belgium has supported crime prevention projects in the form of the so-called 'security contracts'. These contracts have two main strategies (van den Broeck, 2002): 1) the opportunities for crime has to be reduced by more control on the street and better protection of private and public property; and 2) better integration of groups considered 'at risk' (youth, unemployed, ethnic minority) has to reduce crime rates. The federal government stimulated the setting up of integral policies on prostitution and on drugs, among other things.

The regional Flemish government financed various projects in problem neighbourhoods with their Social Impulse Fund. With the Social Impulse Fund Decree of 14 May 1996, the Flemish Community set out to help cities and municipalities carry out a policy intended to restore the living and environmental quality of the city and the backward neighbourhoods and to raise prosperity and fight deprivation (Ministerie van de Vlaamse Gemeenschap, 2000).

According to van den Broeck (2002, p. 175), as a consequence of the plethora of projects, top-down municipal initiatives are developed without any knowledge of the local situation, which results in 'collateral damage' when they collide with existing bottom-up initiatives. For instance, new neighbourhood facilities are opened in spite of existing infrastructure and networking of local residents. On the other hand, places that lack such a bottom-up grown network are neglected by municipal policy. It appears that this top-down policy leads to 'tutelage' and wasted money. Given the slow progress of the projects, tangible results do not follow (van den Broeck, 2002, p. 175).

The involvement of several policy layers with several projects and evaluation requirements hinders a holistic approach. There seems to be no incentive for integration of projects and for setting up tailor-made bottom-up approaches.

4.5.3 Fragmented Security Policy within the City of Antwerp

Not only does the mayor have a large say in security issues, but there is a separate alderman for integral safety care. This has, however, generated discussions on the respective responsibilities of the mayor and alderman regarding safety issues. Before the political decision was made to appoint an alderman for safety issues, no decisions were made regarding the division of tasks and responsibilities between the mayor and the alderman. The alderman wanted to develop an integral safety policy. This however turned out to be impossible because of a competency discussion between the mayor and the alderman and a lack of financial means.

As well as coordination problems between the five different vertical government layers, and the mayor and the alderman, there are also coordination problems within the administration of the City of Antwerp, where 8,000 civil servants work for the local administration within 10 business units. This administrative system is, however, highly compartmentalized and there appears to be hardly any interdepartmental cooperation.

A modest step towards improving the cooperation between involved actors and integrating projects was to appoint a Nuisance Manager in Antwerp. This Nuisance Manager was appointed to coordinate measures to reduce nuisance in designated areas. One of the aims of appointing the Nuisance Manager and designating nuisance areas is to integrate police and other services. Currently, there are three nuisance areas: *Kruger en Den Drink* (*Borgerhout-Noord*), *Provinciestraat* (*Borgerhout-Zuid*) and

Kiel (*Antwerpen-Zuid*). A fourth nuisance area may be added: *Koningsplein* (close to the central station area). Priorities in tackling the nuisance in the designated areas are: 1) run-down houses; 2) drug nuisance; 3) problem youths; and 4) garbage dumping. Because there is only one Nuisance Manager and there is such a large fragmentation of policies, it cannot be expected that substantial improvements to integrate safety policies will be achieved with this policy measure.

4.5.4 New Safety Policy since January 2005

In 2004, after the administrative crisis, a new safety policy was designed, presented to and approved by the City Council. Since 1 January 2005 this new policy has been implemented. The dissatisfaction and discomfort among the residents of Antwerp remained high and there was a growing consciousness within the City Council that something had to change. The main change is that safety policy is no longer a broad and fragmented policy. The new policy is a core policy which emphatically focuses on a few safety-related issues. The core issues are related to problems of security, lliving conditions and integration. The objective of the City Council is that residents from Antwerp can and will feel safe again in their own neighbourhood.

The new policy focuses on a few priorities, which are either neighbourhood- or person-oriented. The City of Antwerp has appointed 10 neighbourhoods and five streets as 'hot-spots'. These are areas where safety and liveability problems have become relatively strong and complex. There is also a person-oriented approach which focuses on young persistent offenders, young group followers, children from the Balkans, addicted persistent offenders, risk families, and people littering on the streets.

The approach of the current safety policy is project-based. The supervision lies within the new Project Unit Safety. In 2005, the budget for urban non-police activities is €6.9 million. In addition, the police, who are one of the main actors of the safety policy, have an operational budget of €136 million and an extra budget for investments of €6.3 million.

At the time of writing, the new safety policy is only just being implemented and clear results are not yet available.

4.5.5 Police Image Problem

The Antwerp police seem to have a relatively bad image among the population (Danneels and Tuerlinckx, 2002). This appears to be due to relatively high crime rates, among other things. The local population and the media accuse the local police for not having undertaken the right measures to fight crime in particular. The media tries to find out every possible reprehensible police actions (for instance, misuse of public means) to strengthen the negative image of the Anwerp police. It appears that whatever project the police develop, they will receive largely critical comments from the population and the media.

Moreover, because of the large political power of the 'Flemish Front' and their focus on insecurity, there is a considerable amount of pressure to achieve short-term results in fighting crime. This pressure sometimes paralyzes a more structural comprehensive approach towards fighting insecurity. It invites the police to undertake particularly repressive actions, to be able to show results on the short term. One of the reactions of an organization of all more recently arrived inhabitants (AEL, Arabic-European Liga) was to control the actual activities of police surveillances. This might further hinder an effective police operation in Antwerp.

As well as the federal police, about 2,340 officers work for the local police organization. The City Council wants to increase this number to 2,630 (van de Perre et al., 2002). For the local police it is difficult to recruit sufficient police officers. Many (potential) officers prefer to work in the green suburbs rather than in the central urban areas with the larger urban problems. The €250 monthly premium for working in the central urban area does not help in this respect. There are relatively many supervisory employees, mostly financed by the federal government. Examples are the 'auxiliary police' (pale blue uniform), the 'neighbourhood supervisors' (green uniform), the 'city wardens' (purple uniform) and the 'park supervisors' (green uniform) (van den Broeck, 2002, p. 174). These employees are, however, often poorly educated and do not have the communication skills of regular police officers. Consequently, they have difficulty with intervening in the frequently-occurring social conflicts. The local population, however, associates these supervisory employees with the regular police force. As a result, their interventions can weaken the image of the Antwerp police.

4.5.6 Best Practice 1: Approach to the Drug Problem: Urban Consultation Network

There is relatively little drug nuisance in Antwerp. Most of this nuisance is concentrated in the *Provinciestraat* and the *Koningsplein* (two drug clinics are located here). Nuisance concerns 'hanging-around' behaviour and noise nuisance. In Antwerp crime rates are seldom related to drug use. Solutions to drug problems in particular are approached from a social perspective, rather than a repressive one.

An urban consultation network has been set up to be more effective in reducing drug nuisance and helping drug addicts. In the SODA (*Stedelijk Overleg Drugs Antwerpen*, Urban Consultation Drugs Antwerp) network there are, amongst other organizations, the judiciary, the Social Department, aid organizations, psychiatric organizations and hospitals. Moreover, since 1996, there has been a single drug coordinator, financed by federal funds.

The network is meant for exchange of information and for signalling of problems in particular. The idea is that the visions, strategies and approaches of the partners have to be mutually attuned, cooperation has to be stimulated and a clear task division has to be implemented. Moreover, the SODA collects data on which to judge the proposed policy options.

Partly thanks to the network, there are good connections between the judiciary, aid organizations and the city administration regarding the approach to the drug problem. The existence of the SODA network helps to institutionalize these connections. The judiciary in particular appears to cooperate in a constructive way to reduce drug nuisance.

The network designed the Strategic Antwerp Drugs Plan in 1998, the first drug policy for the City of Antwerp. By 2004 this plan had been renewed. The four priorities of the renewed plan are prevention, improving care facilities for the drug addicted, guaranteeing good living conditions for residents and a strict repression of drug dealing (SODA, 2004).

4.5.7 Best Practice 2: Line-Spotting in Public Transport Project (Lijnspotting)

Lijnspotting is one of the projects within the security contract with the federal government. The aim of the project is to increase both the objective and subjective security of drivers and passengers. With help of the available funds, 'line-spotters' are appointed. They are put into service in particular on those lines on which passengers feel unsafe. These are often lines which are used by students of secondary school students or lines through underprivileged neighbourhoods in which relatively many immigrants live. Feelings of insecurity are caused by thefts, aggression within public transport, quarrelling and fighting. These problems can be positioned in a broader societal phenomenon: increasing intolerance within the society.

The line-spotters do not have the same competences as the police agents have: they are however in particular active as social workers. These persons help old people and people with baby carriages to get in and off buses and they speak to people who behave in an antisocial way. When things escalate they can call the police directly by a radio connection: the police then normally arrive within 10 minutes. So line-spotters help and inform passengers and prevent and signal crime. In the period of our investigation there were more than 40 line-spotters active. They have to be highly-motivated people with good verbal skills: they receive full training to become line-spotters. The *Lijnspotting* project is considered to be quite successful. People feel safer in public transport vehicles with line-spotters. In many cases when the line-spotters operate, the police do not have to assist. Moreover, the project generates jobs for unemployed people.

Since 2003, a formalization of the cooperation between *Lijnspotting*, police and schools has taken place in order to be able to address nuisance by secondary school students. It appears that only a few students cause nuisance, but the problems can be very persistent. By involving police and schools, it is easier to access and penalize the students. The cooperation consists of regular meetings between the three institutions to discuss the relevant problems and solutions.

The results of the project are positive. The number of interventions by line-spotters has significantly increased over the last few years. This does not mean, however, that crime and nuisance increased. On the contrary, the continuous increase of the number of incidents aggression has been halted and in 2003 even seemed to decrease. The decrease in aggression cannot be accredited solely to the presence of the line-spotters. Other aspects, such as camera supervision, new trams, ticket inspectors and the cooperation with the police have contributed as well (De Lijn, undated).

At the end of 2004 the City of Antwerp and the public transport company *De Lijn* agreed on continuation of the *Lijnspotting* project.

4.5.8 Best Practice 3: BIN Networks

The BIN network is considered to be a best practice for enhancing security perception in neighbourhoods. A BIN (*Buurt informatie netwerk*, neigbourhood information network) is a kind of neighbourhood watch, inspired by English examples. The project was set up in Belgium in 1994 after the frequent robberies in fashion shops (by the 'Kappa 1 gang'). A BIN is a structural partnership between citizens and the local police in a delineated area that contributes to the following three aims: to enhance the general security perception; to stimulate the social control; and to disseminate prevention ideas (Vzw Buurtinformatienetwerk, 2003, p. 5).

The BIN networks work as follows. Citizens within a certain neighbourhood can inform the local police that they want to set up a BIN network. BINs have to be clearly delineated areas. They can be delineated by, for instance, large infrastructure, parks or woods. The police subsequently assess the nature of the problems that confront such a neigbourhood. The BIN is meant only for external safety problems in neighbourhoods: to signal, for instance, suspicious persons entering the neighbourhoods concerned. It can be considered to be a *virtual fence or shield* around a neighbourhood. A BIN is no solution for, for instance, cohesion problems within a district – quarrels, riots or pollution in districts have to be solved by other means. After assessing whether there are external safety problems, the voluntary members have to be registered and vetted for criminal records. One of the civilian members of the network will then be chosen as the coordinator and will have direct contact with a BIN contact person of the local police.

In a BIN there has to be a certain bond between the inhabitants. The BINs also can help to enhance social cohesion in neighbourhoods, because the members have regular meetings where they can exchange information and experiences. This social-cohesion goal is explicitly considered to be one of the aims of the project.

The members of the BIN network operate as *the eyes and the ears* of a neighbourhood. When they notice criminal acts, like burglaries or car thefts, or suspicious persons they can report them to the police (see Figure 4.2). The BIN contact-person of the local police assesses and verifies the obtained information and decides whether they will send colleagues to the neighbourhood. The police can consequently inform the (civil) BIN coordinator what the police have done and what has been observed: the coordinator then informs the BIN-members in the neighbourhood (see Figure 4.3). BINs thus help the police with getting information on (potential) criminal acts, and explicitly give civilians responsibilities to achieve this. The inhabitants also get a better insight into the actions undertaken by the local police. This might help to improve citizens' trust in the capabilities of the police.

There are also BINs of shop owners, who can inform the BIN network of observed thefts within shops. Shoplifters often remain in a shopping area after they have stolen something, because they might get arrested by the police when they leave the area. Through the information of the BIN network, other shop owners can be alerted to the shoplifter and they will be keen on spotting him or her in their shops.

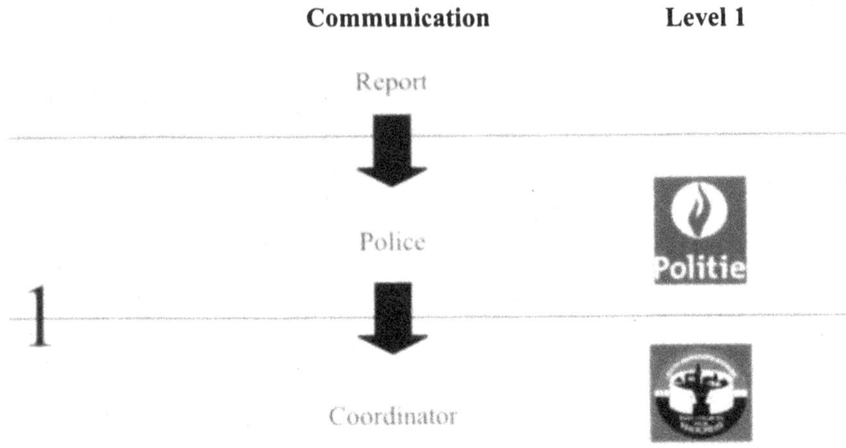

Figure 4.2 Communication within BIN networks via the police

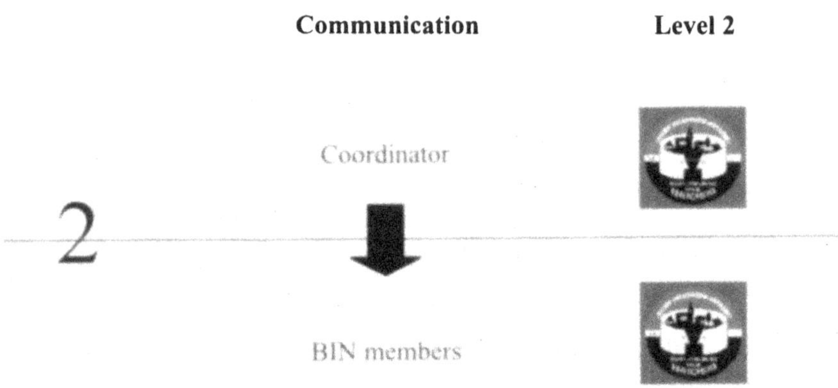

Figure 4.3 Communication within BIN networks from the coordinator to the BIN-members

Communication by the police to the BIN coordinator and the other BIN members can be done via a fax or a semaphone (see Figure 4.4). The passing on of information within the BIN network can take place via a telephone pyramid.

Currently there are 11 BINs in Antwerp. Up to the time of writing, there has been no quantitative evaluation of the BIN instrument. However, an improvement of the safety perception in the BIN neighbourhoods has been noticed. In particular, the BINs of shop owners seem to be successful. Thanks to its BIN network, shoplifting in the major shopping street *De Meir* decreased by between 30–40 per cent. It turns out that shoplifting can shift to other areas after setting up a BIN network. It is hoped,

Figure 4.4 Communication within BIN networks via a semaphone

however, that the total amount of thefts and shoplifting in the city will decrease thanks to this new approach.

A disadvantage of the BIN approach might be that only districts with the lowest crime rates are helped. It appears that those neighbourhoods with the most severe safety problems (the underprivileged neighbourhoods) have set up hardly any such BIN networks, because the necessary societal support is missing.

4.5.9 Best Practice 4: A Comprehensive Policy on Prostitution

In recent years, the City of Antwerp has been quite successful in decreasing the nuisance of the prostitution sector. There was window prostitution on 17 streets distributed over two areas: the station environment and the *Schipperskwartier*. Moreover, there was streetwalking in the *Atheneumbuurt*. The prostitution generated relatively much nuisance, such as circulating cars, noise nuisance, garbage dumping and many crimes. Moreover, in the Schipperskwartier, there were many complementary phenomena generating nuisance, such as human trafficking (often illegal, where foreign women were forced into prostitution); mafia members from Albany controlled the windows, using violence to show their power; many fights and shootings took place; there was illegal trade (in particular at and around Falcon Square); and there was rack renting – high rents for windows were demanded and the working circumstances for the prostitutes were quite bad.

As from 1999, the residents of the involved and surrounding areas were no longer prepared to accept the nuisance. They presented a petition to the City Council demanding proactive policies to reduce the nuisance of prostitution and to improve the living conditions in the neighbourhood.

In a reaction to this the City of Antwerp developed an integral plan to fight the nuisance of prostitution. It was a comprehensive plan in order to do more than just fight the symptoms of the nuisance. The aim was not to completely ban prostitution, but to control the situation. The quality of life for residents in the areas involved had to be improved substantially. To achieve that, the City chose to concentrate window prostitution in three streets (a reduction from 300 to a planned 200 windows, but which seems to have resulted in 250 windows) and to forbid streetwalking. Moreover, streets and areas no longer used by prostitutes had to be redeveloped. The prostitution zone was made car free and there was more attention placed by the cleaning department on the prostitution zone. Furthermore the working and health circumstances of the prostitutes had to be improved substantially. Two specific police teams were installed to achieve the envisaged goals.

The new integral city policy turned out to be quite successful. Indeed, the prostitution zone can potentially be reduced to three streets. There was a sharp decline in crime rates: total crime rates in the Schipperskwartier decreased by 40 per cent. The Albanian mafia lost control of the windows. Illegal trade at Falcon Square disappeared (Danneels and Tuerlinckx, 2002). There was an increased safety perception by local inhabitants and better working circumstances for the prostitutes. The traffic nuisance was also substantially reduced, though there are still some parking problems in adjacent neighbourhoods. Some of the prostitution problems have been transferred to other cities, such as Brussels, Liège and Lille.

Redevelopment of the area has taken place. Every house-owner in the area is obliged to invest in their property, but in 2005 only half of the owners actually invested. The city has also invested in the quality of the public space. With help from European URBAN funds some old prostitution buildings in the station area have been transformed into a design centre (see Figure 4.5). More urban plans have been made and presented to upgrade the old prostitution zone. The intention is to attract new inhabitants (for instance students) and to restore the social fabric in the area.

The actors involved in the comprehensive prostitution policy indicated as factors which might help to explain the success so far now of the new approach:

- setting up a clear and balanced plan – based upon a good vision – to tackle the problems in an effective way;
- generating sufficient political support for the plans;
- the willingness of the involved actors to stick to the chosen policies, also when facing problems;
- having sound communication between all involved partners;
- having sufficient financial means (to invest in physical elements and to pay salaries).

It appears that exactly these success factors should be present in the overall urban safety policy.

Figure 4.5 Reconversion of old prostitution buildings into a design centre

Source: J. Wils and K. Haine, Powerpoint presentation 'De integrale aanpak van de prostitutie in Antwerpen'.

4.6 Synthesis

4.6.1 Safety Perception

In Antwerp, urban insecurity is a topical subject. In the local media relatively much is written on perceived urban insecurity and often on the lack of good policy answers. During the previous decade crime rates rose continuously: at the beginning of the new millennium there was, however, a stabilization of crime. In addition, perceptions of safety in Antwerp are relatively strong, especially compared to other Flemish cities. Local inhabitants appear to complain particularly about problems with living conditions, such as nuisance and pollution problems.

Some argue that the increased fear of crime is mainly due to the lack of social cohesion. As well as the increasing individualism, the presence of many different population groups is considered to be an important reason for the decrease in mutual communication between inhabitants. For many newly-arrived inhabitants appear to be badly integrated within the urban social fabric. Moreover, in recent years immigrants from Eastern European countries who were involved in illegal activities generated relatively many problems in Antwerp. It is expected that such problems could increase with the further enlargement of the European Union.

4.6.2 Urban Attractiveness and Spatial Behaviour

In Antwerp, as in many other Western cities, a selective emigration process has taken place. People who could afford it moved to suburban locations, leaving relatively poor people behind. Several central urban areas of Antwerp house high concentrations of low income groups who are incapable of investing in their environment. In these neighbourhoods, there are relatively high unemployment rates and their residents are often low-skilled or unskilled. In and around these districts, relatively many offences and felonies take place. It appears that it is this combination and concentration of problems which causes perceived insecurity, in particular among the inhabitants in such neighbourhoods.

4.6.3 Policy Reactions

In Chapter 2 we stated that we expect that security will increasingly become an integrating concept for urban governance, because it seems that the desire for more security gets high priority in many cities. In Antwerp, it is indeed the case that crime rates instead of, for example, unemployment, has become a major criterion in the allocation of financial resources to the neighbourhoods (van den Broeck, 2002, p. 184). However, there is as yet no sufficient comprehensive approach to the perceived urban insecurity. In Antwerp there are five governmental levels active each with their own responsibilities, policy programmes and related evaluation requirements. This hinders a comprehensive approach towards urban insecurity and causes a lack of transparency regarding policy projects undertaken. Often there is the complaint that safety issues are approached too much in a top-down way. It appears that sometimes safety projects are started with very little knowledge of the local situation or they frustrate programmes that were already in progress. Furthermore, some issues are not debatable:there are taboos, such as, amongst others, the role of minorities and the existence of problem neighbourhoods. Consequently, it is difficult to develop specific policies on such topics.

In 2004, a first but major step was taken towards a more comprehensive approach to urban safety. A new safety policy was designed. The former fragmented approach seems to be being replaced by a more coherent approach, although specifically focused on a selected amount of safety issues. The focus is twofold: neighbourhood-oriented and person-oriented. A selection of 10 hot-spot areas, five hot-spot streets and six target groups was made. The City of Antwerp's Unit Safety Project has a central role in the implementation of this new policy.

4.6.4 *Organizing Capacity of the Antwerp Safety Policy*

In Antwerp one of the core problems in tackling the perceived urban insecurity appears to be a lack of leadership. There seems to be no actor who is able and willing to lead in an effective and decisive way to tackle the most important problems. Nobody seems to be able to take the lead in the tangle of governmental institutions, political parties and bureaucratic organizations involved and nobody appears to take the political responsibility of breaking the actual stalemate. As a consequence, there is no comprehensive vision on how to improve perceived security. This is also complicated because some problems cannot be explicitly indicated as a result of existing (political) taboos.

Many actors are involved in safety policies at the five different governmental levels but also in the business units within the City administration. However, they do not form strategic networks. They operate in the field of their formulated responsibilities and appear not to be interested in achieving synergetic effects by cooperation. Again this might be due to a lack of leadership, as an effective leadership can be very helpful to stimulate actors to work together.

There appears to be no broad political support for measures to improve the urban governance. A major hindrance to this is the large variety of interests within the governmental coalition. The *Cordon Sanitair* seems to imply relatively large differences of opinions on the nature of the real problems and the proper solutions. Consequently, there is a lack of political support on many topics. The lack of decisiveness of political institutions strengthens the mistrust of the local inhabitants in the urban government.

Another consequence seems to be the bad image of the local police. In the eyes of the local inhabitants, it should be the major actor in increasing perceived safety. Many inhabitants feel, however, that they do not act in an effective way.

Communication concerning urban insecurity appears to be led by the (local) media. They often stress the security problems and the inability of local government and the police to improve the situation. Because of this, people will feel less secure within the city. The more (media) draw attention to insecurity, the more inhabitants will feel insecure.

With the approval and implementation of the new safety policy, organizing capacity seems to be improving. A clear vision and target has been put forward under the lead of the Safety Project team. Whether or not the different involved actors will start to cross their own institutionalized borders and tackle the safety issue collectively remains to be seen, but the first signs appear to be positive.

4.6.5 *Best Practices*

In this case of the city of Antwerp, we discussed four 'best practices'. Although the urban level much has to be done to achieve an effective, comprehensive, security policy, there are some individual examples of projects through which the perceived security could be improved. According to our discussion partners these examples show how, through an improved organizing capacity, the actors involved can contribute to an urban environment that is perceived as safer than before.

The first one is the approach to the drug problem. By setting up an urban consultation network cooperation and the dissemination of available information between the actors involved have been improved. One of the benefits of this new approach has been a better task division. As a result the relatively little drug nuisance in Antwerp could be further reduced.

Another best practice is the Line-Spotting in Public Transport project. By employing 'line-spotters' on problematic lines, people feel safer in public transport. To tackle some of the problems related to students of secondary schools more effectively, the line-spotters have started to cooperate more actively with police and schools. Because of the positive results, the project has been extended.

Another successful project to improve the perceived urban safety is the BIN network, a kind of neighbourhood watch. Inhabitants in districts that have set up such a network feel safer and in some of those districts a decline of crime rates has been noticeable. The BIN networks are also aimed at enhancing social cohesion within districts: lack of social cohesion is considered one of the major causes of heightened feelings of insecurity.

A fourth best practice is the integral approach to the nuisance of the prostitution sector. After substantial protests from the local inhabitants, a comprehensive plan was set up to reduce this nuisance. The aim was not to completely ban prostitution, but to control it and to improve the working and health circumstances of the prostitutes, together with the quality of life of the local inhabitants. The city government managed to reduce the prostitution zone from 17 to three streets, to ban the involved Albanian mafia and to substantially reduce the crime rates. The already-mentioned success factors of this plan– vision, support, willingness, communication and finances – seem, however, to be lacking in the broader urban safety policy. This project could therefore serve as an example for that broader policy.

4.6.6 Recommendations

It would be better if safety policies would take into account that most of the complaints of the local inhabitants concerning perceived insecurity are related to nuisance and pollution. To improve the perceived urban safety it is thus not only necessary to fight crime but also, and even more importantly, to improve the quality of life and mutual communication between inhabitants. Instead of a local governance of crime there is perhaps simply a need for better local government which stops the degradation of neighbourhoods and improves the quality of life. This requires a more integrated, coordinated and accountable policy by the city (van den Broeck, p. 176).

In this respect there appears to be a need for one clear leading actor to obtain a more comprehensive approach in this field. Moreover, there is a need for coordination of the large number of programmes and the large number of actors involved. To clearly define the most urgent problems and relate them to targets at the level of the urban region would be an important step forward. At the same time, there is also a need for a better balance between top-down and bottom-up approaches. Local needs and initiatives should be better taken into account to be more effective and to obtain more social support. In this respect, much could be learned from the success factors of the comprehensive approach of reducing the nuisance of the prostitution sector. The Unit Safety Project appointed under the new safety policy appears to provide for the need for coordination of the large number of programmes and the large number of actors involved. As this new policy is still being implemented at the time of writing, the results remain to be seen.

Notes

1 Part of this section has been taken from van den Berg et al., 2003.
2 Part of this section has been taken from van den Berg et al., 1998, pp. 39–40.
3 Part of this section has been taken from van den Berg et al., 2003.

Chapter 5

The Case of Glasgow

5.1 Introduction

In this case study we focus on the social security in the city of Glasgow. Section 5.2 gives a concise profile of this urban region. In Section 5.3 we deal with the perception of security in Glasgow and the possible causes of feelings of insecurity. Next, in Section 5.4, we will go into the related spatial behaviour of local inhabitants. Section 5.5 goes into policy reactions regarding urban unsafety. In this section we will give specific attention to some *best practices*. Our focus for Glasgow is on community safety problems related to the city centre. Finally, Section 5.6 presents conclusions and some recommendations.

5.2 Profile of Glasgow

The city of Glasgow is an old industrial city, situated in the southwest of Scotland on the bank of the River Clyde: the 'central belt of Scotland'. Glasgow is the centre of the Strathclyde Region. At the beginning of the Industrial Revolution, Glasgow was very prosperous. But, after the decline of the traditional industries in the 1960s, the city faced severe economic and social problems. Ever since, Glasgow is perceived to be a city with high-unemployment rates, high social problems and high crime rates. And although half of the total population is living in deprived areas (41 of the 79 wards Glasgow counts belong to the top-100 most deprived areas of Scotland) things have started to change for the better in the last decade. Glasgow's economy is slowly recovering and the city is trying to improve its image.

5.2.1 Population

In 2001, Glasgow city had 578,000 inhabitants and in the same period Glasgow region had a total population of 629,500 (General Register Office for Scotland, 2004). This is about 12 per cent of the population of Scotland (Scottish Enterprise, 2004a). The population density is almost 33 persons per hectare (General Register Office for Scotland, 2004). For a long time now, the population of Glasgow has been declining. Over the period 1990–2000 the population has decreased by 3.8 per cent (Scottish Enterprise Glasgow, 2002). This decline is caused by both a natural population decline and a net out-migration of citizens. What is striking is that the decline of the female population was more (–4.5 per cent) than the decline of the male population (–3.1 per

Figure 5.1 Geographical position of the city of Glasgow in Europe

cent) in the period 1990–2000, while the share of women in the total urban population (53 per cent) is higher than the share of men (47 per cent) (General Register Office for Scotland, 2004). There are signs however, that the population decline is coming to an end. In the year 2001 there was a small migration surplus of in total 4,000 people (General Register Office for Scotland, 2004).

Compared to Scotland, Glasgow has a slightly higher percentage of people in the age-band 16–44 years and a slightly lower percentage of 45–59-year-olds (General Register Office for Scotland, 2004). Most of the citizens are Scottish (89 per cent), a minority is born in England, Wales, Ireland, or Europe and about 3 per cent of the citizens are born elsewhere (General Register Office for Scotland, 2004). According to another source, the Glasgow City Council, the minority ethnic group now makes up 5.4 per cent of Glasgow's total population. There is, for example, a significant

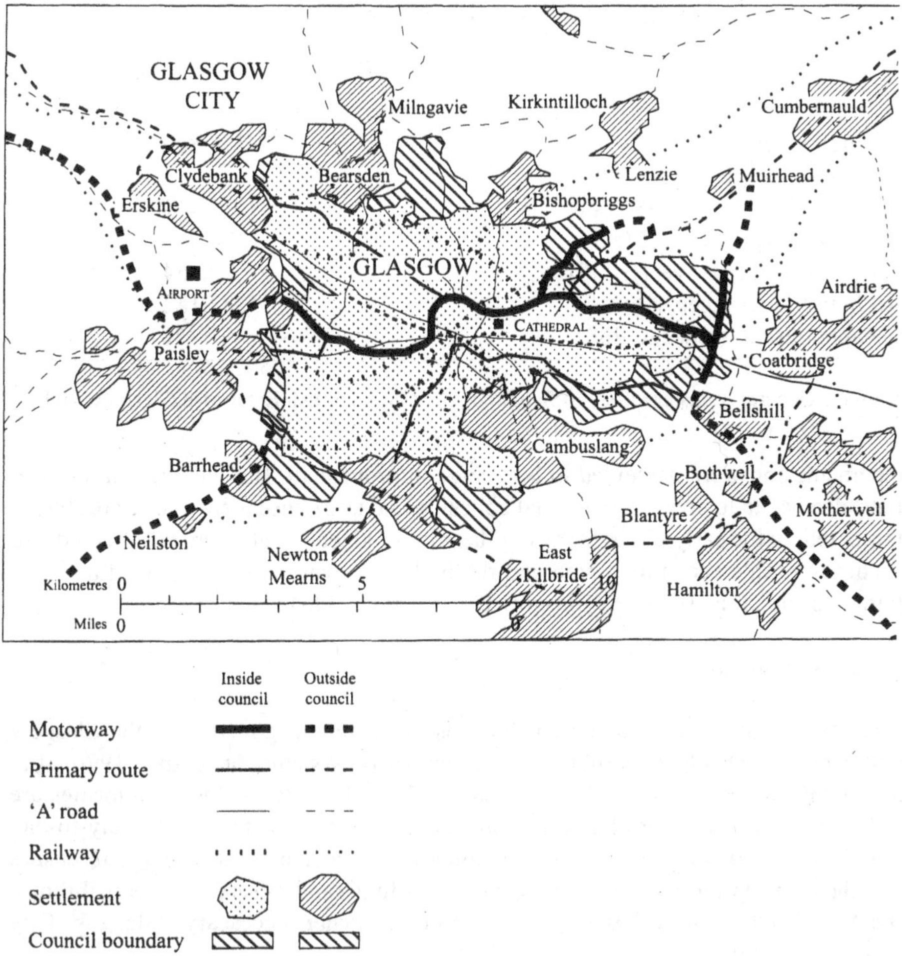

Figure 5.2 Map of the city of Glasgow

Asian population group and a thriving Chinese community (Glasgow City Council, 2004a).

A relatively high share of the citizens (especially by British standards) lives in rented housing. Almost half of the residents (49.7 per cent) occupy their own house, while the other half of the residents (45.8 per cent) rents their house either from public housing or privately, and another 4.5 per cent lives rent free (General Register Office for Scotland, 2004). Around 4 per cent of the total housing stock was vacant in 2001 (General Register Office for Scotland, 2004). This is relatively low, but it is highly likely that there may be differences within the city. The housing stock is characterized by a large share of high-rise flats, the 'tower blocks', built after World War II to solve the acute shortage of accommodation. These flats replaced the small old stone

Table 5.1 Demographic data for Glasgow

	Glasgow
Population, 2001	577,869
Population density (ha.), 2001	33
Population growth, 1990–2000	–4%
Inmigration (past year), 2001	24,768
Out-migration (past year), 2001	20,454
All household spaces, 2001	282,182
Vacant household spaces, 2001	4%

Sources: General Register Office of Scotland, 2004 and Scottish Enterprise Glasgow, 2002.

tenements and were perceived to be a huge improvement. But the large, individual flats also began to break down social cohesion and as a consequence social problems increased. In the early 1980s many of Glasgow's old tenements were refurbished into highly desirable accommodation and the high-rises were largely replaced by more human-scale urban housing (Glasgow City Council, 2004b).

5.2.2 Administrative System

The city of Glasgow is divided into 79 wards and is directly governed by the Glasgow City Council. This local authority was established by statute on 1 April 1996, after a reorganization of local government in Scotland. Essentially, local authorities are independent of the central government and the management of their day-to-day business is for them to conduct as they think is the most appropriate way. To ensure that the local authority is properly managing its funds and its service responsibilities, the Scottish Executive has powers to intervene when necessary (Glasgow City Council, 2004c).

The Glasgow City Council consists of 79 elected members: one member for each ward. The last elections were in June 2004. The members of the City Council develop policies for service delivery and manage these through a structure of committees and subcommittees. Principal committees include, for example, the Policy and Resources Committee, the Audit and Ethics Committee and committees responsible for overseeing each of the Council's services.

The Policy and Resources Committee is the key Council Committee regarding safety policies. This committee guides the Council in the formation of its policy objectives and priorities, develops and supervises the Council's Best Value Review arrangements and reviews the effectiveness of the Council's performance. One of its subcommittees is the Community Safety and Health Committee. This subcommittee is important for this case study, because of its role in the safety developments in the city in general and in the city centre in particular.

Figure 5.3 presents the structure diagram of the Community Safety and Health Committee. This diagram shows that the Community Safety and Health Committee consists of the Community Safety Partnership Board (CSPB), which brings together representatives of the police, several council services, national health services, volunteer groups, etc. They meet four times annually and provide the strategic framework for community safety. Then there is the Community Safety Forum Steering Group (CSFSG) which makes the link between the strategic level of the CSPB and the operational level. At the operational level there are 11 Safety Forums for 11 geographical areas within Glasgow. In these local forums, representatives of statutory bodies, local voluntary groups and local residents meet regularly to discuss the community safety development in their area.

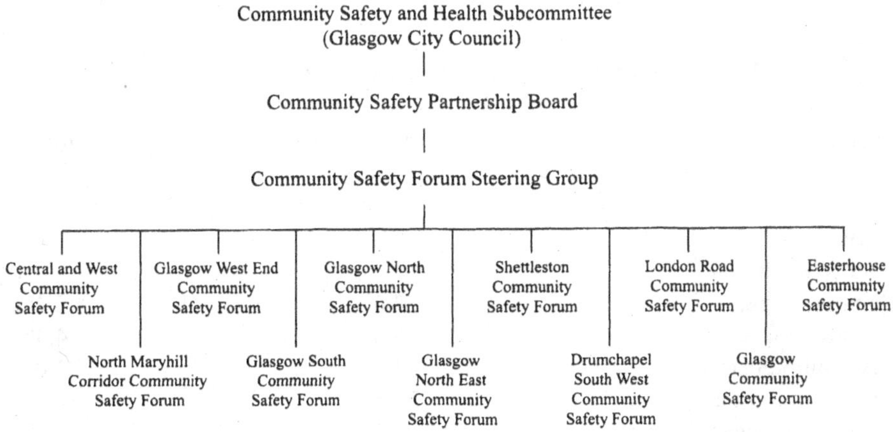

Figure 5.3 Structure diagram of the Community Safety and Health Committee

Source: Development and Regeneration Services, 2004.

As stated before, the administrative region of Glasgow consists of 79 wards. This administrative region of Glasgow is limited. Some of the wealthier suburbs along the border of the council are not included in the administrative region. The wards belonging to the City of Glasgow are relatively poor, meaning that the City of Glasgow has relatively low financial means to operate their service responsibilities. Because citizens of the neighbouring suburbs use these services as well, there are discussions going on about whether or not the borders of the administrative region of the Glasgow City Council will be extended. However, these discussions are long term, which meets much resistance. It is not very likely that there will be an agreement on this point on the short term.

5.2.3 Economy and Employment

During the previous decade Glasgow's economy finally began to recover from the industrial decline of the 1960s. The city has developed itself as commercial capital of Scotland, is now one of Europe's top 20 financial centres. In addition, Glasgow ranks as the second UK retail centre after London's West End and the tourism sector is increasing in importance for the regional economy (Scottish Enterprise Glasgow, 2004b). In 2001, the gross value added was £11.1 billion (€15.8 billion), which was 16 per cent of Scotland's gross output (Scottish Enterprise Glasgow, 2004b). The key economic sectors are business services, communication, biosciences, optoelectronics, software, creative industries, health, retail and tourism. There are over 21,000 business units in Glasgow, among which are BT Scotland, Scottish Power, Abbey National, National and the BBC (Scottish Enterprise Glasgow, 2004b).

Table 5.2 Employment by sector in Glasgow, 2002

Sector	2002 in thousands	2002 %
Agriculture	0.2	0.1%
Energy/water	4.0	1.0%
Manufacturing	27.6	7.2%
Construction	16.6	4.3%
Distribution/catering	84.7	22.0%
Transport/communications	23.5	6.1%
Financial/business services	89.4	23.2%
Public services	117.7	30.6%
Other services	21.2	5.5%
Total employees	384.9	100.0%

Source: Scottish Enterprise Glasgow, 2004b

Currently, the economic growth rate of Glasgow is higher than the average for Scotland and even higher than UK average. In the year 2002, the economy grew by 2.4 per cent and the expansion of the Glasgow's economy continues: the medium growth rate over the period 2002–2007 is estimated at 3.1 per cent (Scottish Enterprise Glasgow, 2004b). In the wider metropolitan area of Glasgow, the working age population is around 1.1 million and in the city of Glasgow itself, it is approximately 338,000 people (Scottish Enterprise Glasgow, 2004b). Over the last decade employment grew to approximately 400,000 jobs in 2002 (Scottish Enterprise Glasgow, 2004b). In 2000 over 30 per cent of jobs were in public administration, education and health. Financial and business services accounted for 24 per cent of employment and another 20 per cent of employment in Glasgow was in distribution, hotels and restaurants (Scottish Enterprise Glasgow, 2004b). Unemployment is not as high as it used to be: in the past decade it has decreased significantly. At the time or writing, the unemployment rate was estimated at 4.7 per cent (Scottish Enterprise Glasgow, 2002). But unemployment still remains above the Scottish and British average (Scottish Enterprise Glasgow, 2004b). Furthermore, the percentage of Glasgow's working age population in employment was 59.7 per cent, significantly below the Scottish and British levels of 73.1 per cent and 74.6 per cent respectively (Glasgow City Council, 2003). Average gross weekly earnings for a full-time job also remain below British average: £418 (€596) in Glasgow against £444 (€634) in Britain (Scottish Enterprise Glasgow, 2002).

5.3 The Perception of Security in Glasgow

There are differences in crime rates and safety perceptions between the city centre and the suburbs of Glasgow. As in most European cities, crime rates are higher in the city centre than in other parts of the city. This is due to the spatial concentration of people and economic activities which makes it a very attractive site for criminal activities like shoplifting and theft and which makes it a very vulnerable site for social disorder such as (alcohol-related) violence. At the same time the city centre is the 'show-piece' of the city for tourists and other visitors and it is therefore essential to create a space where people feel safe. This case study of the city of Glasgow will focus on crime problems and safety perceptions in the city centre. In this section, most figures about crime and safety are for the entire city of Glasgow (or the wider region) and not just the city centre, but this information will be supplemented with the general vision and opinion of experts about the safety situation in the city centre of Glasgow, as acquired via interviews.

5.3.1 Crime

In the city of Glasgow, the total number of recorded crime was 79,000 in the year 2003/2004, which are approximately 140 recorded crimes per 1,000 inhabitants. This number decreased in the past few years with around 2 per cent annually (Community Services, undated(a): Strathclyde Police Authority, 2004). In the city centre a concentration of certain types of crime is visible. In Glasgow Central and West, the are of which the city centre forms part, there are relatively high reports of crime and offences of theft by shoplifting, other theft, petty assault and breach of the peace (MORI, 2003). The reasons for this are twofold. Firstly, as the second retail centre after London's West End, Glasgow's city centre is considered to be a haven for shoplifting and pickpocketing. Secondly, with its many pubs and clubs the city centre has a very attractive night-time economy and attracts many visitors. But because of an insufficient transport system, it is difficult to transfer all the people who want to go home after the pubs and clubs close during the weekend, making it a hotbed for disorder. Keeping in mind that there is a 'knife-culture' among young people going out in Glasgow, it is not surprising that there is a lot of (violent) crime in the city centre, especially during the Thursday, Friday and Saturday nights.

According to the Scottish Executive (2003), Scottish businesses face a cost of £670m (€956m) each year as a result of crime. Shoplifting and disorders after closing times of pubs and clubs are not the only causes of these costs but they contribute substantially to this burden. However bad the situation in the city centre is, the police have stressed that crime has decreased in the past few years.

Table 5.3 Crime figures Glasgow

Glasgow	2000–01	2001–02	2002–03	2003–04
Crime development	−2.1%	−1.4%	−2.0%	−4.8%
Recorded crime	86,053	84,808	83,057	79,096
Violent crime	9%	9%	10%	–
Housebreaking	12%	5%	5%	–
Vandalism	16%	17%	19%	–
Drug misuse	10%	11%	12%	–
Racist incidents	1%	1%	1%	–
Domestic abuse	–	8%	8%	–
Road accidents	8%	8%	9%	–
Road casualties	3%	3%	3%	–
Unknown	40%	37%	34%	–

Source: Community Services, undated(a).

5.3.2 Safety Perceptions

In general, the perceptions of the citizens of Glasgow were rather positive in 2003, with 90 per cent satisfied with Glasgow as a place to live (MORI, 2003). However, being satisfied does not automatically mean that nothing can be improved. And indeed, the citizens of Glasgow would like to see some things improved. Their top three recommendations for making Glasgow a better place to live are cleanliness, more/better policing and a reduction in the crime rates (MORI, 2003). All three aspects are related to safety perceptions. This top three do not actually reveal anything about the safety perceptions of the citizens, but they do indicate that citizens think that safety in Glasgow could be improved.

According to experts, the safety perceptions are an issue in Glasgow. Bad safety perceptions are especially focused on the city centre, although there might be more reason to negative safety perceptions to be focused on some of the neighbourhoods outside the city centre. Feelings of insecurity mainly occur among old people: they are easily intimidated by the 'threatening' behaviour of youths. But research shows that young people as well (sometimes) feel unsafe. What threatens them most are 'gangs', drugs users, 'rough' areas, dark areas and drunken people on the streets (Community Services, undated(a)).

Of course, as will become clear from the next section, safety perceptions are influenced by the image of the city, and Glasgow has had an image of being a 'rough city' for a long time now. But another factor influencing feelings of unsafety among certain population groups is believed to be the media. The credo is: 'Bad news sells'. The local media in particular, but also national media, tend to report everything about any criminal act in the city in the hope of selling more newspapers. However, the result of such an overload of negative news, without being balanced about any positive elements (which of course happen in the city as well), is that it is difficult for citizens to put things in perspective and consequently feelings of insecurity increase.

5.4 Urban Attractiveness and Spatial Behaviour

Outsiders such as (business) visitors and tourists do not have a particularly positive perception of Glasgow's urban attractiveness. For a long time Glasgow has been perceived as grey, violent and very unattractive. This image is even communicated in novels and movies (Pacione, 1995). An in-depth analysis of Glasgow's image revealed that of 50 attributes on an adjectival checklist, the first 21, referred to by more than 40 per cent of respondents, were all unfavourable. Glasgow is characterized by people from outside Scotland as having a good deal of unemployment, many slums and depressed, large council estates and as being working-class city, violent, and aggressive (Pacione, 1995). However, inhabitants of Glasgow perceive their city more positively. As stated before, in 2003 the perceptions of the citizens of Glasgow were in general rather positive: 90 per cent are satisfied with Glasgow as a place to live with 5 per cent dissatisfied (MORI, 2003). The perceptions about the *neighbourhoods* they live in are less good, but still positive: 79 per cent are satisfied and 15 per cent are dissatisfied with their neighbourhood as a place to live (MORI, 2003). There are strong differences between the citizens' perceptions about their own neighbourhoods. Those differences can be linked to the average household income. More people are satisfied in 'rich' neighbourhoods with an average income above £25,000 (€35,675) than in 'poor' neighbourhoods.

Recently, the city of Glasgow appears to become more attractive as a place to live and as a place to spend time. The first to notice are the inhabitants, but visitors and tourists are also slowly gaining interest in Glasgow. Since the 1980s Glasgow has been promoting itself as an attractive centre of culture and leisure. This offensive started in 1983 with the campaign 'Glasgow Miles Better' and was followed by campaigns and events like Glasgow Garden Festival (1988), European City of Culture (1990) and openings of the Scottish Exhibition and Conference Centre, Glasgow Royal Concert Hall, Gallery of Modern Art and Glasgow Auditorium (Glasgow City Council, 2004d). The city promotion seems to have had an effect: the number of tourists increased in the past decade and the retail centre has become the most attractive in the UK after

London's West End. In addition, Glasgow has a vibrant night economy that attracts many (young) people, from outside the city as well. However, this nightlife has a dual influence on Glasgow's image. On the one hand it increases its vibrancy but on the other hand it is a threat to the perceived security: the aggression and violence that come with the nightlife are confirming the image of Glasgow as a dangerous city.

The city centre is gaining in attractiveness not only for tourists and visitors but also for inhabitants. Some people even talk about an 'urban renaissance' with many people moving back into the city from the dormitory suburbs (Safer City Centre Initiative, 2004). In the city centre, housing projects have been initiated and more residents are now live in this area, although the mixture of people in this area is not representative as mainly rich people live there.

However, not all parts of the city are actually very attractive yet. In many suburbs there are major social and economic problems. Of Glasgow's 79 wards, 41 still belong to the top 100 most deprived areas in Scotland (Scottish Executive, 2004) and in 2002 the Child Poverty Action Group announced that the three most deprived areas in the United Kingdom were all located in Glasgow (BBC News, 2002). Those areas are characterized by unattractive tower blocks, high vacancy rates and high unemployment rates as well.

Negative safety perceptions may influence the spatial behaviour of residents and visitors. Visitors may decide not to come at all, residents may adapt their spatial behaviour by avoiding certain places or they may even decide to move away from the city. The same applies to companies. This may have economic, social and spatial consequences as well. It is obvious that a loss of companies and inhabitants is not good for urban development. According to the experts interviewed, the negative safety perceptions are not a direct threat to urban development in Glasgow's city centre. During the day at least, most people have a positive perception of safety: most people do feel safe in the city centre. (MORI, 2003). During the night, however, these perceptions are less good. There are people who tend to avoid the city centre after dark because they do feel afraid. A major cause for this is the night economy and the (alcohol-)related problems. Around 2 a.m. all pubs and clubs are closing and everyone wants to go home at the same time (this is not a specific Glaswegian problem, but more a typical problem in British' cities). The transport system in the city is not sufficient to get everyone out immediately: it takes about two-and-a-half hours. During this period irritation among visitors may rise and aggression and violence are often the answer. Although the city centre is less safe (both actually and perceptually) during the night and is avoided by some people, it is still a very popular place to go out for young people.

5.5 Policy Reactions

In Glasgow, community safety is a very important political issue. It is highly prioritized in the council objectives. The draft version of the Council Plan 2003–2007 of Glasgow City Council states five key objectives for the coming period: 1) to provide accountable, accessible Council Services that are effective and offer value for money; 2) to create a cleaner, safer city and more sustainable environment; 3) to promote social inclusion, tackle poverty and promote health and well-being; 4) to sustain the physical, social, economic, cultural and environmental regeneration of Glasgow; 5) to develop Glasgow's metropolitan role, quality of life, heritage and services (Glasgow City Council, 2003). The people of Glasgow had a strong input in prioritizing the cities' policies. On behalf of the Glasgow City Council, MORI (a research company) performed a survey among the citizens of Glasgow. A recurring theme in the responses to this survey was the need for greater community safety. The 2002 outcomes of the survey revealed that the most important issues for improving the quality of life for the people of Glasgow were 'reducing crime', 'making the city safer', and 'making the city cleaner and more attractive' (MORI, 2003). Glasgow City Council took the outcomes of this survey into account when making the draft Council Plan for the period 2003–2007.

The City Council have taken several initiatives in order to create a cleaner and safer city and a more sustainable environment. These include the implementation of a Community Safety Action Plan (improving community safety, tackling vandalism, reducing accidents), the establishment Restorative Justice Project (tackling youth crime), the development of effective policies and practices as a means of tackling antisocial behaviour together with other agencies and a focus on antisocial behaviour in children (developing Safetown by 2004/5), continuing CCTV surveillance to reduce crime and fear of crime and several other initiatives related to creating a more sustainable environment (Glasgow City Council, 2003). A very important aspect is cooperation between the several municipal departments and with other involved institutions and organizations. Getting private actors involved is an objective (Public Private Partnerships) but this is still difficult when it concerns social problems. In crime and safety issues, many companies think it is a matter for the City Council and that they do not need to be involved. In 1998 Glasgow City Council formed the Community Safety Partnership to harness the efforts of all the different City Council departments and external agencies from the public, private and voluntary sectors that have an interest in making Glasgow a safer place (see also Section 5.2.2, Administrative System) (Glasgow City Council, 2004e).

Next, three best practices regarding initiatives for improving community safety, especially in the city centre, will be discussed.

5.5.1 Best Practice 1: Safer City Centre Initiative

In March 2002, Glasgow City Centre Partnership examined the feasibility of developing a business-led community safety and crime reduction partnership for the City of Glasgow in order to address the safety problems in the city centre commonly. One year later, formally in November 2003, the Safer City Centre Initiative was founded. Objectives related to the reduction of crime, the increase of feelings of safety and gathering of intelligence and the expansion of the programme were formulated (Safer City Centre Initiative, 2004).

The aim of this Initiative is to develop a range of measures to reduce the cost and incidence of crime and fear of crime and to provide effective remedies which affect residents, visitors, tourists and the business community. One of the main activities is creating a radio link between shop-owners related to the initiative. Currently there are 128 radios, including six used by Strathclyde Police. The Radiolink system is useful as an early warning system (for shoplifting or other criminal activities), an intelligence-gathering tool and a means for ensuring the safety of security staff. To improve the strength of the tool, the central CCTV-monitoring complex has also been connected to the radio link since January 2004. The advantage of this link is that CCTV cameras can not only monitor problems with their cameras in streets and public areas, they can also learn about problems and therefore be more proactive in the operation of the cameras. Working in partnership and sharing information is an essential part of the Safer City Centre programme (Safer City Centre Initiative, 2004). The communication links between the members are short and direct and therefore very effective.

The Safer City Centre Initiative is organized as an independent company with initial funding for a period of three years covered by the Scottish Executive. It is a not-for-profit company but must be able to continue to maintain its viability. A Programme Manager assisted by a Membership Officer administers the programme. At the start of the programme, there were approximately 60 members. This steadily increased to 198 members in 2003 and the aim for 2004/2005 is to increase this number by 30 per cent. The membership comprises retail outlets, city centre car parks, universities, hotels, a restaurant, transport operators and the major shopping centres. Monthly meetings are held with members at which matters that affect them in relation to crime and social issues are discussed (Safer City Centre Initiative, 2004).

The Initiative is considered by the discussion partners as being a legitimate and successful means of reducing crime and addressing community issues through bringing all partners together to address the special problems which affect the city centre. Therefore, the Safer City Centre Initiative can be regarded as a best practice. The Scottish Executive is so positive about the programme that they promote the programme in the whole of Scotland.

It is considered essential that the programme continues to expand. Future strategy must continue to concentrate on partnership working with particular emphasis on closer ties with Streetwatch and the Community Safety Partnership. In the long term this may even lead to a merger between the Safer City Centre Initiative into the Community Safety Partnership.

5.5.2 Best Practice 2: CCTV

In the UK 86.1 per cent of all local authorities have installed CCTV in public spaces and 64.4 per cent intend to extend existing systems (Glasgow City Council, 2001). In Glasgow as well CCTV cameras have been installed in many public spaces. In total there are 360 cameras throughout the city and this number is increasing. Most of these cameras are situated in the city centre, but cameras have also been placed in some suburbs known to be problem areas.

CCTV is being used as a tool to help the police tackle crime and disorder. The cameras are in direct contact with the police. In the CCTV Centre, monitors connected to all cameras are watched 24 hours per day. When something unusual is monitored, the police will be contacted to go to the location. It is not only the police who can contact CCTV – citizens can also get help, for example through the Help Points in the city centre. These Help Points are in direct contact with the CCTV Centre.

CCTV is not only used as a tool to tackle crime and disorder. It is seen as a broader tool – as a 'community resource' which helps to address wider social, economic, environmental and cultural concerns. The employees of the CCTV Centre can, for example, watch the behaviour of groups of young children hanging around. If there is evidence that they should be in school or that they are causing nuisance, the CCTV Centre can contact a local police officer to check the situation locally. Another example is that of the child that was lost in the city centre. The mother of the child contacted the Help Point and with help of CCTV the child was located and brought back to the mother. With CCTV it is also possible to locate graffiti, to see who is creating it and to send somebody to clean it up again.

All these examples show that CCTV can be used in many ways to tackle crime and disorder and to keep the city clean and safe. The CCTV system is considered successful: citizens actually make requests for cameras in their neighbourhood. They say they feel safer in areas with cameras than in areas without, not only because cameras give evidence in case something happens, but also because cameras work preventively: offenders think twice about committing a crime in front of a camera. Public surveys do seem to show that CCTV cameras do influence the safety perceptions of residents in a positive way (Glasgow City Council, 2001). It is this enthusiasm of the citizens that makes CCTV a success in the fight against actual crime and fear of crime.

At the time of writing Glasgow is trying to extend the use of CCTV by making direct links from the CCTV Centre to the Fire Brigade and the Ambulance Service. In addition, as stated in the previous 'best practice' section, a link has been made with Radiolink, an information system among shopkeepers to warn each other of shoplifters. Employees of the CCTV Centre can directly follow a shoplifter through the streets of Glasgow and inform the police.

However, urban governors should also be aware of possible problems related to CCTV. First of all there may be problems with civil liberties and human rights. In the UK, there was initial resistance against CCTV as well. The Human Rights Act of 1998 and the Data Protection Act of 1998 now safeguard the privacy rights of the population. Another problem that may arise relates to the feeling of residents that the police will no longer come to their neighbourhood after a camera has been placed. In addition, there are fears that crime and disorder will actually disperse and not be solved. Moreover, there must also be sufficient and appropriate police reactions after CCTV reports. Otherwise, the trust in the system might substantially decrease.

5.5.3 Best Practice 3: Restorative Justice Service

The Restorative Justice Service (RJS) is a pioneering scheme to tackle youth crime in Glasgow. The official launch was on 27 August 2003 after a short pilot period of one month (Community Services, undated(d)). In this multi-agency partnership, the City Council, Strathclyde Police, British Transport Police, Strathclyde Fire Brigade, Greater Glasgow NHS and Children's Reporter work together in order to tackle youth crime in Glasgow (Community Services, 2004). Where in the past no formal action has been taken, with restorative justice it is possible to target action on offending by young people. This is necessary because young people have increasingly been referred to the Children's Reporter: between November 2002 and April 2003 more than 1,800 young people were referred for more than 4,000 offences and many of them were aged between 12 and 15 years. The majority of these crimes are considered 'low-level offences' (or 'petty crime') such as theft, assault and vandalism (Community Services, 2004). The target group for RJS is young people under the age of 16 who are predominantly in the early stages of offending.

The Restorative Justice Service has three main components (Community Services, 2004). First, *Restorative Cautioning* which is delivered by trained police officers. They caution young people who have committed one or two crimes with no significant impact on a victim. The focus is on the effect of the young offenders' behaviour. Second, there is *Restorative Conferencing*: a meeting between the offender and the victim in a safe environment. When young offenders come face-to-face with the victim (either a person or a company who has suffered some kind of damage), they become aware of the effects and take responsibility for their actions, for example by helping repair the harm caused or writing a letter of apology. And third, there is the *Restorative Justice Programme*, which is focused on young people who are starting to develop a pattern of offending, having committed three to five crimes or offences. They participate in a four week programme of three two-hour modules each week. The programme is delivered by a number of agencies. In the later stages, the young people have the opportunity to complete a Community Challenge, where they can put something positive back into their local community, giving them some sense of value (Community Service, 2004).

In the first half year of the service, 550 young people were referred of whom 85 per cent participated in the programme and over 70 per cent of the victims agreed to be involved in the process (Community Services, undated(d)). A strong point of the service is the appointment of a researcher with responsibility for the monitoring and evaluation of the service. A nationally-used evaluation tool called ASSET is used to gather and evaluate data on the key areas of lifestyle, relationships, education, neighbourhoods, health and behaviour. This evaluation will provide specific information relative to the profiles of young people in the early stages of offending, helping the partners of RJS to improve the service and better tackle the problem of youth crime (Community Services, undated(d)).

The Restorative Justice Service is considered to be a best practice by most discussion partners. The most important reasons for this are that the RJS approach encourages young people to accept responsibility for their actions and helps to make amends to both victims and communities (Community Services, 2004). The service tries to prevent young people from becoming persistent offenders by confronting them with the effects of their actions. Young people are often unaware of the implications of certain behaviour. When they do realize, they are often sorry for their behaviour and willing to take responsibility.

5.6 Synthesis

This section recapitulates the most important conclusions for the city of Glasgow. Subsection 5.6.1 focuses on the perception of safety; subsections 5.6.2 and 5.6.3 deal respectively with the spatial behaviour of inhabitants as consequence of changing urban attractiveness and with the policing adopted by the city with an illustration of the best practices. The organizing capacity of the city is briefly mentioned in 5.6.4. We conclude by formulating some recommendations in subsection 5.6.5.

5.6.1 Safety Perception

As in most other European cities, crime rates are relatively high in the city centre, although compared to other European cities, they are relatively higher in Glasgow. The main types of crime are related to shoplifting, theft, petty assault and 'breach of the peace' (MORI, 2003). The city centre, with its many shops, clubs/pubs and visitors, offers the perfect conditions for criminals and other trouble-seeking persons to steal, rob and 'breach the peace'. As stated before, this is the case in many cities and Glasgow is no exception. However, crime figures from the municipality show that crime is actually decreasing. Over the past few years the crime rate fell by 2 per cent annually (Community Services, undated(a)). Of course there are some differences between different kinds of crime, but overall crime decreased and actual safety improved. Even so, the perception of safety among citizens is particularly good and has not improved over the past few years, meaning that a discrepancy exists between actual safety and perceived safety in Glasgow and that this discrepancy is increasing. These feelings of insecurity are also focused on the city centre. The vibrant night economy is one of the main factors influencing the negative safety perceptions. Although the night-life in Glasgow is very attractive to a certain population group, it is also strongly related to feelings of safety. In Glasgow in particular there is a culture of (binge) drinking. Combined with the fact that all pubs and clubs close at 2 a.m. (which causes a major pressure on the public transport and taxi services), it is a hotbed for trouble. This also strongly influences the safety perceptions of citizens. Every weekend they read in the newspapers and hear on the local radio that people have been fighting. As the city centre is the 'showpiece' for the whole city to the rest of the world, it is important to ensure the perceptions of the safety in city centre are good.

5.6.2 Urban Attractiveness and Spatial Behaviour

Glasgow's urban attractiveness was not perceived to be very high by either visitors or citizens. For a long time Glasgow's image was one of being grey, violent and very unattractive (Pacione, 1995). This image, however, is slowly changing for the better. Since the 1990s, the City Council has invested in improving the attractiveness of the city: housing projects have been initiated to improve the quality of the housing supply, safety programmes like Community Safety Partnership have been initiated to tackle crime and to improve the safety perceptions and investment in city promotion projects like 'Glasgow Miles Better' and 'European City of Culture 1990' all seem to have contributed to a more positive image of Glasgow by both visitors and citizens (Glasgow City Council, 2004d). The rising number of visitors (business people, tourists, one-day visitors) underlines this. It can be concluded, therefore, that the city of Glasgow is at a turning point regarding attractiveness. At least for the city centre, attractiveness has improved significantly and the spatial behaviour of people is adapting to it. However, the city does not only include the city centre – the suburbs are also part of it. Because half of these wards belong to the top 100 of most deprived areas in Scotland, it is obvious that the attractiveness of these parts of the city is still poor. Tackling the problems in these areas and improving attractiveness may be the next step for the City of Glasgow to improve the overall quality of the living environment in the city.

5.6.3 Policy Reactions

As already mentioned, safety is high on the priority list of Glasgow City Council. Through a public survey held in name of the City Council, the citizens of Glasgow pointed identified their three most important issues. These issues are reducing crime, making the city safer and making the city cleaner and more attractive (MORI, 2003). When preparing the drafts for the Council Plan of 2003–2007, the City Council took the outcomes of this public survey into account. They are now prioritizing delivering good Council Services, creating a more attractive and safe city, promoting social inclusion, stimulating reurbanization and developing Glasgow's metropolitan role. These objectives show that safety and attractiveness are priorities for Glasgow City Council.

There are already several projects running aimed at improving safety and attractiveness. A few best practices are described in this case study. First, there is the Safer City Centre Initiative, a cooperation between the City Council and the business community in the city centre and aimed at developing a range of measures to reduce the cost and incidence of crime and fear of crime and to provide effective remedies which affect residents, visitors, tourists and the business community. One of the main activities is creating a radio link between members (usually shop-owners). Second, there is CCTV, which is used as a tool to help the police tackle crime and disorder. Throughout the city centre, many cameras have been placed which are monitored from the CCTV Centre. There is a direct link from the CCTV Centre to the police. This measure is used in many UK cities. In other European cities there is still some resistance to CCTV because of civil liberty and human rights issues, but here as well the trend is towards increasing use of cameras. The third best practice is the Restorative Justice Service, a multi-agency partnership aimed at tackling youth crime. The programme is focused on young people (under the age of 16) who are in an early stage of offending. The service consists of three components: restorative cautioning (showing the effects of their behaviour), restorative conferencing (meeting between the offender and victim), and restorative justice programme (a four-week programme focused on young people who have developeda pattern of offending). In the first half year, 85 per cent of the 550 young people referred and 70 per cent of the victims participated in the project. The strength of the programme is that it encourages the young offenders to take responsibility and it raises awareness of the impact of their actions, which prevents them from continuing with criminal behaviour.

5.6.4 Organizing Capacity with Respect to the Community Safety Partnership

It is not only Glasgow that places a strong focus on safety: the national government has also had a strong focus on this issue since the beginning of the 1990s. It could be argued that in the UK there is a clear *vision and strategy* carried out by the national government in the fight against crime and antisocial behaviour. This vision and strategy are implemented in Glasgow by the Community Safety Partnership, which is a *strategic partnership* between City Council and the public and private sectors.

As a consequence of the strong focus of the central government on security, the safety policy adopted by the city has *political support*, although because of the economic situation economic development has a high priority as well. The situation is different with regard to *societal support*: while the business community and some social organizations participate actively in the implementation of the city's safety plan, the citizens' community seems to be less involved.

5.6.5 Recommendations

Partnerships: from project approach to a structural approach

Proper partnerships appear to be key in making Glasgow safer and more attractive. It is clear that in the three best practices discussed – the Safer City Centre Initiative, the CCTV system and the Restorative Justice Service (RJS) – the forming of new partnerships contributed substantially to successful results in tackling actual crime. It shows that substantially better results can be achieved through good cooperation between partners than through operating independently. Many urban partners involved in urban security have often been quite inwardly-directed: they were insufficiently stimulated to cooperate with others. The new projects, however did stimulate them to work together with their natural partners. The mentioned examples with good cooperation between partners thus show the positive results of cooperation. The next step is that these cooperations are to be institutionalized within the city. They should not be a stop-gap measure but rather a structural approach for tackling safety problems.

Nightlife problems

Glasgow appears to have become quite safe during day-time hours. Most of the safety problems happen during the night. These problems seem to be related to restricted opening and closing hours of pubs and clubs and to alcohol misuse. This is not, however, a specific problem for Glasgow but rather a problem for many British cities. It seems, therefore, more logical, effective and efficient to develop solutions for this problem at national level. The national government appears to be the most appropriate government level to come up with policies to tackle this problem. However, this does not mean that cities such as Glasgow do not have to do anything to solve or reduce this problem. They can still take measures (for the short term) to reduce the seriousness of the nightlife problems (for instance, by good CCTV systems and police surveillance). In addition, cities can come up with appropriate initiatives for structural solutions to reduce this problem in the long term. This makes sense because local authorities are confronted daily with the related problems and thus stimulated to find proper solutions and they normally have abundant know-how about this particular problem.

Youth problems

In Glasgow, after acknowledging that youth crime is becoming a more serious crime problem, it has been admitted that youth crime should receive particular attention. It turns out that through better cooperation between police, the Children's Reporter and the Restorative Justice Service this problem can be tackled in a more effective and efficient way. Important elements include influencing the behaviour of young people, confronting them with the consequences of their criminal acts and/or lettin them undertake compensatory activities. One important aim is to limit the number of crimes committed by young people. However, it is even more important to prevent these young people from becoming persistent offenders and even real criminals. This latter goal appears to be so important for the actual and perceived safety of the city that it is recommended that the RJS approach be incorporated within the basic package of safety measures of this city and even to broaden this package with other supportive measures and possible desirable partners like public prosecution, social care, schools and sporting clubs.

Further differentiation of urban functions in city centre is recommended

To improve the safety perception of the city centre of Glasgow, it is important that there is sufficient activity on the streets during both day and night. The best and only way to achieve this is by sound function mixing. To Jane Jacobs (1961) the diversified city is *the* key to a socioeconomically successful *and* attractive metropolitan area. Only those urban areas that are sufficiently diversified will continually attract inhabitants, companies and visitors. A long-term approach to improving the perceived security should thus be to further differentiate the urban functions in the city centre in such a way that the Glasgow centre becomes lively during all times of day and on working days as well as at weekends. The city centre of Glasgow already has quite a diversified mix of functions except for one: living. The amount of people who live in the city centre is rising, but is still very low. The existing plans to extend the housing supply further in the city centre and to improve its attractiveness as a place to live can be considered as a step in the right direction.

Chapter 6

The Case of The Hague

6.1 Introduction

In this case study, we focus on the social security in the city of The Hague, The Netherlands. Section 6.2 gives a concise profile of this urban region. In Section 6.3, we deal with possible causes of feelings of insecurity within the city of The Hague. Next, in Section 6.4, we will go into the related spatial behaviour of local inhabitants. Section 6.5 goes into policy reactions regarding urban insecurity. In this section we will give specific attention to some *best practices*. Our focus for The Hague is on the developments within Laak, an 'underprivileged neighbourhood'. Finally, Section 6.6 presents conclusions and some recommendations.

6.2 Profile of The Hague

6.2.1 Situation and Demography

The Hague is situated in the western part of The Netherlands along the coast. Its wider region, Haaglanden, has about 963,000 inhabitants and consists of Delft, Westland, Rijswijk, Wassenaar and some other municipalities. The region of Haaglanden is located next to Rotterdam. Together with Amsterdam, Rotterdam and Utrecht, The Hague belongs to the Randstad conurbation (or the Deltametropool).

The Hague itself has 463,000 inhabitants. This number has decreased since the 1970s, when there were 600,000 inhabitants. A selective suburbanization of mostly middle-class people caused this outflow. About 29 per cent of the inhabitants of The Hague have a non-Dutch background (CBS, 2003). Most of them originate from Surinam, Turkey or Morocco (Buurtmonitor, 2004).

The district of Laak is situated in the west of The Hague next to the inner city. It is located between a railway line, the *Haagse Trekvliet* canal and the municipal border with Rijswijk. Laak is characterized by a high concentration of buildings, a little amount of green space and a relatively high population density, although this is changing slightly with the implementation of renovation projects (for example, in the framework of the European Program URBAN). Part of Laak (around the Holland Spoor train station) was a so-called 'emergency area' which has received extra attention from police and policy-makers. The problems were focused in the 'prostitution zone' where prostitutes walked the streets, causing inconvenience.

Figure 6.1 Geographical position of The Hague in Europe

For our analysis we will consider the Laak district divided into three main areas (see Figure 6.2): Laak-Noord, Laak-Centraal and Spoorwijk. Laak has a little more than 37,000 inhabitants and this number is, as in the rest of The Hague, declining. Many people are moving out of this district, often to the newly-built district Leidschenveen-Ypenburg. The outflow is quite high: in Laak this out-migration was 15.5 per cent in 2001 (see Table 6.1) (Den Haag, 2002b). The total decrease in the population is smaller: the population in Laak fell by –3.6 per cent over the period of 1993–2003 (CBS, 2004).

In-migration to Laak consists of mainly foreign people. In The Netherlands foreign people are defined as 'all people of whom [one of] the parents is born in a foreign country'. This is in contradiction to most other European countries, where foreign people are defined as 'people who are born in a foreign country'. The

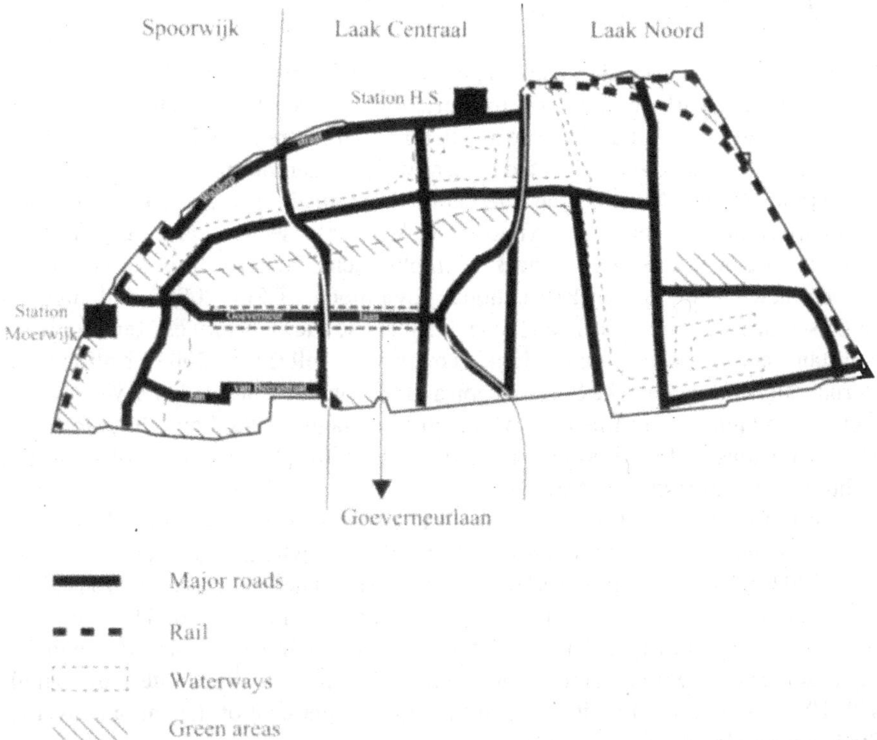

Figure 6.2 Map of the Laak district

Source: Den Haag, 2004.

percentage of inhabitants with a non-Dutch background in the Laak district is rather high (49 per cent) compare to the city of The Hague (29 per cent) (CBS, 2004). The main group of foreign people is from Surinam (Buurtmonitor, 2004). There are also people from Easter European countries such as Poland and Rumania coming to The Hague. They often stay only for a few months, for example to work in horticulture in the 'Westland' (the agricultural area between Rotterdam and The Hague) during the high season.

The population of Laak is relatively young compared to The Hague. Only 9 per cent of the population is older than 65 years, while the average for The Hague is 14 per cent (see also Table 6.1). The share of 0–19 and 20–64-year-olds is higher in Laak than in the entire The Hague (Buurtmonitor, 2004).

6.2.2 *Economy and Employment*

Historically, The Hague is the centre of politics and administration in The Netherlands. The government, parliament and the ministries are located here. The Hague is not only a national centre for politics, but also an international centre for politics and law. Most embassies and consulates are located here, as well as international institutions like the International Court of Justice, the International Criminal Court and the International Criminal Tribunal for the former Yugoslavia. The public sector, therefore, is the most important sector in this city in terms of employment: 22 per cent of all employees in The Hague work for local or national government (DSO, 2003). Although the public sector is dominant in The Hague, business services, health care and trade are important sectors for the local/regional economy as well (DSO, 2003). National and international companies like Shell, Aegon and Nationale Nederlanden have an office, or even headquarters, in this city. Although The Hague is the home base for some large companies and institutions, it is still a city with a large amount of small and medium-sized companies (SMEs).

Two-thirds of all working people from The Hague also work within the city, the rest works outside the city, mainly in Rotterdam, Rijswijk and Zoetermeer (Den Haag, 2002a). Next to employees from the city itself, The Hague serves as a regional employment centre. Half of all employees do not live in the city of The Hague but in the wider region of Haaglanden (Stadsgewest Haaglanden, 2004). Although The Hague serves as a regional employment centre, the unemployment rate is quite high. With 10.9 per cent in 2002, it is higher than the 4.1 per cent of the national average (Stadsgewest Haaglanden, 2002).

Table 6.1 Data of metropolitan profile The Hague

Characteristics	Haaglanden	The Hague	Laak
Population (2003)	963.000	463,000	37,000
Average growth of city population (%, 1993–2003)		4.3	–3.6
without annexation of 2002 (%, 1993–2001)		–0.5	–
0–19 years (%, 2003)		23.0	27.0
20–64 years (%, 2003)		63.0	64.0
65+ years (%, 2003)		14.0	9.0
Share of the population of foreign extraction (%, 2003)		29.0	49.0
Outmigration (%, 2001)		15.4	15.5
Unemployment (%, 2002)		10.9	11.0
Average gross monthly household income (€, 2002)		2,135	1,667

Sources: CBS, 2004; Den Haag, 2002a, 2002b; Buurtmonitor, 2004.

In The Hague there are huge differences between the average net monthly household incomes per district. These average household incomes range from €1,535 to €3,072 net per month (Den Haag, 2002b). This makes The Hague a relatively segregated city.

District Laak belongs to the three poorest areas of the city. It has an (estimated) average household income of €1,667 net per month and an unemployment rate of 11 per cent. The area is characterized by a high degree of movements out of the area (16 per cent) and because of that there is a decreasing basis for local shops and retail (Den Haag, 2002b; Buurtmonitor, 2004). The newly-built shopping mall *MegaStores* is supposed to stimulate new economic activities in Laak. In the old port area, a renovated business district has grown up which attracts new companies and institutions like the The Hague University of Professional Education (*Haagse Hogeschool*).

6.2.3 *Administration*

As previously noted, The Hague is the political centre of The Netherlands. The Hague is, like every other municipality in The Netherlands, financially dependent on the state. Only a small part of its income comes from the municipality itself. Despite this financial dependence, the city has a high autonomy; it is free to formulate its own policies and to spend its own budget.

The City Council consists of the Lord Mayor and the Aldermen. The contemporary City Council has had roughly the same composition for the last 12 years or so (VVD; liberals, PvdA; socialists and CDA; Christian democrats). The Hague is divided in seven districts. Since 2002 The Hague has extended to an eighth, newly-built district: Leidschenveen-Ypenburg. Unlike Amsterdam and Rotterdam, the districts of The Hague do not have their own elected governors, although they do have a *stadsdeelwethouder* (District Alderman). This person is responsible for the composition and implementation of the annual district policy plan, a local implementation plan based on policies for the entire city.

Municipal policy in The Hague is based on the *Grotestedenbeleid* (GSB, Major-City Policy), initiated by the state in 1994. The city-oriented grants, subsidies and city policies from nine ministries are clustered and coordinated by this Major-City Policy. The cities involved in the programme (the 30 largest cities in The Netherlands) have to draw up an integrated urban strategy that has to be approved by the state. Depending on the strength of the implementation and evaluation of the city's strategy, contracts are signed between the local and national authorities (DSO, 2003).

6.3 The Perception of Security in The Hague

Every two years the city of The Hague monitors the perception of its inhabitants on all aspects of the living environment. For 2002 this monitor concluded that most inhabitants always felt safe (62 per cent), but there were also people who (sometimes) felt unsafe in the city (10 per cent) and more than a quarter (28 per cent) of the inhabitants (sometimes) felt unsafe in the borough or district they live in. Since 1998, the number of people who (sometimes) feel unsafe in their own borough has increased. Feelings of insecurity stem from several different causes ranging from threat of actual crime to a damaged and unclean built environment (Den Haag, 2002b).

Although there is often a paradox that sees a deterioration of the perception of safety going together with a decrease in reported crimes, this is not the case for The Hague. Indeed, over the period 1996–2002 the total amount of crime reports in the city increased by 15 per cent and over the last year by 5 per cent. Most reports belong to the characterization 'crime against property without violence'. The other three crime categories are crime against property with violence, violent crime and other crime. About 33 per cent of all arrested persons in 2001 were younger than 24 years and one out of 10 persons was even under the age of 18 (Den Haag, 2003b). This increase crime numbers is also proved by a small research project on 'zinloos geweld' (useless violence) from the regional police department. This research indicated several reasons as possible causes for the increase in crime numbers. These include not only an actual increase in offences, but also a higher willingness to report crime, better recording methods by the police, or better research methods, all of which can increase the number of crime reports (Politie Haaglanden, 1999).

As stated, The Hague is a segregated city with respect to average household incomes. With respect to safety and safety perception the same division can be seen. There are relatively good and relatively bad districts. In the 'good' (or rich) districts only 15 per cent of the inhabitants (sometimes) feel unsafe, while this percentage is almost 40 per cent in the less good districts (Den Haag, 2002b). The differentiating factor between the 'good' and the 'bad' neighbourhoods is the perception of threat. This perception is graded at 1.9 (0 = never, 10 = very often) for the entire city of The Hague, which means that the inhabitants almost never feel threatened. This grade is quite low for the city as a whole, but there are remarkable differences within the city. In the best districts the grade is 0.5, in the worst districts the grade is 3.6 (Den Haag, 2002b). It is not only the perception of safety that shows this division within the city, but the 'objective' data on cleanliness of the streets, reporting crimes, etc. also underline this segregation (Den Haag, 2002b).

The perception of safety in Laak is worse than in other parts of The Hague; about 38 per cent of all people (sometimes) feel unsafe in their own district (see Table 6.2). The perception of deterioration is 5.4 for The Hague and 6.1 in Laak. These numbers show the grade people give to deterioration in their district (0 = 'never', 10 = 'very often'). Victimization is also higher in Laak than in The Hague (Den Haag, 2002b) Objective data show the same. The number of crime reports in Laak is relatively high compared to other districts. In the period 1996–2002 this number increased, but in contrast with The Hague the number declined in the year 2002 (Den Haag, 2003b). This might indicate a small improvement in the actual safety situation in Laak. According to the monitor, the inhabitants of Laak see theft of bicycles or from cars, rubbish on the streets and dog dirt as the main problems of the district, and not (as perhaps was expected) the crime rates (Den Haag, 2002b). The relatively large inflow of people

Table 6.2 Data perception on safety, The Hague, 2002

		Safety			% Victims					
		Perception crime against property	*Perception threat*	*% (sometimes) feels unsafe*	*Car-related offences*	*House-breaking*	*Vandalism*	*Violence*	*Theft of wallet/ purse*	*Other theft*
The Hague	1996	4.8	1.4	26	29	12	9	9	8	–
	1998	4.9	1.6	23	24	13	12	7	6	15
	2000	4.9	1.6	24	30	12	10	5	5	13
	2002	5.2	1.9	28	34	10	11	7	6	15
District Laak	2002	6.2	2.3	38	38	14	12	7	6	16

Note: 0 = never, 10 = very often.

Source: The Hague (2002b).

from outside The Hague in the last decade and the presence of a prostitution zone are aspects influencing the feelings of insecurity in this district

6.4 Urban Attractiveness and Spatial Behaviour

6.4.1 Underprivileged Neighbourhoods

As reported in Section 6.2, the Laak district is one of the three poorest neighbourhoods in The Hague. Even if low income, high unemployment, a high concentration of ethnic minorities and a high percentage of out-migration characterize the whole borough, some differences can be found among the three main areas that compose the neighbourhood.

Laak Centraal is probably the borough with the best image among the three. It was built during the 1930s and 1940s and the area has been recently renewed. Nowadays the presence of the *Megastore* shopping mall (the largest in The Hague), the The Hague University of Professional Education (*Haagse Hogeschool*) and a recently-renovated business district has improved the attractiveness of the area. Although a lot of attention has been given to the housing stock in order to attract the middle class, the problem of illegal housing is still an issue in the neighbourhood. The presence of the *Haagse Hogeschool*, the largest higher education institute in The Hague, is very important for the area since it contributes to linking this neighbourhood with the rest of the city, but there is still the feeling that this institute's contribution of to the improvement of the area could be larger.

Spoorwijk, located in the southwest part of the Laak district, can be considered as a work-in-progress. Indeed, at the moment about one third of the borough is under construction and this produces a double effect on its functioning. On the one hand, the many ongoing renewal projects can contribute to create a better image for the future and to lay the groundwork for economic growth in the area. On the other hand, these renewal projects have created a temporary lack of demand for the retail sector, since one third of the inhabitants have moved. As a consequence some of the shops had to close, leaving behind vacant buildings, with a negative impact on the perceived safety.

Laak Noord is one of the weakest areas of the city and surely the most difficult neighbourhood of Laak district. This area has always had the image of a problematic neighbourhood especially regarding dirtiness, criminality and vandalism. The local authority has invested a lot in the area in the attempt to change the situation but it seems that is still a lot of work to be done. The large number of different ethnic groups living in the area (up to 37 different nationalities) and the poor conditions of the physical environment do not facilitate the work of the local authority. Illegal housing (fed by the illegal labour market), drugs, criminality and the cultural barriers that prevent the immigrants' involvement in the renewal process of the area are the main reasons that hinder the improvement of the borough's image.

6.4.2 Urban Attractiveness and Spatial Behaviour

The Laak district has two main strengths: its location and its public transport infrastructure. Located at short distance from The Hague city centre (between the core and the hard ring of the city) and well linked to it by public transport, equipped with a railway station with direct links to Rotterdam, Schiphol Airport and Amsterdam, Laak district has the potential to become a new central location in The Hague metropolitan area. The presence of the *Megastore* shopping mall, the Haagse Hogeschool and the new business area in Laakshaven represents some of the attempts made by the local authority to move in this direction. Nevertheless, for different reasons, these three huge investments made in the area still do not pay back in terms of image and attractiveness of the area: indeed the outflow from Laak is still high (see Section 6.2).

The neighbourhood's weak points concern mainly the housing stock and the huge presence of low-income groups (often belonging to ethnic minorities) who, for different reasons, are not willing or able to fully integrate themselves into society. The problem related to the housing stock has different aspects. Firstly, many believe that at the moment there is too much social housing in Laak:[1] this has the consequence of attracting mainly low-income (foreign) groups. It is argued that this kind of tenant cares much less about the physical conditions of their house and their surroundings than house owners do. This appears to be particularly true for the lower rental level market. This often leads to badly-maintained houses, dirty streets and pavements, contributing to the impoverishment of the local living environment and, as a consequence, to a worst perception of safety.

Another problem concerns the so-called 'slum landlords': these are landlords who rent the same house to several (often illegal) people in order to maximize the rental income. They usually rent houses 'per bed' instead of per room or per family. Even if there are no official data on this phenomenon, the illegal room-rental activity is recognized as one of the neighbourhood's biggest unsolved problem by the local authority (Den Haag, 2002e). Connected to this there is also the problem of illegal people living in Laak. These people, usually illegally employed in the building or horticulture sectors, contribute to enhancing the feeling of insecurity in the area because, given their illegal status, they do not try to be involved or integrated into the society. According to our discussion partners a further problem concerns the housing conditions in Laak; most of houses of the area are poorly maintained and this, as we have already noted, contributes to creating the kind of poor living environments that enhances feelings of insecurity. Based on the idea that, in order to enhance the quality of life of an area, medium and high-income groups should be attracted there, the city has undertaken huge plans to renew the housing stock (i.e. in Spoorwijk alone almost one third of the houses will be renovated) and this will probably contribute to changing the image of the neighbourhood in the long run. At the moment, though, it seems that this renewal policy is giving different results: while it seems to be working well in Spoorwijk, in Laak Noord the present effects are not satisfactory. In this area, for the moment, this policy has had a double negative effect. On one side, it is not attracting medium and high-income groups from other parts of the city because the people who can afford these kinds of houses prefer to buy a house in other locations, such as the newly-annexed locations of Leidschenveen-Ypenburg. Laak has probably not yet achieved an image able to attract medium or high-income groups. On the other hand, this policy creates a lack of affordable houses for those low-income groups who have been living in Laak for a while, are well integrated in the area and would like to invest in a house. This kind of person, usually the immigrants who are best integrated in the society, are forced to leave the neighbourhood because they cannot afford the new planned houses.

The second problem affecting the Laak district appears to be the large presence of low income groups, often of ethnic minorities. On the one hand these groups have relatively low purchasing power and this prevents the economic development of the neighbourhood. On the other hand, low income groups very often also have lower education and poorer socioeconomic perspectives. This usually means that they have other concerns than to be fully involved in initiatives that aim at improving the quality of life and the safety of the neighbourhood. Therefore, although there are a number of good examples of citizens participation in the area,[2] the Laak district has the lowest grade of 'attachment to the neighbourhood' of the whole The Hague (Den Haag, 2003).

The consequent spatial behaviour in Laak district is clear: along with the rest of the city of The Hague, Laak has been losing population in recent years (3.6 per cent in the last 10 years, see Table 6.1). The constant loss of inhabitants has inevitably impoverished the economic base of the area. As we can see from Table 6.3, many indicators concerning the shopping activity in the area – such as the purchasing power spent in the district, the flow of customers and the floor productivity – show the deterioration of Laak's economic base. This impoverishment of the neighbourhood has created unemployment that, in its turn, makes room for illegal activities. All this negatively affects the image of the area; not only do fewer people want to live there, but also fewer people are willing to go shopping in the area. This is confirmed by the 18 per cent decrease in the turnover generated by non-local customers in the district in the period 1994–2000. An example of the impoverishment of the local shopping activity is represented by Goeverneurlaan (highlighted in Figure 6.2) which can be considered the central street of the area. Untili a few years ago it was full of different kind of shops and clearly represented the centre of the local economic activity. Nowadays few shops are open and the street has become the symbol of the neighbourhood's decay. The overall decrease in the quality of life and of the living environment has translated into a deterioration of the perception of safety both by local and non-local residents and, as a consequence, into a deterioration of the borough's image. This leads to that loss of inhabitants and impoverished economic base that start the above-mentioned vicious circle. The main challenge for Laak district now is how to break this vicious circle.

Table 6.3 Shopping in Laak district, period 1994–2000

	Daily shopping			Non-daily shopping			Total		
Indicators	*2000*	*1994*	*Change 1994–2000*	*2000*	*1994*	*Change 1994–2000*	*2000*	*1994*	*Change 1994–2000*
Purchasing power spent in the district (in %)	78%	73%	7%	20%	27%	-25%	46%	48%	–5%
Flow of customers (in %)	25%	43%	–42%	63%	58%	9%	40%	48%	–17%
Turnover generated by local customers in the district (in €m)	115	95	21%	37	40	-6%	152	135	13%
Turnover generated by non-local customers in the district (in €m)	38	71	–46%	64	54	17%	102	125	–18%
Total turnover (in €m)	154	166	–7%	101	94	7%	255	260	–2%
Number of shops	74	98	–24%	191	163	17%	265	261	2%
Floor productivity	6382	7370	-13%	410	1234	–67%	942	2634	–64%

Source: adapted from Den Haag, 2002e.

6.5 Policy Reactions

Although at the moment most of the policy measures concerning safety are decided by the national government, cities in The Netherlands do have a responsibility for urban safety as an institutional task. In the political agenda of the city of The Hague safety plays a very important role: since the last political elections in 2002, it has become the number one priorityf or the City Council. The main aim is to achieve a 25 per cent reduction in criminality and antisocial behaviour in public spaces by 2006 (Den Haag, 2002d). Compared to the city of Rotterdam, which also has safety as the highest priority on its political agenda, The Hague has chosen what we could define as a 'low key approach' to the urban safety problem. Indeed, instead of communicating (improved) data on safety, The Hague decided to communicate mainly the 'positive actions', which means informing the general public about the initiatives undertaken to improve the quality of the living environment. This choice has been made possible because The Hague has a good image among people and, generally speaking, is not perceived as an unsafe place to live. This is in contrast to Rotterdam, which has to fight hard to change its image in people's perception since it is often (wrongly) considered to be the most criminal city of The Netherlands.

The Hague's safety policy is included in the 'Een veilig Den Haag: een opdracht aan alle Hagenaren' plan ('A Safe The Hague: A Task for all the City's Citizens'), where the City Council has specified the objectives that must be achieved by 2006. The approach is characterized by strong cooperation bewteen the local authority (the City Council), the residents and all other important actors operating in the city such as the police, social organizations and entrepreneurs. The plan sets up the guidelines for the safety policy that has to be carried out in the city. The day-to-day application of these guidelines is described in the different districts' Master Plans ('*stadsdeelplannen*'), in the Master Plan of the police, in the programmes of the Major Cities Policy ('*Grotestedenbeleid*') and in other theme-specific and area-based programmes. The approach used by the city of The Hague is in line with the national approach to (lack of) safety. In The Hague special attention is given to unsafe public places and young people.

The practical day-to-day application of the safety policy takes place in the eight districts of the city. At this level the local authority, the police, some social organizations, entrepreneurs and residents work together to find solutions to local problems: all these actors together produce a list of priorities in terms of district safety.

The huge commitment of the City Council on safety has translated into extra funding for the safety policy in the city. In 2003 €2.5 million additional funding was especially meant for youth criminality and maintenance and surveillance of the living environment. In the same year the structural funds for safety also got an extra €4.2 million: €2.7 for public order and (fire-) safety and €1.5 for projects concerning drug-related problems. The total amount of the structural funds for safety in the year 2003 was €6.9 million (Den Haag, 2002d).

6.5.1 Cooperation (The Triangle)

In The Netherlands the local authority has, as institutional task, a special responsibility for safety in the city. However, this does not mean that the municipality is the only actor involved in the safety policy. A safe city is a concern of all urban actors, from inhabitants to entrepreneurs, from the police to the city's administration. This cooperative approach is also followed by the city of The Hague, as stated in its safety master plan: 'a successful approach to urban safety requires the willingness and the skills of all actors involved in it to cooperate' (Den Haag, 2002d, p. 39).

In large Dutch cities the main three actors involved in the cooperation over urban safety are: the local authority, the police and the Public Prosecutor.

- The policy plan elaborated by the *Mayor* for the period 2002–2006 has five priorities: safety (as priority number one); commitment to the city; spatial and urban development; social cohesion; and culture and sport (Den Haag, 2002c). The Safety Plan shows the main guidelines of the approach the city uses to enhance the (perception of) safety. The policy undertaken consists of a combination of repressive and preventive measures, efficient cooperation between all municipal institutions and a combination of theme-specific and area-based approaches. The Safety Plan has six main priorities: 1) youth criminality; 2) violence; 3) problems caused by drug addicts; 4) safety in public space; 5) maintenance, supervision and control; and 6) improving mentality in terms of norms and values (Den Haag, 2002d).
- In The Netherlands, the *police force* is divided into several departments that operate quite independently. The police unit operating in The Hague covers the whole region of Haaglanden; this unit is divided, in its turn, into districts. Laak is one of these districts and therefore has its own district police team. Depending on the different problems concerning safety, the police can play a role as a major actor, a pioneer actor or just as support for other actors including residents, business and social organizations. The main targets for the Haaglanden police for 2003 were: a decrease in violence, a decrease in youth criminality and a decrease in recidivism (Den Haag, 2003b). The interrelation between the police master plan and the master plans of the different districts of the city has become more intensive in recent years. The local police districts are continuously involved as partners in safety-related projects elaborated by the local authority and other social organizations. Examples of this collaboration are the 'father-neighbourhood project' and the 'night prevention project' (Den Haag, 2002d).
- The *Public Prosecutor's Office* is the only authority in The Netherlands with the power to bring suspects to criminal judgement. Its primary duty is to assure that crimes are investigated and prosecuted: in order to pursue this duty the Public Prosecutor cooperates with the police and the other Public Prosecutors in The Netherlands. The Public Prosecutor's Office is a national organization with 19 branches overall the country, one of which is based in The Hague and covers the area of two police units – Haaglanden and Hollands Midden. The Public Prosecutor

of The Hague together with the City Council and the police annually draw up a working plan where the objectives that have to be achieved in terms of safety are set up.

Generally speaking this cooperation between institutional actors on the issue of safety is often seen as an example of best practice. Nevertheless, there are still some issues that could be improved in terms of the quality of the cooperation (Den Haag, 2002d). First of all, there is a concern about the fact that the approach adopted by the city is still too repressive, while it should be more preventive. Secondly, the expectations of the different partners involved are very often not made explicit. Moreover, the outputs and the social effects of the cooperation are sometimes formulated vaguely, bringing no concrete results. Finally, there is a strong dependence on the local authority for the financial element of the cooperation although, at least for the moment, this does not seem to be a big problem.

The city is trying to improve the quality of the cooperation by focusing especially on a clear formulation of outputs and the relative desired social effects and by improving its operational (day-to-day) aspect (Den Haag, 2002d).

6.5.2 Safety Policy in Laak

According to the local Master Plan 2004–2005 special attention in Laak district is given to some important issues regarding safety and its perception such as violent crimes, house burglaries, unsafe public spaces and different sort of nuisances (Den Haag, 2003c). In order to solve these problems, priority has been given to the promotion of 'social control' under the supervision of the local police. This measure is in line with the approach adopted by the city of The Hague; indeed, in the Policy Plan 'Kracht van Den Haag' (Den Haag, 1999), elaborated within the framework of the national Major Cities Policy, there is a special focus on integral safety in order to diminish and prevent violence and trouble in public spaces, diminish and prevent youth crime and strengthen supervision and maintenance. Moreover, strong participation of residents in safety-related projects is an example of the promotion of the 'social control'. Also in Laak district the safety policy consists of a combination of repressive and preventive measures, of cooperation between different institutional actors and a combination of theme-specific and area-based approaches. In the local safety policy some best practices can be found.

Best practice 1: the street representative

The Laak police team, together with the local authority, decided to start a street representative initiative (*straatvertegenwoordiger*). For each street the police look for a resident who can keep a 'special eye' on the street itself. The street-representative initiative is based on the willingness of people to give their time voluntarily and especially on the anonymity of the service so that the people involved in it do not feel afraid of possible repercussions for reporting antisocial behaviour in their streets. The street representative is asked to report possible antisocial behaviour in his/her street of residence such as drug dealers, child abuse, noise, receiving stolen goods or anything similar. The possibility of reporting the presence of possible slum-landlords in the street, perceived as one of the worst problems concerning the housing stock in Laak, is also very important.

If the street representative notes (possible) antisocial behaviour in his/her street, he/she can call a free telephone number and report it. Afterwards the police will check the reported situation. Each month an evaluation is asked from the street representative in order to evaluate the initiative.

Often cited as one of the best practices of the Laak district, the street-representative initiative has a double advantage. On one hand, these people help and support the police tasks, allowing the police team to focus its resources on other priorities. On the other hand, this initiative has proved to have a very important effect on the feelings of the residents involved in it: the feeling of 'being responsible' for their streets increases their feeling of 'attachment to the neighbourhood' and motivates them to stay. In June 2003 this initiative received an official acknowledgment ('*het Compliment*') issued each month by the city of The Hague: the motivation that justified this acknowledgment was 'the street-representative is a good example of local inhabitants that made something to improve the security and the quality of life in their neighbourhood by focusing on the improvement of norms and values' (Den Haag, 2004).

Best practice 2: the hot-spots policy

Hot-spots are defined as 'places in the city characterized by high criminality and concentration of problems for a long time' (Den Haag, 2002d). The city of The Hague is committed to tackling these hot-spots with specific measures. The main aim of the 'hot-spots policy' is to normalize the situation in these areas that can be considered as the most unsafe areas of the city. At present in The Hague there are 26 hot-spots located in the 25 less safe places of the city. The hot-spots list is a dynamic list, meaning that it can change over time: whenever the situation in one hot-spot is improved it will be removed from the list (and if necessary others will be added). The main characteristics of the hot-spot policy are special attention for a minimum of four months per hot-spot, cooperation bewteen local authority, police, social organizations, entrepreneurs and local residents and periodical evaluation of the results (Den Haag, 2002d).

The hot-spot policy is a good example of that cooperation between different urban actors often mentioned as best practice in The Hague. In order to evaluate the effect of this policy every four monthsthe local authority asks the police to make an evaluation report of the situation in each hot-spot with the help of some specific indicators. The data collected in the first four months of the hot-spot policy are used as starting point for future evaluations. The evaluation part represents, for some, the weak and risky side of the programme since it carries the risk that these data could be used for political purposes: indeed, as we have seen, the main aim of the city's strategy is to become 25 per cent safer by 2006 and this could create some pressure in order to focus on some specific facts that would influence the indicators used to measure insecurity.

Three hot-spots have been identified in Laak: the Tippelzone Waldorpstraat, Paets van Troostwijkstraat and Wenckebachstraat/'t Kikkertje. The *Tippelzone* is the prostitution area of The Hague; most of the prostitutes have drug problems and/or they are in the country illegally. The main problem is that this area generates a lot of criminality and problems. Here the police and the local authority cooperate with a social organization that helps prostitutes (Stichting Hulpverlening Opvang Prostituees) in order to decrease the criminality in the area, to provide medical help and advice to the addicted prostitutes and to avoid the spreading of the problems to the contiguous areas.

Some young people using the public spaces to loiter, especially in the summer period, characterize the other two hot-spots of Laak, the Paets van Troostwijkstraat and the Wenckebachstraat. This brings nuisance, vandalism, dirtiness and sometimes car thefts since some of these young people also commit criminal activities. In this area the main aim of the cooperation between the local authority, the police and some youth organizations is to reduce the troubles caused by these young people and to avoid their moving to other locations.

There are some critics of the hot-spots policy and they focus mainly on the risk that such a policy will not solve the problems but simply move or spread them from the hot-spots to other places. However the local authority is aware of this possible side effect, which is considered when the different hot-spot policies are elaborated.

Best practice 3: the JTT (Youth Supervision Team, Jongeren Toezicht Team*) Laak*

The JTT project is a joint initiative of the Municipality of The Hague and the Police Haaglanden; the local authority finances the project and the police execute it. This initiative is now active in three districts of the city, among which are the district of Laak. The aim of the JTT project is twofold: it aims at improving (the perception of) safety in the area and it helps young people who have dropped out school and lack any particular skill to enable them to gain any work experience and to develop their skills for the labour market. The JTT can be considered as a sort of training school: young people working in the JTT must develop their skills and think about what they would like to do in the future, with the help of their supervisors. It any case it has to be considered as a permanent job because young people can stay for maximum one year on the team and, during this period, they can also apply for other jobs or for schools. Young people work 32 hours a week under the supervision of two police agents: before starting the job they are trained to deal with possible dangerous situations.

The young people working for JTT Laak patrol, wearing a recognizable red uniform, the port area (*Laakhavengebied*) and the *Megastore* shopping mall; they report issues such as rubbish on the street, broken traffic signs, abandoned vehicles or bicycles and similar. In the shopping mall they also patrol the parking lot and this has proved to be very effective, since the number of reported thefts from cars parked in the shopping mall has dramatically decreased. The local police office then takes care of solving the reported problems.

This initiative has several positive effects: it supports the police patrols, allowing the police to focus on other priorities; it improves the living environment of the neighbourhood; it helps potential socially-excluded young people to build a base for their future; and it contributes to a safer environment.

6.6 Synthesis

This section recapitulates the most important conclusions for the city of The Hague. Subsection 6.6.1 focuses on the perception of safety; subsections 6.6.2 and 6.6.3 deal respectively with the spatial behaviour of inhabitants as consequence of changing urban attractiveness and with the policies adopted by the city, with an illustration of the best practices. Subsection 6.6.4 describes the organizing capacity with respect to safety policy in The Hague. We conclude by formulating some recommendations in subsection 6.6.5.

6.6.1 Safety Perception

The Hague can be considered as a relatively safe place to live in: in 2002 only 28 per cent of its inhabitants felt unsafe sometimes in the district or borough of residence. Nevertheless this percentage has been increasing since 1998 and this trend could, in the long run, jeopardize the positive image that people have of the city.

As previously stated, considering the average household income The Hague is a segregated city: the three richest and the three poorest neighbourhoods of the country are located within the municipal borders. The same segregation can be noticed also with respect to safety and its perception. In the safer (and richer) districts only 15 per cent of the local inhabitants sometimes feel unsafe, while this percentage is almost 40 per cent in the less safe districts. The perception of safety in the Laak district, the district that represents the focus of this case study, is quite poor: 38 per cent of its inhabitants sometimes feel unsafe in the district. The number of reported crimes in Laak is relatively high compared to other districts of the city but, in contrast with the general performance of The Hague, this number has decreased in 2003.

6.6.2 Urban Attractiveness and Spatial Behaviour

The above-mentioned segregation, both in terms of average household income and perception of safety, has an influence on the urban attractiveness of the city's boroughs and on the consequent spatial behaviour of the inhabitants. In the period 1993–2003 both the city of The Hague and the Laak district lost population. In particular, Laak district lost 3.6 per cent of its inhabitants (see Table 6.1).

The Laak district has two main strengths – its central location and its good public transport infrastructure – and two main problems – the relative bad housing stock (especially the related phenomenon of the 'slum landlords') and the large presence of low-income groups (often from ethnic minorities).

The local authority has invested heavily in public infrastructure and the presence of the *Megastore* shopping mall, the *Haagse Hogeschool* and the new business area in Laakshaven represents a good potential for the future development of the neighbourhood. Nevertheless, it seems that the district is in a kind of transition phase where the new investments are not yet able to pay back in terms of image and attractiveness. It is of crucial importance for the local authority to manage this transition stage in a proactive way.

The housing stock is surely one of the most important reasons that pushed many people to move out of the neighbourhood. Problems such as the *slum landlords*, poor housing conditions, the (sometimes) inadequate selling policy[3] of new houses together with a huge presence of social houses represent a push-factor for moving out of Laak. The large ongoing housing redevelopment project in Spoorwijk will probably improve the situation but, at the moment, it reinforces the status of transition stage of the neighbourhood.

6.6.3 Policy Reactions

Since the last political elections in 2002 safety has become the highest priority for the City Council of The Hague. The main target set up by the City Council is to achieve a 25 per cent reduction in criminality and antisocial behaviour in public spaces by 2006 (Den Haag, 2002d). The Hague has chosen a 'low key approach' to the urban safety problem: the main focus of communication is on the positive actions such as investments made to improve the quality of the living environment in public spaces, rather than on safety data.

The safety plan elaborated by the City Council consists of a combination of repressive and preventive measures, theme-specific and area-based approaches and improving cooperation between municipal institutions. Particular attention is paid to youth criminality and safety in public spaces.

Following the idea that a safe city is a concern of all urban actors, the safety Master Plan states that 'a successful approach to urban safety requires the willingness and the skills of all actors involved in it to cooperate' (Den Haag, 2002d). This has led to an intensive cooperation between the City Council, the Police and the Public Prosecutor at city level (the so called 'Triangle') and, more specifically for the district Laak, to the Management Team Laak.

As a result of this integral approach some best practices can be identified:

- the *street-representative* initiative allows some people to be anonymously 'guardians' of their streets; they are asked to report any kind of crime or antisocial behaviour that takes place on the streets where they live;
- the *hot-spots policy* is a special policy adopted by the City Council in order to normalize the situation in those areas considered as the most unsafe of the city. Each hot-spot (26 in the whole city of The Hague, three in the Laak district) gets a special attention from the police for a minimum of four months and a periodical evaluation of the results. Strong cooperation between local authority, police, social organizations, entrepreneurs and local residents is the main characteristic of the hot-spot policy;

- the *JTT (Youth Supervision Team,* Jongeren Toezicht Team*)* project is a joint initiative of the municipality and the police. It has a twofold aim: to improve the perception of the safety in the area and to help young people who have dropped out of school to develop their skills in order to prepare themselves for the labour market. This initiative is now active in three boroughs of The Hague, one of which is Laak district.

6.6.4 Organizing Capacity with Respect to the Safety Plan

A clear *vision* underlines the safety policy of the city and its boroughs: by 2006 a 25 per cent reduction in criminality and antisocial behaviour has to be achieved. The City Council of The Hague plays a *leading* role in the implementation of the safety policy, because safety has become the highest priority on its political agenda since the last political elections in 2002. The city has been able to stimulate *strategic partnerships* with the major actors involved in urban safety: not only is the cooperation with the police and the Public Prosecutor effective but also social organizations, entrepreneurs and citizens actively cooperate. This has led to a good *political and societal support* for the safety plan.

Communication plays an important role in the implementation of the safety policy. The low key approach adopted by the city – focused on communication of the initiatives undertaken rather than on the diffusion of data about safety – has been possible because of the relative good *socioeconomic conditions* and image of the city.

In the district of Laak the *societal support* is ambiguous: on one side there is a element among local inhabitants that cooperates in many initiatives related to urban safety and, therefore, fully supports the strategy of the neighbourhood's Master Plan. For example, the street-representative initiative received a huge consensus among local residents. On the other hand there are many citizens who belong to the low-income groups, sometimes with an illegal status, who are either unable or unwilling to integrate fully into society and, therefore, who do not take part in the local safety-related initiatives. The poor societal support of part of the low-income groups (often of ethnic minorities) living in Laak has a negative influence on the rest of the local population and on the image of the neighbourhood. This, in turn, translates into a poor *performance* by the area from an economic and social point of view.

6.6.5 Recommendations

It is well known that the attractiveness of a neighbourhood, both for potential newcomers and for local residents, is highly influenced by its image. At the moment Laak district clearly has a bad image. It is perceived as a poor neighbourhood witha high percentage of ethnic minorities and high rates of criminality. The two main problems of the district – poor housing stock and the large presence of low income groups – generate a negative spiral effect on the image and on the economic base of the area: the worsening of the image produces an impoverishment of the economic base that, in its turn, generates an even worse image of the neighbourhood. There is no doubt that the main challenge for the local authority is to stop and invert this vicious circle.

The local authority has worked hard in recent years to try to improve the perception of the quality of life in the area and to break the above-mentioned vicious circle. Many theme-specific and area-based initiatives have proved successful, but their impact is usually limited to the very local (street or block) level. These initiatives represent fundamental steps in the construction of a solid base for future development of the area but, unfortunately, they have not yet been able to produce the substantial change in the neighbourhood's image that is required. This is also due to the particular transitional phase in which the neighbourhood at present finds itself: the huge redevelopment of the housing stock in Spoorwijk will surely have positive effects in the future.

The adoption of a proactive policy that focuses on the solution of existing problems and prevention of future problems and on the possibility of turning these problems into opportunities for development is fundamental for Laak. The JTT project is an example of such a proactive policy. It shows how a problem – young people who have dropped out of school – can be turned into an opportunity – producing a service for the community and at the same time helping these young people to develop skills for the labour market.

In Laak there are a number of potential 'image-improvers' such as the The Hague University of Professional Education and the *Megastore* shopping mall. Unfortunately they have not yet produced the expected change of image. The Hague University of Professional Education is the largest higher education institute in The Hague and it should try to attract more students living in the Laak area. It has been recognized that in many European cities the academic and student community can represent a driving force for urban development (van den Berg and Russo, 2003). This institute could play an important role in the redevelopment of the neighbourhood and represent a significant link between Laak district and the city centre. It could contribute to fighting the two main problems: on one hand, it can attract students to live in the area with the consequent positive stimulus of the local economic base. On the other hand, together with other local education institutes such as the *Mondriaancollege*, it could help many low-income immigrants to integrate into the society by offering language courses, increasing the possibility that these groups will become more interested and willing to participate in neighbourhood renewal projects.

More attention to programmes that prevent youth criminality, such as the JTT programme, and a deeper involvement of the local university in the neighbourhood's safety plan could help Laak district to complete its ongoing process of urban renewal.

A final recommendation concerns the general approach undertaken by the local authority in the attempt to redevelop the Laak district. Considering the two main problems of the area – the poor quality of the housing stock and the low average household income – it seems that in recent years the city has focused mostly on the attempt to solve the first problem, by investing massively in physical infrastructure. Nevertheless, a clear vision on how to attract the middle-income group to the neighbourhood is still lacking. The formulation of such a vision should be considered as important as the investment in infrastructure.

Notes

1 By social housing we mean rented houses with monthly rents below €597. For these houses the level of the rent price is determined by the government.

2 In Spoorwijk and Laak-Noord alone there are six immigrant associations and the initiatives known as the 'fathers' centre' and the 'mothers' centre' – associations set up to help parents who have problems in their families – are very successful.

3 Sometimes relatively expensive houses are sold in relatively poor neighbourhoods. This can lead to two problems: the difficulty of attracting the middle-income groups who, for the same price, can buy a house in a better neighbourhood and the difficulty for people already living in the area who would be willing to invest in a house to afford this investment.

Chapter 7

The Case of Helsinki

7.1 Introduction

In this case study, we focus on the social security in the city of Helsinki, Finland. Section 7.2 gives a concise profile of this urban region. In Section 7.3, we deal with possible causes of feelings of insecurity within the city of Helsinki. Next, in Section 7.4, we will go into the related spatial behaviour of local inhabitants. Section 7.5 goes into policy reactions regarding urban insecurity. In this section we will give specific attention to some *best practices*. Our focus for Helsinki is on the (housing) developments within Mellunkylä and Myllypuro in the Eastern Major District, 'underprivileged' districts. Finally, Section 7.6 presents conclusions and some recommendations.

7.2 Profile of Helsinki

7.2.1 Situation and Demography

Helsinki, the capital of Finland, is situated in the Uusimaa region in the south of the country. The city is built on a narrow peninsula in the Baltic Sea and clamped in between the city of Espoo on the west and the city of Vantaa on the north (see Figure 7.2). From a European perspective, Helsinki is quite peripheral. However, it is well connected to the rest of Europe: it has an international airport (Helsinki-Vantaa International Airport) and several ferry links to cities along the Baltic Sea. The domestic rail, road and air connections are very good as well. The urban area of Helsinki follows a finger-like structure along the railways and main roads leading to the rest of the country. The city is part of two larger geographical entities. Together with Espoo, Vantaa, and Kauniainen, Helsinki forms the Helsinki Metropolitan Area (HMA). In addition, there is the wider Helsinki Region. This entity contains the HMA and eight other neighbouring cities. Most of the data that will be used in this case study come from Helsinki city and the Helsinki Region.

In 2003 the city of Helsinki had approximately 559,700 inhabitants, while the whole region of Helsinki had approximately 1.2 million inhabitants in the same year, which is almost one fifth of the total national population (Urban Facts, 2004a). The population Helsinki is growing. Between 1990 and 2003 Helsinki's population increased by 14 per cent. Traditionally, the region has a domestic migration surplus, mostly young and well-educated people moving to the city to study and to start a career (van der Meer

Figure 7.1 Geographical position of Helsinki in Europe

et.al., 2004). Early in 2004 the Helsinki city population declined, while the Helsinki Region increased (City of Helsinki, 2004b). This phenomenon is explained by the fact that (mainly) families moved to the outer ring, because families were growing and wanted to live in larger dwellings in an area where housing was cheaper. This is not a new phenomenon: in 1989 more people moved away from than into the Helsinki Metropolitan Area (Urban Facts, 2004). This history of immigration and the relatively high fertility connected to it leads to a fairly young population age structure (Van der Meer et.al., 2004). Helsinki city is quite densely populated. The total land area of Helsinki city is 184.5 km^2, the population density in 2003 was slightly more than 3,000 inhabitants per km^2 (Urban Facts, 2004). This is higher than European cities like Glasgow or Rotterdam, for example. There is a relatively low share of people who do not have Finnish nationality. In an international perspective, Helsinki has a relatively

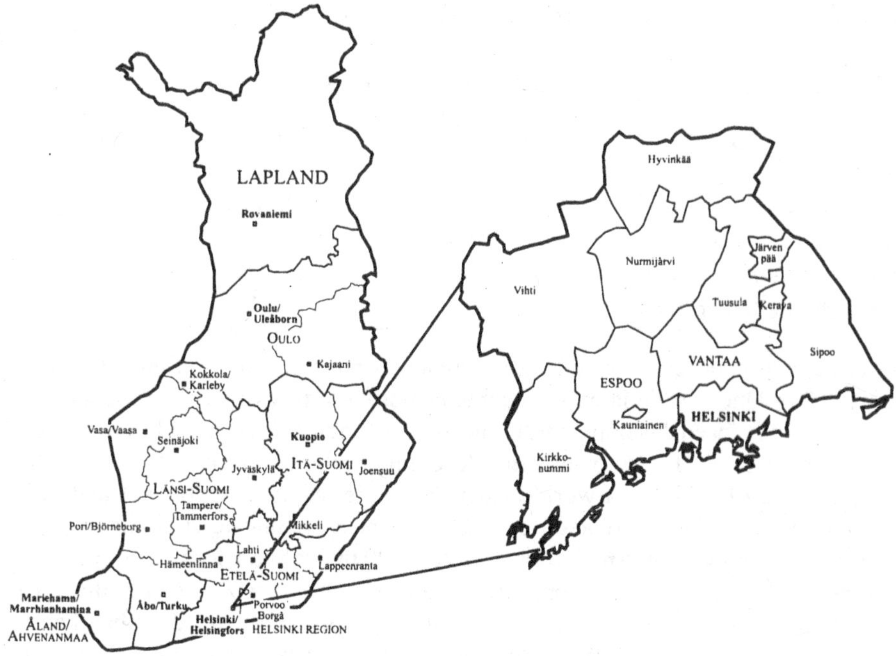

Figure 7.2 Map of Finland and Helsinki Region, 2004

Sources: GeoHive, 2004; Transport Plus, 2004.

low share of people without Finnish nationality. The share of non-Finnish persons in the total population was 5.1 per cent in 2002/03. However, in a national perspective this percentage is relatively high. In the whole country of Finland, only 2 per cent of the total population does not have Finnish nationality (Urban Facts, undated). Most inhabitants of Helsinki speak Finnish, but there is also a Swedish-speaking population group. With 6.3 per cent of the population, this group is not very large (Urban Facts, 2004). However, Swedish is the second official language and all official documents in Finland are bilingual.

7.2.2 Economy and Employment

Until World War II the Finnish economy was predominantly characterized by agriculture and some concentrations of industry. After WWII there was a rapid development into a complex market economy with the USSR as an important trade partner (van den Berg and Russo, 2004). After the fall of the Berlin Wall, the USSR fell away as a trade partner and Finland faced a severe economic recession during the 1990s. Unemployment rates rose dramatically and long-term unemployment was high.

Table 7.1 Demographic figures Helsinki and Finland, 2003

Demography/geography	Helsinki City	Helsinki Region	Finland
Population, #, 2003	559,700	1,224,100	5,206,300
Population growth, %, 1990–2003	14.0	–	–
Total area land, km^2, 2003	185	2,970	304,590
Population density per km^2, 2003	3,034	412	17
Finnish nationality, %, 2003	94.9	96.0	98.0
Other nationality, %, 2003	5.1	4.0	2.0

The social consequences related to this were a new phenomenon for Finland (Urban Facts, 2004). One decade later, the economy started to recover. This recovery was based on the advanced developments in specific post-industrial sectors like production and the application of state-of-the-art telecommunication services and new media services. Today Finland is a world leader in mobile phones, the internet and new media services (van den Berg and Russo, 2004). The economic heart of Finland is in the Helsinki Metropolitan Area. Approximately 700,000 jobs are located here, which is 30 per cent of the total job supply in Finland. The gross value added of this area is €40 billion, which is 34 per cent of the national gross value added (Urban Facts, 2004b). The economy of Helsinki Metropolitan Region has been doing well the last few years (production shows a growth of 2.6 per cent over 2003 and net sales show an annual growth of 5 per cent (City of Helsinki, 2004b)), although there are some signs of stagnation of the growth as well.

At the time of writing, the Helsinki Metropolitan Area is heavily dependent on business and financial services, trade and logistics, culture and leisure services, research and development, high technology manufacturing services, higher education and national level administration. In 2002 most people were working in the sectors public services (35 per cent), business activities (14 per cent), trade (14 per cent) and manufacturing (12 per cent) (Urban Facts, 2004a). As previously stated, the high unemployment rates of the beginning of the 1990s are over, but in the last few years, following the European economic development, unemployment is rising again. In 2001, the unemployment rate was 5.7 per cent (Urban Facts, undated). Two years later, it had risen to 6.9 per cent and in the beginning of 2004 it was estimated at 7.5 per cent. Even so, the unemployment rate in Helsinki is lower than for Finland as a whole, where it was estimated at 9.3 per cent in the beginning of 2004 (Urban Facts, 2004a). Because of Helsinki's strong dependency on the ICT cluster, It is often said that that the city needs to develop new industrial clusters to complement the ICT cluster and traditional industries and to make the industrial basis of the city more versatile. This is needed to eliminate the risks of the strong volatility of the global ICT business and modest growth prospects (Urban Facts, 2004b). Another problem Finland is facing is the ageing of the population. Although Helsinki is characterized by a relatively young population structure, in the next few years more people will leave than enter the labour market. As in many Western European countries, the age cohort after World War II is slowly beginning to retire, leaving many vacancies as a consequence. This development requires adaptation on the part of employers, for example, by settling for a smaller number of jobs or importing labour from abroad (Urban Facts, 2004a). The strong point of the labour market in Helsinki is that the education level is relatively high. As much as one third of the population of 15 years and older has a university degree (City of Helsinki, 2003).

Table 7.2 Economic figures for Helsinki and Finland

Economy	Helsinki City	Finland
Jobs, #, 2001	376,700	2,251,200
Enterprises, #, 2000	32,700	223,500
Unemployment rate, 2004	7.5	9.3
Shares employed labour force, 2002:		
Public and other services	34.8	32
Manufacturing	11.8	20.7
Trade	13.7	11.9
Business activities	14.2	8.2
Agriculture and forestry	0.3	5.3
Other	25.2	21.9

7.2.3 Housing

As housing is an important topic in this case study, a short overview of the housing supply and development in Helsinki will be presented. In order to prevent shortages and social segregation, housing policies in Helsinki are connected to social policies. A strong city planning together with the model of the 'Nordic welfare state' (aimed at keeping income differences at a minimum) resulted in a very balanced socioeconomic situation within the city.

The total housing stock consisted of about 300,700 dwellings in 2001 (Urban Facts, undated). This supply is still increasing. Since 1990 the number of dwellings has grown by 40,000 (City of Helsinki, 2003). There is a large share of rented housing (46 per cent) of which most is supplied by the city or by housing organizations – very few apartments are privately rented. Another 43 per cent of the housing supply is owner-occupied (Urban Facts, undated). Whoever can afford it will buy their own house, meaning that those who rent houses often can be characterized by low incomes and unemployment. Despite the increase in social housing in the past decade there is still a shortage of housing: only 30 per cent of the applicants for social housing received a flat in 2003 (Urban Facts, 2004a). Although there are, of course, differences between the districts, generally Helsinki's housing stock can be characterized by apartment buildings; just 17 per cent of the supply is detached housing (Urban Facts, undated). When walking through any living area in Helsinki it is hard to tell which apartment blocks are social housing and which are owner-occupied. Because of the use of high quality and diversified architecture, most districts show a very attractive and diversified housing stock.

7.2.4 *Administration*

Finland is a centrally governed welfare state where all cities and municipalities obey the same laws and procedures. Balanced regional development has been one of the main concerns. It is considered to be so important that, for example, measures have been taken to transfer resources from Helsinki Region to the rest of the country, because the economic growth of those other regions lags behind Helsinki Region. Municipalities in Finland have an exceptionally strong autonomy: they have, for example, the right to levy tax of 15 per cent to 20 per cent of people's personal income (Holstila, 2004). This autonomy makes the City of Helsinki a considerable economic and political actor.

The highest decision-making organ in Helsinki is the City Council, which consists of 85 members who are elected by municipal elections every fourth year (City of Helsinki, 2004a). The latest election was in 2004. Currently, the largest parties are National Coalition (conservatives, 25 seats), the Social Democrats (21 seats) and the Green League of Finland (17 seats) (Urban Facts, undated). The City Council decides on all important financial matters such as budget and income tax percentages. In addition, the City Council is responsible for organizing the city administration, appointing the city organs and filling its most important posts as well. Another important city organ is the City Board, which is responsible for such areas as the management of the city administration, the preparation of the agenda of the City Council, the execution of the Council's decisions and the supervision of the legality of the Council's decisions. The members of the City Board are elected by the City Council for a period of two years (City of Helsinki, 2004a). The City of Helsinki is organized in sectors, meaning that subjects such as city planning and real estate, public works and environmental affairs and social affairs and public health are addressed in separate departments. The subject of safety relates to all these topics, but there is no official safety policy agreement. One of the consequences is that there is no central person (for example, a councillor) responsible for the topic of safety. This may create difficulties regarding organizing safety policies.

7.2.5 *Mellunkylä and Myllypuro*

Figure 7.3 shows all 33 districts in Helsinki. The Eastern Major district (*Itäinen*) contains the districts of Mellunkylä, Myllypuro, Vuosaari, and Vartiokylä. This case study focuses on the two 'underprivileged' districts Mellunkylä and Myllypuro and some extra information about these two districts will be presented here. Almost one fifth of the Helsinki population lives in Itäinen (97,200 people) and this population is growing. Over the period 1990–2003, the population increased by 28 per cent (City of Helsinki, 2003). Approximately 9,200 people live in Myllypuro, 36,600 in

Mellunkylä and 51,400 in the other parts of Itäinen. In Mellunkylä, population growth was lower than for the whole of Itäinen (15 per cent). In Myllypuro the population even decreased by 9 per cent over the same period (City of Helsinki, 2003). The declining population is related to both a natural decline and an outflow of people. Young people leaving their parents' house in particular often move away to other districts. This results in a population structure strongly dominated by the elderly (Schulman and Bäcklund, 2003).

The districts in Itäinen are definitely not slums as they are known in, for instance, American cities, but the district is less well-off than the average for Helsinki. Economic development in Itäinen lags behind the city's average; the economy is recovering relatively slowly there, resulting in a relatively large proportion of unemployed (Schulman and Bäcklund, 2003). Related to this is the relatively high share of persons receiving income from social security. In Helsinki the average of people with this income is 11 per cent, while in Itäinen it is 15 per cent. Mellunkylä and Myllypuro have even higher shares (16 per cent and 17 per cent respectively) (City of Helsinki, 2003). Next to a lower economic position and higher share of income from social security, the population of Itäinen seems to be less educated as well. The share of persons older than 15 years with an academic degree is 25 per cent, compared to 34 per cent in Helsinki (City of Helisnki, 2004c) and in Myllypuro and Mellynkylä, these shares are even lower: 23 per cent and 20 per cent respectively (City of Helsinki, 2004c).

The housing stock of Itäinen consists of 47,600 dwellings: 4,800 in Myllypuro and 18,000 in Mellunkylä. In Itäinen, the share of social housing is higher than in the city as a whole. In Mellunkylä more than half of the total housing stock is social housing. The total housing supply in Itäinen has increased by 35 per cent in the last decade. Especially in Mellunkylä many new dwellings have been built (City of Helsinki, 2003). A lot of money has been invested in renovating existing apartment blocks as well as in building new dwellings. This has been done with financial subsidies from the Housing Fund of Finland (the state has supported the renovation of private housing companies and given loans to rental housing companies).

7.3 The Perception of Security in Helsinki

7.3.1 Actual Security in Helsinki is High

By international standards, Helsinki is regarded as a safe city (City of Helsinki, 2002). The total number of offences in the police district of Helsinki was 99,200 in 2002, which is 177.3 offences per 1,000 of the population on average (Urban Facts, 2004b). Compared to other European cities like Glasgow, Rotterdam and The Hague, this crime rate seems very high. Of course, there are large differences in definitions of crime rates and in the readiness of the citizens to record crime. This makes international comparisons of crime rates complicated. Helsinki's high crime rate is believed to be related to the high degree of willingness of the population to report crime. This is related to the demands of the insurance companies to provide a police report before

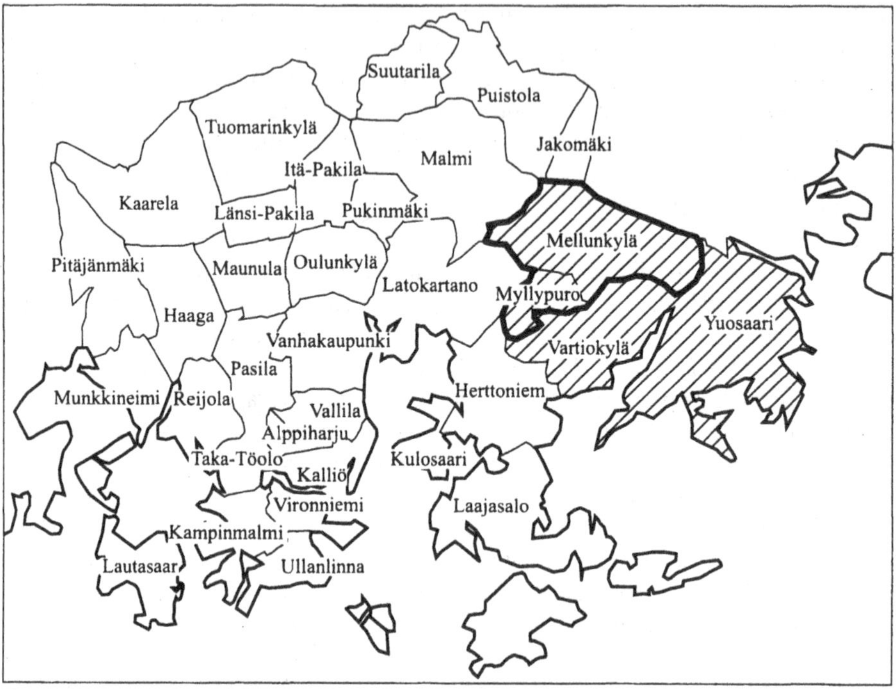

Figure 7.3 The districts in Helsinki, including Itäinen

Note: hatched area = Itäinen

Source: Urban Facts, 2004b.

Table 7.3 Facts and figures of Itäinen and sub-districts Myllypuro and Mellunkylä

Demography and economy	Itäinen	Myllypuro	Mellunkylä
Population, #, 2003	97,200	9,200	36,600
Population, % of Helsinki City, 2003	17	2	7
Population growth, %, 1990–2003	28.8	–9.3	15.2
Housing stock, 2003	47,600	4,800	18,000
Share social housing, %, 2003	48	42	51
Income security, % of population, 2002	14.5	16.6	15.6

paying the indemnities. Although the recorded crime rate in Helsinki is high compared to other European cities, actual safety is expected to be better than other European cities, as in those cities the actual crime rate is estimated to be much higher than the recorded crime rate.

On a national perspective as well, Helsinki is a safe city, although there is relatively more crime in Helsinki compared to other major Finnish cities. Residents of Helsinki have actually experienced violence and/or the threat of violence more often than in other cities in Finland (Heiskanen et al., 2004). The highest crime rates in Helsinki are found in the city centre. Violence in particular occurs relatively frequently in this area. Within the city centre there is a clear concentration of crime around the central station. This is the area where, on Thursday, Friday and Saturday evenings, people take public transport to go back home after a night of partying. A spatial concentration of drunken people can be a breeding ground for problems, in particular breach of the peace and violence. Other locations with relatively high concentrations of crime are metro and railway stations. Because the number of metro stations is lower than the number of, for example, bus stations, these sites are characterized by larger numbers of people leaving and entering the premises. Again, a concentration of people can be a breeding ground for problems, especially when a majority of is under the influence of alcohol after a night of partying (Tuominen, 1999).

As in other European countries, there is a strong relationship between violence and alcohol abuse in Finland. Alcohol abuse is a hot topic in Finland. As in the other Nordic countries, taxes on alcohol have always been very high to reduce alcohol consumption among the population. At the beginning of 2004, however, alcohol taxes came down. With the accession of Estonia to the European Union it has become very easy for Finnish to take the ferry to Estonia's capital, Tallinn, and import wine, beer and liquors at much lower prices. The fact that alcohol prices have come down and that it is easier to buy alcohol for even lower rates only one-and-a-half hours' journey away from Helsinki may have consequences for alcohol misuse and related crime and violence in Helsinki. But what these consequences will be is not clear: there are no figures on this topic available yet.

Some types of crime have been decreasing, for example, crime involving assault and violence, but other types of crime have been increasing over the last few years, for example, vandalism, drinking in public, disturbance of the peace on the streets, and drugs-related crime (City of Helsinki, 2002). Overall, crime figures in Helsinki have decreased in the past few years; the total number of offences has declined by 4 per cent over the period 1999–2002 (Urban Facts, 2004b). Helsinki's actual security can be regarded as very good and, in the light of the crime figures of the past few years, it seems to be improving. One of the reasons why Helsinki (and Finland) has such low crime figures is believed to be the equality of the social system; Helsinki has relatively small differences in social classes, especially compared to other European cities. In many of the world's large cities it is exactly this difference in social classes that could lead to regional and social segregation, which is a breeding ground for crime (City of Helsinki, 2002).

7.3.2 Safety Perceptions Relatively Low

Although Helsinki in general is regarded as one of the safest cities in the world, not all citizens perceive it as such. There are some differences in opinion about how inhabitants of Helsinki perceive safety. The City of Helsinki, for example, states that many citizens feel unsafe in their city (City of Helsinki, 2002). This statement is based on the outcome of the national poll which says that 90 per cent of the Finns believe that society's internal safety and the amount of crime and violence have changed for the worse in the past few years (City of Helsinki, 2002). Other sources, however, state that the safety perceptions of Helsinki's citizens about are not that bad. Several national public surveys on social safety and urban attractiveness have been held in the past decades and the major cities, including Helsinki, were highlighted. When the outcomes of these public surveys are compared, the safety perceptions have been quite stable in recent years. An useful indicator for safety perceptions is the share of people (sometimes) feeling unsafe in the city centre of their home city. Compared to other major cities in Finland, Helsinki's citizens do not consider their inner city area as more unsafe at night than do citizens of other cities. The differences in shares were very small, meaning that this outcome is not statistically significant (Heiskanen et al., 2004). Within the city of Helsinki, however, there are larger differences in citizens' safety perceptions. In the 'best' district in 2003, 6 per cent of the respondents to a public survey said they (sometimes) felt unsafe in their home district, while in the 'worst' districts this was 35 per cent: the difference between the districts in Helsinki that were considered the safest and the most unsafe is nearly sixfold (Heiskanen et al., 2004). Summarizing this, a distinctions needs to be made regarding the opinion of the City of Helsinki (based on a national poll) that many people feel unsafe in their city; there are considerable differences in safety perceptions between the districts, but, based on a urban public survey, overall perceptions of safety have been stable in the past few years.

There are several possible reasons explaining why the safety perceptions are lower than expected in a very safe city like Helsinki. Safety perceptions have much to do with image or reputation. As stated before, Helsinki was in a severe economic depression in the 1990s. Unemployment rates were very high and economic perspectives were low. This was the first time that the citizens of Helsinki had encountered such a situation and it created grounds for feelings of uncertainty and social problems. In adition, the media influences safety images of districts. The local media in partiuclar give more attention to (local) crime without putting it in perspective. Therefore, people get the feeling that crime is increasing and that the chances of getting involved with crime if increasing for them personally as well. Another factor influencing safety perceptions is the quality of the built environment and public places. A badly-maintained environment can increase feelings of unsafety. In certain districts (for example, the focus areas Myllypuro and Mellunkylä) with many high-rise apartment blocks, the built environment and public places are perceived to be badly maintained. It must be stated here that this is all about perceptions as well, because the overall maintenance of buildings and public places in Helsinki is exceptionally high. In Finland, alcohol

Table 7.4 Security figures in Helsinki

Actual and perceived safety	Helsinki City
Total crime, #, 2002	99,238
Crime development, %, 1999–2002	–4
Lowest share of people (sometimes) feeling unsafe, %, 2003	6
Highest share of people (sometimes) feeling unsafe, %, 2003	35

consumption also strongly influences safety perceptions. With the reduction in taxes on alcohol, people are afraid of large increases of alcohol consumption and the related problems. There is not really a fear of an increase in the number of people addicted to alcohol, but of the problems of existing addicts becoming more severe, meaning that people will drink stronger liquors.

7.3.3 Mellunkylä and Myllypuro

The highest shares of perceptions of insecurity occur in the northeast and east of Helsinki. The latest public survey shows that in these major districts the shares of people saying that they (sometimes) feel unsafe in their home district is high: between 26.8 per cent and 34.7 per cent (Heiskanen et al., 2004). The districts pf Mellunkylä and Myllypuro are located in east and have therefore relatively high perceptions of insecurity. One of the safety problems in the two districts appears to be domestic violence. In contrast to many other European countries (e.g. Germany and The Netherlands), the police have authority and even an obligation to act against domestic violence. This is to make sure that the police can tackle the problem, even when a victim does not want to report their own relative. However, although domestic violence might be a problem for actual safety this does not usually influence safety perceptions in a district strongly, because the crime occurs behind closed doors. What does have an influence on safety perceptions in these two districts is the visible use of drugs and alcohol and young people hanging around (in the shopping mall). People with children are also worried about traffic safety, as strong traffic, noise and pollution (Eronen et al., 2002). A public survey showed that residents were not positive about the safety situation in near future: one third of the interviewed group in the eastern districts believed that the safety situation would become worse in the next few years (Eronen et al., 2002).

7.4 Urban Attractiveness and Spatial Behaviour

7.4.1 The City of Helsinki

Helsinki is an attractive city to live in with a high quality of life. An international comparative study among 215 cities worldwide showed that Helsinki was ranked number 24 in 2004. Two years earlier, Helsinki ranked even higher, at number six, but rectification for climate lowered the ranking (Mercer, 2004). The cold and rainy middle season and the long and dark winter dim the excellent scores of Helsinki on other aspects of quality of life. The supply of leisure facilities, for example, is very good; there is a large variety of opera and theatre performances, cinema, museums, zoo, sports, restaurants, etc. Finland, as other Scandinavian countries, is well-known for its Nordic welfare system: there is relatively little social segregation (a factor often seen as a seedbed for social unrest). Another attraction factor for Helsinki is the quality and maintenance of its built environment. As previously stated, the apartment blocks that characterize most districts all have a similar quality level, whereas the diversity of architecture prevents the districts for becoming homogeneous and boring. The attractiveness of the city is also expressed in the low vacancy rates of housing: housing prices are high and keep on rising and there are waiting lists for social housing up to several years (Urban Facts, 2004a). Rising housing prices are not only a reflection of the attractiveness of the city. Housing prices are also high because of the low interest rates (which make it attractive to buy) and the fact that space in Helsinki city is scarce; the city is enclosed between Vantaa, Espoo and the Baltic Sea and there is not too much land left to be developed.

7.4.2 Mellunkylä and Myllypuro

Within the city of Helsinki, Mellunkylä and Myllypuro are perceived as less attractive living areas. This is mainly due to the lower education levels of the population, lower average household incomes and the lower quality of the built environment. Itäinen was built in the 1950s and 1960s and is characterized by the typical homogeneous and grey high-rise apartment blocks of that era. At that time, most people moving to this district came from rural areas: they were not used to living in small and anonymous apartment blocks. At that time, perceptions of Itäinen as an unattractive and unsafe district arose. This image still exists, although to a lesser extent by inhabitants than by outsiders. As previously stated, the housing stock is homogeneous compared to other districts. A large share of the stock is rented, most of it through housing corporations. The housing stock is perceived as less attractive and worse maintained than in other parts of the city (although this is relative, because the overall level of maintenance is exceptionally high in Helsinki). However, with support from the state, most of the apartment blocks have been renovated and redeveloped in the past few years. Not only has the physical environment been redeveloped, there have also been projects to address the social and economic problems in the district. Although by Helsinki standards the focus district of this case study can be seen as being underprivileged, by international standards it appears not to be really underprivileged.

7.4.3 Consequences for Spatial Behaviour

Urban attractiveness and (perceptions of) insecurity hardly influence spatial behaviour in Helsinki nor Mellunkylä and Myllypuro negatively. The small migration flow out of Helsinki described earlier is due to a lack of available and affordable housing rather than safety reasons. Short-term spatial behaviour might be influenced to some extent: public places like the central station area and metro stations in suburbs may be avoided by residents during night hours.

7.5 Policy Reactions

As is described in the previous section, safety is not a major problem for the City of Helsinki. However, safety is chosen as one of the most important values (City of Helsinki, 2002). One of the reasons why safety is such an important issue for the City of Helsinki is that a competitive economy which is attractive for (foreign) investments requires a safe and attractive environment (City of Helsinki, 2002). Another incentive for putting safety high on the political agenda is the State Council's decision of 1999 that a national crime prevention programme to reduce crime and increase safety should be developed (City of Helsinki, 2002). Therefore, all municipalities in Finland have to design local crime prevention programmes and safety plans. The local crime prevention programmes and safety plans should be based on cooperation of the police and municipal governments with a focus on local crime prevention (City of Helsinki, 2002). The City of Helsinki has a proactive approach towards social safety; although the problem with actual (social) safety and safety perceptions is relatively small, the urban government acknowledges the rise of these problems in other European cities and realizes that they may have to deal with them in the (near) future. Their safety policy is thus preventive, aimed at maintaining safety at a high level.

The actual safety policy of the City of Helsinki is still in the process of being developed. Although a safety policy is not yet available, a safety strategy has been written and accepted by the City Council in May 2001. In September 2004 this strategy was evaluated by the City Council. The main themes of the safety strategy are: peace on the streets, intoxicants, damage to property and domestic peace (City of Helsinki, 2002). The current safety strategy emphasizes that improving safety requires an intensified cooperation between actors involved such as city, police, business community, parishes and residents. In addition, it is necessary to change the current operational cultures (City of Helsinki, 2002). As previously stated, the city is organized into sectors with no-one centrally responsible for safety. Safety is still being addressed by the sectors separately.

In the past few years, several projects have been initiated with the aim of improving (perceptions of) safety, although this often is a more indirect aim of these projects. An example is the project where local residents jointly planted tulip bulbs in public parks and green areas. The direct aim of this project was to create more social cohesion – to bring residents together and increase the commitment with their neighbourhood. The indirect aim is a possible increase in safety perceptions due to, firstly, making the residents less anonymous – they get to know each other by working together – qnd secondly, the public space becoming better maintained and more attractive and therefore perceived as less unsafe. However, all existing projects directly and indirectly aimed at improving (perceptions of) safety are strongly fragmented. There is hardly any coherence between the individual projects. Moreover, the projects are often subsidized for only a limited period of time. After this period of subsidy, the project stops and new projects are initiated. The tacit knowledge gathered during those projects is subsequently often lost. In addition, most projects being developed and implemented are hardly monitored or evaluated, unless they are part of URBAN, when monitoring and evaluation is a requirement. This implies that it may be difficult for the City of Helsinki to measure the impacts of its policy and decide whether or not the chosen direction is worth continuing.

To improve the efficiency and effectiveness of the projects, a coherent safety policy, a strong implementation and organization of this policy and projects and a (mid-term and ex-ante) evaluation of the implemented projects are all necessary. According to van den Berg et al. (1997), the efficiency and effectiveness of policies increase when problems are addressed with the cooperation of all involved actors under the strong leadership of one actor and with a generally accepted vision for future developments as a starting point. The City of Helsinki is indeed stressing the importance of cooperation between involved actors, but a strong vision for future safety developments is still lacking and a strong leader responsible for safety matters is not present either. In addition, the scheme of 'formulation – implementation – evaluation' for designing policies is not always used very consistently in the City of Helsinki.

Over the past few years, the focus districts of this case study have received (and still receive) extra political attention and money from the City Council. Because these districts are seen as 'underprivileged' areas, special policies have been developed to strengthen the socioeconomic situation in this area. Two programmes, URBAN (I and II) and *Lähiö Projekti* (Neighbourhood project), were initiated. Improving safety was not the main objective of these programmes, but it played a role indirectly. The URBAN I and II programmes cover the Myllypuro and Kontula districts in Helsinki and the Koivukylä- Havukoski (URBAN I) and Länsimäki-Hakunila (URBAN II) districts in the neighbouring city Vantaa (URBAN, undated). During URBAN I approximately €10m was invested by the EU Regional Development Fund, the cities of Helsinki and Vantaa and the state. During the URBAN II Programme, approximately €22.5m will be invested by the EU Regional Development Fund, the cities, the state and the private sector (Urban Helsinki-Vantaa, 2003). The objective of URBAN II is to 'revive urban areas economically and socially as well as to enhance sustainable development' (Urban Helsinki-Vantaa, 2003). The *Lähiö Projekti* covers the districts Myllypuro, Kontula, Kivikko, Vesala and Pihlajamäki. It is a cooperation between several administrations (among others, city planning, public works, economic and planning centre, building regulation, social services, sport and youth departments) with the aim of levelling-out disparities between different residential areas by taking local actions. Thus URBAN is more focused on social and economic restructuring, while the *Lähiö Projekti* is focused on physical restructuring. The URBAN II Programme and the *Lähiö Projekti* are coordinated to complement each other (Helsinki Lähiöprojekti, undated). Within these two programmes several projects have been developed that can be seen as best practices in order to improve the attractiveness of the living environment and indirectly to improve social safety. The first best practice that will be described below involves the physical renovations, especially of council housing in the area. The second best practice covers cooperation between police, social workers and Public Prosecutor's Office and the third best practice describes the role of the housing consultant in preventing social problems regarding housing.

7.5.1 Best Practice 1 – Cooperation of Police with the Public Prosecutor and Social Work

Public prosecution is centrally organized in Helsinki. There is one courthouse where all public prosecutors are employed and where all cases are treated. However, in March 2003 public prosecution was partially decentralized. Since then, all four districts of the Helsinki Police host a Public Prosecutor. This has been done in order to improve the cooperation between the two institutions and to increase the decision-making abilities of public prosecution and police together. Now that police and public prosecution are located directly near each other, exchange of information is easier and cooperation comes more naturally, not only on the local level, but also on the management level, where monthly meetings are also held in order to improve cooperation. This better cooperation improves the efficiency and effectiveness of addressing criminal behaviour. For example, it will be easier to prioritize cases of persistent offenders or young offenders who are in danger of becoming persistent offenders. Their trial process can be speeded up and subsequently they can be punished more promptly, because of short mutual communication lines. Both the police and public prosecution regard this cooperation as very positive and effective.

In addition, there is also cooperation between the police and social work departments. In some cases offenders are in need of social help, for example, young offenders who have a problematic social background. A social worker takes a look at this background and helps in case of any problems. Often this prevents the young offender reverting to criminal behaviour. In cases of domestic violence, too, a social worker appears to be more experienced in dealing with difficult social situations. The cooperation between police and social work started as a pilot project in *Itäinen*. One social worker is posted at the police station and is paid by the City of Helsinki. Recently the initiative was introduced in other districts in Helsinki as well.

7.5.2 Best Practice 2 – Physical Renovation Council Housing

One of the most important objectives of the *Lähiö Projekti* is renovating the physical and green environment in Mellunkylä and Myllypuro. The apartment blocks built in the 1960s and 1970s are not an archetype for attractive building. Therefore plans were designed and executed to improve the quality of council housing in these areas during the period 2000–2006. The Housing Production Bureau in the area has played an important role in this process. By 2003 almost all city-owned buildings had been renovated; new elevators were installed, facades of apartment blocks were restructured (new balconies) or at least maintained, etc. (Helsinki Lähiöprojekti, 2003; 2004).

But council housing was only part of the renovation project: public buildings like a metro station (as already noted, a centre of offending/criminal behaviour), an old people's centre, a children's day care centre and a sports park have been renovated or even newly built. The environment, like city parks and other public spaces, were, or are about to be, also renovated (Helsinki Lähiöprojekti, 2003; 2004). Over the period 2000–2004, the total investment made by different city administrations was €49 million. The City Neighbourhood Fund granted an extra €4 million especially for improving public environment in the area (Helsinki Lähiöprojekti, 2004). Because there is no clear evaluation of the outcomes and effects of the project, it cannot be concluded that the project was a success. However, it appears that all improvements have added substantially to the quality of the living environment of the area and subsequently improved the feelings of safety among the residents.

7.5.3 Best Practice 3 – The Housing Adviser

The large high-rise apartment blocks characterizing Itäinen are generally seen as negative contributors to feelings of insecurity among the residents. In Kontula, too – a neighbourhood within the focus district – the large complexes of (mainly) council housing were not regarded as popular by residents. The feeling of anonymity contributed to social problems. Housing corporations were increasingly faced not only with poor upkeeping, nuisance, but also with problems like rent arrears. Therefore, under the umbrella of URBAN I, a housing adviser was employed by the municipal real estate company. A housing adviser is a social worker employed by the housing corporation who intervenes in social problems related to housing (for example unpaid rents, disorder, nuisance etc.) The main focus of a housing adviser it quite broad: their task is to help tenants get control over their own lives and to develop measures that will help diminish social exclusion (Haapanen, 2004). The project was carried out during the period November 1999–December 2002 (URBAN, undated).

From the results of the discussions held with key persons, this project has been chosen as a best practice because of the positive contribution to the quality of the living environment. The success of the project lies in two elements of the work of the housing adviser. First, a working network emerged in which the housing adviser connected all related service providers to an individual client, enabling a more efficient and effective service. The clients included mentally disabled, aged, substance abusers, immigrants or families with children in crisis. Although a few clients were unwilling to cooperate, most were positive about the received help (URBAN, undated). The second element was the steering group. Here, the chief of the local social services unit, the director of the housing company and some other crucial actors were brought together, creating a strong commitment to solving the housing-related problems.

The direct results of this project are a considerable decrease in the amount of evictions and the amount of court cases. The housing adviser and the related chain of services brought cost saving to the clients, the real estate companies, the social and health services and other involved services. In addition, the quality of the living environment increased considerably.

Because of the good experiences, the city council decided to start working with housing advisers on a permanent base. At the time of writing, a proposition on how this should be organized is being prepared. This is a complex process because of the many different stakeholders (several independent housing corporations, real estate department, social services departments and tenant organizations are involved). Most housing companies are positive about the results and therefore also positive about the appointment of a housing adviser in the company. However, some housing companies are critical about their social role. They believe that this field of work belongs to the Social Services Department and that housing companies should stick to their core business: the technical and economical aspects of housing. The fact that housing corporations have to make a financial contribution might also cause initial resistance.

The success of the housing adviser has been widespread. A national network of housing authorities and companies, which discusses and spreads this model and comparing it with other models, has emerged. Housing corporations in several other Finnish cities have already adopted the model.

7.6 Synthesis

This section recapitulates the most important conclusions for the city of Helsinki. Subsection 7.6.1 focuses on the perception of safety; subsections 7.6.2 and 7.6.3 deal, respectively, with the spatial behaviour of inhabitants as consequence of changing urban attractiveness and with the policies adopted by the city, with an illustration of the best practices. The city's organizing capacity is briefly mentioned in 7.6.4. We conclude with formulating some recommendations in subsection 7.6.5.

7.6.1 Safety Perception

From an international perspective, Helsinki can be regarded as a safe city. On the national level as well, Helsinki is a safe city, although relatively more crime occurs in Helsinki than in other major Finnish cities. Within Helsinki there is a clear concentration of (violent) crime in the city centre and at metro stations, especially during the night on Thursday, Friday and Saturday evenings. In general, the crime level is not high and crime actually is decreasing. Over the period 1999–2000, crime fell by 4 per cent (Urban Facts, 2004b). In spite of the high safety standard in the city of Helsinki, the perceptions of safety among the residents are not as good as expected. Nationwide, 90 per cent of the people even believe that society's internal safety and the amount of crime and violence have changed for the worst (City of Helsinki, 2002). Other sources state that safety perceptions within Helsinki have stayed on the same level over the past few years. Helsinki's residents do not feel less safe (in their inner city) than residents of other major Finnish cities do (in their inner city) (Heiskanen et al., 2004). However, within Helsinki there are some differences regarding safety perceptions. In the best districts, only 6 per cent of the residents said they (sometimes) felt unsafe in their own district. But there is a large difference in the worst districts: here, up to 35 per cent of the residents (sometimes) feel unsafe. In East Helsinki, where the focus districts of this case study (Mellunkylä and Myllypuro) are located, the safety perceptions are not too good: between 26.8 per cent and 34.7 per cent of the residents (sometimes) feel unsafe (Heiskanen et al., 2004). There is no clear reason for the large discrepancy between the actual safety situation and the safety perceptions in Helsinki. An explanation may be found in (an after-effect of) the economic depression of the 1990s, the strong and negative attention on crime by the (local) media, poorer maintenance and quality of the built environment and the public abuse of alcohol.

7.6.2 Urban Attractiveness and Spatial Behaviour

Helsinki is well known as a city with an attractive living environment where all daily and leisure facilities required are available. The housing stock and all public space throughout the city is of a high standard. The overall level of quality can be regarded as high. The City of Helsinki has a policy aimed at minimizing social differences. The level of segregation is therefore remarkably low, especially compared to other European cities. However, there are of course popular and less popular districts within the city. The focus districts of this case study are perceived to be the city's 'underprivileged' districts. Here, the population is relatively less well off than in other districts; the unemployment rates are higher, the income levels are lower, the share of well-educated people is lower and social problems are greater. The quality of the built environment is relatively lower too. However, it must be kept in mind that these differences are relative. Overall, the quality of the living environment still reaches a good standard. It can be concluded that the urban attractiveness of the City of Helsinki is high. There are no clear signs of changed spatial behaviour, either in the form of avoiding places during the night or in the form of people moving away to safer districts, due to unattractiveness or bad safety perceptions.

7.6.3 Policy Reactions

As previously stated, crime and safety perceptions are not a major problem in Helsinki. Nevertheless, safety has been chosen as one of the most important values for the City of Helsinki. The State Council placed it high on the political agenda and the city followed this example. One of the reasons for making safety an important political topic while actual safety problems are small is the conviction that safety is essential for an attractive environment and a competitive economy. This proactive approach by the City of Helsinki towards social safety is aimed at maintaining safety at a high level instead of waiting until crime and safety perceptions have become worse. Despite the proactive approach and the high importance of social safety for the city, an actual safety policy is still in process of being developed. The only policy document available is a safety strategy, which will be the starting point for the safety policy. The strategy is based on the belief that the complexity of safety issues requires an intensified cooperation between all actors involved (city, police, business, parishes and residents). However, the projects (indirectly) aimed at improving the social safety situation in the city that are already in operation under the safety strategy are fragmented. A coherent safety vision is lacking: subsidized projects often end as soon as the period of subsidy is over and hardly any evaluations of the projects are being made. Therefore, the effectiveness of the projects is often not clear and knowledge gained throughout the project is being lost.

In the past few years the focus districts have received extra political attention and financial means to improve their quality of life. With help of URBAN I and II and the *Lähiö Projekti*, extra investments have been made in improving the quality of the built environment and public space and to stimulate socioeconomic developments. Under the umbrella of these subsidy programmes, several projects were implemented that were successful in upgrading the social safety situation. A best practice in this regard is the cooperation of the police with both public prosecution and social work agencies. All four police districts now host a Public Prosecutor who specifically works at the local level. The police in the Itäinen district cooperate with both a Public Prosecutor and a social worker. Some difficult cases, mainly concerning domestic crime or people with psychological problems, are helped by the presence of a social worker. Geographical proximity greatly improves cooperation between the two institutions and therefore improves the effectiveness of their work. A second best practice is the physical renovations of council houses and public space in the district, with help from the *Lähiö Projekti*. These physical renovations improved the quality of the built environment, with a positive effect on safety perceptions in the area. The appointment of a housing adviser – a social worker focusing on social problems among the residents in council housing apartment blocks – also had a positive effect on safety perceptions in the district. This appointment can be seen as a best practice. However, it is also an example of a project being implemented with subsidies and being ended as soon as the subsidy period was over.

7.6.4 Organizing Capacity with Respect to Safety Policy

Safety is highly prioritized by the City Council of Helsinki. The *political support* for safety can be regarded as good. *Societal support* as well is high, as many people in the city perceive safety as deteriorating. However, the current safety strategy consists of many individual projects and lacks an integral *vision*. This safety strategy is proactive and aimed at maintaining the high safety level, but it is not a coherent safety policy. Several projects aiming to tackle parts of the complex (safety) problem have been initiated. In some of these projects several involved actors try to address the safety issues commonly, creating the basis for *strategic networks*. One aspect of organizing capacity requires special attention – *leadership*. At the time of writing, there is no real leader in safety issues in Helsinki. At the same time, nobody is really responsible for the safety topic in the city. This all shows that some elements of organizing capacity are present in the safety issue in Helsinki, but the essential elements of *leadership* and *vision* could be further developed.

7.6.5 Recommendations

The awareness of the City of Helsinki that social safety is an important element for future socioeconomic development of the city can be regarded as very positive. This case study showed that the City of Helsinki already has some good examples of projects aimed at improving social safety. To improve the effectiveness of the social safety initiatives, and to influence safety perceptions of the residents in a positive way, some recommendations can be made.

Considering the relatively small role of social safety in Helsinki it appears to be unnecessary to dramatically increase political attention on social safety. However, it could be advantageous to appoint one person to be responsible for social safety matters. This person would have a bird's eye view of the problems related to social safety in Helsinki and could motivate the involved institutions and persons to address these problems. Because safety is typically a topic that requires a more integral approach, this person also could try and stimulate cooperation between the involved administrative departments to overcome the current strict separation between the different departments.

As stated, there are already projects implemented in Helsinki aiming to improve social safety and living conditions. What also has been stated is that most projects stand alone; there is no coherence between them. In addition, there is insufficient overview of the results and effects of the projects, because there is little ex-post monitoring. Furthermore, many subsidized projects tend to finish at the end of the subsidy period. To improve the effects of the projects and to sustain the knowledge gained during the projects, it would be recommendable to better monitor and evaluate the course and outcomes of the independent safety projects and to stimulate the continuation of projects that proved successful.

A last recommendation concerns the city's communication strategy. Currently many residents in Helsinki perceive safety as deteriorating, despite the fact that Helsinki is a safe city. One of the aspects strongly influencing safety perceptions of people is the often negative news coverage by the (local) media. In order to gradually alter the current negative safety perceptions, news coverage should give a more realistic picture of the safety situation in Helsinki and should therefore cover the positive stories as well. A clear communication strategy by the City of Helsinki could contribute to restoring this balance between positive and negative news coverage.

Chapter 8

The Case of Heerlen

8.1 Introduction

In this case study we focus on the social security in the city of Heerlen. Section 8.2 gives a concise profile of this urban region. In Section 8.3, we deal with the perception of security in Heerlen and the possible causes of feelings og insecurity. Next, in Section 8.4, we will go into the related spatial behaviour of local inhabitants. Section 8.5 examines policy reactions regarding urban insecurity. In this section we will give specific attention to some *best practices*. The focus of this case study is on the city centre and mainly on the problems related to drugs and insecurity. There is special attention on '*Operatie Hartslag*' (Operation Heartbeat), a project aimed at tackling the severe problems related to drugs misuse in the city centre. Finally, Section 8.6 presents conclusions and some recommendations.

8.2 Profile of Heerlen

8.2.1 Geographical and Historical Development: The Influence of the Mining Industry

Heerlen is located in the south of The Netherlands, close to the borders with Germany and Belgium. Together with the cities of Brunssum, Kerkrade, and Landgraaf, it forms a strongly urbanized area with approximately 250,000 inhabitants (Bureau Onderzoek and Statistiek, 2004a). The urban development of Heerlen is remarkable. In the twentieth century, the city was one of the most prosperous in The Netherlands, thanks to its successful mining industry. During that time, the city grew rapidly: several smaller mining villages were incorporated and the total population number increased five times within 25 years. The closure of the mines in the 1970s had enormous consequences for the socioeconomic urban development of Heerlen and marked the end of the prosperous era. Because of the strong economic dependency on mining, a severe economic crisis with high unemployment rates and related social problems arose. Despite national subsidies, special redevelopment programmes and even the relocation of some large national public organizations, the region never fully recovered.

The city of Heerlen is divided into 23 districts. As stated, the city grew rapidly in the early twentieth century, incorporating several smaller mining villages. The

Figure 8.1 Geographical position of Heerlen in Europe

characteristics of these former villages are still visible in the current districts. A second period with strong influence on the development of the city was the period after the closing of the mines. Old industrial sites and buildings and low-quality housing estates were demolished as they lost their original function and quality. In the city centre in particular, urban revitalization resulted in a large number of new and modern architectural estates typical of the 1980s and 1990s.

8.2.2 Population: A Declining City

In 2004, the city of Heerlen had almost 95,000 inhabitants (Bureau Onderzoek en Statistiek, 2004a). Unlike many other Dutch cities, Heerlen has a declining population number: over the past decade, the city has lost almost 3 per cent of its population

(CBS, 2004). This population decline is caused by both a natural decline and a net out-migration of people. As the population ages, with the birth rates smaller than death rates, there is a natural population decline (Bureau Onderzoek and Statistiek, 2004c). In addition, a small negative migration balance contributes to the decline of the population. There is a small inflow of people, mostly foreigners. The number of non-Western foreigners increased from 4,500 in 1996 to 6,500 in 2004 (CBS, 2004). In total, the share of non-Western foreigners in the total population is approximately 7 per cent. This share is very small compared to other Dutch cities like, for example, Rotterdam, where the share of non-Western foreigners was 47 per cent in 2003 (CBS, 2004). Nevertheless there are larger numbers of people moving out of Heerlen. The socioeconomic situation is believed to be a major reason for this outflow; people are trying to find their niche elsewhere. However, it appears to be a relatively small population group that actually migrates out of Heerlen compared to other (European) cities with a long-term weak economic performance. A possible reason for this relatively small out-migration could be the high dependency of many people on public institutions. Heerlen has a large share of the population (up to 40 per cent) receiving some form of financial support from general means. For decades, the mining industry had a strong influence on the personal lives of residents. Everything, 'from cradle to to the grave', was organized for the mine-workers, resulting in a culture/mentality where people are not used and not able to take initiatives and create opportunities. People who are moving away are often the better-educated and independent people, leaving a higher share of socioeconomically weaker persons in the city (Gemeente Heerlen, 2004b).

As stated, the focus area of this case study is the city centre. There are about 4,500 inhabitants in the city centre. This number of residents is relatively small. As a result, it can become very quiet in the streets after the shops close. Another consequence is that the supply of daily facilities (grocery, bakery, greengrocers, etc.) appears to be poor. The population in the city centre is characterized by a strong concentration of people of 65 years and older: in 2003, 30 per cent of the residents belonged to this age cohort. Most residents in the city centre live in single-person households. The housing stock in the city centre consists of mainly apartments above the shops. Most apartments (70 per cent) are rented (Bureau Onderzoek and Statistiek, 2004b).

8.2.3 Administrative System

The City Council is directly elected by the residents and has 37 members. They determine the main lines of the municipal policy plan and decide on important issues such as the budget. The coalition for the period 2002–2006 is made up of the political parties CDA (Christen Democrats), SP (Socialist Party), Stadspartij Heerlen (local political party) and PvdA (Labour). Daily government is in hands of the Mayor and the Aldermen. The Aldermen are elected by the City Council: the Mayor is appointed by the Crown. He or she also chairs the City Council and is responsible for public order and safety.

In common with all municipalities in The Netherlands Heerlen is financially dependent on the state. Only a small part of its income is derived from the

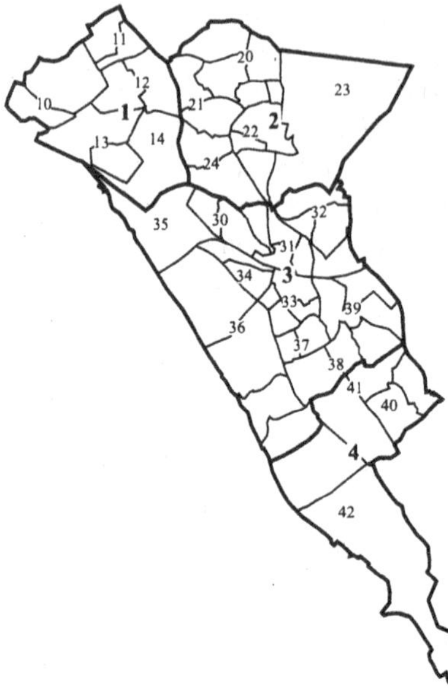

City areas

1 Hoensbroek
2 Heerlerheide
3 Heerlen-Stad
4 Heerlerbaan

City neighbourhoods

10 Maria Gewanden-Terschuren
11 Mariarade
12 Hoensbroek – De Dem
13 Nieuw Lotbroek
14 De Koumen
20 Vrieheide – De Stack
21 Heerlerheide – Passart
22 Heksenberg
23 De Hei
24 Rennemig – Beersdal
30 Zeswegen – Nieuw Husken
31 Schandelen – Grasbroek
32 Meezenbroek – Schaesbergv. – Palemig
33 Heerlen-Centrum
34 Eikenderveld
35 Woonboulevard – Ten Esschen
36 Welten – Benzenrade
37 Bekkerveld – Aarveld
38 Caumerveld – Duove Weien
39 Molenberg
40 Heerlerbaan – Centrum
41 Heerlerbaan – Schil
42 De Beitel

Figure 8.2 Map of the districts in the city of Heerlen

municipality itself. The city has some autonomy to formulate its own policies and to spend its own budget. However, municipal policy in Heerlen is strongly based on the *Grotestedenbeleid* (GSB, Large Cities Policy); a policy initiated by the National Government in 1994, which clusters city-oriented grants, subsidies and city policies from nine ministries. The cities involved in the programme (the 30 largest cities of The Netherlands) draw up an integrated urban strategy. As there are large subsidies involved, the municipal policy plan for the elected period has to be in line with the main aims and objectives of the *Grotestedenbeleid.*

The urban government of Heerlen operates in a so-called 'service model' which is strongly focused on the geographical level of districts and neighbourhoods. In total there are seven 'service centres' (Gemeente Heerlen, 2004a):

- Staff Department (providing the Council with legal advice and responsible for public order and safety, district-oriented approach, HRM, communication and finance);
- Department of Internal and External Services;
- Department of Public Work, Sport and Recreation;
- Department of Urban Development;
- Department for Welfare, Employment and Social Affairs;
- Music School;
- Heerlen Public Library.

At the time of writing, the City of Heerlen is reorganizing and is planning to change its service model to a more pragmatic model with a theme- and area-based approach.

In the service model there is another important organization, the Office for Public Order and Safety (OOV), set up in 1994. Civil servants from various municipal departments working on safety-related topics cooperate in this office. This independent organization has become an integrated department of the municipality. This department consists of the Policy and Planning division and the Supervision and Order Maintenance division. The divisions are not located on the same premises, but there is a close cooperation between the divisions.

Table 8.1 Facts and figures for Heerlen

Characteristics	Heerlen
Population, #, 2004	95,000
Population growth, %, 1995–2004	–3%
Population density per km², 2003	2,000
Non-Western foreigners, %, 2004	7%
Employment per sector, %, 2003	
Business services	18%
Health and social care	16%
Trade	13%
Industry	12%
Other	41%
Unemployment, %, 2004	10%
Highly-educated, BA/MA, older than 18y, %, 2003	21%

8.2.4 Difficult Economic Development and Relatively High Unemployment Rates

As already noted, Heerlen faced a severe economic crisis after the closure of the mines in the 1970s. The national government subsidized the region in several ways. One of them was to relocate the public institutions CBS (Statistics Netherlands) and ABP (a pension fund) to Heerlen in order to provide extra employment. However, these companies need highly-educated employees and the share of highly-educated people in Heerlen is low: 21 per cent of the population of 18 years and older has a degree comparable to a BA or MA (Bureau Onderzoek and Statistiek, 2004c). The mismatch between a large demand of better-educated people and a large supply of lower-educated people results in a relatively high unemployment rate. In 2004 unemployment was 10 per cent, which is 2 per cent higher than the previous year (Parkstad Limburg, 2004). Compared to the national average of 4.5 per cent in the first period of 2004 this is very high, but compared to other large Dutch cities, the unemployment rate is average (CBS, 2004).

In total there are almost 4,000 companies in Heerlen. About 32 per cent of the companies are active in trade, 20 per cent in commercial services and another 10 per cent in other services. Most people work in business services (18 per cent), health and social care (16 per cent), trade (13 per cent) and industry (12 per cent) (Bureau Onderzoek and Statistiek, 2004c). However, according to the City of Heerlen, the city lacks a clear economic profile. There is no obvious specialization in one or more economic sectors. To improve this, the City of Heerlen would like to attract more ICT, 'medtech' activities, and SMEs (small and medium-sized enterprises) in the near future (Gemeente Heerlen, 2002). All these problems resulted in Heerlen falling behind other Dutch cities. In the period 1994–2002, the City could not manage to restore this deficit. The emphasis of economic policies, therefore, lies on stimulating the growth of business activities: (re)developing high quality business parks in order to create space for business activities (a good example in this respect is Avantis Business Park, a cooperation between the City of Heerlen and the City of Aachen); increasing retail attractiveness; and strengthening the knowledge exchange between government, business and knowledge institutions (Gemeente Heerlen, 2002).

In the city centre, the focus area of this case study, the economy is dominated by retail, as are most city centres. The retail supply contains mostly fashion in the lower and middle-priced sectors. The city centre of Heerlen is perceived to be an attractive shopping area for people from the wider region. With the construction of a new shopping mall, Corio, the total floor area was expanded in 1998. In the last few years, the retail sector in Heerlen has lacked dynamism. Since the opening of Corio, not much has changed in the retail supply in the city centre. Some retailers have ceased trading (in Heerlen) and it appeared to be difficult to fill these empty shops again. One of the main losses has been the supermarket. Residents in the city centre now have to buy their daily groceries outside their neighbourhood.

8.3 The Perception of Security in Heerlen

8.3.1 Drug-related Crime and Other Crime Developments

In Heerlen, actual crime and general nuisance are more or less on the same level as in other Dutch cities. However, the perceptions of safety are worse in comparison to other cities; aspects of living conditions and safety – such as social cohesion – are much lower (Gemeente Heerlen, 2002). The City of Heerlen states that the actual safety situation improved over the past few years (Gemeente Heerlen, 2004b). This statement is based on the outcomes of surveys regarding victimization. Police recordings of crime, however, show a growing crime rate, from 17,000 recorded occurences in 2000 to 22,000 in 2003, an increase of 32 per cent over the total period. Looking at annual changes, there is a clear slow-down of the increase of crime rates: between 2000 and 2001 the increase was 13 per cent while in 2002–2003 there was an increase of 6 per cent (Bureau Onderzoek and Statistiek, 2004c). In the city centre as well there was an increase in crime in the period 2001–2003. The number of recorded crimes increased by approximately 38 per cent (Bureau Onderzoek and Statistiek, 2004a). However, a rise of crime recordings does not always reflect an actual increase in crime. Many crimes stay unrecorded due to the victims' unwillingness to report crime to the police.

The recorded increase in crime in Heerlen could just as easily be due to an increase in victims' willingness to report crime to the police, particularly in the light of the increased police attention in respect of the project *Operatie Hartslag*.

The most apparent safety problems in Heerlen appear to be burglary/theft and nuisance. These two types of crime make up 68 per cent of the total crime rate in Heerlen. Burglary rates seem to be improving, as they have been decreasing since 2001. Nuisance, however, is increasing, with drug-related nuisance in particular showing a strong increase from 900 reports in 2000 to 4,000 reports in 2003 (Bureau Onderzoek and Statistiek, 2004c). The location of Heerlen close to the borders with Germany and Belgium and the tolerant drug policy may contribute to the problems with drug nuisance. The Dutch drug policy has a special position in Europe. Possession, trade, dealing and production of all types of drug are illegal in The Netherlands. There is, however, a tolerant attitude towards soft drugs (hashish, weed) and they can be bought and used in coffee shops. In border regions like Heerlen this may attract 'drug tourists' – people visiting The Netherlands to buy and use drugs. A decade ago, an increase in the number of hard drug users (cocaine, heroine, etc.) in and around the central station was noticed. This resulted in an increase in public use and dealing of drugs, quarrels, noise, people crowding together, etc. For a large part the drug tourists were causing these nuisances (Gemeente Heerlen, 2001). The drug problems in Heerlen appear to be of a different kind than in other border cities like Venlo and Maastricht. Regarding drugs, Heerlen can be characterized by a 'hard drug' market, where in other cities mainly soft drugs are sold. This causes different kinds of nuisance: for example, addicts using cocaine are more aggressive than people using marijuana.

As in many other European cities, there is a concentration of safety-related problems in Heerlen's city centre. Next to the city centre there are also two districts in the north and east of the city where relatively much (petty) crime and nuisance takes place (Gemeente Heerlen, 2002). In the city centre, the central station area used to be particularly disreputable as a result of the presence of the '*harddrugscene*' (Gemeente Heerlen, 2001). The national railway company (*NS*) even declared the station to be the one of most unsafe train stations in The Netherlands. However, over the past few years the situation has improved tremendously. During the day there is now very little visible drug nuisance.

8.3.2 Large Gap between Actual and Perceived Safety

Another problem in Heerlen is the perceived safety: there is a relatively large gap between the actual safety situation and safety perceptions. The actual safety situation is comparable to other Dutch cities. Safety perceptions, however, are relatively bad: feelings of insecurity are twice as high in Heerlen as in other large cities in The Netherlands (Gemeente Heerlen, 2004b). In a public survey held in 2003 43 per cent of the residents said they (sometimes) felt unsafe in their own neighbourhood and 51 per cent of the residents said they (sometimes) even felt unsafe in Heerlen in general (Bureau Onderzoek and Statistiek, 2004a). These are high shares, but there is a discernible positive development since the last poll in 2001 and the shares of

Table 8.2 Figures of crime rates and safety perception in Heerlen

Heerlen characteristics	2000	2001	2002	2003	2004
Actual crime					
Total recorded crime rate, #	16,931	19,147	21,115	22,342	17,888
Crime per 1,000 of the population	178	201	222	238	191
Change recorded crime compared to previous year, %	–	13	10	6	–20
Several types of crimes					
Recorded burglaries/theft, #	8,910	9,141	9,098	8,062	6,725
Recorded nuisances, #	4,841	6,315	7,419	9,340	6,697
Recordings drugs (dealing and use), #	1,269	2,122	3,430	4,826	2,335
Perceptions of crime					
Share of residents (sometimes) feeling unsafe in own district, %	–	–	–	51	–
Share of residents (sometimes) feeling unsafe in Heerlen, %	–	–	–	43	–

Source: Bureau Onderzoek and Statistiek, 2004a.

people (sometimes) feeling unsafe in general and in their own district have come down (Bureau Onderzoek and Statistiek, 2004a). Regarding safety perceptions there have been shifts between the neighbourhoods: some show improved safety perceptions while in other neighbourhoods the perceptions have worsened. In the city centre, the share of people (sometimes) feeling unsafe in general is very high: 80 per cent in 2003, an increase compared with the outcomes of the public survey of 2001 (Bureau Onderzoek and Statistiek, 2004a).

The City of Heerlen is worried about the large gap between safety perceptions and the actual safety situation. As stated, crime rates have improved according to the city's statistics. Safety perceptions, however, have not improved accordingly. In the city centre, safety perceptions have even worsened in the past few years. Consequently there is a relatively large gap between feelings of safety and the actual safety situation, especially compared with other Dutch cities. There is no clear cause for this large gap between actual and perceived safety in Heerlen. Two possible causes may be the high dependency of the population on public institutions and the high expectations of the role of the City Council and the police in improving safety. Other factors, like a low economic performance, high (long-term) unemployment, perceived unattractiveness of the built environment, and negative media attention, may also influence feelings of insecurity.

Residents' involvement in Heerlen appears to be good at the local or district level, but low for the city as a whole. Residents blame the City Council and the police for not being repressive and for tolerating nuisance and crime. Here again, the high dependence of the residents of Heerlen on their government is noticeable (Gemeente Heerlen, 2002). Residents expect the government to solve all safety problems and appear not to acknowledge their own contribution to the solutions of the problem.

8.4 Urban Attractiveness and Spatial Behaviour

8.4.1 Urban Attractiveness

Even though the last mines closed some decades ago, Heerlen remains associated with the mining industry. However, there is very little of the mining industry left, which causes identity problems for the city region. Urban redevelopments in the 1970s and 1980s resulted in the demolishing of the majority of mining fields and historic buildings. Often, these buildings were replaced by modern architecture. At that time there was no clear and consistent vision of what the results of such large-scale urban redevelopment should be, resulting in a hodgepodge of buildings and architectural styles. The current physical urban environment influences the urban identity of Heerlen. The residents of Heerlen tend to identify themselves more with the district they live in than with Heerlen as a whole. This can be explained by the perceived (un)attractiveness of the physical/built environment. Another reason, however, is the historical division of Heerlen into districts, as these districts used to be autonomous villages before the strong urban growth in the early twentieth century.

One of the main factors influencing urban attractiveness is the quality of the built environment. Regarding the housing supply, there is a need for more variety and differentiation in the housing supply, especially in the middle and higher segments. Greater variety and differentiation would improve the quality of the housing supply: better quality and more capacity would stimulate circulation on the housing market (Gemeente Heerlen, 2004b). This would increase the housing supply for middle- and higher-income groups. Because there is a large share of socially weaker residents in Heerlen, it would be beneficial to stimulate the 'stronger' and more prosperous residents to stay in, or even to come to, the city. However, improving the housing supply alone seems to be insufficient to increase the city's attractiveness for this population group. Economic perspectives and city image, for example, also play a role in this perspective.

It is not only the housing supply that influences the quality of the built environment: public buildings and public space also influence the attractiveness. To bring the quality of the public space in the city centre to a higher level, the City of Heerlen has invested, for example, in renovation of the *Glaspaleis* (Glass Palace), an architectural piece of art designed by F.P.J. Peutz and a landmark (one of the few) for the city centre, and in the *pleinenplan*, a policy programme to renovate and refurbish the squares in the city centre (Gemeente Heerlen, 2004b). The green environment – parks and other small green areas in the city – is also important. Research indicates that Heerlen is one of the 'greenest' cities in The Netherlands with respect to presence of (public) green areas. However, residents do not perceive it as such, because many of these public green areas are not accessible (Gemeente Heerlen, 2004b).

In the early years of the twenty-first century, the attractiveness of the city centre seems to have improved. It had long been negatively affected not only by the presence of drug addicts, but also by the relatively low quality of the built environment. Improvements in the city centre's attractiveness were established by a policy programme directly aimed at reducing drug-related nuisance and crime. Another aspect contributing to improvements in the city centre, as stated in the previous paragraph, are the investments made in public buildings and squares. And thirdly, the attractiveness of the city centre is (and was already) positively influenced in the last few years by the retail supply. Although some daily facilities like a supermarket are not present in the city centre, the offer of daily facilities is well appreciated by both residents from Heerlen and visitors from the wider region.

8.4.2 Spatial Behaviour

The safety situation, and especially safety perceptions, appear to influence the spatial behaviour of residents in Heerlen. Approximately 80 per cent of the population in the city centre said they avoided certain places because they perceived them as being unsafe. In the other districts, this share is significantly lower: on average 43 per cent of the population avoided certain places (Bureau Onderzoek and Statistiek, 2004a). During the night, the city centre area becomes quiet, which influences safety perceptions in a negative way. After the shops close, few people visit the city centre, because there are few activities going on. During the day however, the centre can be regarded as safe, in contrast to the situation before 2001.

8.5 Policy Reactions

8.5.1 High Priority for Safety in the City Council Policy Plan 2002–2006

The general policy of the City Council is formulated in the *Meerjarig Bestuurlijk Programma 2002–2006* (MBP 2002–2006, Administrative Programme 2002–2006). The city's ambition is to create 'an optimal living environment in districts and neighbourhoods in which all residents are able to function independently and feel safe, involved and responsible' (Gemeente Heerlen, 2002, p. 9). This administrative programme divides the municipal responsibilities into 10 different programmes. There are seven programmes containing the programmes: 1) living conditions and safety; 2) economic structure; 3) social infrastructure; 4) education and labour participation; 5) construction, living and environment; 6) accessibility; and 7) culture. The remaining three programmes include the structural responsibilities and activities of the City: public services, administration, and government/management (Gemeente Heerlen, 2002, p. 5). The thematic projects in particular require an integral approach and the cooperation of all involved municipal departments. The available financial means are being distributed over the 10 programmes annually. The 'living conditions and safety' category receives few structural means from the municipality. Most financial means are derived from incidental national and international subsidy programmes like URBAN, ISV (Investments Urban Renewal) and GSB (Large City Policy). The total budget for the period 2003–2006 is €5.5 million approximately (Gemeente Heerlen, 2002).

New policy developments can be seen in the new long-term development plan *Meerjaren Ontwikkelingsprogramma* (MOP, long-term development programme), which was designed within the framework of the Large Cities Policy 2005–2009. This report describes the desired long-term developments for the city of Heerlen and formulates objectives to achieve for the Large Cities Policy III. The outcome objectives for all Dutch cities joining the Large Cities Policy are to improve objective and subjective safety, the living environment and social quality. In addition, they have to attract middle- and higher-income groups to the city and increase their economic strength (Gemeente Heerlen, 2004b). The City of Heerlen formulated its long-term objectives for the Large Cities Policy as follows: increasing the ability of people to cope for themselves; increasing business dynamics; strengthening the city centre's position as the heart of city and region; developing the city's identity; and strengthening the regional position (Gemeente Heerlen, 2004b). This shows that safety is stilln important policy priority for the City of Heerlen, but that economic development has gained in importance as well.

However, the MOP report was published in October 2004 and did not have a direct effect on the current policy from the City of Heerlen yet. In the current general policy, safety is one of the City of Heerlen's top priorities. A safety coordinator has been appointed and the OOV (Office for Public Order and Safety) has started to design a safety strategy. The City sees the lack of social cohesion as one of the main problems for safety and living conditions at the city level. Four main directions for solutions have been formulated in the MBP 2002–2006. With respect to improving safety, there is a need for more maintenance of the public environment and for policies aimed at improving perceptions. Another direction is social cohesion and the consciousness of social responsibility among the population. Both aspects need to be strengthened. The district level is regarded as the best level to begin with in this respect. The third direction is communication regarding safety and living conditions. At the time of writing, the City did not have an explicit PR policy on safety, because it feared that too much public attention would have an adverse affect on safety perceptions. However, we believe that in some cases improving communication concerning safety-related topics could also benefit safety perceptions: it can create more realistic expectations of the role of the city in improving social safety and therefore improve the support for socially difficult measures. Previously, the ambitions of the City Council were high. The achieved results therefore contrasted badly with the expectations that had been raised amongst the residents. The last direction for improving safety lies in the combination approach of both repressive and preventive measures. Previously, the emphasis was on repression, but now there is more awareness of the complexity of the safety problem. Repression can only counter the symptoms of unsafety, not the causes: prevention and care are now considered important aspects as well. All four solutions need an integral approach in which involved departments cooperate. The leading role in this respect would be for the City Council (Gemeente Heerlen, 2002).

For the city centre, the main problem to address is drugs-related crime and nuisance. It is considered important in this respect that the police operate a more repressive regime. At the same time, there must be a social care system to avoid drug addicts or young criminals falling back in their bad habits. The drug policy of the City of Heerlen is based on both the reduction of nuisance from drug addicts and on the improvement of social care for drug addicts to help them tackle their personal problems. Regarding repressive measures, the police focus on the trade in hard drugs (cocaine, heroin, etc.) and nuisance from drug addicts. Social care is provided in the form of several services like day- and night-care facilities and special programmes to help addicts to come off drugs and to assist resocialization, etc. (Gemeente Heerlen, 2004a). In the case of severe (hard) drug addicts in particular, this problem is complex and difficult to resolve. The police and the institutions for social care have started to cooperate more closely in the *Operatie Hartslag* project (Gemeente Heerlen, 2001). This cooperation has proved to be effective. However, many existing regulations (such as privacy regulations) hinder efficient and effective cooperation. Regarding persistent offenders (which most severe drug addicts are), better legislation would help to facilitate both police repression and social care. However, stronger legislation also raises ethical questions and necessitates social and political discussions.

The next paragraph describes the project *Operatie Hartslag* (Operation Heartbeat) as best practice of the City of Heerlen. In contrast to other case studies of SecurCity, this will be the only best practice described, although not because Heerlen has no other best practices – the project of two Moroccan police officers giving special attention to problem children and their parents in Moroccan society in Heerlen, for example, appears to be very successful. The newly-implemented project of district teams is also promising. The district teams promote stronger cooperation between the district contact persons, the police, the City and the residents on the district level in 13-week projects. During these 13 weeks, special objectives are formulated and extra attention is given to these districts.

Operatie Harstlag is a large project with many different aspects. In particular, the inter-relation of these aspects and the cooperation between all involved actors is essential for the success of the project.

Best practice: Operatie Hartslag (Operation Heartbeat)

As already noted, the city centre of Heerlen has been strongly dominated by a group of drug addicts and the related persons and activities around them: dealers, runners, drug tourists, crime, quarrels, nuisance, etc. The area around the central train station in particular demonstrated a concentration of this 'hard drug scene'. However, it was not only the city centre that was affected: drug related nuisance was also reported from residents in other parts of the city. In 1993, an increase of drug nuisance was noticed and in response to that a care and advice centre (OAC, *Opvang- en Adviescentrum*) was established. The OAC was an easily-accessible service centre which received much interest from the target group: obviously the OAC served a clear need. But the expected result – a decrease of drug nuisance – did not materialize. More repressive measures were used to bring down incidences of drug nuisance (Gemeente Heerlen, 2001). At first this seemed to help, but after a few years, drug nuisance increased again. In summer 2000 there was an overload of drug addicts and other people from the hard drug scene in the city centre. The normal capacity of police and social care was insufficient to solve the problem and the need for a more structural approach became much more apparent. There was obviously a clear need for cooperation to address the drug problems and all involved partners were aware of this need and were willing to cooperate. In addition, several developments offered better opportunities to tackle nuisance and drug-related crime. For example, a new reception centre, legislative care for addicts, a growing awareness of residents that the police could not solve this problem on their own and the will of involved actors to address the problems integrally and reduce nuisance and crime (Gemeente Heerlen, 2001).

These were the incentives to start the project *Operatie Hartslag*. Initially, the project was due to start in June 2001 and finish just over three years later in September 2004. Because of a slight delay in the official start the project lasted until May 2005. The aim of the project was 'the ability to control drug nuisance on the streets of Heerlen'. Although some citizens appeared to have interpreted this as 'eliminating all drugs nuisance from the streets of Heerlen', the objective has always been to create a city centre with the same level of actual and perceived crime and drug nuisance as comparable Dutch cities (Gemeeente Heerlen, 2001). While the integral approach to the drug problem and cooperation of all involved actors was new, it was also a prerequisite for dealing with the complexity of the problems. The actors involved in the project were the local authority (the Mayor, the responsible counsellor and the OOV), the police, public prosecution, social care institutions (Mondriaan Zorggroep, Stuurgroep Vangnet, GGD OZL, etc.). The project was organized in several administrative layers. First, there was the *Regiegroep Integrale Veiligheid* (RIV, Integral Safety Direction Group), which placed all existing (safety) projects, memorandums and policies into a wider context in order to integrate the work of all different actors and set out the main direction of the project. In addition, in the start-up period there was a *Bestuurlijke Begeleidingsgroep* (Administrative Supervision Group) to help the different actors involved to cooperate. The second layer consisted of the Project group – the people who actually executed all measures and plans. This group was assisted by the Working Group, who collected information and worked out the plans. Communication between all layers, but also communication to the population, was a crucial part of the project for a clear understanding of the aims and objectives of the project and of the way in which the method and measures used could increase public support.

The main measures taken were: further development of a regionally-differentiated and coherent supply of 24-hour care facilities; better use of criminal and administrative law and intensification of repression of dealers, runners, drug tourists and addicts; intensifying cooperation between several local institutions; investing in the quality of the physical environment (Gemeente Heerlen, 2001). One practical example is the more diversified social care facilities set up by the social care institutions with the help of the local authorities. Adjacent to the day-care facilities, a night-care facility for homeless and addicted people was created. Although there have been problems in the decision on the location of the facility, it has contributed to decreasing the nuisance from drug addicts by taking them off the streets. To avoid attracting drug addicts from all over The Netherlands and abroad, only drug users related to the city of Heerlen could use these care facilities. With the care provision at a certain standard, repressive measures could be increased. For tackling drug problems, it was essential to make sure that care and repression harmonize with each other in order to have the maximum effect. It would be useless to increase repression without giving the addicts social care. At the same time, drug addicts often need an incentive to ask for care. Repression can be a good incentive. To give an example, the police have become stricter on the law that forbids dealing or using (hard) drugs in public. However, the need for addicted people to obtain and use their drugs remains. The day-care centres offer a place to use, keeping the drug addicts of the streets and decreasing the drug nuisance in the streets. To help the police keep order in the streets, CCTV was introduced. About 130 cameras were placed throughout the city centre. These cameras are not monitored 24 hours a day, but approximately 90 hours per week (mainly during the nights and weekends). The remaining time the videos were taped. CCTV is used as a preventive tool and as a source of evidence in case of troubles. Positive effects have been the downturn of both shoplifting and the number of drug users and dealers in the area covered by the cameras.

Of course, there has also been criticism, especially related to the anti-drug approach. One of the main criticisms concerns the hypocrisy of national policy for legalizing the sale of soft drugs but not their production. Another concerns the hypocrisy of banning hard drugs by law and at the same time providing facilities for drug use. Keeping drug addicts of the streets most of the day may reduce direct drug nuisance, but it will not prevent the addicts from housebreaking and theft in order to fund their drug needs. Providing methadone is part of a solution, but this is only a substitute for heroin use and many addicts use cocaine or both. Another criticism is related to the location of the day- and night-care facilities, as many residents protest against the possibility of having one of these facilities in their neighbourhood. Some actors believe it to be important to locate both facilities in the vicinity of the city centre (as drug addicts would not use the facility if it is too far away), but not to locate the facilities at the same location (as it will keep them 'busy' with organizing their daily care). From interviews we learned that day- and night-care facilities appear to be important for decreasing the overall level of nuisance in the city and making it controllable for social workers and the police. This location dilemma might be reduced with help of good communication with the local residents and good support from police and social workers. However, this is a very contentious issue for the City of Heerlen and has caused several aldermen to resign.

After three years of executing the project, it can be concluded that some positive results were measured. The cooperation between all involved partners proved to be an essential added value. Under the lead of the mayor at that time, the enthusiasm and belief that it could work out well grew among all partners involved. The cooperation between social care and police especially improved, thanks to the direct contact between the involved persons. The key point in tackling drug problems is the right mix of repression and care. The result of all efforts has been a noticeable decrease in nuisance caused by the 'hard drug scene' in the city centre. People visiting the city centre and central train station indicate that they have noticed these improvements. The approach of *Operatie Hartslag* is new in The Netherlands and because of its integral approach was named the best urban project of 2004 among the 26 largest cities in The Netherlands (Gemeente Heerlen, 2004).

8.6 Synthesis

This section recapitulates the most important conclusions for the city of Heerlen. Subsection 8.6.1 focuses on the perception of safety; subsections 8.6.2 and 8.6.3 deal respectively with the spatial behaviour of inhabitants as consequence of changing urban attractiveness and with the policies adopted by the city, with an illustration of the best practices. We briefly describe the organizing capacity with respect to *Operatie Hartslag* in subsection 8.6.4. Finally, we conclude with formulating some recommendations in subsection 8.6.5.

8.6.1 Safety Perceptions

Compared with other Dutch cities, the crime rates in Heerlen are more or less on the same level. The main problem was drug nuisance and related crime. This problem can be related to the geographical location of Heerlen near the borders with both Germany and Belgium. Heerlen has a large 'hard drug scene' and attracts relatively many drug tourists; the drug-related problems appear to be greater than in other cities along the Dutch border. Relatively high rates of theft, robberies, threat/intimidation (so-called high-impact criminality) and large problems with drug nuisance had a negative effect on safety perceptions of the local population. Heerlen was associated with drug nuisance not only in the city itself but nationwide as well. The perceptions of safety were therefore very low; half of the local population said they (sometimes) felt unsafe in Heerlen. This share is up twice as high as other Dutch cities, creating a relatively large gap between actual and perceived security in Heerlen.

In the past few years improvements have been made in the city centre. Drug nuisance decreased visibly, but the safety perceptions have not (yet) improved accordingly. It is difficult to explain this large gap between actual and perceived safety. One possible explanation may be that the residents expected the drug problems to be completely solved by the City Council. Although considerable improvements have been made, the problem is not completely solved: there will always be some addicted and homeless people. This problem appears to be inherent to cities.

8.6.2 Urban Attractiveness and Spatial Behaviour

For more than half a century Heerlen was a mining area. The first mines were opened early in the twentieth century. The city grew and flourished, but this all came to an end with the closing of the last mine in the 1970s. Because of the high economic dependency on the mining industry, the impact was tremendous. Economically, the city lost its foundations and unemployment rates were high. But also from an urban perspective too, the city faced many changes. First, with the growth of the mining industry, the city grew too large to become a unity. After the closure of the mines, most elements that harked back to the mining era were erased. Industrial buildings no longer functioned and were replaced by modern architecture. This resulted in a city without a visible history and identity and a built environment without spatial unity. Residents tend to identify themselves with the district they lived in rather than with the whole city of Heerlen.

The attractiveness of the city was long undermined by the nuisance caused not only by drug addicts, but also by drug tourists, runners, dealers, etc. The deteriorating attractiveness also influenced spatial behaviour: residents started to avoid certain places. Although improvements have been made in the actual safety situation, safety perceptions are relatively low and this is shown by the fact that during the night 80 per cent of the residents in the city centre said they avoided certain places because they perceived them as being unsafe (Bureau Onderzoek and Statistiek, 2004a). Residents adapted their spatial behaviour: in the whole city of Heerlen 43 per cent of residents said they avoided certain places because of perceived insecurity (Bureau Onderzoek and Statistiek, 2004a).

8.6.3 Policy Reactions

The large gap between actual and perceived safety and the drug nuisance and related crime put safety high on the City of Heerlen's priority list. The main aim of the City Council Plan 2002–2006 is to 'create an optimal living environment in districts and neighbourhoods in which all residents are able to function independently and feel safe, involved and responsible' (Gemeente Heerlen, 2002, p. 9). The directions that should help achieve this aim are:

- increasing maintenance and improving policies aimed at increasing safety perceptions;
- increasing social cohesion and consciousness of social responsibility;
- improving the City Council's communication strategy regarding safety and living conditions, and;
- changing the emphasis on repression in safety policies to a combination of repression and prevention (Gemeente Heerlen, 2002).

As already noted, in the city centre in particular, where many of the problems regarding safety were concentrated, improvements have been made. The 'hard drug scene' is causing fewer nuisances.

8.6.4 Best Practice

The project *Operatie Hartslag* is believed to have had a positive effect on the safety and the attractiveness of the city centre. This project was initiated in the summer of 2000 as a direct reaction to the unacceptable level of crime and drug nuisance. Under lead of the mayor at the time, several involved actors were called together to formulate an integral approach for tackling the complex problems of drug nuisance and related crime. Police, city, public prosecution and social care institutions started to cooperate more closely. Those directly involved got to know each other and their functions better and short communication lines were established. The aim of this project was to 'be able to control drug nuisance from the streets of Heerlen' (Gemeente Heerlen, 2001). The first objective was to increase and improve the social care provisions for drug users: day- and night-care, provision of methadone, etc. As soon as the social care reached a certain level, the police became less tolerant and repressive measures were intensified. Not only repression and care were provided but extra investments were (or are being) made in the public places in the city centre – maintenance, cleanliness, improving the squares, etc. A direct result is fewer nuisances from the hard drug scene in the city centre; drug users are seen less on the streets and more in the day- and night-care facilities. To achieve this result, cooperation between the involved partners appeared to be essential: instead of just working alongside each other (and sometimes interfering with each other), police, social workers, public prosecution and City Council now try to combine their knowledge and powers.

Of course, there are critical voices as well. One of the elements of *Operatie Hartslag* is the provision of day- and night-care facilities for drug addicts. These are safe places where all facilities to use drugs are available, except for the drug itself, because hard drug are illegal. Although these day- and night-care facilities keep the drug addicts off the streets (at least for part of the day) and therefore reduce the nuisance, critics find it hypocritical to support hard drug use (which is illegal) by providing all necessary means except the drug itself.

8.6.5 Organizing Capacity with Respect to the Operatie Hartslag Programme

The safety policy, and especially the 'anti-drug' approach of the City of Heerlen, was initiated under the strong *leadership* of the mayor of Heerlen at that time, Mr Sakkers. His *vision* was to improve the safety and attractiveness of the city centre by decreasing the nuisance caused by drug trade and use. Because of the urgency of this problem, *political support* was guaranteed. Under the leadership of the mayor a *strategic network* was created in which all relevant actors took part. Not only the City Council, police and public prosecution, but also care providers and representatives of the citizens were brought together in order to tackle drug-related problems. The result was *Operatie Hartslag*. The *societal support* for this programme is high, although there are some problems in this respect as well: for some reasons citizens' expectations of the outcomes were so high that they could never have been met. A clear communication towards the citizens might have helped in this respect.

8.6.6 Recommendations

The City of Heerlen has high ambitions in tackling the drug-related problem in the city centre. At first the aim was to reduce as much as possible drug nuisance from the streets in order to increase the (perceptions of) safety. The results of the measures taken in the past few years seem to be good. However, despite the reductions of drug nuisance, residents' perceptions of safety in the city (centre) have not improved accordingly (yet). Although the City of Heerlen's ambition was to decrease the drug-related problems in the city centre significantly, the citizens seemed to expect a complete elimination of the problems. The expectations of citizens turned out to be so high that the (remarkable) end results to date compare unfavourably to them. This case shows that a city must be aware of the expectations raised by its formulated policy. A sound communication strategy could influence this positively.

Another aspect influencing safety perceptions is the socioeconomic situation. In a situation where people feel they have less self-control over their lives due to, for example, long-term unemployment and low incomes, safety perceptions are often low. This not only appears to be the case in Heerlen – the case of Gera, for example, is similar. Clark and Oswald (1994) have stated that in Britain the unemployed have significantly lower levels of mental well-being than employed people. Improving employment and the socioeconomic situation in general is expected to increase perspectives and therefore to increase perceptions of safety among the population.

As (long-term) unemployment is Heerlen is relatively high and the socioeconomic situation is worse than the general situation in The Netherlands, paying extra attention to economic development is to be recommended. New policy documents already show a change towards regional economic stimulation, which can be regarded as a positive development.

As *Operatie Hartslag* proved to have made a significant contribution to the improvement of the quality of the city centre and diminishing the drug nuisance and related problems, it is important to tie in the integral cooperation more strongly with the daily activities of the involved partners. In addition, it would be advisable to extend the reach of the programme to other districts within the city of Heerlen. The quality of the urban environment has improved in the city centre, but other districts also need extra attention to address safety-related problems. This becomes even more important taking into account the fact that citizens of Heerlen often identify themselves with the ward they live in.

A last recommendation regarding the (perceived) safety situation in the city centre of Heerlen concerns urban functions in this area. As Jane Jacobs (1961) stated, a balanced mix of urban functions (living, working, and leisure) improve the quality of the living environment. The number of residents living in the city centre is relatively small, meaning that as soon as the shops close, the streets look deserted, which influences safety perceptions negatively. A more diverse mix of functions in the city centre is expected to attract more people which would increase the vibrancy of the area. That might contribute substantially to the safety perceptions of the city.

Chapter 9

The Case of Leeds

9.1 Introduction

In this case study we focus on the social security in the city of Leeds, United Kingdom. Section 9.2 gives a concise profile of this urban region. In Section 9.3, we deal with possible causes of insecurity feelings within the city of Leeds. Next, in Section 9.4, we will go into the related spatial behaviour of local inhabitants. Section 9.5 goes into policy reactions regarding urban unsafety. In this section we will give specific attention to some *best practices*. Our focus for Leeds is on problems related to drugs and insecurity. Finally, Section 9.6 presents conclusions and some recommendations.

9.2 Profile of Leeds

9.2.1 Situation and Demography

The urban system of the United Kingdom is characterized by one absolute centre: London. Besides London there are also several 'second cities'. Together with cities such as Birmingham and Manchester, Leeds is one of them. Being the capital of Yorkshire and the Humberside Region, Leeds has an important regional function. It is situated in the middle of Britain, between London and Edinburgh. The city of Leeds counts approximately 715,000 inhabitants (Leeds Initiative, 2003). Leeds consists of 33 diverse communities or wards and covers 217 square miles (349km^2). Leeds is surrounded by extensive suburban and rural areas containing freestanding towns such as Garforth, Wetherby, Rothwell, Morley and Otley as well as numerous small villages (Leeds Initiative, 2004). The city centre lies in the ward of City and Holbeck. The city centre is not the same as the inner city, which covers a wider region. The city centre has a low population density, but a very high density of jobs.

Over the period 1991–2001 Leeds had a population growth of 1.2 per cent in total. This corresponds with the average population growth of the whole of Yorkshire and the Humber (Leeds Initiative, 2003). A relatively large student population characterizes the demography of Leeds. About 10 per cent of the total population are students (Leeds Initiative, 2003). The 'non-white population' in Leeds is around 8 per cent of the total population. The total black and ethnic minority population (including 'non-white population') is 10 per cent of the total population. This percentage increased in the last decade but is still relatively low. Pakistanis form the largest ethnicity group (Leeds Initiative, 2003). Overall the black and ethnic minority group in Leeds is

Figure 9.1 Geographical position of Leeds in Europe

quite small, but there are large differences between the wards in Leeds. In Harehills for example the percentage of 'non-white population' is 40.4 per cent and in Chapel Allerton, 33 per cent (Leeds City Council, 2003).

In the last few decades of the twentieth century the United Kingdom was characterized by a 'flow southwards'. Many people moved from the northern cities in Britain southwards to (the region of) London. Leeds is one of the few cities that did not show an outflow of inhabitants (Lewis, undated). There is even a small inflow: in 2001 the surplus of people moving to Leeds was 8,000 people, around 1 per cent of the total population (Leeds Initiative, 2003).

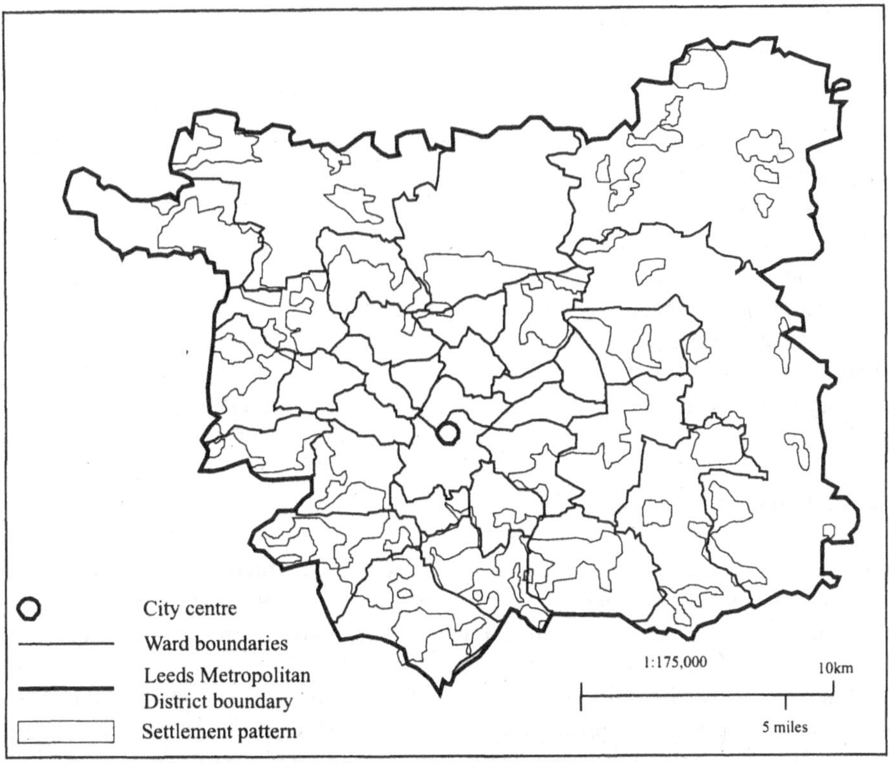

Figure 9.2 Map of the wards in Leeds, 2004

Source: Leeds City Council.

9.2.2 Administration

The Leeds Metropolitan Region has several different administrative divisions. First there is Leeds City Council, which divides Leeds into 33 wards. Then there is the Primary Care Trust (PCT) divisions, for health services, which divides Leeds into five regions. In addition, there is also the police divisions, which consist of four regions (Weetwood/Pudsey, Chapeltown, Killingbeck, and City and Holbeck). This used to be six regions, but in 2003 there was a regional restructuring.

The main body for daily governance is the Leeds City Council. Next to this institution there is also the Leeds Initiative, a partnership founded in 1990 and led by the City Council. Its aim is to provide a strategic approach for the city's long-term development (Leeds Initiative, 2004). The Leeds Initiative therefore formulated a Vision, which has six main themes: 1) competing in a global economy; 2) making the most of people; 3) integrated transport; 4) looking after the environment; 5) creating better neighbourhoods and confident communities; and 6) a planned approach to technology. A Strategy Group has been created for each of these themes to work

Table 9.1 Demographic data of Leeds

Characteristics	Year	Leeds
Population number	2001	715,402
Population growth	1991–2001	1.20%
Ethnicity white as % of total population	2001	91.80%
Ethnicity non-white as % of total population	2001	8.20%
Black and minority as % of total population	2001	10.80%
Inmigration as % of total population	2001	1.12%
Surface in square miles	2004	217
Wards	2004	33
Primary Care Trusts	2004	5
Police Divisions	2004	4

Source: Leeds Initiative, 2003.

out that part of the vision. Next to the Strategy Groups there are also Partnership Groups, working out segments of the themes (see Figure 9.3). The segmentation is not exclusive, with several groups having influence and interest in more than one strategy area (Leeds Initiative, 2004).

One of the Partnership Groups is Leeds Community Safety. Together with Community Leeds and Regenerating Leeds they are working on the fifth theme: making better neighbourhoods and confident communities. Every three years Leeds Community Safety produces a strategy for tackling crime in the city (Leeds Initiative, 2004). The key priorities for the 2002–2005 period are domestic burglary, antisocial behaviour by young people, drugs and violent crime (Leeds City Council, 2003).

9.2.3 Economy and Employment

At the time of writing, the economy in Leeds is flourishing. Leeds was one of the economic centres in the Industrial Revolution. Thanks to a diversified economic basis, the city was less affected by the industrial reorganization and restructuring which began in the 1950s. The production and processing of textiles and clothing characterized the local economy, but commerce and other activities were important as well. In the decades after the industrial decline, employment in industry decreased dramatically, being replaced by increased employment in the financial sector. Since the 1980s this sector has grown, and the city now ranks third in national financial and business services. Although the service sector (business and public) accounts for more than half the workforce, many people are also employed in distribution, manufacturing, construction and transport and communications (Leeds City Council, 2003c). Almost 38 per cent of all employees work in managerial or professional occupations. This percentage is higher than in the rest of the Yorkshire and Humber region, but lower than in England/Wales (Leeds Initiative, 2003).

THE LEEDS INITIATIVE:	**Leeds Initiative Board** Non-executive	**Leeds Initiative Executive** Executive management and planning	**Leeds Initiative Office** Management coordination and facilitation
STRATEGY GROUPS:	**Leeds Economy** Vision theme: competing in a global economy **Transport Leeds** Vision theme: integrated transport	**Environment Leeds** Vision theme: looking after the environment **Leeds Connected** Vision theme: a planned apporach to technology	**Learning Leeds** Vision theme: making the most of people **Renegeration Leeds** Vision theme: better neighbourhoods and confident communities
PARTNERSHIP GROUPS:	**Leeds Financial Services** **City Centre Leeds** **Leeds Arts**	**Leeds Manufacturing** **International Leeds** **Leeds Community Safety** **Regenerating Leeds**	**Leeds Media** **Leeds Architecture and Design** **Community Leeds**

Figure 9.3 Leeds Initiative organization chart

Source: Leeds Initiative, undated (b).

In total there were about 429,000 persons working in Leeds in 2001, with about 383,000 employed persons and 46,000 self-employed persons. By 2005 this number had grown by 10 per cent (Leeds City Council, 2003c). The total population aged between 16 and 74 was 520,000 in 2001 (Leeds Initiative, 2003). Around 31 per cent of the jobs in Leeds are located in the city centre (Leeds City Council, 2003c). Leeds is also increasingly attracting labour from outside the area as many people are travelling greater distances to work. In the period 1981 to 1991 commuter flows to Leeds increased from 52,000 to 74,000, while the commuter flows out of Leeds only increased from 35,000 to 38,000 (Leeds City Council, 2003c).

In the last few years Leeds has had a persistent period of employment growth and low unemployment (Leeds City Council, 2003c). The unemployment rate of people aged between 16 and 74 in 2002 was 5.3 per cent, which is quite low. Long-term unemployment was only 1 per cent (Leeds Initiative, 2003). However, there are differences between the different wards within Leeds. In the city there are seven wards that belong to the worst 10 per cent nationally according to the Oxford Deprivation Index 2000. In these wards the unemployment rate is 12 per cent, significantly higher than the average for Leeds. Also, unemployment is significantly higher among the black and ethnic minority group, at about 10 per cent in 2003 (Leeds City Council, 2003c).

Table 9.2 Economic data Leeds

Characteristics	Year	Leeds
Population in age band 16–74	2001	520,000
Employment		
Total number	2001	429,000
Employed	2001	383,000
Self-employed	2001	46,000
Employment per economic sector		
Manufacturing	2003	21%
Construction	2003	6%
Distribution	2003	22%
Transport and communications	2003	6%
Services	2003	53%
Other	2003	1%
Unemployment		
Unemployment rate	2002	5.3%
Long-term unemployment	2001	1%
Unemployment in 7 worst wards	2001	12%
Unemployment among black and ethnic minority group	2001	10%

Sources: Leeds Initiative, 2003; Leeds City Council, 2003c.

9.3 The Perception of Security in Leeds

9.3.1 Safety Development

In the last five years Britain has shown a remarkable fall in crime. Between 1997 and the period 2002/2003, the British Crime Survey measured a fall in crime of 25 per cent. Crime recorded by the police also decreased with 3 per cent in the period 2002/2003 (Home Office Statistical Bulletin, 2003). But the police do not record all crimes, meaning that the actual crime rates might be higher than the official rates and that the fall in crime might be different as well.

In the city of Leeds, 97,000 crimes were recorded in 2003 – approximately 136 crimes per 1,000 of the population. Several types of crime appear to be decreasing. For example, the number of robberies, burglaries, theft of and from cars all decreased. However, the number of reports of, for example, violent crimes has increased over the past few years (Leeds Community Safety, undated). Drugs crime is relatively low and in the period 1998–2001 it fell by 34 per cent (Leeds City Council, 2003b).

9.3.2 Safety Perception

According to the British Crime Survey the risk of becoming a victim of crime in Leeds was at an historic minimum of 27 per cent in the period 2002/2003. This is one-third of the risk measured in 1995 (Home Office Statistical Bulletin, 2003). Nevertheless, in the same period almost three-quarters of the public still believed that the national crime rate was rising (Home Office Statistical Bulletin, 2003). In 13 wards of Leeds there was a decrease in crime rates but the majority of the people did not think this was the case. In some wards the residents even believed that the crime rate had increased rather than decreased (Leeds Community Safety, 2002). Residents' perception of safety of does not seem to correspond with reality. However, most people do feel safe in Leeds, especially during the daytime. A public survey revealed that 96 per cent of the residents felt 'fairly safe' or 'very safe' during the day whilst outside in the local authority area. After dark the percentage of residents feeling 'fairly safe' or 'very safe' is much lower: 51 per cent (Leeds Community Safety, undated).

According to Community Involvement Team Survey among residents, the priorities for a safer community should be burglary, youth crime and a safer environment. Drugs are in fourth position in this survey (Leeds City Council, 2003b). The priorities set by the Leeds Community Safety Partnership for the period 2002–2005 do take into account the opinion of the residents. The priorities are burglary, drugs, violent crime, and young people and antisocial behaviour (Leeds Community Safety, undated).

9.3.3 Drugs and Crime

Drug use is a dominant factor in, and very often even a cause of, crime. Not only is the use of drugs itself a problem, but more important are drug-related crimes. The police usually test all those arrested for property crime. Of everyone tested, approximately 50 per cent test positive: however, the percentage of people who admit to using drugs is significantly higher. This is mainly due to the high threshold of the drug-testing equipment. Therefore drug use is one of the highest priorities for the Leeds Community Safety Partnership in the contemporary period.

According to the Drug Action Team (DAT) the problems in Leeds are begging, drug use, prostitution and crime. In 2003 almost 29,000 adult arrests were made in Leeds: officially there are around 5,000 in Leeds with drug-related problems (although some believe this number could be higher) and around 746 drug users referred themselves to agencies (Leeds Community Safety, 2002). The average drug user is male, aged 20–24. This is quite young, especially compared with the national picture where the majority of the drug users are 30 or older (see Table 9.3). In a DrugsScope report it was suggested that in the period 2001/02 there could be 3,694 long-standing/regular users of opiates, cocaine and/or amphetamines among the population aged 15–64 (Leeds City Council, 2003b). By another measure the same report suggested the figure could be 2,778 'problematic drugs users'.

Table 9.3 Crime and safety perception data

Characteristics	Year	Leeds
Actual crime		
All recorded crime	2002/3	97,000
All recorded crime, per 1000 of the population	2002/3	136
Crime decrease	2001	1.8%
Risk of becoming a victim	2002/3	27%
Increase number of crimes per type		
Robbery	2002/3–2003/4	–32%
Burglary	2002/3–2003/4	–23%
Theft of vehicle	2002/3–2003/4	–22%
Theft from vehicle	2002/3–2003/4	–22%
Violent crime	2002/3–2003/4	12%
Drugs-related crime		
Number of people arrested for drug misuse	2003	29,000
Arrested people tested positive for drugs	2003	53%
Average age of drug abusers	2003	20–24
Safety perceptions		
Perception: increasing local crime rates	2004	43%
Perception: feeling fairly/very safe during daytime	2004	96%
Perception: feeling fairly/very safe during nighttime	2004	51%

Sources: Home Office Statistical Bulletin, 2003; Leeds Community Safety, 2002 and undated.

9.4 Urban Attractiveness and Spatial Behaviour

9.4.1 Leeds: A City with a Double Identity

With over 1,000 shops in the city centre distributed over a variety of shopping streets such as malls and historic shopping arcades – many of which are pedestrianized – the city of Leeds represents the regional shopping centre for the whole of Yorkshire and the Humberside Region and one of the top four retail centres in the country. During the shops' opening hours – approximately from 9.00 a.m. to 5.30 p.m. – the city centre is used by all categories of inhabitant (young, elders and families) and visitors. The fact that many jobs are concentrated there contributes to keeping the central area very busy during working hours. During this part of the day people feel quite safe since the streets are crowded. Moreover, beggars and rough sleepers (two of the categories that affect the perception of safety most negatively) are less visible or, in the case of beggars, exhibit non-aggressive behaviour.

After 5.30 p.m. the atmosphere of the city changes. Most of the visitors, shoppers and workers leave the city centre as shops and offices close. This natural process of emptying, which takes place in many other European cities, combined with the fact that few people live in the central area – mostly students or young urban professionals (YUPs) – creates empty streets and squares that make people feel unsafe (see section 9.3). Moreover, begging becomes more noticeable in the evening and more bogus *Big Issue* vendors (http://www.bigissue.com)[1] are seen: this contributes to the deterioration in people's perception of safety. In addition, Leeds Community Safety has stated that the city centre suffers from a widespread perception of poor safety in the evenings (Chesterton, 2003). In order to overcome this process of depopulation, the Council, together with local retailers, has launched the initiative 'Leeds Alive After Five'. This campaign has gain momentum and after six months there were over 70 shops staying open until 7 p.m. or 8 p.m. on Thursday, Friday and/or Saturday nights.

The streets become busy again in some parts of the city centre after 8.00 p.m. when mostly young people go out for a drink or to a club. Even if these people do not apparently feel unsafe they are often, especially students (http://www.crime-reduction.gov.uk),victims of urban crime.

This vibrant nightlife in Leeds has positive effects both for the economy and the image of the city: it attracts many young people from the whole of Yorkshire and the Humberside Region and it is one of the main reasons why many students in the UK choose to study at Leeds' universities. Leeds has the second largest UK student population outside London (after Birmingham); in 2001 Leeds had more than 55,000 students – a 125 per cent increase compare to 1991 (http://www.healheadingley.org.uk). Most of the students live in the ward of Headingley where a process of 'studentification' has taken place in recent years, with considerable repercussions on the local property market (*The Economist*, 2004). Nevertheless, the vibrant nightlife of the city also brings some problems in terms of perception of urban safety. Since all pubs and clubs close at the same time (respectively at 11.00 p.m. and 2.00 a.m.), many large groups of (often drunken) people congregate in several parts of the city looking for a transport mode to go home. Unfortunately there is no public transport running at that time and there are insufficient taxis to satisfy this demand for transport.[2] Very often people become aggressive and occasionally fight to get into one of the few taxis available. This leads to large groups loitering or walking around, which represents antisocial behaviour that intimidates some other people.

The double identity of the central area of Leeds reflects the spatial behaviour of the different urban actors. While most of the retail and business sectors are attracted by the city centre, only few people live there: in October 2002 the estimated population of the city centre was 5,200 (City Centre Leeds, 2003). Even if recently there has been a dramatic growth in the number of city centre residents and the expectations are that its population will double by 2010,[3] this part of the city remains populated mainly by students and young urban professionals. Indeed, the city centre still lacks some basic facilities for residents such as the corner shops for groceries, doctors and most of the facilities for children. Most families and the elderly prefer to live in the suburbs where housing prices are more affordable, there are more facilities and space for children and where even after 5.30 p.m. people do not feel unsafe.

9.5 Policy Reactions

Since the beginning of the 1990s antisocial behaviour and crime have had a high priority in the Labour government's political agenda. This political focus on security has a double origin. On the one hand, safety has been recognized as one of the main factors affecting quality of life in urban areas: a safe physical and social environment can have a positive effect on the economic performance of cities, attracting residents, visitors and investors. On the other hand, there is a pure financial/economic reason to focus on safety: it has been proved that investing in prevention is cheaper than spending on repression. More precisely, for each £1 invested in treatment, up to £3 can be saved in criminal justice costs (Home Office Drugs Strategy Directorate, 2003).

The Home Office is the government department responsible for national safety policy. The government's emphasis on the safety issue has created a record number of police officers on the streets of UK communities (Home Office, 2004). In the UK crime is tackled at local level by Crime and Disorder Reduction Partnerships (CDRPs): these are 'a combination of police, local authorities and other organizations and businesses who have banded together to develop and implement strategies for tackling crime and disorder on the local level' (http://www.homeoffice.gov.uk). Each CDRP produces a strategy for its local area.

Thus, in recent years, the more rigorous action against street crime in UK cities has become a direct order from the national government, which sets the targets that local authorities must fulfil. This national attention on safety-related problems in urban areas has brought two main consequences for cities. The first (positive) consequence is that local authorities have more (financial) resources to invest in safety. The second (less positive) effect is that this focus on safety is quite centrally oriented; this means that central government sets the main targets and guidelines of action and the local authority has little room to adapt this policy to its local circumstances. This second consequence can be considered less positive for a number of reasons. First of all, the specific local problems are not taken into consideration by the national government. Moreover, the lack of independence of the local authorities can generate a sense of frustration in them (especially in the police) since they cannot always tackle crime in the way they would like and that they believe would be more appropriate for the local circumstances. Finally, politics (even if not only on the national level) is usually led by short-term results that can get the media and public attention and this can induce some deficiencies affecting the long-run strategy of the local authority. In Leeds it has already been noticed that the strong focus on safety has led to fewer resources available for investment in other sectors, such as health and education, which can also play an important role in the fight against crime.

Nevertheless, the increased attention of the UK central government on the safety issue has led the city of Leeds to adopt safety as its top priority, something that probably would not have happened without the pressure coming from London.

9.5.1 The Partnership

Leeds began to embrace the concept of partnership at the beginning of the 1990s through informal meetings among several local institutions. Since then the 'partnership culture' has improved dramatically: the result of this is the Leeds Initiative (see also Section 9.2). Founded in 1990 and led by the Leeds City Council, the Initiative has become a very effective body that provides a strategic approach to the city's long-term development. The Leeds Initiative has grown from the eight founder partners and nowadays represents 20 large organizations or sectors in the city among which are the two local universities, the retail and business sector, the West Yorkshire Police and the five Leeds Primary Care Trusts (Health).

One of the Leeds Initiative Partnership Groups is Leeds Community Safety, which represents the local Crime and Disorder Reduction Partnership. Formed under the provision of the Crime and Disorder Act 1998, it has the overall aim to secure sustainable reductions in crime and disorder and address fear of crime in the city of Leeds (Leeds Initiative, undated). The key priorities of the Leeds Community Safety for the period 2002–2005 are domestic burglary, antisocial behaviour by young people, drugs, and violent crime (Leeds City Council, 2003). Leeds Community Safety has a clear commitment to ensuring that the city centre is a safe environment for residents, visitors and businesses.

9.5.2 West Yorkshire Police Authority

One of the prime roles of the regional Police Authority is to tackle crime. According to the 2003–2004 Policy Plan the priority in tackling crime is to investigate, detect and prevent priority crime (West Yorkshire Police Authority, 2003). The targets are to reduce robbery, house burglary, thefts of and from vehicles and to increase the overall number of offenders brought to justice. The two main objectives of the plan are to combat drugs misuse and to tackle crime against vulnerable victims.

The national focus on safety has had a huge influence on the functioning of the police in Leeds. Firstly, the police are now stricter than before against antisocial behaviour:[4] while, for instance, begging is forbidden by previous legislation, the police have only recently stopped tolerating it. Moreover, the police have now embraced the partnership approach – quite a dramatic change for a civil service that was not used to working permanently in partnership with other institutions (apart from other police authorities). It seems that the police force in Leeds is doing very well in this new context of partnership and that they are enjoying this new way of tackling urban crime; they are now on the front line in promoting new collaborations with other local agencies. The work of the police also has a more proactive approach: their main focus is on the prevention of crime, especially by drug users. Unfortunately there is also a negative aspect to the central government's emphasis on safety. As well as the fact that the Police Authority has little influence on the selection of the targets (which are selected in London), they also have more 'paper-work' to do in order to fulfil the requirements set by the central government. These extra bureaucratic tasks could represent a problem in terms of resources to be dedicated to the usual police work.

Best practice 1: rough sleepers

A clear link has been noticed between rough sleepers and criminal activities such as robbery, shoplifting, violent crime and other street activities such as begging, street drinking and prostitution, with some people engaging in more than one of these activities. In addition, many rough sleepers are addicted to class A drugs (such as heroin, Ecstasy and cocaine). Since rough sleeping and the related criminal activities have a huge influence on people's perception of safety, the city of Leeds has worked hard in recent years to tackle this issue.

In December 2002 Leeds Community Safety chaired the National Rough Sleeping Summit, whose main finding was confirmation of the need for a strong multi-agency approach to fight this issue. This multi-agency approach should be focused on the reduction of all the abovementioned antisocial street activities in order to reduce or prevent rough sleeping.

The current approach is centred on the Rough Sleepers Support Team, a multi-agency team that works to improve access to health care, benefits and social support for people sleeping rough. There are also specific posts dealing with mental health and drugs related to those who are sleeping rough. A particular emphasis has been maintained on improving the level of the volume of people accessing treatment.

The strategic approach adopted by the multi-agency team to fight the problem is twofold. It aims firstly at assuring that those engaged in rough sleeping or other street-based activities have opportunities to access appropriate services to improve their living conditions. Moreover, it also aims to disrupt and challenge illegal and antisocial street behaviour. The overall target of the strategy is to reduce rough sleeping to as near to zero as possible. Recent head counts have shown encouraging but controversial results: from the 43 rough sleepers counted in October 2002 only four were found in March 2004. While these numbers show the success of the approach they might also suggest that some rough sleepers are moving out of the city centre or hiding themselves more successfully. In order to diminish the spread of rough sleepers over a larger area, the city extended the counting area beyond the city centre.

Best practice 2: Drug Action Team

The Drug Action Team (DAT) is a national programme funded in 1995 in order to tackle drugs problems and to build a better Britain. Under the assumption that most acquisition crime[5] is committed by drug-addicted people, the top 40 British acquisition crime areas (areas with high drugs-related crimes) became 25 DAT areas. DAT Leeds covers two of these top 40 areas: Holbeck and Headingly.

Until recently the DAT was not an particularly active institution. It was only when the national political focus shifted towards urban safety in the 1990s that this multi-agency team began to receive more attention. Since 2001 this has resulted in more financial resources being made available, thanks to the National Drug Strategy.

Originally the focus of the DAT was mainly on treatment of people (drug users) and less on criminal justice: however, in 2002 the DAT came under the supervision of the Home Office Department and the focus changed towards criminal justice. Since 2002, as a consequence of the increased financial resources involved, DAT has become more responsible and accountable in its functioning through a series of performance indicators that helped both politicians, by having visible results to be used for the public and media attention, and the people involved in the project, by having a precise target to be reached. It seems that this performance-oriented management has had positive results, especially in terms of efficiency.

DAT Leeds is a multi-agency partnership which includes more than ten different institutions. The financial resources available (more than £7.8m for the period 2003/04) are allocated to the partnership which, in turn, decides how to allocate them among the different agencies. This allows for a degree of flexibility in the budget allocations: for instance, what is saved in one sector can be invested into another one.

DAT Leeds is performing quite well at the time of writing. Plenty of resources have been invested in education, awareness and training through the HEAT programme (Health, Education, Awareness and Training) whose main aim is to produce an holistic approach towards drugs/crime issues. Foundations have been set to improve access to drug services for black and minority ethnic groups and facilities for safe disposal of needles have been increased. Nevertheless there is still plenty of room for improvement. In recent years the DAT has particularly improved in its 'visibility' both among the city's institutions and among people involved in it. Some of the existing bottlenecks concern:

- the range of treatments available: they would like to have a larger variety of treatments to stop people using drugs;
- the difficulty of finding skilled people (as therapists, doctors, etc.) willing to work with drug-addicted people;
- the difficulty of involving black and ethnic minorities in treatment because of both cultural problems and the lack of awareness of the services provided among these categories;
- the difficulty of encouraging women to be treated because most of the medical service providers are men;
- the concentration of all services provided by DAT in the city centre: this attracts most of the drug addicts living in the region to the city.

In order to overcome the last-mentioned bottleneck there are plans to redistribute the services to all five parts of the region. This initiative has a double aim: to avoid all drug users coming to the city centre and to make the service more accessible to everybody.

Best practice 3: Criminal Justice Intervention Programme (renamed Drug Intervention Programme)

One of the main aims of the British government's updated Drug Strategy 2002 is to break the links between drugs and crime by extending, enhancing and integrating a range of criminal justice interventions (Home Office Drugs Strategy Directorate, 2002). The Criminal Justice Intervention Programme (CJIP) is a nationwide project started as a pilot project in 25 British cities corresponding to the 25 DAT areas. In April 2004 the project was extended to 40 areas.

The CJIP is based on the concept of treatment. Treatment is not considered a soft option: under orders imposed by the courts, some drug users are directed towards treatment in addition to prison rather than instead of it. The National Treatment Outcomes Research Study, better known as the NTORS report, demonstrates that treatment is effective in reducing criminal offending. The CJIP, which represents a typical example of the 'carrot and stick' approach adopted by Leeds, aims at moving drug-abusing offenders into and through the drug treatment system, through criminal justice interventions. These interventions cover the whole criminal justice system, including police custody, courts and probation, prison, treatment, through care and aftercare. The programme 'ensures that expansion of individual interventions is accompanied by a definite move towards providing a beginning-to-end support system for dealing with drug-misusing offenders' (http://www.drugs.gov.uk/NationalStrategy/CriminalJusticeInterventionsProgramme, official website of the Home Office Drugs Strategy Directorate). Since CJIP attempts to get drug-addicted offenders into treatment and out of their bad habits, it can be considered as a good example of a proactive policy to stop drug-related crime at its source.

CJIP is also about partnership: many institutions and agencies work together, even if this cooperation does not always work smoothly (especially in the field of exchanging information). The CJIP in Leeds received over 900 referrals in 2004: around one third of all referrals from prison have accommodation problems, a number of people have been given assistance with accommodation and some have now moved into full-time work. One of the main bottlenecks of CJIP Leeds is the lack of capacity in respect to drug treatment; CJIP aims to increase capacity so that more drug-addicted offenders can access treatment.

9.6 Synthesis

The purpose of this section is to sum up the most important conclusions for the case of Leeds. After reviewing the perception of safety and the relative spatial behaviour of its inhabitants, a brief summary of the policy measures undertaken by the local authority will be made. Some recommendations will conclude the section.

9.6.1 Security Perception

In recent years crime figures for the UK have shown a remarkable decrease. In Leeds too crime has decreased, even if over the whole spectrum: while drugs crimes fell by 34 per cent in the period 1998–2001, domestic burglaries increased in the year 2002. Despite the fact that the risk of becoming a victim of crime in Leeds was at its historic minimum in the period 2002/03, most people believed crime rates had increased in the area. This discrepancy between the deterioration in the perception of safety and the parallel reduction in crime rates has been observed in other cities.[6] In any case, Leeds is characterized by the fact that people's perception of safety changes dramatically during the day: while during working hours (from 9.00 a.m. to 5.00 p.m.) most of the people feel safe, after dark the majority feel unsafe.

According to residents, the priorities in the fight against crime should focus on burglary, youth crime, the quality of the living environment and drug-related problems. The local authority considers drugs as one of the highest priorities in safety because there are many crimes related to the use of drugs – such as begging, vehicle crimes, domestic burglaries and prostitution – that have a negative influence on the perception of safety.

9.6.2 Urban Attractiveness and Spatial Behaviour

As well as the safety perception of its inhabitants, Leeds city centre's attractiveness also changes considerably during the day. From 9.00 a.m. to 5.30 p.m. the city is crowded with different groups of people who work, shop or just visit the centre. After 5.30 p.m. streets start to empty: most shops and offices close and people return to their homes, mostly located outside the central area. At this time of the day beggars and *Big Issue* vendors become more visible (and are perceived as more aggressive) and this has a negative effect on people's perception of safety. After 8.00 p.m. some parts of the city centre become busy again as the large student community (the second largest in the UK outside London) and the YUPs (young urban professionals) living in the area go out to pubs and clubs. This creates a vibrant nightlife in the city, which has both positive and negative consequences. On one hand, it attracts many young people and students to the city, benefiting the local economy and the image of Leeds. On the other hand, it keeps families and the elderly out of town and creates safety problems late at night when pubs close and large groups of (often drunken) people search for the limited number of available taxis to take them home.

Even if at the time of writing the city is performing well in terms of economic activity and employment, the double identity of Leeds city centre – perceived as quite safe until 5.30 p.m. and less safe afterwards; very attractive as living location for students and YUPs, not attractive at all for families and elders – carries the risk of bringing the city unbalanced growth in the future.

9.6.3 Policy Response

Since the beginning of the 1990s antisocial behaviour and crime has represented one of the highest priorities of the Labour government's political agenda. There are two main reasons for this: on one hand, safety has been recognized as one of the main factors affecting quality of life in and the functioning of cities; on the other hand, it has been realized that investing in prevention of crime is cheaper than its repression. Therefore, the greater emphasis on the fight against street crime that has been taking place in UK cities in recent years represents a direct order from national government. The consequence of this for Leeds is that safety represents the number one priority in the *city*'s political agenda too.

Regarding safety there are two local key actors: Leeds City Council and the Leeds Initiative. The latter is a partnership founded in 1990 and led by the City Council, whose aim is to provide a strategic approach for the city's long-term development. One of the Leeds Initiative Partnership Groups is Leeds Community Safety, which has the overall aim of securing sustainable reductions in crime and addressing fear of crime in the city.

One of the main aims of the city's safety policy is to combat drug abuse and the antisocial behaviour that it generates. The safety policy adopted by the city, and implemented by the Leeds Community Safety, has two main characteristics. Firstly, it has a multi-agency approach; not only is Leeds Community Safety based on this approach but also most of the safety policy measures are developed and implemented through the cooperation of different institutional actors. Secondly, it is characterized by the 'carrot and stick' approach, which results in a combination of preventive and repressive measures. The following best practices have, indeed, both characteristics.

- *Rough sleepers*: the strategic approach adopted by the Leeds Community Safety and carried out by the Rough Sleepers Support Team to fight this problem is twofold. It aims firstly at ensuring that rough sleepers have the opportunity to access appropriate services to improve their living conditions and, secondly, it aims at disrupting antisocial street behaviour. Recent head counts have shown encouraging but controversial results: from 43 rough sleepers counted in October 2002 only four were found in March 2004. These numbers show the success of the approach but may also suggest that some rough sleepers are moving out of the city centre or hiding themselves more successfully. In order to diminish the spread of rough sleepers over a larger area, the city extended the counting area beyond the city centre.
- *DAT*: the Drug Action Team (DAT) is a national programme founded in 1995 in order to tackle drugs problems in Britain: the top 40 British acquisition crime areas (areas with high drug-related crimes) became 25 DAT areas. Originally focused on treatment of people, from 2002 DAT changed its focus towards criminal justice. DAT Leeds is a multi-agency partnership including more than ten different institutions. It has invested considerable resources in education, awareness and training and it is working on the improvement of access to drug services for black people and minority ethnic groups.
- CJIP: the Criminal Justice Intervention Programme (CJIP) is a nationwide project started as pilot project in 25 British cities corresponding to the 25 DAT areas. The CJIP, which is a typical example of the 'carrot and stick' approach, is based on the concept of treatment (but not as a soft option): under orders imposed by a court, some drug users are directed towards treatment in addition to prison rather than instead of it. The CJIP Leeds aims at moving drug-abusing offenders into

and through the drug treatment system, through criminal justice interventions. In April 2004 the CJIP Leeds had 125 persons on its books, 20 of whom had been housed on release from prison, with three of them having full-time jobs.

9.6.4 Organizing Capacity with Respect to the Safety Plan

The analysis of Leeds' present urban safety policy cannot leave out of consideration the strong focus that the national government has placed on this issue since the beginning of the 1990s. It could be argued that in UK there is a clear *vision and strategy* carried out by the national government in the fight against crime and antisocial behaviour. This vision and strategy is implemented in Leeds by two actors who have *leadership* in the city's safety policy: the City Council and the Leeds Community Safety. The latter is the expression of a *strategic partnership* (the Leeds Initiative) that involves both the public and the private sectors.

As consequence of central government's strong focus on security (which could be considered as the initiator of the fight against urban crime), the safety policy adopted by the city has strong *political support*. The situation is different with regard to *societal support*: while the business community and some social organizations participate actively in the implementation of the city's safety plan, the citizen's community seems to be less involved.

The flourishing economic activity, low unemployment rate and image of a young and vibrant city give Leeds good *spatial-economic conditions* that have helped the *performance* of the safety policy. In the period 2002/03 the possibility of becoming a victim of a crime in Leeds was at a historic low point. Nevertheless, the perception of safety among the inhabitants has decreased and this could be a consequence of the double identity of the city.

9.6.5 Recommendations

The city of Leeds can be considered as a pleasant place with a flourishing economy, low unemployment rate and an image of a young and vibrant city. Nevertheless, one trend that could jeopardize the future development of the city can be identified – the unbalanced growth within the city centre, characterized by a strong double identity (very safe until 5:30 p.m., relatively unsafe afterwards) and by an intensive and vibrant nightlife. Both characteristics lead to a specific spatial behaviour of the main urban actors: while students, young urban professionals and businesses do want to locate in the city centre, most families and the elderly do not want to live there.

In order to ameliorate this double identity, the local authority could work in two directions. On one side something should be done to keep the city alive after 5:30 p.m.The 'Leeds Alive After Five' initiative is a good example of how the local authority can stimulate people to stay in the city centre after work. Even if this initiative is successful, it is still not able to create the critical mass that would be able to keep at least some areas of the city centre alive after 5:30 p.m. The involvement of some of the several shopping malls located in the centre in this initiative could contribute to better results; in this case some synergies with the large student and YUP population existing in the city are possible. Indeed, students represent a relatively cheap and flexible workforce that would be willing to work as shop assistants or in the hotel and catering industry after 5:30 p.m. and the young urban professionals are probably willing to shop after working hours and/or to eat outside since they have relative high incomes.[7]

On the other side, the local authority could develop policies to attract a wider target group than just students and young urban professionals. The approach here could be twofold: firstly, through improved facilities for families such as corner shops for groceries, doctors and most of the facilities for children and secondly, through an improved perception of safety for families and the elderly by reducing that antisocial behaviour that most affects it. An enhancement of the street warden service could improve safety perception during the day – once again some synergies with the large student population could be found.[8] A solution to the transport problem that occurs at night when pubs and clubs close could improve the perception of safety at night. A geographical dispersion of new pubs could help to solve this problem even if it would not change the situation for existing pubs and clubs. In this case the local authority should try to involve the pubs and clubs and persuade them to take more responsibility regarding their customers' behaviour outside the pub.

A final remark concerns the strong focus on safety taking place both at national and local level. While it has brought more (financial) resources for safety issues, it has inevitably also led to fewer resources invested in other sectors – such as education and health – which also have a strong impact on urban safety. More involvement of these sectors in the partnership – from a financial point of view also – could contribute to overcomiing the safety problem.

Notes

1 *The Big Issue* is a weekly magazine usually sold by homeless and socially-excluded people: legimate sellers are licensed.

2 In Leeds there are two different kinds of taxis: 'black and white' and private hire. The former are registered by the City Council and must stop when hailed as well as being available at designated taxi ranks. The second are privately owned and can only be sent from their office to a designated address (legally, they cannot be hailed on the street). The problem is that there are not enough 'black and white' taxis available at night because few drivers are willing to work at that time since they are worried they will be assaulted by drunken people.

3 According to City Centre Leeds, one of the partnership groups of the Leeds Initiative, in April 2004 there were about 6,000 people living in the city centre and this number is expected to grow to 10,000 by the year 2010.

4 There is a difference between crime and antisocial behaviour. While criminal behaviour covers an action that is prohibited by law (such as theft or robbery) and therefore is always persecuted by the police, antisocial behaviour is an action not specifically covered by legislation but which detracts from the quality of life that can be expected by an average

member of the public (e.g. gangs prowling around a neighbourhood or persistent annoyance of a small number of people by individuals).

5 Acquisitive crime is defined by Schedule 6 Criminal Justice and Court Services Act 2000 as theft, robbery, burglary, aggravated burglary, taking a motor vehicle without consent, aggravated vehicle taking, obtaining property by deception and going equipped for stealing.

6 Concerning the UK only, the Home Office annual report confirms that despite the fact that crime has been reduced by 25 per cent since 1997 in UK and the chance of being a victim is at its lowest for over 20 years, too many people still live in fear of crime (Home Office, 2004).

7 In many European countries shopping malls have extended opening times (usually from 9.00–10.00 a.m. to 8.00–9.00 p.m.). As a result they have become crowded with people who shop, eat, meet or just go for a walk at any time of the day.

8 Other cities have some kind of street-patrol services by civilians and students who could be hired to patrol the streets late in the afternoon when the normal street-warden service would be more expensive and staff less available.

Chapter 10

The Case of Bari

10.1 Introduction

In this case study, we focus on urban safety in the city of Bari, Italy. Section 10.2 gives a concise profile of the metropolitan area. In Section 10.3, we describe the actual and perceived safety situation of the city. Next, in Section 10.4, we will go into the related spatial behaviour of local inhabitants. Section 10.5 goes into policy reactions regarding urban unsafety. In this section we will give specific attention to some *best practices*; the focus for Bari is on youth crime. Finally, Section 10.6 presents conclusions and some recommendations.

10.2 Profile of Bari

10.2.1 Situation and Demography

The city of Bari is the capital of Puglia, a region of approximately four million inhabitants on the southeastern corner of Italy. The original city centre, a 1.3km^2 area known as 'Bari Vecchia', has developed during the years in a hemispheric way. Today, with a population of more than 330,000 inhabitants (in 2001) and a size of 116km^2, Bari can be considered as the centre of a metropolitan area (the Province of Bari) that includes 44 municipalities and is home of more than 1.5 million people.

While the last decade has seen a growth of the population of the entire Province, mainly due to the immigration, the population of the city in recent year has decreased and aged.

One of the main challenges for the city in recent years has been the inflow of migrants from non-EU countries, especially illegal immigrants from – or arriving through – Albania and ex-Yugoslavia.

10.2.2 Administration

Italy is divided in 20 regions, each of which is divided into provinces. The Region of Puglia includes five provinces – Bari, Brindisi, Foggia, Lecce and Taranto. The city of Bari, administrative capital of Puglia, is divided into nine districts and 20 neighbourhoods.

In Italy different police forces operate at national level; the most important ones for public safety are the State Police, the Carabinieri Corp (member of the Armed

Figure 10.1 Geographical position of Bari in Europe

Forces) and the Guardia di Finanza. While the State Police and the Carabinieri perform the functions of public order and security policing, the Guardia di Finanza is mainly involved in the fight against smuggling and financial fraud. At local level safety policy is decided by the Provincial Committee for Security, a multi-agency team composed of the Prefect, the Mayor, the President of the Province of Bari and other local authorities involved in safety.

10.2.3 Economy and Employment

Bari's economy is balanced and diverse. The primary (agricultural) sector of the Province is larger than the national average. However it is undersized compared with that of other cities in the Puglia region (van der Meer et al., 2004). Retail, traditional

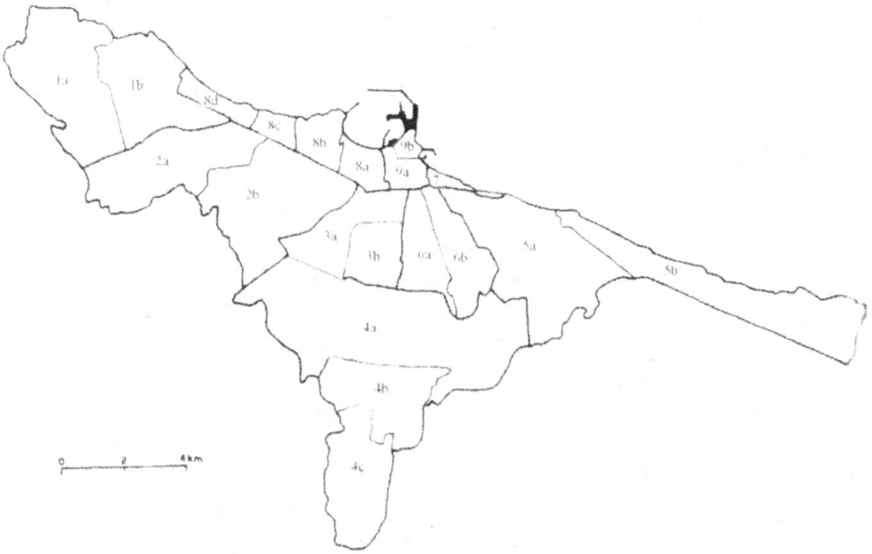

1: Santo Spirito (a) – Palese (b); 2: San Paolo (a), Stanic (b); 3: Picone (a) – Poggiofranco (b); 4: Carbonara (a) – Ceglie (b) – Loseto (c); 5: Japigia (a) – Torre a Mare (b); 6: Carrassi (a) – San Pasquale (b); 7: Madonnella; 8: Libertà (a) – Marconi (b) – San Girolamo (c) – Fesca (d); 9: Murat (a) – San Nicola (b).

Figure 10.2 Inner city of Bari

'light' manufacturing (such as textile, shoes and food), building and real estate sectors are the main economic activities of the city; more recently the service sector and ICT-related activities have developed rapidly (Palma et al., 2003).

In 1999 the Province's unemployment rate was 16.7 per cent, more than five points above the national average and almost four times the rate in the northeast of the country. The situation becomes much worse when the youth sector is considered, with a juvenile unemployment rate of 40.8 per cent (http://www.istat.it).

An analysis of the national and international c*ompetitiveness of the city* gives controversial results. According to Palma (2003) the city of Bari scores quite badly in national surveys regarding the quality of the living environment (Legambiente, 2001), the presence of cultural assets, human capital and public administration (Emmanuel and Governa, 1997) and the economic base of the urban system. Paradoxically some international surveys show improvements. DATAR (1989) classified Bari as a city with a strong R&D (research and development) sector and with an international orientation. A study conducted by Equipe Paris (1994) classified Bari as an important regional centre but still far from being a centre with an international orientation. The tertiary sector and the poor quality of life were considered the two main weaknesses.

Finally, Bari also scores badly according to a research undertaken by the Centro Studi EUROPOLIS (in Palma, 2003) and a more recent study of DATAR (2003), where the city gets a worse score compared to a similar study carried out in 1989.

Strong points of the city are the university sector and the port activities. With a first-class knowledge infrastructure (the University of Bari and the Polytechnic) Bari is one of the most important student centres of Southern Italy. In recent years, many investments have taken place in the port area (more than €60m in the period 1998–2003), which a dramatic increase in traffic both of passengers and goods. Closely linked to the development of the port, Bari plays now a strategic role in the development of the Trans-European Network 'Corridor No. 8' (the so called 'Highway of the Sea') as centre of a new trans-Adriatic region which includes the countries of ex-Yugoslavia, Greece and Albania and which will have a fundamental importance in the openness of the EU towards the Balkans.

The 1990s were certainly the most important period for the redevelopment of the city, since many huge projects with a strategic importance of the city took place. Most of these projects were related to the two big events that Bari hosted in that period: the football World Cup in 1990 and the Mediterranean Games in 1997 (Palma, 2003).

10.3 The Perception of Security in Bari

10.3.1 Development of Crime in Bari

In order to describe the development of criminal activity in Bari it is necessary to make a distinction between ordinary crime and organized crime. While ordinary crime is committed by people operating alone, organized crime is committed by members of a specific organization. Usually each organization is controlled by one 'family': in the metropolitan area of Bari organized crime is controlled by five 'families'.

Criminality, especially organized crime, in Bari and in the Region of Puglia has changed a lot in the last few decades. Because of its strategic position on the Mediterranean coast, the region has for a long time been a smuggling centre for the south of Italy; the contraband trade represented a source of income for many families (and children) and it had a relatively non-violent impact on social activities. Local people never perceived smuggling as a real criminal activity that could jeopardize their lives.

At the beginning of the 1990s two fundamental developments changed the region's criminal activity. On one side the loosening of border restrictions with Eastern Europe brought more competition in smuggling activities and this led to a progressive reduction of the contraband trade of Puglia. This, in its turn, had the main consequence that an important source of income progressively disappeared from the area. On the other had, during the same period several convicted bosses belonging to the Camorra (the Mafia from Naples) were transferred to local prisons in Puglia for two main reasons: firstly, because jails in the area of Naples did not have enough capacity for all the arrested members of the Camorra and secondly, to prevent these people from keeping active contact with their organizations. The consequence was that the bosses of the Camorra contacted local criminals and the result was that the model of organized crime that existed in the Naples region was imported and established in Puglia also.

Until a few years ago Bari was well known for burglaries, pickpocketing and smuggling. Even if most crimes had cyclical pattern it could be argued that the contraband trade had almost disappeared in 2000, following a large police operation called 'Primavera'. Pickpocketing and burglaries decreased dramatically in the 1990s and at the time of writing are more or less stable, though official data show an increase for the city of Bari (see Table 10.1). The number of robberies has been constantly increasing because they have become the alternative source of income for many people previously employed in smuggling activities.

Many areas located outside the city centre are characterized by a high level of social, cultural and economic deprivation. These areas are not under the control of the legal system but under the control of organized crime, managed by a few families each controlling a different part of the city. In these areas organized crime represents the 'social winning model' especially when it is able to control important economic activities. The five most dangerous neighbourhoods of the city are Enziteto, S. Paolo, Carbonara, Ceglie and Japigia.

10.3.2 Safety Perception

Observations about the perception of safety in Bari are very difficult to make. At local level there is a complete lack of data concerning how people (or other urban actors) perceive the problem of insecurity in the city. At national level a 2003 survey on perception of crime (Il Sole 24 ore, 2004) reports a very negative result for the city. With 35.7 per cent of people considering crime a very serious problem, Bari is 97th (out of 103) in the rank of Italian cities – where Naples is the 103rd. Moreover the few data over recorded crime (see Table 10.1) available probably represent a very small part or the real situation since most of the crimes are not reported to the authorities (some estimates the reported crime as 10 per cent of the total criminal activity of the city[1]). From a qualitative point of view the situation does not improve. At institutional level there is a large discrepancy between different actors: for some Bari is a relative safe city, for others the city competes with Naples for the title of most dangerous Italian city.

It seems that, on the one hand, people are used to (some) criminality that has become part of their everyday life; people know the areas that should be avoided at certain times of the day and how to behave in specific circumstances. On the other hand, it seems that people are not happy with the actual situation, especially concerning youth crime, but they have accepted it because of lack of any alternative and trust in the governmental organizations. As a consequence organized crime is perceived by people as a *substitute for the institutions*, not only in the management of many public goods – it is well known, for example, that social houses in Bari are controlled by organized crime – but paradoxically also for security. If a car is stolen, it might be easier for the owner to contact the illegal network, pay a small charge and get the car back rather than to report it to the authorities.

Table 10.1 Crimes reported to the judicial authority by the State Police, Carabinieri Corp and Guardia di Finanza

	2001		**2002**		**2003**		**Difference 2001–2003**	
	Province	*Bari*	*Province*	*Bari*	*Province*	*Bari*	*Province*	*Bari*
Murder	30	10	30	7	27	11	-10%	+10%
Attempted murder	85	27	50	6	80	33	-5.8%	+2.2%
Violence against persons	1,293	266	1,390	228	1,326	198	+2.5%	–25.6%
Sexual violence	66	18	52	15	57	10	–9%	–44.4%
Burglary and pickpocketing	32,402	8,991	32,772	9,791	32,851	10,547	-1.3%	+17.3%
Robbery	985	433	1,007	408	1020	481	+3.5%	+11%
Arson	380	50	384	67	411	35	+8.2%	–30%
Drug-related crimes	844	283	725	284	825	421	–2.3%	+48.7%
Total recorded crimes	**50,838**	**15,624**	**51,369**	**16,301**	**61,003**	**20,415**	**+20%**	**+30.7%**

Source: Municipality of Bari, 2004.

10.3.3 Youth Crime

Also youth crime has changed a lot in the last decades and, of course, these changes are mostly related with the evolution of criminal activity in the city. Three main developments regarding youth criminality can be identified in Bari. Firstly, while in the past most youth crime was connected with smuggling activity, nowadays most of it is connected with organized crime activities such as robberies, drug trafficking and sometimes even homicides. Secondly, while in the past youth criminality referred almost exclusively to the lower and poorer class of the society, nowadays it has become a universal phenomenon: youth criminals belong to low-income as well as medium- and high-income groups. This is supported by the 'well-being/malaise' theory elaborated by Occhiogrosso,[2] President of the Court for Minors of the city of Bari. Thirdly, it seems that youth criminals are becoming younger and are committing more serious crimes; whereas ten years ago pickpocketing was the first crime committed by youngsters, today the 'entry-level' has become a robbery.

There are different reasons that push young people to commit criminal activities. First of all most of the children want to have more consumer goods; they want to wear expensive fashionable clothes and to have the latest model of mobile phone. The easiest way to get the money needed to maintain this standard of living is to be involved in some criminal activity. A second reason is given by the lifestyle that criminality (especially organized crime) has to offer: it is seen by young people as a successful lifestyle model and, most importantly, with no alternatives based on legality. This 'winning social model' is very attractive for the youngsters and it has, unfortunately, a strong 'contagious capacity'. Not only do young people already belonging to the organized crime like it, but also their friends and schoolmates. Unfortunately schools are not able to offer an alternative attractive lifestyle model based on legality. Moreover, the culture of illegality is widespread throughout the city at different levels of the society: from families (who do not care whether their children attend school or not) to social and institutional organizations. The problem linked to the culture of illegality is so diffused that sometimes young criminals do not even know that their activities are illegal.[3] Finally, another reason why youth criminality is so diffused in Bari is due to a practical need of organized crime: nowadays most of its members are in jail and this forces them to recruit new members. The easiest way to do this is to attract the youngsters living in the most deprived areas of the city. The soft jurisdiction (and related sentences) for minors does not help to reverse this trend.

10.4 Urban Attractiveness and Spatial Behaviour

10.4.1 Unbalanced Spatial Development

Since the 1960s the city of Bari has focused almost exclusively on the renewal of one area – the core of the city centre known as 'Bari Vecchia' (the Old Bari) – to the detriment of the rest of the city. This process begun when the local authority forced many (poor) inhabitants of Bari Vecchia to relocate to more peripheral areas. This policy led to the creation of specific neighbourhoods, like S. Paolo, containing the most vulnerable and poorest part of society where criminality easily took root. The renewal policy of Bari Vecchia reached its climax with the URBAN I project in the mid-1990s. At that time the area was one of the most dangerous parts of the city and it was considered a 'no-go area' even for the police force. European funds have been used to renovate the whole area – many buildings have been restored, many shops have opened and it has become an attractive area of the city with a good quality of life and relatively low criminality.

Figure 10.3 Bari Vecchia

10.4.2 Impact of Safety on the Spatial Behaviour of the Urban Actors

It is not easy to say whether the spatial behaviour of the *inhabitants* is influenced by safety and its perception. On the one hand, very few people appear to relocate or move from one neighbourhood to another because of perceived insecurity, firstly, because local inhabitants have more or less learnt to coexist with criminality and, secondly, because there are no valid alternatives. Indeed the only good neighbourhood is Bari Vecchia but it is also the most expensive area to live in: the other parts of the city do not differ from each other enough to justify relocation. On the other hand, citizens have adapted their daily spatial behaviour on the basis of the existing 'no-go areas' of the city.

Regarding the *business sector*, we have to distinguish between small and medium-sized enterprises and large businesses. The first group is usually forced to pay the so called *pizzo*[4] to local criminal organizations – this is a quite common and long-established practice that has been more or less accepted by local entrepreneurs, who take it into consideration when creating a business plan. In any case, this phenomenon must represent a restraint on the development of local small and medium-sized enterprises. Indeed, small or medium entrepreneurs are very often unwilling to grow further because this would automatically be translated into a higher *pizzo* to pay to local criminal organizations and most of them are not willing to take this risk. This happened a few years ago, for example, when specific European funds meant to help local small entrepreneurs to renew and/or improve their activity were largely unused.

Contrary to what one might expect, large companies – such as Bosch, Getrag and Ikea – are not influenced by local criminal organizations. Indeed, it would be too risky and complicated for organized crime to extort money from large companies both because of the lack of a physical entrepreneur/owner of the business and because the fierce reaction they would get from the police forces. Therefore in the region of Puglia criminality does not represent as much of a restraint on large investments as is commonly thought, although the Bari Metropolitan Area still appears to have an image problem, which might hinder the attraction of new large companies.

10.5 Policy Reactions

10.5.1 The Actors Involved

The Minister of the Interior is responsible for public order and security maintenance. In carrying out this department's function, the minister is supported by the Public Order and Security Committee, an advisory body consisting of an Undersecretary of the Interior (deputy chairman), the Chief of Police (General Director of Public Security) and of the heads of the other police forces. At central level the function of public security administration is exercised by the Public Security Department and at local level by provincial and local authorities, public security officials and officers. The following are the public security provincial authorities: the Prefect, in charge of the Territorial Government Office, with general responsibility for public order and security; and the Questore, the senior official of the State Police, responsible for the direction and technical and operational coordination of public order and security services and of police force employment (http://www.poliziadistato.it).

In Italy different police forces operate at national and local level; the most important ones for public safety are the State Police, the Carabinieri Corp and the Guardia di Finanza.

At local level safety policy is decided by the Provincial Committee for Security, a multi-agency team composed of the Prefect, the Mayor, the President of the Province of Bari and other local authorities involved in safety. This Committee is an advisory team for the Prefect who, in recent years, has acted as the leader. He set up a network among the main actors involved in urban safety and asked them to participate in the process of creation of the city's safety policy. The leadership of the Prefect in the local safety policy has also been favoured by the fact that the previous administration did not consider safety as high priority for the city.

10.5.2 Safety Policy in Bari

Bari's safety policy changed dramatically in June 2004 when Mr Emiliano, a former judge, won the election and became Mayor, representating the centre-left party. The previous administration had a rather controversial impact on the safety situation in the city. On the one hand they denied the existence of organized crime in the city and did not consider safety a priority for the city. On the other hand they joined two European programmes which had and could in future have an important impact on the safety situation in Bari. The first is the already-mentioned URBAN I programme, whose main contribution was to clean up the medieval-historical part of the city (Bari Vecchia), transforming one of the most dangerous 'no-go' areas of the city into an attractive and liveable one. The second is participation in the SecurCity project of URBACT on which this comparative study is based. Even if the opponents of the previous administration support the idea that both programmes were undertaken for purposes other than safety (real estate speculation for the URBAN I project and public relations for the URBACT programme), the positive role they had and will have on the safety situation of the city cannot be denied. However, the regeneration of Bari Vecchia has also some negative aspects: most of the criminality originally located in the central historical area has not disappeared but instead has largely moved to other areas of the city, making them even more dangerous than before.

As former anti-Mafia magistrate, the present Mayor has made safety one of the highest priorities for the city. Bari's current safety policy is a combination of repressive and preventive measures.

The *repressive measures* are developed by the Prefettura and carried out by the magistrature through the police forces. They consist of a huge intelligence work (more than 180 people work in intelligence) aimed at the capture of members of the highest levels of organized crime. This policy has a double effect: on one side to keep a constant pressure on organized crime to show that local authorities are firmly committed to fight it and, on the other side, to show citizens the effort being made and commitment that local authorities have against criminality. The latter can also help to fight the 'winning social model' represented by organized crime that influences many young people to start a criminal career.

The *preventive measures* are carried out by the different police forces in cooperation with other local authorities. The main aim is to erode the base of organized crime by trying to prevent many (especially young) people from joining. The momentum is favourable since the criminal situation in Bari now is in a relative calm phase, in contrast to what is happening in Naples, for example.[5] There are two kinds of preventive policies mainly carried out by local authorities. Firstly there is a special focus on those people that have just finished serving their time in jail trying to support them to reintigrate into legal society. The first positive results are now becoming visible: a larger number of ex-detainees are willing to give up a criminal career, more people are willing to help them in doing it and some local entrepreneurs are willing to offer them a job. Good examples are institutions such as the 'Cooperativa Vita Nuova' and the 'Cooperativa Obiettivo', which help ex-detainees to get back into (legal) society.

Secondly there is special attention on young children in the attempt to avoid them coming into contact with (and usually being 'employed' by) the organized crime. The latter surely represents the most difficult challenge for local authorities. Strong efforts will be dedicated to the development of specific school programmes where judges and members of the police forces will be involved in trying to teach young people the culture of legality and showing them the existence of an alternative lifestyle based on legality.

Another preventive measure is based on the development of 'Bari Citta' Sicura' (Bari Safe City), a sort of partnership between different local authorities (police forces, municipality, schools, etc.) whose aim is to improve the perception of safety in the city. Specifically focused on preventive measures, it represents a first step towards the multi-agency approach proved to be quite successful in the UK and its final aim is the creation of a local agency for security.

Best practice 1: URBAN I Initiative

In 1994 the European Commission decided to launch the Community Initiative URBAN with the aim of tackling issues of urban regeneration and cohesion. The Initiative, which covered the period 1994–1999, targeted neighbourhoods with extreme deprivation, addressing the problems of poverty and social exclusion through investments aimed at the creation of a better physical and social environment. The URBAN I Initiative in Bari covered the 32 hectares of the historical centre Bari which in 1994 had a population of approximately 8,000 inhabitants. Though Bari Vecchia was considered a high density area, in previous years there had been a major reduction in the resident population. The area was characterized by socio-economic distress and urban decay; the proportion of population over 60 was higher than the urban average and the unemployment rate was about 25 per cent. There was a high rate of youth at risk, with 37 per cent of young people aged between 18 and 29 who did not complete school (URBAN I Initiative, 2004). The whole area was considered a 'no-go' area even for the police forces and there was the highest rate of youth crime in the city.

Approximately €20m was invested over four years in a twofold strategy aimed at: 1) stopping and reversing the trend of loss of economic activities; and 2) reducing the main social problems in the area – namely high unemployment and youth at risk. Support was given for the development of new economic activities, especially in the hotel, restaurant and catering industry and craftwork sectors, in order to promote tourism and leisure activities.

Nowadays the result of the URBAN I Initiative is quite evident. What was previously one of the most dangerous areas of the city completely controlled by local crime organizations and considered 'no-go' area even by the police forces is nowadays an attractive part of Bari. Several cafes and restaurants make Bari Vecchia a vibrant place. Criminality has almost disappeared from the area, although unfortunately it did not completely disappear from the city, since some of the criminal activities once located in the historical centre have simply moved in other neighbourhoods. The renewal of Bari Vecchia can be seen as an example of how the (re)development of the economic base of an area can promote safety. Thanks to the huge investments

– provided in this case by European funding – one of the most beautiful areas of the city was extracted from the control of local organized crime and given back to the framework of legality. Nevertheless, it should be noticed that large groups of cruise tourists are still escorted by the police when they walk through Bari Vecchia.

Best practice 2: restorative justice project for young people

In 1989 CRISI (Centro Ricerche Interventi Stress Interpersonale) was founded by a group of volunteers in response to the need to set up a centre for safety in the province of Bari. In 1995 CRISI received the juridical status of a social organization and from 1998 it has been financially supported by local authorities.

Programmes of restorative justice represent the main activity of CRISI, which deals both with penal and social disputes using mediation in order to rehabilitate the relationship between the offender and the victim and between the offender and society. The focus is on mediation rather than on 'social repression/punishment' because in Bari it is still quite difficult for the offender to be reintegrated into society. In 1996 this project was brought under the umbrella of the Courts of Minors which helped the development of many relationships with other local authorities involved in safety – such as the municipality, the police forces, the magistrate etc. – and transformed the centre started by a group of volunteers in a multi-agency team for restorative justice.

Through the process of mediation they try to explain to the offender why his/her behaviour damaged the victim and why this is not acceptable in modern society. Mediation seems to be a powerful tool, especially in the prevention of re-offending of young people. With an budget of approximately €85,000, in 2004 CRISI managed over 150 cases, of which 41 per cent had a positive outcome from mediation.

10.6 Synthesis

10.6.1 Security Perception

It is quite difficult to make judgments on safety perception in Bari. On the one hand, there is a lack of quantitative data about the perception of safety and on the other hand, the few official data available on recorded crime represent a small percentage of the real criminal activity and are therefore not useful for an interpretation of security perception. The qualitative information collected by our discussion partners the situation does not clarify the situtation: some consider Bari a relatively safe city, while others consider it to be one of the most dangerous cities in Italy.

In any case, it can be argued that people are used to certain level of criminality and, even if they are not satisfied with the situation, they accept it basically because of lack of alternatives and trust in governmental institutions. The consequence of this is that very often organized crime is perceived as a substitute for regular institutions.

10.6.2 Urban Attractiveness and Spatial Behaviour

In the last 40 years the city's spatial policy has been focused on the redevelopment of the old historical centre, the area called Bari Vecchia. This intensive attention on the city centre has created huge socio-economical differences between this part of the city and the rest, with relatively large consequences on the level of safety. Bari Vecchia, a former 'no-go' area even for the police, has become an attractive area of the city. The huge investments made by the URBAN I project to stimulate the economic activity, the openness of the area for cruise tourists and the relatively strong presence of the police forced organized crime to leave this area. On the other side many suburban areas – like S. Paolo, Enziteto, Carbonara, Ceglie and Japigia – have become economically and socially very deprived. In these areas of the city the culture of illegality is very developed and, very often, organized crime 'replaces' local and national institutions.

The spatial behaviour of both citizens and business activities is not really influenced by organized crime. In both cases the main reason is the lack of alternative locations with a better quality of life and/or business climate. Organized crime affects small and medium-sized entrepreneurs particularly, since they are forced to pay a price (the *pizzo*) in order to do business. It has been noticed that this can prevent local entrepreneurs from enlarging their business because this would translate in a higher price to be paid to local criminal organizations.

10.6.3 Policy Response

The attention paid to urban safety in Bari changed dramatically after the political election of June 2004. Previously, the city's administration had a controversial approach to local safety. On the one hand they denied the presence of organized crime, simply ignoring the problem. On the other hand, thanks to the URBAN I project, they have transformed the city centre from one of the most dangerous areas of the city into an attractive one.

The newly-elected Mayor, a former magistrate, has put safety high on the local political agenda. The city's current safety policy is a combination of repressive and preventive measures. The repressive measures consist mainly of a huge intelligence operation aimed at the capture of members representing the highest levels of organized crime. Preventive measures have the aim of eroding the basis of organized crime, by preventing many (young) people from joining it. Special attention is paid to children to avoid them to coming into contact with (and usually being 'employed' by) organized crime and on those (young) people who have just finished serving their time in jail in order to help them to get back into the legal society.

10.6.4 Organizing Capacity with Respect to the Safety Plan

Since the political elections of June 2004 the local authority appears to have developed a clear *strategy* on how to tackle the problem of urban safety. What is less clear is the *vision* concerning the future development of the city as a whole. Until 2004 the (informal) leader of the local safety policy has been the Prefect, who set up informal relationships among local authorities involved in safety – such us the three police forces, the city and the Public Prosecutor – and who created those *strategic networks* necessary to develop a multi-agency approach towards urban crime. Nowadays the *leadership* seems to have been taken by the new Mayor, a former judge, who has put safety high on the local political agenda and intends to continue the work initiated by the Prefect. The new elected city administration seems also to provide local safety policy with that *political support* that was previously missing. It seems more difficult to get *societal support* from the inhabitants; during the last decades local authorities have done little to prevent organized crime to spread over the area and to impose illegality as a social winning model. As a consequence many people have lost their trust in local institutions and see organized crime as a substitute of them.

The *spatial-economic conditions* of the city are characterized by strong internal differences; while the historical centre has a flourishing economic activity, most of the suburban areas are highly deprived. This unequal distribution of wealth reflects directly the crime *performance*; while Bari Vecchia is a relative safe place, some suburban areas are completely controlled by organized crime.

10.6.5 Recommendations

The first recommendation concerns the availability of data. Considering the 11 cities involved in this comparative study on urban safety Bari scores relatively poorly on the availability of data and policy documents. No single policy document concerning either the safety situation or safety policy has been produced by the city in recent years. Also simple data on the demographic and economic situation of the city are very difficult to obtain: even the official website of the city is very short of information. The development of an information system is fundamental both to setting up a comprehensive policy and to communicating it to the citizens. It has been highlighted several times that perceived safety is probably more important than objective safety when considering policy options. Very different opinions have been collected from our discussion partners on this subject: some consider the city a 'relatively safe place', others think it is 'the most dangerous Italian city together with Naples'. This reflects not only the complete lack of knowledge on how people perceive the safety situation in the city but also the relatively little attention being paid to this issue at policy level. It is therefore advisable to invest some resources into the attempt to investigate the feelings of people with regard to urban security.

Secondly, it should be realized that currently there is momentum for the city to take the leadership and the initiative in the local safety policy. The newly-elected Mayor, a former magistrate, has the characteristics to be the new leader – he has a strong image among citizens, considerable knowledge about the problem of organized crime and he can rely on skilled management. This appears to offer good momentum to set up the basis for a long-term effective policy and the proposed creation of the 'agency for security' is the first necessary step towards it.

Another recommendation concerns the economic development of the city. In the past attention has been paid mainly to the redevelopment of the historical centre – Bari Vecchia – ignoring the rest of the city. This has produced huge internal differences and the creation of many deprived areas. Unemployment in the city is much higher than the national average and the juvenile unemployment rate is over 40 per cent. This weak economic situation favours the development of crime. For young people in particular it is easier to find a job in organized crime rather than on the regular job market.

Finally, more attention and resources should be put into the education system: most of the children are easily attracted by the social winning model offered by organized crime and the phenomenon of truancy is too great. Unfortunately teachers are not trained to deal with this situation. One positive element is the initiative to invite members of the police forces and of the Public Prosecutor's Office to teach children that in the long term legality pays better than crime does. We suggest extending this kind of teaching activity to schoolteachers in order to train them to deal with children who are easily attracted by crime.

Notes

1 Internal source of the Carabinieri – one of the two main police forces operating in Italy.

2 The original concept of the 'Teoria del benessere-malessere' can be found in Occhiogrosso, 2002.

3 In Bari, for example, illegal parking is normal and it is mostly tolerated by the local police. Nowadays it has become so normal to park the car in an illegal way that people do not even know the difference between an authorized parking space and an unauthorized one. This (not criminal) behaviour contributes also to the diffusion of the culture of illegality especially among young people.

4 *Pizzo* is a regular (usually monthly) payment that local entrepreneurs have to make to organized crime as a kind of insurance. For this they get the 'protection' of and from organized crime itself.

5 At the moment of writing (end 2004 and beginning 2005) a bloody war is going on in Naples among the members of one of the families that control the local organized crime. Dozens of people have been killed within a few weeks.

Chapter 11

The Case of Birmingham

11.1 Introduction

The subjec of this chapter is the city of Birmingham, United Kingdom. Section 11.2 gives a concise profile of this urban region. In Section 11.3 we deal with possible causes of feelings of insecurity within the city of Birmingham. Next, in Section 11.4, we will go into the related spatial behaviour of local inhabitants. Section 11.5 goes into policy reactions regarding urban safety. In this section we will give specific attention to some *best practices*. Our focus for the city of Birmingham is on youth crime. Finally, Section 11.6 presents conclusions and some recommendations.

11.2 Profile of Birmingham

11.2.1 Situation and Demography

Birmingham is the second city of the UK and the capital of the West Midlands Region. The city, which covers approximately 267.8 km^2, is located in the centre of England and represents a national transport junction. With a population of over one million Birmingham is a very young and multicultural city: according to the 2001 census (Birmingham City Council, 2003) about 44 per cent of the city's residents are under 30 years of age (where the national average is 38 per cent) and 30 per cent of the population belongs to ethnic minorities.

After three decades of negative or zero population growth – in the period 1971–2001 the population dropped from over 1.1 million to slightly under one million – in recent years Birmingham has experienced an increase in the number of its inhabitants. In 2003 the city had approximately 992,000 inhabitants.

11.2.2 Administration

Since the abolishment in 1986 of the West Midlands Metropolitan County Council the local authority responsible for the governance of the city is Birmingham City Council. Local authority services are organized around wards boundaries (there are 39 wards in the local authority area, see Figure 11.2), while the police, fire and probation services operate on a West Midlands wide basis and encompass seven local authority areas. West Midlands Police service is organized into 21 Operational Command Unit areas (OCUs). There are nine OCUs in the Birmingham area, although none

Figure 11.1 Geographical position of Birmingham in Europe

of them correspond to local authority boundaries (Birmingham Community Safety Partnership, 2002b).

The Birmingham Community Safety Partnership, established in 1998 in response to the 1998 Crime and Disorder Act, is the local authority charged with the monitoring of local crime and the preparation of the city's crime reduction strategy. The Birmingham Partnership comprises the statutory Crime and Disorder Reduction Partnership between Birmingham City Council and West Midlands Police, together with other local agencies such as West Midlands Fire Service, the National Probation Service and Birmingham health services (Birmingham Community Safety Partnership, 2002b).

Figure 11.2 Wards in Birmingham

Source: Boundary Committee for England, 2003.

11.2.3 Economy and Employment

Birmingham was one of the main centres of the Industrial Revolution thanks to its metal and weapon industries and the production of jewellery. In the twentieth century the city developed itself as the centre of the automobile industry of England with the presence of car manufacturers such as Rover, MG and Jaguar (Braun, 2004). The jewellery sector is still very important since half of the jewellery made in the UK is created in the Jewellery Quarter, one of the most fascinating neighbourhoods of Birmingham.

Like many other European industrial cities Birmingham in the 1970s and 1980s had to face the transition from an industrial to a service society. Between 1971 and 1987 there was a decrease in the number of jobs in the industrial sector of 46 per cent and in the total employment of 25 per cent (Baber, 2001). The automobile industry and the related sectors, at that time the main pillars of the regional economy, were hit especially hard.

From the 1970s the city began to focus on the diversification of the economic base. Birmingham's already weak position in the service sector was reinforced by its unattractive inner city and bad (international) image. In the 1980s a new City Centre Strategy was developed, was focused on the revitalization of the inner city as a catalyst for the regional economy. The main pillars of this strategy were the improvement of the internal accessibility (especially for pedestrians), the creation of so-called 'distinctive quarters' (neighbourhoods with a distinctly different profile) and the development of the International Conference Centre (Braun, 2004). More recently some major redevelopments have begun the process of opening up adjacent inner city areas, effectively doubling the size of the actual city centre (Birmingham Community Safety Partnership, 2002b). Among other things, the £60 million Selfridges store located in the Bull Ring shopping area is an example of how Birmingham is trying to be recognized and admired. The Armadillo, as it is called by locals due to its 15.000 circular, shiny aluminium discs, has already become a landmark for the city.

Nowadays Birmingham is a regional centre that acts as a major site of employment and leisure activity; the city has become the strongest British business and financial centre outside London. The economic base of the city is more diversified: 36 per cent of the city's working residents in 2001 were employed in the management, professional and associate professional groups, a figure similar to the national 40 per cent (Birmingham City Council, 2003).

Despite the economic renaissance of the last years, Birmingham coexists with continuing levels of poverty and deprivation. There are high inequalities in health, housing quality, educational attainments and between all of the city's various ethnic groups. The Birmingham local authority district, the largest in the country, ranked 15th in the National Index of Multiple Deprivation in 2002,[1] with two of its wards in the top 1 per cent of deprived wards in the country, and a further eight within the top 5 per cent (Birmingham Community Safety Partnership, 2002b). The unemployment rate is still higher than the regional average: in 2004 it was 5.1 per cent compared to the regional 2.6 per cent.

11.3 The Perception of Security in Birmingham

11.3.1 Safety Development

Among the different tasks that the already-mentioned 1998 Crime and Disorder Act requires from local partnerships is the auditing of existing crime and disorder data to be carried out every three years. The first Audit was held in 1999 based on figures of 1997–1998; the second Audit was held in 2002 based on 2000–2001 figures; the third one is taking place at the time of writing (February 2005) and is based on 2003–2004 figures.

According to the British Crime Survey (BCS), in the period 1997/98–2002/03 Britain has seen a remarkable 25 per cent fall in crime (Home Office Statistical Bulletin, 2003). The same Survey also says that crime reported to the police is rising. Despite the findings of the BCS, the comparison between the first and second Audit showed that the overall 'recorded' crime increased in Birmingham in the period 1999–2002. Nevertheless, data concerning the periods 2002/03 and 2003/04 have shown a reduction in the total crime of the city, as can be seen in Figure 11.3.

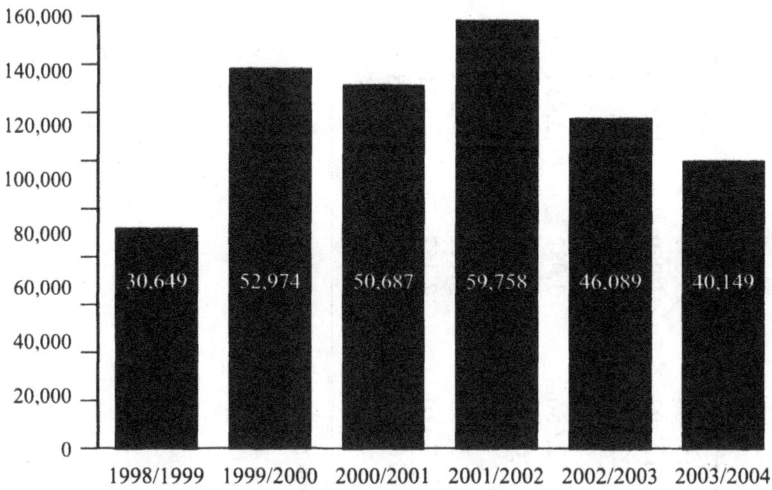

Figure 11.3 Total recorded crime in Birmingham, period 1998–2004

Source: Birmingham Community Safety Partnership

Certain types of crime such as criminal damage, drugs-related crimes, sexual offences and violence against the person have increased; others such as burglary, robbery, theft from persons and from shops have fallen after a period of growth (see Table 11.1). It should be noticed that some figures have been inflated by the new recording practices introduced in April 1998.[2]

Crime in Birmingham is not evenly distributed throughout the city: it seems there is an apparently intractable mix of crime, criminal behaviours and specific neighbourhoods which constitutes 'the crime problem' in different ways and in different places (Birmingham Community Safety Partnership, 2002a). Results from

Table 11.1 Trends of some types of crime in Birmingham in the period 1998–2004

Type of crime	1998/99	1999/2000	2000/2001	2001/2002	2002/2003	2003/2004	Difference 1998–2004
Burglary – dwelling	17,185	15,734	13,659	14,270	11,803	12,086	–29.7%
Burglary – other	12,056	12,292	11,269	11,905	11,116	9,771	–19.0%
Criminal damage	17,683	22,601	20,714	23,089	21,639	22,196	+25.5%
Drugs – trafficking	510	475	593	574	719	595	+16.7%
Drugs – other	2,898	2,686	3,082	3,433	3,781	3,759	+29.7%
Robbery	4,394	6,377	6,739	7,823	5,953	6,131	+39.5%
Sexual offences	780	903	977	1,184	1,207	1,198	+53.6%
Theft from person	2,281	3,430	4,111	4,394	3,019	2,576	+12.9%
Theft from shops	6,228	7,110	7,467	7,641	6,869	6,705	+7.6%
Violence against the person	12,428	16,617	19,485	22,838	21,793	23,336	+87.7%
Total crime	130,649	152,974	150,687	159,758	140,149	n.a.	–12.27%

Source: Birmingham Community Safety Partnership.

the 2005 Audit confirm that crime is spatially differentiated since the distribution of the Community Safety core priorities are not evenly distributed within the Birmingham wards (Birmingham Community Safety Partnership, 2005).

11.3.2 Safety Perception

Birmingham is a good example to illustrate the safety paradox. Despite the fact that in the period 2002/2003 crime dropped more than 12 per cent compared to the previous year and that the West Midlands Police is the best-performing police force in the country, the fear of crime has constantly increased since 2001.

The Birmingham Community Safety Partnership is clearly aware of the existence of this reassurance gap and is firmly committed to tackle it. The Crime and Disorder Audit 2002 states that 'there is no straightforward link between risk of crime and fear of crime, so telling someone that evidence shows they are very unlikely to be a victim of a crime may do little to ease their fears' (Birmingham Community Safety Partnership, 2002b, p. 10). Annual polls confirm that crime is the citizens' principal concern in Birmingham.

Table 11.2 Top five priorities to be tackled according to respondents (not stated in order of importance)

1999*	2001**	2002***	2005^
Burglary	Burglary	Burglary	Antisocial behaviour
Robbery	Robbery	Street crime/robbery	Clean streets and neighbourhoods
Muggings	Vehicle crimes	Sex offences	Drugs related crimes
Car stolen	Young people hanging around	Illegal drugs	Preventing youth crime
Vandalism	Drug dealing	Violent assaults	Muggings

Sources: * Crime and Disorder Audit 1999; ** Survey commissioned by West Midlands Police; *** Crime and Disorder Audit 2002; ^ Crime and Disorder Audit 2005.

Table 11.2 summaries the results of the Crime Audits and independent surveys conducted by the West Midlands Police regarding the top five priorities that Birmingham's citizens would like to see tackled. The category 'Burglary' is a further confirmation of the reassurance gap: while the number of burglaries has been falling since 1998/1999 (see Table 11.1) people continued to consider it as one of the main problems. The research 'Feeling the Difference' conducted by the West Midlands Police in July 2004 confirmed that almost 90 per cent of the respondents who gave an opinion believed that crime levels over the previous 12 months had stayed the same or increased, despite the fact that in the period December 2002–November

2004 Birmingham experienced continued and strong reduction of recorded crime (Birmingham Community Safety Partnership, 2005). Moreover, in January 2002 more than 1,300 questionnaires were collected among the residents of all 39 wards of the city. The results showed that the majority of respondents felt that the area in which they lived had stayed the same (46.7 per cent) or become worse (42.5 per cent) in terms of safety in the previous three years (Birmingham Community Safety Partnership, 2002b). It seems that drug-related problems especially are starting to emerge as one of the citizens' main concerns.

Finally, according to over 220 organizations operating in Birmingham, the four main priorities that should be tackled are burglary, antisocial behaviour, street crime and illegal drugs (Birmingham Community Safety Partnership, 2002b).

11.3.3 Youth Crime

In recent years problems related to youth crime emerged as one of the top priorities for the citizens of Birmingham. The period 1998/1999–2000/2001 saw a very dramatic change in youth crime since young people increased as a percentage both of offenders and victims, with an increasing percentage of females involved in offending (Birmingham Community Safety Partnership, 2002b).

The majority of crimes committed by young people are against other young people; phenomena such as bullying and stealing mobile phones have become quite common in many schools in the city. Among young offenders there is an increase in the type of offences concerned with violence and criminal damage; shoplifting seems to be committed mostly by young females. The fact that youth crime – especially bullying and street crime affecting youngsters – is still under-reported contributed to the choice of the Birmingham Community Safety Partnership to consider it as one of the highest priorities.

A recent survey conducted among schools and youth organizations in Birmingham reveals that many young people feel unsafe when travelling around the area where they live, when going to the city centre and when travelling on public transport (Birmingham Community Safety Partnership, 2002b).

The results of the last Audit (2005) have confirmed that youth crime is a priority both in terms of young people at risk of becoming potential offenders and also as the fastest growing age group being victimized (Birmingham Community Safety Partnership, 2005). The 2005 Audit data highlight two other important considerations. Firstly, there has been a dramatic increase in the percentage of young offenders using drugs; this is indirectly confirmed by the emergence of 'drug-related crimes' as one of the main concerns of citizens. Secondly, contrary to other types of crime, youth crime is not an area-based problem but a phenomenon that is spread all over the city's wards (with the possible exception of the four northern wards of Sutton). Nevertheless, youth crime can still be considered as a classproblem since most of the young offenders belong to the most vulnerable and poor parts of the society.

A clear link has been established between truancy and young offenders – most of the pupils who are frequently (unauthorized to be) absent from school are also young offenders. This has been a serious problem in Birmingham but in recent years figures of school attendance have improved thanks to the fact that the police can now stop children during school time and question them as to why they are not at school (and the parents of persistent truants can be punished).

11.4 Urban Attractiveness and Spatial Behaviour

The 1998 Crime and Disorder Act and the new City Centre Strategy developed by the city in the 1980s represent the two most important factors that have influenced Birmingham's attractiveness in the last decade. This process of renewal has led to two main spatial consequences.

The first is that the city centre has become a very attractive place for living, working, shopping and recreation. During the 1960s and the 1970s many people left the city centre, leaving deserted areas that soon became perceived as very unsafe. This unattractive situation changed after the active urban policy undertaken by the local authority from the 1980s. Nowadays some 5,000 properties are located in the city centre – with the number set to double by the end of the decade – and over 100,000 people come to work there each day (Birmingham City Centre Partnership, 2004). Besides the already-mentioned Selfridges – considered the biggest urban shopping centre of Europe – a huge number of shops and leisure facilities are concentrated in the central area, especially in the Bull Ring. This attracts thousands of people each day from the whole West Midlands Region[3] and, together with the increased number of people living and working in the area, has contributed to reducing the level of crime in the city centre. This trend has been reinforced by the recent commitment of the Birmingham City Centre Partnership to set up two Business Improvement Districts (BIDs) in the central area: one in Broad Street – where most of the nightlife of the city takes place – and one in the Central area – which includes most of the shopping facilities. A BID is a partnership between the city and the private business sector established following a local ballot whose aim is to have cleaner, safer, friendly, attractive, vibrant and economically stronger city districts.

The second spatial development that has taken place in Birmingham is that, in previous decades, few investments were made outside the central area, with the consequence that the attractiveness of some wards was not improved at all. Indeed, even if the local economy is flourishing compare to the past, the rate of unemployment in Birmingham is above the national average – 7.6 per cent compare to 3.2 per cent in January 2002 (Birmingham Community Safety Partnership, 2002b) – and a quarter of its wards are in the top 5 per cent of the national Index of Multiple Deprivation. One of the priorities of the Birmingham Community Safety Partnership in the next few years is 'cleaner and safer neighbourhoods'. This will improve the situation of some of the worst areas, since this policy is directed towards the whole city and not just to the central areas as the BID, but it has to be supported from adequate and parallel investments aimed at improving the attractiveness of the most deprived wards.

Figure 11.4 The Selfridges store (top) and of the Rotunda in the Bull Ring area (bottom)

11.5 Policy Reactions

11.5.1 Birmingham Community Safety Partnership

The 1998 Crime and Disorder Act required from major UK cities the creation of crime and disorder partnerships that could play a new role in the area of local crime reduction. In response to this, in 1998 the Birmingham Community Safety Partnership was established between the Birmingham City Council and West Midlands Police. Other local authorities agencies are also involved in the Partnership, such as the West Midlands Fire Service, the National Probation Service West Midlands, Birmingham Voluntary Service Council and Birmingham Health Service (Birmingham Community Safety Partnership, 2002b).

The main philosophy behind the Partnership's work is to pursue long-term actions to tackle the root causes of criminality and increase public confidence. After some initial difficulties related to the complexity of the management of people belonging to different organizations (with different needs and priorities), the multi-agency approach introduced by the Partnership has proved to be absolutely indispensable to facing a complex problem such as urban safety. In 2002 the Birmingham Crime and Disorder Strategy stated that 'Partnership working with people drawn from different professional and organizational backgrounds remains a challenge' (Birmingham Community Safety Partnership, 2002c, p. 5). Nevertheless, the Partnership has allowed the development of contacts between the different actors involved in the safety policy of the city that did not take place before. Nowadays there is intense communication and exchange of information and knowledge between these actors which has led to more efficiency in crime prevention and reduction. As a matter of fact, total crime has dramatically reduced in the city; the Partnership has achieved two exceptionally challenging Public Service Agreement targets to reduce house burglary and to reduce the death and injury through house fire. Additionally, the West Midlands Police Force is the best-performing police force in the country.

11.5.2 Local Safety Strategy

Since the late 1990s safety has become the highest priority for the Birmingham City Council. The safety policy adopted by the city can be seen as a combination of repressive and preventive measures that leads to a firm policy based on the provision of public services.

The 1998 Crime and Disorder Act required a three year planning and action process in which each Community Safety Partnership should produce a Crime and Disorder Audit and a Crime Reduction Strategy, with the strategy being the direct outcome of the audit (at least from the second strategy period on). Up to the time of writing there have been three strategy periods: 1999–2002, 2002–2005 and 2005–2008.

At the same time as the first strategy was produced the government advised local crime reduction partnerships to identify between five and seven priorities for crime reduction in their areas. Since (urban) safety is a very wide issue, the aim of the government was to provide a framework within which local partnerships would operate rather than to provide a complete approach to all areas of crime reduction. For the period 1999–2002 Birmingham Community Safety Partnership selected the following priorities: domestic burglary, car crime, safety in public places, domestic violence, racially-aggravated crime, young people as offenders and victims and illegal drugs (Birmingham Community Safety Partnership, 2002c).

The 2002–2005 crime and disorder reduction strategy was organized around three main issues:

1. the reduction of crime and violence, which addresses crimes such as burglary, car crime, robbery, violence, antisocial behaviour and youth crime;

Table 11.3 Top priorities of Birmingham's crime and disorder strategies

1999–2002	2002–2005	2005–2008
Domestic burglary	Response support	Cleaner and safer neighbourhoods
Car crime	Priority neighbourhoods and places	Offender management and drug treatment
Safety in public places	Supporting victims and public reassurance	Violence and vulnerability
Domestic violence	Youth offending and social inclusion	Young people
Racially-aggravated crime	Illegal drugs and substance misuse	Reduction of gang violence
Young people	Information and intelligence development	Illegal drugs

Source: Birmingham Community Safety Partnership (2002b, 2005).

2 the reduction in the fear of crime, which considers a new Partnership approach to the health and environmental aspects of crime;
3 the development of local capacity particularly by improving Partnership intelligence, information gathering and analysis of problems (Birmingham Community Safety Partnership, 2002a).

The second strategy took into consideration all aspects of the crime and disorder problem, namely victims, offenders and locations. The Partnership therefore recognized the importance of tackling crime within specific areas that could be defined as high-risk neighbourhoods. The issue of youth crime emerged as a higher priority in this second strategy than it had in the first. One of the main aims of the 2002–2005 strategy was also to improve cooperation among partners according to the idea that more can be achieved jointly than separately. The six priorities of the second crime and reduction strategy were response support, priority neighbourhoods and places, supporting victims and public reassurance, youth offending and social inclusion, illegal drugs and substance misuse and information and intelligence development (Birmingham Community Safety Partnership, 2002a).

Some of the problems that most challenged the functioning of the Partnership were the city's size (Birmingham has the largest Community Safety Partnership in the country) and the mismatch among partners organizational boundaries. In order to address this problem in 2004 the Partnership reorganized its structure and Local Delivery Groups were created to determine and deliver the community safety agenda in each district area. For the 2005–2008 period the five priorities of the crime and disorder reduction strategy were cleaner and safer neighbourhoods, offender management and drug treatment, violence and vulnerability, young people and the reduction of gang violence (Birmingham Community Safety Partnership, 2005). From Table 11.3 it can be seen that the importance of the quality of the built environment in the perception of safety had been recognized. Indeed, initiatives aimed at having cleaner streets and neighbourhoods can play an important role in the level of safety perceived by inhabitants.

In Table 11.3 we can see the top priorities of the strategies adopted by the Partnership in the three periods. Comparing this information with that in Table 11.2 it can be noticed how the strategy is build upon the results of the audit. Indeed, on the one hand car crime was a citizen's priority until 2001 and it was also a strategy priority for the first period only. On the other hand, drug-related crime and young people (both as offenders and as victims) have been a priority for citizens since 2001 and have also always been a priority for the Partnership's strategies.

As the problem linked to the 'reassurance gap' emerged from the beginning of both the strategy periods 2002–2005 and 2005–2008, strategies were focused on the fear of crime with 'supporting victims and public reassurance' and 'cleaner and safer neighbourhoods' respectively. Recent polls highlighted that among the residents of the ward Aston the main cause for the feeling of insecurity was 'fly-tipping and litter' (Birmingham Community Safety Partnership, 2005). Through its 'Re:generate' programme Birmingham Community Safety Partnership has made use of the latest technology (GIS and GPRS) to map perception and to tackle the fear of crime at its root causes.

11.5.3 Youth Offending Service

Birmingham Youth Offending Service (YOS) is a partnership between Birmingham Social Services, National Probation Service – West Midlands, West Midlands Police, Birmingham Education Department and Birmingham Health Authority (http://www.birmingham-yot.org.uk). The overall aim of the YOS is to prevent offending and re-offending by children and young people in the city. Birmingham YOS is the largest in the country. With over 300 employees, it is divided into five multi-agency teams across the city and four specialist YOTs (Youth Offending Teams) (Intensive Supervision and Surveillance Programme (ISSP), Youth Inclusion Support Team (YIST), Inappropriate Sexual Behaviour (ISB) and Bail and Remand) based on the city council wards, which deliver a range of interventions to young people. Each team includes members from a broad range of backgrounds among which are social workers, YOT officers, probation officers, police officers, drugs workers, voluntary workers and mentors. They work together to address all the factors that can contribute to the risk of offending behaviour, from poor educational attainment to drug abuse and from lack of family support to sexual or health problems.

The teams work in a number of ways: by confronting young people with the consequences of their (offending) behaviour, by offering young people new skills and opportunities, by supporting families in taking responsibility for their children and by ensuring that court orders are proportionate to the seriousness of the crime (Birmingham Youth Offending Service, 2004a). The work carried out by the YOS can be seen as an example of how a repressive measure – i.e. a court sentence – can be transformed into a preventive measure (to prevent re-offending) thanks to the partnership approach which has once more proved to be highly successful.

As with many other recent safety-oriented initiatives, the YOS was set up by the national government under the 1998 Crime and Disorder Act. Birmingham YOS is considered quite successful, particularly for its methods of intervention and for intervening earlier in youth crime. The initial budget has increased by three times thanks to entrepreneurial management which has been able to attract different kind of funds and grants. In the year 2004/05 the total direct funding of the YOS Birmingham was £9,881,000, almost 20 per cent of which came from grant funding streams (Birmingham Youth Offending Service, 2004b).

A negative aspect of the YOS is that the organization can work only with young offenders to prevent re-offending – it cannot target those young people who are at risk of offending but are not yet offenders.

The Youth Inclusion and Support Programme (YISP) established in October 2003 is an initiative aimed at preventing children aged 8–13 years from committing crimes and entering into the criminal justice system. Facilitated by the Youth Inclusion Support Team (YIS Team), comprising of family support workers, programme coordinators and a Development Board, the YISP operates citywide in response to referrals from a range of statutory agencies. Some of the initiatives of the YISP are the YOS Activity Programme, the Looked After children prevention service and the Prevention Through Sport initiative. All these interventions are targeted at prioritizing young people who fall into specifically defined risk factor categories, but they are also available to children living in the locality of schemes around the city. Children referred to the Programme and its subsidiary initiatives are closely monitored and supported by the YIS Team and its multi-agency partners.

Best practice 1: ISSP

The Intensive Supervision and Surveillance Programme (ISSP) is considered the most robust community programme available for young offenders in England and Wales (Moore et al., 2004). The targets of the programme are persistent young offenders or those young offenders who have committed more serious offences. In 2001 the national government initiated this programme with the specific aim of tackling young persistent offenders, that is to say the 3 per cent of young offenders who commit 25 per cent of youth crime. The special commitment of national government is also supported by an economic argument; indeed, to keep a young offender in custody is more expensive than to keep him/her in the community.

ISSP has a multi-agency approach and combines supervision with surveillance in an attempt to ensure the programme completion and to bring some discipline to young offenders' lives. The ultimate aim of the programme is to reduce the frequency and seriousness of their offending (Moore et al., 2004). The Youth Offending Service is responsible for delivering ISSPs.

An ISSP lasts six months and is divided into two parts: in the first three months there is intensive supervision (25 hours per week), whilst in the second three months supervision is reduced (with a minimum of five hours per week). On completion of an ISSP the young person will continue to be supervised for the remaining period of the Supervision Order. A key element of the programme is community surveillance, which ensures that the offenders are aware that their behaviour is being closely monitored. This helps to give more structure to young people's lives, which have often been chaotic.

In the period April–December 2004, 132 people started the ISSP in Birmingham and Solihull with 58 per cent of them successfully completing the programme. The core elements of the programme, which employs around 30 staff members, are supervision and surveillance. *Supervision* takes different forms. Education is provided if the young person is not at school, training is provided for young people over 16 years old and assistance is sometimes given to find a job. Moreover, each young person also attends two hours of reparation per week in order to make indirect reparation to the community in which they live. Other elements of the supervision include 'one-to-one offence confrontation work', family support, drug awareness and/or treatment, help with accommodation and special activities such as football, music and drama. *Surveillance* takes the form of tagging (electronic monitoring of the young person) and tracking (all young people are tracked whilst on the programme).

Even if an official evaluation of the ISSP does not yet exist, the case of Birmingham can be considered a success story. Indeed, a preliminary evaluation carried out by Oxford University[4] indicates that Birmingham ISSP led to a reduction of 66 per cent in the number of recorded offences committed by those young people who were evaluated (looking at six months prior to ISSP and six months post-ISSP). Moreover, those who continued re-offending committed less serious crimes and with lower frequency. One of the most positive aspects of the Birmingham ISSP is that the young offender involved in the programme can, during special activities such as football or drama playing, stop behaving as he/she 'has to' in the gangs and start to be him/herself. This is considered to be one of the crucial elements in reducing youth crime.

Best practice 2: Safer School Partnership

The Safer School Partnership (SSP) is a joint initiative between the Department for Education and Skills and the Youth Justice Board. Launched in September 2002, the programme aims at reducing problem behaviour by young people both in and around schools, and improving schools as places to learn (Bhabra et al., 2004). The programme provides a well-focused approach to addressing the high level of crime and antisocial behaviour committed by and against children and young people in and around schools.

The SSP involves support of a dedicated full-time police officer based in a selected secondary school and in some instances its feeder primary schools. The role of this officer is to work in partnership with children, young people and school staff. Its role differs very much from existing and traditional police work within schools, where police officers undertake an essentially teaching role. Taking a more operational policing approach enables the police officer to become more proactive in working with partners to reduce truancy and exclusion, victimization and antisocial behaviour within the school and its community, to identify and work with children at risk of becoming victims or offenders, to ensure full-time education of young offenders and to support school staff in dealing with incidents (Bhabra et al., 2004).

A successful example of the SSP in Birmingham is the Holte School, a comprehensive school educating boys and girls in the age range 11–16. There are more than 900 pupils at the school, the majority of whom have English as an additional language. Located in the ward of Aston, one of the poorest of Birmingham, the Holte School had problems with truancy, bullying and other antisocial behaviour. Since the school joined the SSP programme and became part of the Behaviour Improvement Programme, it has successfully reduced the number of episodes involving antisocial behaviour; moreover, truancy has been reduced and the overall educational attainment of the pupils has improved. Most of this success is due to multi-agency work. The School Police Officer especially has been able to involve the parents of the pupils also and this has proved to be quite effective in reducing antisocial behaviour (especially bullying) and in increasing the feeling of safety in and around the school. Nowadays the school is perceived as a safe place where the children can learn.

Best practice 3: St George's Post-16 Centre

St George's is an Education and Training Centre set up in 1996 as a partnership of the Diocesan Board of Education, the former South Aston and Newtown City Challenge, Birmingham City Council and City College Birmingham. The centre is financially sound and it offers a wide range of courses in response to local youngsters' needs and is used by more than 1,200 students. The centre has worked in partnership with the Youth Justice Board, the Youth Offending Service and Birmingham Children's Fund to respond to the more informal educational needs of local young people. Most of this work is focused around holiday programmes with specific summer activities.

The work carried out by St George's Centre can be considered a preventive measure against youth crime. Working together with the youngest children who are at most risk of offending, they try to teach them some discipline. Young people can go to the centre and play football or music or take part in other kinds of activities which prevent them being on the streets (often in a street-gang) and, therefore, at risk of offending or being a victim. Over the years the Centre has become increasingly involved in the local community, strengthening the relation with the local residents' group. The Centre is a good example of working in partnership and is quite successful, thanks to the employment of former criminals who can better understand the mentality of young offenders or young people at risk of offending.

A limitation of the Centre is due to the fact that they can work only with young people until they are 17, despite the fact that usually these youngsters also need assistance later at the age of 18–19. The St George's Centre begins the work of preventing young people to become criminals but someone (i.e. the local authority) has to look after them once they leave the Centre. Indeed, at that age they are still at risk of being on the streets and becoming criminals. Therefore there seems to be a serious gap regarding the provision of sound services for this age group.

11.6 Synthesis

11.6.1 Security Perception

In the most recent years total recorded crime in Birmingham has fallen dramatically. In the same period West Midlands Police has scored as the best-performing police force in the country. Nevertheless, the fear of crime has constantly increased since 2001. The safety paradox deriving from the mismatch between objective and perceived safety is currently one of the most difficult challenges the local authority has to face.

Since 1999 Birmingham Community Safety Partnership has carried out a Crime Audit every three years that highlights the main priorities that Birmingham's citizens would like to see tackled. Burglary, robbery, drug-related crimes and youth crime are issues that have always had the maximum importance for local inhabitants. Recently issues such as antisocial behaviour and the quality of the living environment have also become top priorities for the residents.

In recent years youth crime has emerged as one of the biggest problems concerning safety in Birmingham; the number of young people involved in crimes and antisocial behaviour both as offender and as victim has increased. The majority of crimes committed by young people is against other young people; bullying is a widespread phenomenon. Two important issues emerge from the 2005 Crime Audit data. Firstly, there has been a dramatic increase in the percentage of young offenders using drugs. Secondly youth crime, contrary to other crimes, is not an area-based problem but a phenomenon spread across all wards of Birmingham.

11.6.2 Urban Attractiveness and Spatial Behaviour

Since the 1980s the new City Centre Strategy has contributed to reshaping the central area of Birmingham, transforming it from an old and deserted post-industrial city centre to one of the most vibrant in the UK. Huge projects as the Selfridge store (the city's new landmark), the Bull Ring and the Mailbox have contributed to changing the identity and the image of the city centre dramatically. Nowadays it is a very attractive place to live, work and shop, with an enhanced level of safety.

On the other hand, in the last few decades little investment has taken place outside the central area. The consequence of this inner-city-focused spatial policy was that the poorest wards did not improve their situation and their image (and the related safety perception) worsened. It is no coincidence that a quarter of Birmingham's wards are in the top 5 per cent of the national Index of Multiple Deprivation.

11.6.3 Policy Response

Since the late 1990s safety has become the highest priority for Birmingham, as it has for many other UK cities and towns, due to the rise of people's concern about safety and the related special commitment by the national government. The result of this commitment was the creation of the Birmingham Community Safety Partnership as cooperation between the City Council, West Midlands Police and other local authorities involved in safety. The main aim of the Partnership is to pursue long-term actions to tackle the root causes of criminality and increase public confidence. After some initial difficulties, the multi-agency approach has proved to be very effective and indispensable in fighting crime.

Every three years since 1999 the Birmingham Community Safety Partnership has to produce, on the basis of the results of the Crime Audit, a Crime Reduction Strategy setting out the main priorities of the safety policy of the city. At the time of writing Birmingham Community Safety Partnership has a firm policy which combines repressive and preventive measures. Among the main priorities for the 2005–2008 strategy are measures to increase public reassurance and to reduce young criminality.

With regard to youth crime, the Birmingham Youth Offending Service (also a multi-agency organization) has been established with the specific aim of preventing offending and re-offending by children and young people.

11.6.4 Organizing Capacity with Respect to the Safety Plan

In the city's safety policy the *leadership* role is clearly played by Birmingham Community Safety Partnership. It provides those *strategic networks* among all local authorities involved in safety that form the multi-agency approach proved to be absolutely indispensable to fight crime.

While the *vision* in terms of safety has been provided by national government, the *strategy* to implement it has been developed by the City Council through Birmingham Community Safety Partnership. The national government's strong commitment provides the right *political support* needed to allow the City Council to put safety at the top of its agenda. *Societal support* is more difficult to evaluate. On one hand the growing feeling of insecurity in the population creates the basis for strong support for any initiative aimed at reducing crime. On the other hand, it also reduces the effectiveness of safety policy and police work in citizens' eyes. The private sector is generally not involved in Birmingham's safety policy; initiatives such as the Business Improvement Districts (BIDs), which also have an influence on the actual and perceived safety, could represent a first approach to the greater involvement of private actors in the safety policy of the city.

The *spatial economic conditions* of the city reflect the safety *performance* in the different parts of the city. Flourishing economic activity, a low unemployment rate and a vibrant image make the city centre a relatively safe place to live, work and shop. On the other hand, many wards still suffer from high unemployment rates and the few investments made in the last decades have contributed to worsening their image and the related perception of safety.

11.6.5 Recommendations

Two trends characterize the city of Birmingham at the time of writing. Firstly the city has previously had a highly segregated spatial policy which has resulted in a flourishing, vibrant and attractive city centre and many wards ranking high in the national Index of Multiple Deprivation. It is clear that there has been too much focus – from an economic point of view – on the central area and little attention to the other wards. Considering Birmingham's situation at the beginning of the 1980s it is clear that this extreme focus on the city centre was necessary. The fact that nowadays Birmingham has a positive national and international image is due to the new City Centre Strategy elaborated in the 1980s. Nevertheless, it is now probably time to consider investments in other parts of the city also. Normally speaking a sound local economic base contributes to increasing the quality of the living environment and, therefore, the perceived safety.

The second trend concerns crime: while total recorded crime has been decreasing in the last few years, the fear of crime continues to grow. As we stated above, the city has invested a lot in improving its national and international image and has undoubtedly succeeded Nevertheless, it seems that less attention has been given to the communication of this improved quality of life (and less criminality) to the citizens. Probably too much has been invested in marketing at the external level and too little at the internal level. The city of Birmingham has been very effective in reducing crime but less effective in communicating this to its inhabitants. A marketing strategy more focused on the needs of local inhabitants would probably help to communicate the progress made by the city in terms of safety. Moreover, more involvement of the private sector in the safety policy could make it easier to reach the citizens. Initiatives such as the Business Improvement Districts can easily enhance the feeling of safety of those involved simply (i.e. shop owners) because they get to know what the city does for them.

Another important issue that has to be addressed by the city concerns the education system. On the one side, it offers an example of best practice in terms of safety policy (see the Holte School or St George's Centre). On the other hand, it also represents a dangerous bottleneck in the process undertaken by the Birmingham Community Safety Partnership of fighting crime at its root causes, especially with regard to youth crime. It seems indeed that the whole effort set up by Birmingham to reduce youth crime is effective for young people only until they are 16–17. Once they reach adulthood (18 years old) young people cannot take part in most of the programmes and initiatives that have helped to keep them away from the streets and from criminal activities. At this stage, the education system plays a fundamental role since it has to continue the work initiated by others. Indeed, at the age of 18 young people are still at risk of (re-) offending. Unfortunately colleges are not involved in Birmingham Community Safety Partnership's multi-agency approach. Head teachers of the colleges have a good deal of power over admission and if they refuse to accept young people with a criminal record there is the risk that these youngsters will be back on the streets (maybe in a street gang). This could jeopardize the good work undertaken by other organizations which by law can work only with teenagers. The lack of an organization to reunite the city's colleges makes it more difficult for the Birmingham Community Safety Partnership to face this issue, since they have to deal with each school independently.

A final remark is based on the fact that both the City Council and the Birmingham Community Safety Partnership should be prepared for a possible change in central government policy. Indeed, at the moment the whole safety policy is based on a huge (also financially speaking) commitment by national government. It is advisable to look after the financial sustainability of the safety strategy and to think about a 'worst-case scenario' option in which the existing or new government decides to shift its focus from safety to other issues.

Notes

1 The Index of Multiple Deprivation (IMD) is a national index constructed by combining data on income, employment, health deprivation and disability, education, housing and accessibility to services.

2 There were two main changes in the counting rules. Firstly certain offences were 'added up' rather differently, to reflect that there may be a number of separate, unrelated victims, of what would previously have been described as one continuous offence. Secondly, from April 1998 new categories of recording were included in the crime figures for the first time (Birmingham Community Safety Partnership, 2002b).

3 Birmingham is one of those cities that do not have large shopping centres located at the edge of the urban area: almost all shopping capacity of the city is located in the city centre.

4 At the moment of writing this evaluation has not yet been published.

Chapter 12

The Case of Gera

12.1 Introduction

In this case study, we focus on the social security in the city of Gera. Section 12.2 gives a concise profile of this urban region. In Section 12.3 we deal with the perception of security in Gera and the possible causes of feelings of insecurity. Next, in Section 12.4, we will go into the related spatial behaviour of local inhabitants. Section 12.5 goes into policy reactions regarding urban insecurity. In this section we will give specific attention to some *best practices*. Our focus for Gera is on problems related to tackling youth crime in the deprived area of Bieblach with special attention for the role of the Youth Station. Finally, Section 12.6 presents conclusions and some recommendations.

12.2 Profile of Gera

12.2.1 Population: A Historical but Declining City

Gera is a German city of approximately 107,000 inhabitants (Thüringer Landesamt für Statistik, 2004). It is located in the heart of Germany, in the federal state of Thuringia, between the cities of Leipzig and Erfurt, the latter city being the capital of Thuringia (see Figure 12.2). With its location close to the intersection between the two motorways A9 Berlin-München and A4 Dresden-Frankfurt am Main and with Erfurt Airport within one hour's distance, Gera is relatively accessible. Compared with most other cities in this research, Gera is a quite small city, but within the federal state of Thuringia it is the largest city after Erfurt. The municipality of Gera extends over 152 km^2 and at 707 inhabitants per km^2 the population density is quite high (Stadt Gera, 2004).

Gera is an old city with a long history. One of the most fortunate times was the 1920s, the 'roaring twenties'. At that time, Gera was the third richest city in the whole German Empire. Although some of the buildings have deteriorated, this is still visible in the characteristic architecture of many buildings. But during the First and Second World Wars and the Communist era, the city of Gera deteriorated and new, grey, high-rise apartment buildings became part of Gera's identity as well. A large share (35–50 per cent) of the citizens lives in these areas. A good example of an area with high-rise apartment buildings is the borough of Bieblach. Bieblach, divided into Bieblacher Hang and Bieblach-Ost, is the 'home base' of the Youth Station, one of the focus points of this case study.

Figure 12.1 Geographical position of Gera in Europe

In the last decade, the population of Gera has been decreasing rapidly. In the period 1998–2003, for example, the total population decreased by 8 per cent (Thüringer Landesamt für Statistik, 2004). This population decline is due to both a negative natural growth and a net out-migration from the city. Every year hundreds of citizens, mostly young people, leave Gera to look for better job opportunities in the western part of Germany. The population composition is characterized by a gap in the age band 25–30 years, meaning that there are relatively few people in this age band. The reason for this gap is that many people aged between 25–30 are moving away in search for better job opportunities. This is a threat for both economic and future population development.

Most of the inhabitants of Gera have German nationality. Only 1.4 per cent of the inhabitants are foreign (Thüringer Landesamt für Statistik, 2004). This percentage is

Table 12.1 Demographic data

Population	2002	2003
Surface in km²	152	152
Inhabitants per km²	711	707
Population	108,082	107413
Population development 1998–2003		–7.74%
Foreigners, percentage	1.37%	
In-migration	2741	
Out-migration	4039	
Net migration	–1298	
Migration as % of population	–1.20%	
Births	732	
Deaths	1256	
Natural growth	–524	
Education (% of total population)		
% primary school	24.80%	25.40%
% secondary school	35.30%	36.90%
% high school/prof. education	15.10%	15.50%
% other	24.80%	22.20%

Sources: Thüringen Landesamt für Statistik, 2004 and Gera Stadt, 2004.

quite low, especially compared to other cities in this SecurCity research. Part of the foreign population consists of *Aussiedler* (evacuees) – people who migrated from Russia, and who officially have German nationality because their ancestors were German. The fact that they have lived in Russia for such a long time means there are difficulties with integration.

12.2.2 Administrative System

Germany is a democratic parliamentary federal state. The Federal Government possesses the principal legislative competences. It is built up out of 16 federal states (*Länder*) of which Thuringia is one. The federal states have a great deal of autonomy. They have most of the executive power. They also have responsibility for the organization and functioning of local government and for housing, urban and regional development. Every four years a new parliament for the federal state is elected (van den Berg et al., 1993). The most recent elections were in June 2004.

After central government and the federal state, the third administrative tier is that of local government. There are three types of local government: the municipality (*Gemeinde*), the '*Kreis*' and the autonomous city (*kreisfreie Stadt*). In principle the municipality is the basis of local government. They fulfil tasks primarily concerned with their own territory. But when their municipal scale is too small for certain tasks,

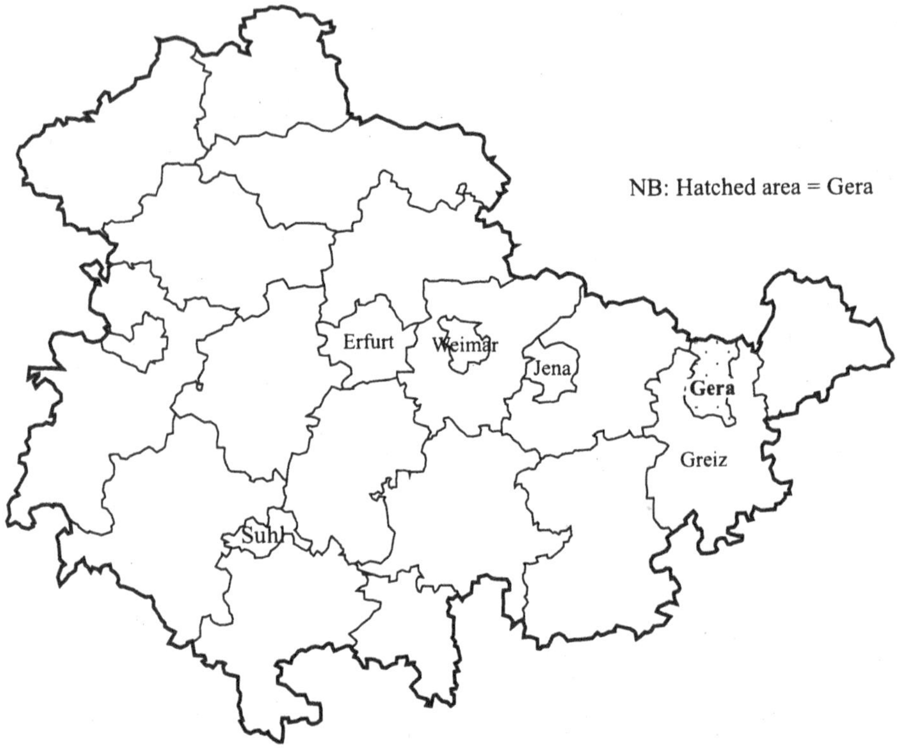

Figure 12.2 Map of Gera in Thuringia

these tasks are performed in partnership with other municipalities. These (mandatory) partnerships are called '*Kreise*'. Next to that, there are also cities which are large enough (in population size, economic position, etc.) to perform all local administration tasks themselves. This form of local government is called the autonomous city (*kreisfreie Stadt*) (van den Berg et al., 1993). Gera is such an autonomous city. It is divided into 40 boroughs, but these boroughs do not have any autonomy. The tasks of the city are performed by the local government, which in Gera consists of four political parties (CDU, PDS, SPD, *Arbeit für Gera*). There is no single coalition in Gera, but for every political theme such as youth care, economic development, etc, new coalitions are formed.

The administrative system of the police is different than that of the state administrative system. The Gera police district falls under the authority of the federal state of Thuringia. This police district is divided in four police regions: Police Inspection North, Police Inspection South, Police Inspection Greiz and Police Inspection Altenburger Land. The city of Gera lies in two of these police regions. About 75 per cent of the city belongs to Police Inspection North, the rest belongs to Police Inspection South. These two police regions do not only cover the city of Gera, but also the wider region.

12.2.3 Economy and Employment

Gera used to be a typical industrial city. Until 1990 industry's main branches were textile industry, machinery industry, electronics and mechanics/optical industry. Most citizens at that time were working in industry or agriculture. From the early 1990s the local economy changed. Industry declined and the service economy became more important. The most important branches in the early twenty-first century are the service sector, the motor industry, machinery industry, optical industry and environmental technology (Stadt Gera, 2004). Most of these sectors are still strongly linked with industry.

Table 12.2 Economic figures for the city of Gera, 1991 and 2001

Economy	1991	2001
Employees	71,700	51,700
Unemployment	–	17.4%
GDP per person, €	–	19,340
Disposable household income per inhabitant, €	–	14,749
Branches	Textile industry	Service sector
	Machinery industry	Motor industry
	Electronics	Machinery industry
	Mechanics/optical	Optical industry
		Environmental technology

Source: Thüringen Landesamt für Statistik, 2004.

The economic situation in Gera, in common with the rest of Thuringia, is not really flourishing. In 2002 there were in total 50,000 employees in Gera (Thüringer Landesamt für Statistik, 2004). The largest employer was the hospital with 2,000 employees. In addition, there were a few medium-sized companies of 100–500 employees, but most of the companies in Gera were small. In the last decade the number of employees has decreased almost every year. A consequence is that unemployment has been increasing and reached a high 18.5 per cent in 2004. Moreover, there are no signs of improvement in the near future (Thüringer Landesamt für Statistik, 2004). This poor economic situation has major consequences, both for the economy and for the society as a whole.

The disposable annual household income is €14,749 per inhabitant. This is average compared to other cities in Thuringia. Not only are the average household incomes quite low, the financial means of the City are quite low too. In last few years, the city ended the financial year with debts, which makes it even more difficult for the city to set up policies to stimulate the local economy and to improve the perceived safety.

12.2.4 Bieblach

This case study focuses on problems related to tackling youth crime in the deprived area of Bieblach, with special attention for the role of the Youth Station. The Bieblach district is situated in the east of Gera and consists of two neighbourhoods: Bieblach-Ost and Bieblacher-Hang. About 16,000 people live in this district, but this number is rapidly decreasing. Many (young) people are moving away to areas with better economic opportunities. The consequence is that there are high vacancy rates. In the high-rise apartment blocks that characterize the built environment of Bieblach, this causes feelings of insecurity. Since many residents of Bieblach are unemployed, often for a long time, there are many social and safety problems. The hopelessness and the lack of economic opportunities cause social problems and decrease the social cohesion in the district.

12.3 The Perception of Safety in Gera

12.3.1 Crime Development

In 2003 there were 99.7 crime reports per 1,000 inhabitants in Gera (Veröffentlichungen BKA, LKA zur PKS, 2004). According to the *Landespolizei Thüringen Polizeidirektion Gera* (2004) this crime rate was a little lower: 87.0 in the same year. Compared to other cities in the region, Gera has a very low crime rate. Erfurt, for example, had a crime rate of 132.1 and Jena 104.1 per 1,000 inhabitants in the same period (Landespolizei Thüringen Polizeidirektion Gera, 2004). Compared to other European cities like Leeds, Glasgow and The Hague as well, the crime rate for Gera is very low.

The crime-solving rate in Gera is very high, almost 70 per cent. This applies not only to Gera, but the whole of Germany. The definition of the solution of a crime is one of the reasons for such an exceptionally high rate. In Germany, the solving rate differs from other European countries in that it also includes mior criminal offences such as fare dodging, ignoring red traffic signs, etc. These crimes are relatively easy to solve.

Since 1995 the crime rate has been more or less stable in Gera: in the period 1995–1999 the crime rate had decreased, but after this period crime increased a little again (Veröffentlichungen BKA, LKA zur PKS, 2004). This is in contrast with a downward trend in crime rates in most European cities. There seems to be a convergence of crime rates going on in European cities: cities with relatively high crime rates show decreasing crime figures, cities with relatively low crime rates show increasing crime figures.

According to the police, organized crime is the biggest threat to the safety of the inhabitants of Gera. The citizens, however, are often hardly aware of the existence of organized crime. Therefore, they do not feel threatened by it. What troubles citizens and what influences their feelings of safety are burglary, theft, demolition, fare dodging, and physical injury (Landespolizei Thüringen Polizeidirektion Gera, 2004). Another problem in Gera is crime related to extremism, both right and left wing. Right-wing extremism is more visible to the population (because of demonstrations and the intimidating behaviour of its followers) and therefore this may be more threatening. The presence of right-wing extremism in this area might seem very strange, because the share of foreigners in the total population is only 1.4 per cent in Gera (Landesamt für Statistik, 2004). However, the same phenomenon was visible during the 1980s in France, where the right-wing party *Front National* gained many voters in districts with low shares of foreigners in particular. It appears to be the irrational fear of a possible threat from criminal foreigners that made residents vote for the *Front National* (Mayer, 1986).

12.3.2 Youth Crime

One of the major problems related to crime is youth crime. In 2001 almost 40 per cent of all crime was committed by people under the age of 21 and this share is rather high (Veröffentlichungen BKA, LKA zur PKS, 2004a). Most youth crime is related to theft and criminal damage. Therefore, youth crime is now one of the main priorities for the Gera police (North Division). Special measures have been taken with the establishment of the Youth Station; an office where police, public prosecution and youth legal aid cooperate in judging young offenders. It seems that this extra political and police attention on youth crime is effective, because the number of offenders under the age of 21 decreased in 2004.

12.3.3 Safety Perception

Although Gera is a relatively safe city, the perceptions of citizens about safety are poor. All persons interviewed indicated that the elderly in particular are afraid to go out on the streets in the evening. This fear is spatially spread all over the city, but is particularly strong on public transport. The fear is often caused by young people grouping together and drinking alcohol in the streets or on public transport. They are perceived to be a threat.

One important reason for this increase in fear of crime in Gera has to do with the political changes since 1989. During the Communist period, there was a strong police presence on the streets. This gave people the feeling that they were being controlled, but it also gave a feeling of security. If criminal events took place most people did not know because the media was not allowed to report it. After the fall of the Berlin Wall the whole situation changed. There were fewer police on the streets which meant that criminals could more easily commit crimes without being caught. At the same time, newspapers and TV programmes reported more crimes because their reports were no longer censored. For the population of former East Germany it appears that crime has risen tremendously since 1989.

Another reason for the increasing fear of crime has to do with the socio-economic situation in Gera. As stated, Gera has a difficult economic situation with high unemployment rates. This can have an (indirect) influence on safety in two different

Table 12.3 Data on crime and safety perception in Gera, 2000–2003

Crime and safety	2000	2001	2002	2003	Growth 2000–2003
All recorded crime	9,548	9,821	10,706	10,773	12.8%
Crime per 100,000 inhabitants	8,323	8,704	9,739	9,967	19.8%
Solved, %	65.7%	63.8%	66.2%	69.3%	
Suspects younger than 14 years	414	343	238	240	–42.0%
Suspects between 14–18 years	770	719	706	683	–11.3%
Suspects between 18–21 years	668	639	651	644	–3.6%
Total offenders under age of 21	1,852	1,701	1,595	1,567	–15.4%
Total % suspects under age of 21	40%	–	–	–	–
Types of crime					
shoplifting		22.10%	21.40%		
theft (serious)		3.40%	12.70%		
financial misappropriation (various)		17.20%	27.30%		
vandalism		12.80%	9.10%		

Sources: Veröffentlichungen BKA, LKA zur PKS, 2004: Gera Stadt, 2004: Auswertung Jugendstation Gera 2001–2002: Polizei Direction Gera, 2001.

ways. Firstly, high unemployment brings a lack of perspective; it makes people feel desperate and futureless. These negative feelings may be expressed through (domestic) violence or through a growing popularity of right-/left-wing extremism. These negative feelings also make people less interested in their living environment. Because of their personal problems, they do not want to invest time and attention in their community and social cohesion breaks down as a result. Secondly, the economic situation has a negative influence on safety because many (young) people move away, looking for jobs. The community falls apart, causing a second threat for social cohesion.

12.4 Urban Attractiveness and Spatial Behaviour

12.4.1 Urban Attractiveness

The city of Gera lies in an attractive environment; it is a widespread city surrounded by forests and fields in the hilly environment of Thuringia. The city itself has a rich history characterized by both very prosperous and very difficult times. This is can be seen in the varying communities in the city. On the one hand is the old inner city, with some very attractive architecture: although some of these buildings need renovation, the atmosphere in this part of the city can be characterized as friendly and orderly. On the other hand there are the suburbs like Bieblach and Lusan with high-rise and drab apartment buildings. Many houses are left vacant because of population outflow to the western part of Germany. These areas are perceived to be less attractive. The attractiveness of the living environment in the city is threatened by the loss of daily facilities. Shopping facilities are disappearing in the suburbs because of the population decrease.

12.4.2 Spatial Behaviour

As already noted, there is a strong outflow of people moving westwards. The high unemployment, caused by the structural economic problems, forcespeople to seek work elsewhere. Young people in particular are becoming frustrated by the lack of economic opportunities and are moving to former West German states, where the unemployment rates are significantly lower.

This effect on the spatial behaviour of the citizens of Gera therefore has little to do with perceptions of insecurity. However, the people who stay in the city do adapt their spatial behaviour as well. They tend not to go out in the streets after dark and are afraid of opening the door to strangers. If they go out, they tend to avoid certain places or public transport. This behaviour is a reaction on the feelings of insecurity some people have. Older people in particular feel intimidated and frightened by groups of young people hanging around and by the frequent articles about crime in the local media.

12.5 Policy Reactions

A major disadvantage for the urban government of Gera is represented by its financial situation. There is a lack of financial means because the city has debts. Although the growth rate of the debts is decreasing, the total debts are still increasing annually. One of the causes is the problematic economic situation in the region and the related high unemployment rates. At the same time Gera holds on to its image as a 'social city': for example, all working women with children are supported by the urban government in childcare costs. Although this accounts for a substantial part of the annual budget, it is important for the citizens and therefore for the local government. Because of the disadvantageous financial situation, the city of Gera is more than usually dependent on the federal state, the federal government and on the European Commission. The city receives subsidies and credits from these institutions. Additional financial means also come from public/private partnerships.

The problems with the financial situation also have implications for urban policies in general and safety policy in particular. The number one political priority in Gera (and in the rest of Thuringia) is economic development and the ongoing fall of unemployment. A strong and stable economy with low unemployment rates is essential for urban development in general, but also for safety. Maslow's hierarchy of needs shows that people first need to satisfy their physiological needs like hunger, thirst and housing. The second step in Maslow's pyramid is security (see Chapter 2, Figure 2.2), but people will not pay much attention to security unless their physiological needs are fulfilled and these needs can only be fulfilled when (most) citizens have a job and an income to obtain food, water and accommodation.

Gera's economic policy is focused on attracting and retaining large manufacturing companies. It is aimed at producers of car components, because there are several production sites of, for example, VW, BMW, Opel and Porsche in the wider region. Large manufacturers are likely to provide jobs and may attract other smaller related companies or create spin-offs. A large producer of car components could favour Gera above other places because of its geographical location – near an intersection of two important national motorways and near the regional airport of Erfurt. However, Gera faces competition from other cities in the region in this respect.

Because of the political prioritizing of the economy there has not been much political attention on safety in Gera to date. This is changing, however, because the municipality had realized that safety is important in attracting companies and in retaining citizens. This attention on safety is at an early stage and there is no official safety policy (yet). However, both the city and the federal state have initiated several projects that contribute to decreasing youth crime and thereby to improving safety perceptions among the citizens of Gera. For example, a law has been passed that makes it possible to fine people who throw litter on the streets and a *Bürgerbeamte* (a kind of district officer) has been engaged to improve the relationship between citizens and police. Three projects in particular are considered best practices by many of our discussion partners in tackling the problems in Bieblach and especially problems regarding youth crime. First there is the Youth Station, which has proved to be very successful in keeping young children from becoming persistent offenders. The second project is the *JKPP*, which tries to prevent crime and offences committed by (young) children. And last there is the Bieblach District Office: an intermediate stage between the district and the municipality in matters regarding the redevelopment of the area, etc. The best practices in this respect are discussed in in turn.

Best practice 1: Youth Station

The Youth Station (*Jugendstation*) was set up after its introduction by the Minister of Justice of the federal state of Thuringia in 2001. The Minister had seen a project in Stuttgart *(Haus der Jugendrechts*) and decided it could be helpful in tackling the safety problems related to youth crime in the borough of Bieblach in Gera.

The Youth Station started as a pilot project. Three institutions were accommodated in one building: the police, the youth legal aid institution and public prosecution. These three institutions cooperate in order to decrease youth crime (see Figure 12.3). The aim of this project is to accelerate the trial process of people under the age of 21 who have committed a crime and to prevent them from becoming persistent offenders at an early stage. A quick trial and judgment improves the effectiveness of the punishment: the young offenders are directly confronted with the consequences of their behaviour (instead of waiting months for their trial), which may prevent them from committing more crime. The geographical proximity of the institutions in one building leads to a faster and therefore more effective trial process, because the officers involved can easily contact each other about a specific young offender. This is a form of preventive policy, because the institutions aim to prevent young offenders from becoming persistent offenders.

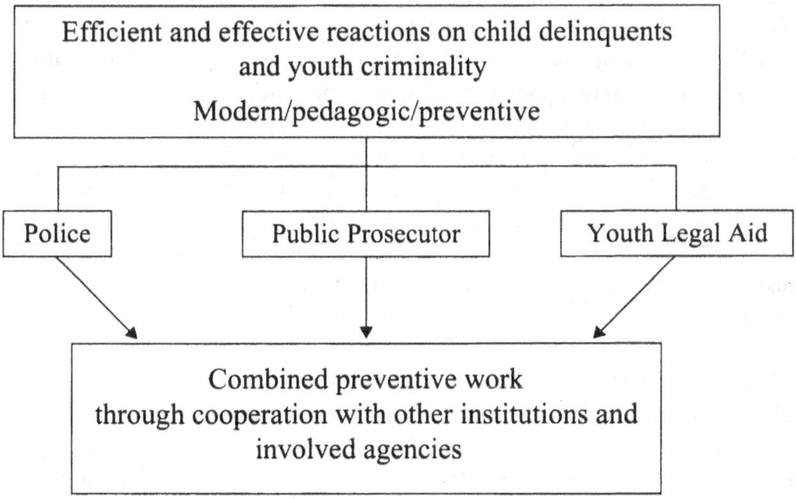

Figure 12.3 Structure of Youth Station Gera

In the Youth Station project, the police arrest children who commit a crime. The police have become stricter in warning and arresting young people. The young offenders are contacted by a youth legal aid officer who offers them and their parents legal aid. They can also bring them into contact with other social services like the *Algemeine Soziale Dienst* (General Social Service), *SOS Kinderdorf International* or the *JKPP* (Youth Crime Prevention Program), etc. Because public prosecution is directly involved in this project, the young offender can be sure that he or she will receive trial and judgment quickly. There are no official outcomes of the performance of the Youth Station project at the time of writing, because it has only been running for three years. However, anecdotal evidence from the officers involved suggests it is a successful project: cooperation is satisfactory and the project seems to be having a positive influence on the number of youth crime and the number of persistent offenders. Since 2000 the number of under age offenders for the age bands up to 14-years-old and between 14–18 and 18–21 has decreased (by up to 42 per cent for the 0–14 age band) (Veröffentlichungen BKA, LKA zur PKS, 2004). The project also has some weak points, however. First of all, the project only involves those children within Police Division North and within the city of Gera who are involved in criminal activities and not all children from the wider region. Young offenders from outside the city or the police division cannot be sent to the Youth Station. This seems to be a consequence of a lack of cooperation between police divisions (who have, as already noted, other territorial division than that of the city). There is hardly any cooperation between the police divisions. Secondly, the project does not deal with children with alcohol or drugs problems or who are involved in serious crimes like murder. These children are most in need of extra help to prevent them for committing crime again. A third point is that the employers of the several institutions are less productive at this Youth Station than they would be in their normal offices, because of the personal and intensive support required for every child. This might be a problem for the Youth Station's future work. When the workload at the main office of one of the institutions becomes too great (which is not a hypothetical situation for public prosecution), the head of that institute may decide to withdraw their officer from the Youth Station.

The future of the Youth Station in Gera is quite uncertain. It started in 2001 as a pilot study and was supposed to be an example for other cities in Thuringia. However, although the pilot phase of the project is over, the project still only operates in Gera and not in other cities. The project is supposed to continue in Gera. Personnel and financial support is still given by the three institutions and the city government, but the subsidy from the federal state is threatened by a changing political situation and a resulting decreased political support for the Youth Station.

Best practice 2: JKPP (Youth Crime Prevention Programme)

As well as the Youth Station, there is another project aimed at diminishing youth crime and preventing young criminals for becoming persistent offenders: JKPP, *Jugendkriminalität Präventionsprojekt* (Youth Crime Prevention Programme). This project started in 1997. Since 2000 it is located in and supported by *SOS-Jugendhilfen* Gera (part of SOS Children's Village[1]). The aim of this project is to give social help to young offenders (up to the age of 14) and their parents. The relationship with the Youth Station is that JKPP receives its information about children committing crime from the Youth Station. The difference between the Youth Station and the JKPP is that the former aims to decrease youth crime by speeding up the trial process while the JKPP aims to decrease youth crime by offering social care. A project staff member approaches the parents of the child for a free consultation about the situation. A meeting with the JKPP is not obligatory, but most of the time parents are interested in a conversation with an outsider who is a professional. During conversations with the parents it often appears that there are more social problems in the family. The JKPP helps the family to find solutions to the problems, gives information about education and raising children, and provides names of other institutions that may be helpful.

As well as this personal approach to the parents and the child itself, there are also other initiatives taken by the JKPP. They pffer information about crime and aggression to children in the form of videos, anti-aggression training, etc., not just to children who have already committed a crime, but also in schools. The JKPP also offers information to, for example, teachers about dealing with criminal behaviour and aggression in children. It is very active in preventing any kind of criminal behaviour among young children. The ideology is that it is better to prevent at a young age, than to 'cure' when it is already too late. At the time of writing the project still focuses on children between 11 and 14 years, but there are offenders who are even younger. Until now, legislation has prohibited approaching children younger than 11, but this might change in the future. One of the institutes that influence this legislation is the Crime Prevention Advisory Committee (*Kriminal Präventiviteit Beirat*). One of the staff members of the JKPP is involved in this, and other, committees.

Best practice 3: Bieblach district office

The district office is part of a federal state programme called 'Social City'. This is a long-term programme aimed at addressing social, physical and economic problems in deprived areas. Bieblach is one of the project areas. In order to communicate the redevelopment plans to the citizens, to receuve feedback from the citizens and to support the citizens with extra social help, the district office was established. The district office is partly subsidized by the urban government and partly by the federal state. It is staffed by a district office manager with help mainly from volunteers. The office building is facilitated by the housing corporation. It functions as a place where citizens can meet the district office manager with questions and worries about spatial and social developments in their district and they can make requests for further improvements. Questions and comments are made about, for example, litter on the streets, information about municipal renovation plans, nuisance, the possibility of playing cards or attending English courses, cycling paths, etc. There is a small budget to finance the residents's ideas and plans. The district office communicates all plans and projects initiated by the city and the federal state to redevelop the district socially, economically and physically, through newsletters and meetings. The residents are directly involved in the development of their own district: their ideas and requests are taken into account by the local and federal government. The district office manager has a central role between the citizens of Bieblach and the local and federal government.

Besides, the district office also facilitates the '*Deutscher Familienverband*' (German Familiy Associate). A staff member of this organization is available once or twice a week and helps the families in the district with all kinds of social problems, such as advice on education, sending schoolchildren on holiday during the summer, care for the elderly, giving information (for example, with videos) on all kinds of social topics, having discussions with children (education), etc.

The aim of district office is not directly to reduce crime rates but rather on addressing social problems and informing people on how to deal with physical changes and economic problems. Involving the residents in the process of development and implementation and providing extra social services to address their personal problems strengthens social cohesion in the district and therefore also positively influences feelings of safety. Particularly in a district where the population is decreasing and the vacancy rates of apartments are high, this appears to be very important. The district office is chosen as a best-practice because of its participation with the residents (best seen in the participation numbers of official and unofficial resident meetings) and its contribution to improving social cohesion.

12.6 Synthesis

12.6.1 Safety Perceptions

The city of Gera is an old city with a rich history. It has had some very prosperous but also some very unfortunate eras. Currently the city is going through some difficult times due to an economic recession accompanied by high unemployment rates. This has implication for safety perceptions and fear of crime has been growing among the residents of Gera. In reality, Gera can still be seen as one of the safest cities in Germany: crime rates are relatively low and rates of solving crimes are relatively high. Within Gera there are a few areas with higher levels of (social) problems, such Bieblach, but there are no strong spatial concentrations of crime, but feelings of insecurity are relatively high in Gera. The elderly in partiuclar feel threatened at night and on the public transport system, mainly due to young people hanging around in groups.

It is not only the economic situation that affects the safety perceptions, but also the historic situation – the transition from communism to liberalism has influenced safety perceptions. Before the fall of the Berlin Wall relatively few crimes occurred thanks to high police control in the streets. Moreover, if anything happened, it was not reported in the newspapers. But nowadays there is less police control and every incident is extensively presented in both the newspapers and on television. This gives many people the feeling that crime has increased tremendously and that the streets of Gera have become unsafe.

There also seems to be a strong relationship between the perceptions of insecurity and the poor economic situation. The lack of perspective related to high (long-term) unemployment rates cause social problems. Domestic violence, for example, is relatively high in Gera. The lack of economic perspective is also a source for sympathy for left- and right-wing extremism among some population groups, which is causing social unrest and fear as well.

12.6.2 Urban Attractiveness and Spatial Behaviour

In Gera there is an out-migration of people. Because of the lack of economic perspective, many (young) people move away and try their luck in cities in the western part of Germany, where the job opportunities are better. This form of spatial behaviour has nothing to do with safety but with attractiveness, and in this case especially with economic attractiveness. In addition, the outflow of people contributes to a decrease in urban attractiveness. In Bieblach, for example, the vacancy rates of apartments are very high. Many empty apartments in high-rise apartment blocks make the environment unattractive for residents, which is an impetus for more out-migration. In the end a vicious circle occurs where urban attractiveness only decreases and people move away. This is exactly what is going on in Gera, and especially in Bieblach.

12.6.3 Policy Reactions

The City of Gera does not have a specific safety policy. There are plans for designing a safety policy, but the problematic financial situation makes it more difficult to find financial means for implementing the policy. However, economic policy is more important than safety policy. Improving the economic development and decreasing the high unemployment rates is the main priority for the City of Gera. Gera's economic policy is focused on attracting and retaining big manufacturing companies, like producers of car components. Big manufacturing companies are likely to create jobs for the local population and may even attract new companies or create spin-offs. A strong and stable economic situation will improve urban development and will also have an effect on crime and safety perceptions.

Although there is no actual safety policy, several projects have been initiated to bring down the crime rates and to improve Gera's residents' feelings of safety. Three of these initiatives have been described in this case study as best practice because of their contribution to the safety situation. First, there is the Youth Station, where the police, public prosecution and youth legal aid work together to speed up the trial process in order to diminish youth crime and to prevent young criminals becoming persistent offenders. Extra attention on youth crime is very relevant in Gera, because 40 per cent of all crime is committed by minors. Related to the Youth Station is the JKPP (Youth Crime Prevention Programme). This is the second best practice example and this project tries to help children and their parents to get back on the right track again. The JKPP gives social help and, if more specialized help is required, has good contacts with other institutions. The third best practice is the Bieblach District Office, which functions as an intermediary between municipality and the residents regarding the redevelopment of the Bieblach district in an attempt to improve social cohesion.

12.6.4 Organizing Capacity with Respect to Safety Policy

We have seen that Gera does not have a safety policy. A clear vision on the desired development of safety – the basis of organizing capacity – is therefore lacking. The mayor can be seen as a leader in trying to get the topic on the political agenda. However, up to the time of writing this has appeared to be difficult. One of the reasons may be that political support for urban safety may be relatively low, not because safety is regarded as unimportant but because other topics such as, for example, economic development, have higher priorities. The difficult financial situation of the City of Gera may also influence political support for a safety policy. Societal support for safety may be higher, as fear of crime is believed to be rising. There is also a basis for strategic networks as in some individual, safety-related projects several involved actors are commonly addressing a specific safety problem. An example in this respect is the Youth Station. The required organizing capacity for a complex issue like safety policy is not (yet) optimal.

12.6.5 Recommendations

The best practices mentioned in this case study are good examples of projects aimed at decreasing crime rates and improving social cohesion. However, these projects are not part of a broader safety policy. For the City of Gera it would be good to integrate the various projects into a coherent safety policy. A coherent policy which integrates the various projects would have a larger effect on improving crime and safety than single projects. In addition, with a concrete safety policy it would be easier for the city to communicate a consistent message about crime reduction and improving safety to its inhabitants. For the City of Gera it is crucial to improve its economic development and this is also important for safety matters. Attracting companies and jobs, decreasing unemployment and increasing incomes will help to stop the vicious circle of people moving away and the districts becoming less attractive as places to live for the remaining residents.

Note

1 SOS Children's Village is an international children's welfare organization providing long-term care for orphans and children in need.

Chapter 13

The Case of Prague

13.1 Introduction

In this case study, we discuss the social security in the city of Prague, Czech Republic. Section 13.2 gives a concise profile of this urban region. In Section 13.3, we deal with possible causes of insecurity feelings within the city of Prague. Next, in Section 13.4, we will go into the related spatial behaviour of local inhabitants. Section 13.5 goes into policy reactions regarding urban unsafety. In this section we will give specific attention to some *best practices*. Finally, Section 13.6 presents conclusions and some recommendations.

13.2 Profile of Prague

13.2.1 Situation and Urban Development

The Czech Republic has a turbulent history. After the First World War, it formed the country Czechoslovakia, together with the current Slovakia. After the Second World War, Czechoslovakia came within the Soviet sphere of influence. For decades, the country had a communist regime. Massive demonstrations in November 1989 (known as the 'Velvet Revolution') were the starting point for dramatic political changes: the Soviet authority collapsed. Eventually, on 1 January 1993, Czechoslovakia was split up into Slovakia and the Czech Republic. Obviously, the changes brought about have had tremendous (socio-economic) impacts. Even today, the citizens of the Czech Republic are influenced by these past developments.

Since 1993 the population number of the Czech Republic appears to be more or less stable and is approximately 10.2 million (OECD, 2004). About 10 per cent of the total population lives in Prague, the capital of the country, located in the northwest.

The city of Prague had approximately 1.1 million citizens in 2003 with a population density of 2,300 persons per km^2 (City of Prague, 2003). Although the labour market in Prague attracts people from all over the country, the city has been losing population through migration since the mid-1990s as well. Especially the class of 'new rich' people moved to newly develop suburban districts just outside the municipal borders (Sykora and Cermak, 1998).

In the eighteenth century six independent urban units on both banks of the river Vltava were unified. Today, these former independent urban units form the six neighbourhoods of the city centre: Stare Mesto (Old Town), Josefov (the preserved part

Figure 13.1 Geographical position of Prague in Europe

of the former Jewish Town), Nove Mesto (New Town), Mala Strana (Lesser Town), Hradcany and Vysehrad. The latest population figures available indicated that about 57,000 citizens live in this area (Sykora and Cermak, 1998).

13.2.2 Economy and Employment

As stated, much has changed in the Czech Republic's economic situation since the fall of the Communist regime in 1989. One of the main economic changes is the large-scale privatization that took place. At first, this privatization resulted in high inflation rates (52 per cent in 1991), but they came down to below 10 per cent after a few years (Landenweb, 2004). The economy of the Czech Republic has grown strongly over the past decade: the GNP per capita increased from \$2,900 (around €2,150) in 1990

Figure 13.2 Map of the districts in the city of Prague

to $4,400 (around €3,300) in 1995 and $5,250 (around €3,900) in 2000 (Worldbank, 2004). The city of Prague is believed to contribute 22 per cent to the total GNP of the Czech Republic (City of Prague, undated (c)).

As in most Western economies, the economic structure in the Prague is dominated by the service sector. Regarding output shares, the largest economic sectors are commercial services, retail and repairs and public administration and services (City of Prague, 2003). The economic sectors of administration, education, healthcare/retail, catering, accommodation and services for business and finance are most important (City of Prague, 2003) for employment.

Unemployment in Prague is low. In the city of Prague, the unemployment rate was approximately 4 per cent of the labour population in 2002 and has been more or less stable over the past few years (City of Prague, 2003). National unemployment rates are significantly higher. In 2001, approximately 8.5 per cent of the Czech labour population was unemployed. In 2002, this number rose to 9.4 per cent (CNB, 2005). A major problem is unemployment among youth. It appears to be difficult for young people to find a job: up to 18 per cent of the labour population under the age of 25 was unemployed in 2003 (OECD, 2004).

Education levels of the population in Prague appear to be good. Approximately 22 per cent of the population older than 15 years in Prague has a college or university degree (City of Prague, 2004). Obviously there are differences between education levels in European cities, but this share of 22 per cent of the population of 15 years

Table 13.1 Demography and economy figures, Czech Republic and Prague

	Czech Republic	Prague
Population number, 2003	10.2 m	1.1 m
Population density, 2003	–	2,300
GNP per capita, €, 2000	3,900	–
Unemployment rate, 2002	9.4%	4.0%
Person older than 15 with university degree, %, 2003	10.0%	22.0%

and older having a college or university degree is not low. The share for the entire Czech Republic is 10 per cent (City of Prague, 2004).

13.2.3 Administration

The Czech Republic is divided into 14 administrative regions, which are often made up of several municipalities. These administrative regions have the autonomy to change certain regional legislation. The municipal border of the city of Prague coincides with an administrative region, giving the City of Prague more legislative power than other Czech cities. This sometimes seems to cause conflicts between the City of Prague and neighbouring municipalities regarding spill-over effects, for example, non-residents using urban facilities while not paying through taxes or stricter drug policies resulting in addicts moving to neighbouring municipalities.

The most recent elections in Prague were in 2002 at which time the 70 members of the Assembly of the City were elected. The Assembly selects the Mayor and the members of the City Council. Currently, the Assembly comprises ODS (Civic Democrats – 30 seats) and the ČSSD (Social Democrats – 12 seats), and some smaller parties (City of Prague, 2002). The departments of the City of Prague cover economy and finance, property affairs, regional and municipal issues (e.g. transport, education, social care and health, etc.), state administration execution in the field of area development and care, administrative issues, city development authority, internal services, internal audit and control and external affairs. Next to these urban departments there are additional governmental bodies important with respect to (social) safety matters: chief executive office, legal and law and crisis management (City of Prague, undated (c)). The two deputy mayors have common responsibility for safety: one for security and the other for crime prevention.

13.3 The Perception of Security in Prague

In Prague, as in other European cities, the gap between actual safety and perceived safety seems to be growing slowly. The actual safety situation seems to be improving, with crime figures coming down. At the same time, perceptions of safety appear to lack behind, although it is a very early conclusion on a situation which is only just changing.

13.3.1 Actual Security in Prague

As in other Eastern European cities and countries, crime took a strong upturn after the fall of the Berlin Wall. People became more free, restrictions less stringent and with a free media, more information about criminality became publicly available. This all has influenced crime and safety perceptions in the last decade. In Prague as well, crime increased after 1990, but in the last few years the crime statistics appear to show more or less stable figures. According to the experts, the safety situation in Prague does not differ significantly from any other large Western European city.

The total recorded number of incidents in 2003 was 999,000. This is approximately 97 crimes per 1,000 of the population. Compared to other (Western) European cities this seems to be lower than average. Related to the previous year (2002), the crime figure dropped by almost 3.7 per cent. Not all types of crime show the same development. Drug-related crime and the level of brutality for example seem to be decreasing, while 'traditional' and economic (white collar) criminality seem to be increasing (City of Prague, undated). Of course, crime rates do not always reflect reality, as not all crimes are reported. It is believed that the current crime figures represent approximately one-third of the total criminality. The outcomes of a public survey confirm this assumption (International Business and Research Services, 1999).

Table 13.2 Crime figures in Prague

	Prague
Recorded crime rate, 2003	999,000
Recorded crime rate per 1,000 inhabitants, 2003	97
Crime development 2002–2003, %	–3.70%

Looking at the crime recordings, one of the main problems in the city of Prague appears to be theft from and of cars. Approximately 42 per cent of the total recorded crime rate involves car crime (City of Prague, undated). As car crime is also one of the most visible types of crime, it is an important factor influencing safety perceptions. However, what is most often recorded may not be the most important actor influencing urban safety. At the Congress of Local Authorities in 2003, the Police of the Czech Republic presented an overview of the main crime problems in Prague, which according to them are juvenile delinquency, serious white-collar crime, terrorism, illegal migration and organized crime (Meeting of the Working Group of Consultants, 25 March 2003).

Juvenile delinquency often starts at an early the age in Prague, sometimes even at the age of 12. It involves petty crime, pickpocketing, car break-ins, etc. There are three supposed reasons why young people in Prague commit crime – boredom, need for extra money or under pressure from adults. For the first reason, boredom, there can be several underlying causes. In Prague there seem to be few leisure facilities for children and adolescents. One could think of playgrounds for the smaller children, sports fields and youth centres for the adolescents. As well as the fact that there is not much diversion for young people in Prague, they seem to be less well supervised by parents and adults. Societal changes since 1990 have meant that women are allowed take paid employment. Moreover, economic changes have meant that women were not only allowed to, but that they actually had to get a job to secure the household income. With both parents working, children receive less supervision. Another reason for youth crime is said to be the need for extra money. Drug use and gambling in particular are reasons for young people to need extra money. It is believed that a high percentage of all youth crime is related to drug use. The drug problem in the Czech Republic has increased. Previously, the nation was a transit country for drug runners and dealers, but with the increase in the welfare level, the use of drugs has increased as well. The problem of youth crime for financial needs for, for example, drug use and youth crime out of boredom are inter-related, as the use of drugs and gambling can also be seen as behaviour sprung from boredom. The last main reason behind youth crime is the most serious one (although perhaps not the one that appears most often). This concerns adolescents who are forced to commit crime by adults. In the Czech Republic responsibility for criminal actions starts at the age of 18. Between the ages of 15 and 18 there is a legal liability but punishments are generally much less harsh than the legal system for adults. For children under the age of 15, there is no legal liability at all. There tend to be people abusing this fact by forcing (their) children to steal or rob. To address this problem, the national government enacted a law stating that parents are responsible at all times for their children's behaviour and that parents are responsible for the education and well-being of their children (Law §31). However, implementation of this law appears to be difficult.

13.3.2 Security Perceptions

It is difficult to characterize the safety perceptions of the citizens of Prague. It seems that safety perceptions have been worsening. In 1999, a public survey was held in the city of Prague, questioning which factors most influenced people's perceptions of safety. It appeared that pickpocketing, physical violence and car/house break-ins were in the top three most worrying criminal activities. Almost one-third of the citizens claimed to have been victim of some kind of crime in the previous two years. This share also included citizens with a member in their household who had been victimized in the past two years. According to the public survey, citizens would like to see more police officers in the streets: 44 per cent of the respondents confirmed this statement (International Business and Research Services, 1999). Other causes may be found in the low level of legal awareness of most citizens: often people do not know what is and what is not allowed and are not aware of the consequences. Obviously, freedom is essential, but a low level of legal awareness, high tolerance levels and no social control can all negatively influence safety perceptions. A zero tolerance attitude by the police is believed to improve legal awareness and therefore security perceptions. For the residents of the Czech Republic, however, less tolerance and more repression are highly sensitive measures, as they are connected with the Communist era.

13.4 Urban Attractiveness and Spatial Behaviour

The city centre of Prague is characterized by a rich history and represents a wide collection of (architectural) monuments in the form of squares, bridges and castles. Parts of the city centre are registered under the UNESCO world cultural and natural heritage register. There is a large variety of cultural activities, such as concerts, theatre, annual festivals (Spring Music Festival) and a large range of restaurants and pubs, which seem to positively influence Prague's attractiveness. In 2002 Prague was named the European City of Culture. All this architectural and cultural pomp and circumstance attracts many people. The city centre therefore can be seen as an attractive leisure site. Obviously, there are negative side effects of this attractiveness as well, such as pickpocketing and overcrowded streets. As stated before, pickpocketing is one of the crimes that is related to youth crime (which does not imply that all pickpocketing is committed by minors). However, tourists are not expected to change their spatial behaviour by avoiding crowded places in order to prevent themselves from becoming victims of pickpocketing.

The majority of the residents live in districts other than the city centre. Little information about the attractiveness of other districts in Prague is available. Whether or not citizens adapt their spatial behaviour, or even move away, for safety reasons is unclear. As stated before, there was a population decrease after the mid-1990s. This outflow of people was caused by a shortage of acceptable housing within the city centre, especially for the 'newly rich'. Evidence of change in spatial behaviour caused by insecurity is not available for Prague.

13.5 Policy Reactions

Security is not a top policy priority for the City of Prague. The policy statement for the period 2002–2006 formulated the goals and priorities of the City Council. The most important elements were general urban development, economic development, housing and transport. As a new member of the European Union, the importance of the integration of Prague into European structures was also stressed (City of Prague, undated (c)). Although not a top priority, security and crime prevention (or 'legislation, security and crime prevention') is part of the policy statement (City of Prague, 2002). In total, the City Council spends approximately 2 per cent of its budget on security matters (City of Prague, undated (c)).

Legislation, security and crime prevention policy are based on a national safety policy formulated in 1993. The main goal of Prague's safety policy is to enhance feelings of safety in the city. The implemented or planned measures taken by the City Council relate to improving public order and reducing crime, improving technical facilities and facilitating staff for the Municipal Police and improving flood prevention and emergency warning systems (City of Prague, undated (c)). This last topic has less to do with general feelings of safety in the city and more with the actual threat of a river flood, following the emergency situation with the River Vltava in August 2002.

The safety policy for the period 2002–2006 paid special attention to crime prevention. At the time of writing the City Council is preparing a special Crime Prevention Programme 2005–2008. Despite the importance given to crime prevention in policy documents, the scope of the actual preventive activities (mainly done by the policy) is small. For example, 25 police officers out of a total of 1,500 of the Prague Municipal Police work on crime prevention programmes. In addition, there are about 300 'district officers' indirectly involved in prevention. It seems that in practice most measures taken are still repressive. Even this characterization does not really do justice to the safety policy in Prague, because the social acceptance of repression is low and both police forces struggle with a negative image, making repression a disputable measure. Again, this resistance against repression appears to relate to the Communist era.

13.5.1 Actors Involved

The main actors involved in security matters in Prague are the City Council and the Police. The organization of the police in Prague needs extra attention. The police in Prague are responsible for public safety, but there are two different police departments, both having their own responsibility. These are the Police of the Czech Republic and the Prague Municipal Police. The former have the legal right to investigate and to arrest offenders. The latter department was established after the political changes in 1990 and are more focused on minor offences like traffic crime. They do not have the right to investigate: they only manage local affairs of public order within the jurisdiction of the city. The Municipal Police has about 1,500 police officers working in the City of Prague. Taken together, all departments of the Municipal Police throughout the Czech Republic are said to have approximately 7,500 officers. Police priorities in both the Czech Republic and Prague are juvenile delinquency, serious white-collar crime, terrorism, illegal migration, organized crime, illegal activities related to drugs, intellectual property crime and cyber crime (Šindlerová, 2004).

The City Council also installed an extra commission on crime prevention. This is an advisory organ for the City Council consisting of all involved actors in crime prevention advising on the effectiveness of preventive measures. The main goals and priorities for crime prevention include analyzing and evaluating the security situation in cooperation with the Municipal Police and Police of the Czech Republic, realizing an educational programme for managers of crime prevention, preparing minimum quality of services offered, completing tasks arising from the Strategy of Crime Prevention 2004–2007 (City of Prague, undated).

13.5.2 Youth Crime

As already noted, youth crime, which involves mainly petty crime such as pickpocketing, car break-ins, etc., is a problem for the city of Prague. It is difficult for the police to tackle youth crime as legal liability starts at the age of 18. Between the age of 15 and 18 there is a legal liability, but punishments are generally much less than for adults. As many young offenders are under the age of 15 (sometimes as young as 12 years old), youth crime is difficult to address. In an attempt to tackle youth crime for offenders under the age of legal liability also, the national government enacted a law stating that parents are responsible at all times for their children's behaviour, their education and their well-being (Law §31). Up to the time of writing, this law has seldom been used and this is not the only law that is enacted but not in use. Alternative sanctions for juvenile delinquency instead of imprisonment have seldom been made use of in Prague either, although they have long been provided for in Czech law. An explanation may be that judges seemed to be opposed to these alternatives for juveniles (Neubacher et al., 1999).

As repressive measures appear to be insufficient to tackle the problem of youth crime, preventive measures are used as well. However, these preventive measures seem to be more focused on the possible victims of (youth) crime than on potential young offenders. An example of a prevention programme for minors is AJAX; an education programme run by the Municipal Police aimed at second and third grade schoolchildren. Over a two year period a local police officer discusses several security-related themes such as safe behaviour, protection of persons and possession, drugs, legal knowledge and also hygiene, traffic education, and harassment (Městká Policie HL.M. Prahy, undated). The programme is based on a personal relationship between police and children, educating them about the risks on the street and presenting the police as friends instead of enemies. In addition to AJAX, several other education programmes focus on other target groups, but there appears to be no information of any aimed at preventing vulnerable minors from becoming offenders or at preventing those who have already committed an offence from become persistent offenders.

Unfortunately, more information about the specific problems related to youth crime in Prague and especially about the implemented policies to reduce youth crime was not available. Therefore we cannot describe a best practice with respect to juvenile delinquency.

13.5.3 Crisis Management

In common with other European cities, Prague has to deal with possible threats like natural disaster, terrorism, disasters, etc. The previously-mentioned river flood in August 2002 proved again that prompt and high-quality information is essential to guarantee the residents' safety when dealing with a city-wide emergency. Direct information on the situation and developments around the emergency enable the city to make the right decisions and to protect the population from further damage. Most large cities already have some form of crisis management, but the City of Prague has an advanced technical system at its disposal. This best practice is described below.

Best practice 1: RSS (Rescue Safety System)
The Rescue Safety System of the City of Prague initially was set up to deal with extraordinary situations and to protect its citizens. The responsibility from safety lies in the first instance with the mayor of the City of Prague, then with the deputy mayor for safety and then with the director of the crisis department. Together with other experts, they form the *crisis staff*. They are the decision-making actors in case of an emergency. In order to make the right decisions, they are informed about the actual situation and expected developments by all involved actors, such as police, fire brigade, transportation group, sanitation and epidemiology, etc. The strength of the RSS lies in the technical assistance from the experts. A private and independent computer network facilitates the collecting and analyzing of information. Information is gained with help of CCTV, a public camera system with approximately 300 cameras throughout the city. Officially, the Czech Republic Police are the main user of CCTV, but the crisis centre is one of its additional users. The crisis centre can also make use of a camera security system throughout the metro network. With all information gained, the crisis staff can warn citizens. The dispersal of information goes through TETRA, a warning system using city radio, TV, repeaters, sirens, etc., which is available even during a power cut.

All technical assistance contributes to successful crisis management, but the most important part is correct communication of information to the right person. In order to train for this, collective exercises are held twice a year. The first real-time exercise was during the 2002 river flood. In this critical situation the information services and dispersal appeared to be working well. Other situations in which RSS appeared to be useful were during a collapse of the public transport system, the threat of poisoning of the drinking water, and also during less critical situations such as the ice hockey World Cup.

13.6 Synthesis

13.6.1 Safety Perception

Crime rates faced a strong upturn after the collapse of Communism in 1989. In recent years, the crime rate in Prague seems to have stabilized. In 2003, the number of recorded incidents was on average 97 crimes per 1,000 inhabitants (City of Prague, undated). However, according to a public survey, this number represents only one-third of the total crime in the city (International Business and Research Services, 1999). The main crime problems in Prague seem to be car crime, youth crime and drug abuse.

Safety perceptions in Prague are more complicated to discuss. The strong upturn in crime rates after the collapse of Communism is believed to have influenced safety perceptions negatively. The current situation and trends regarding safety perceptions are less known. A small public survey has been undertaken, indicating a deterioration in safety perceptions. Factors like pickpocketing, physical violence, car crime/house break-ins, etc. seem to influence safety perceptions most (International Business and Research Services, 1999).

13.6.2 Urban Attractiveness and Spatial Behaviour

Little information on urban attractiveness and spatial behaviour of people in Prague is available. The city seems to be attractive both to residents and visitors. The city centre is well known for its attractive historic environment. This attracts visitors but also generates negative side effects (pickpocketing, unreliable taxi drivers, overcrowding of streets, etc.). Obviously, most citizens live in districts other than the city centre and are not regularly confronted with these negative aspects. There is no evidence available for drastic changes in citizens' spatial behaviour caused by, for example, insecurity. As in other cities, incidents such as robberies or car crime may affect the routes people use, but whether or not this is applies more to Prague than other cities remains uncertain. The above-mentioned migration flows out of the city during the mid-1990s were caused by a shortage of housing in the city and an abundant supply in nearby suburbs: for the 'newly rich' in particular, it appeared to be attractive to move out of the city centre (Sykora, 1998).

13.6.3 Policy Reactions

Security is not a top policy priority for City of Prague. General urban and economic development appears to have a higher priority. Even so, security is part of the policy statement of the current City Council. Approximately 2 per cent of the municipal budget is allocated to security matters. The main actors in urban security matters are the City Council, the Police of the Czech Republic, the Prague Municipal Police and Social Services. The current safety policy can be characterized as mainly repressive, although difficult and sensitive because of the repression during the Communist era. Preventive measures gain in importance as well. The main goal of the current safety policy (which is based on a National Security Act introduced in 1993) is to enhance feelings of safety in the city. In this respect several objectives have been formulated by the City Council. During the current policy period the City Council wants to improve public order and reduce crime, improve technical facilities and facilitate staff for the municipal police and enhance the flood prevention system and the emergency warning system (City of Prague, undated (c)).

The last objective in particular seems to work well in Prague. The city' Rescue Safety System (RSS) is mentioned in this case study as a best practice. A computer network linked to the CCTV system of the Czech Police and to TETRA, a warning system using city radio, TV, repeaters, etc., provides the city with all possible information giving a 'bird's eye view' of the actual crisis situation. The crisis staff – consisting of the mayor, the deputy-mayor, the director of the crisis department together with experts – use this information to make the right decisions in case of an emergency and uses TETRA to inform the citizens. The technical assistance proved its value during the flood of August 2002.

13.6.4 Organizing Capacity with Respect to Safety Policy

The City of Prague definitely has a *vision* on how safety in the city should develop in the (near) future. Although not a top priority, safety issues are part of the 2002–2006 policy statement. The safety policy is aimed particularly at enhancing feelings of safety among the local residents. The city's two deputy mayors are responsible for two different aspects of safety: security and crime prevention. Because there are two people responsible and because in both cases safety is only one of their responsibilities it can be stated that there is no strong *leadership* in safety policy in Prague. The *political support* seems to be relatively good as there is specific attention on the topic in the current City Council Programme, but *societal support* may need to improve. Few societal institutions or residents are actively involved in improving safety. Another less strong point in the organizing capacity regarding safety policy in the City of Prague is the *strategic network*. There is very little cooperation between the several actors involved in safety issues. Crisis management is the only area in which the city council and police cooperate with other institutions like the fire brigade and health care departments. A strong leader who can clearly *communicate* the safety vision to all actors involved in safety issues could improve the organizing capacity regarding safety policy in Prague.

13.6.5 Recommendations

From the available information presented in this case study we can conclude that, as well as repressive measures against crime, preventive measures have also gained more attention in the city of Prague. Crime prevention programmes have been developed by both police forces and special officers for developing prevention policies have been appointed. The existing prevention programmes are often long term and strongly focused on a personal relationship between officer and residents (children). This is a positive development, but some recommendations can be made in this respect as well.

Firstly, most prevention programmes focus on possible victims. Obviously, information and education on how to prevent oneself from becoming a victim of crime is useful. However, existing prevention programmes show hardly any interest in potential offenders. In the case of youth crime especially, attention on possible offenders could be essential. Extra attention on risk groups may prevent young children from becoming offenders, or at least prevent young delinquents from becoming persistent offenders.

Secondly, from the available information it seems that both police forces in the city mostly work alongside each other instead of intensively cooperating with each other. Some documents (e.g., Meeting of the Working Group of Consultants, 25 March 2003) do mention cooperation between Prague Metropolitan Police and the Police of the Czech Republic. In practice, both police forces appear to cooperate very little, at least in the field of (youth) crime and crime prevention. Better cooperation could improve the efficiency and effectiveness of the prevention programmes: when working on programmes that try to prevent young offenders from becoming persistent offenders dedication from both the investigating police force (Police of the Czech Republic) and the police force for public order (Prague Municipal Police) is required.

Another recommendation concerns the involvement of other urban actors in Prague's safety policy, such as the city council, the public prosecution, social services, residents, etc. Crisis management is a good example of several urban actors cooperating in order to commonly address the threat of city-wide emergencies. Institutions like the City Council, police, fire brigade and also transportation, sanitation etc. work together in a strict organizational structure in which every involved person has their own responsibility. Obviously, youth crime prevention does not require such strict organization as crisis management, but more fine-tuning of the policies and measures taken by all different actors involved would increase the effectiveness of the measures taken.

A last recommendation for the City of Prague with respect to safety policy in general and juvenile delinquency in particular is to find a balance between repressive and preventive measures. Without repression, prevention is useless. As stated, preventive measures in Prague are currently being designed and implemented. It is important to continue this development. But repression is important as well. Though we are aware of the high sensitivity to repression in the Czech Republic, it could and should be carried out more strictly. A 'zero tolerance' policy may be a little too ambitious, but the general message to residents should be that criminal behaviour will no longer be tolerated. In a country where crime figures were much lower under a more regulated regime in particular, it is essential to lower the tolerance level in order to show residents that they can count on the police in order to improve safety perceptions.

Chapter 14

Synthesis

14.1 Introduction

In this comparative research we have tried to analyse the role of security in urban development in several European cities. The central research question is: 'What is the role of security in urban development in the twenty-first century and what are the local policy implications?'

To answer this question we have analysed the situation and developments of actual and perceived security and the related policy measures in 11 European cities. Ten of these cities currently form the SecurCity Network of the Urbact Programme.[1] SecurCity officially started in February 2004. The network concentrates on the improvement and effectiveness of policies and actions to combat the (perceived) insecurity in the participant cities. SecurCity addresses one of the main areas of intervention of URBACT: the improvement of safety and the quality of life. Antwerp is the only city in this comparable study not included in the SecurCity Network.

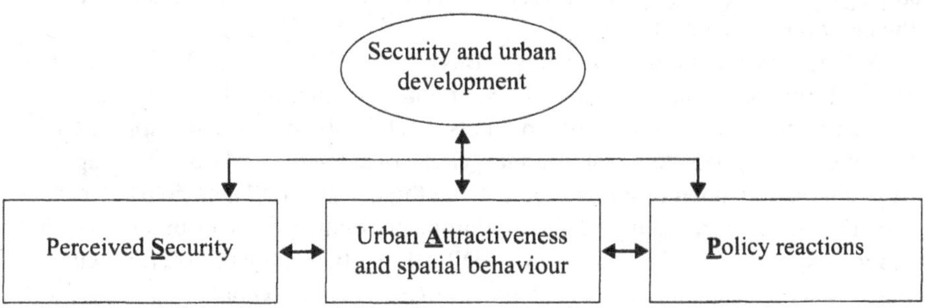

Figure 14.1 The SAP model

The analysis of the case studies is based on the SAP model. This model resulted from a theoretical framework in which we linked safety with urban development. SAP is the acronym for Safety perception, urban Attractiveness, and spatial behaviour and Policy reaction. These three factors influence each other and have impacts on urban development. For the analysis of the policy reactions, we have focused on three specific themes related to urban security: area-based safety policies, drugs and insecurity and youth crime and insecurity.

The SAP model was applied to all case studies and will also be the basis for this synthesis. In this chapter we will start by describing briefly the profiles of the case studies involved (Section 14.2). Section 14.3 describes the actual and perceived security situation and the possible caused underlying changing security perceptions. Subsequently, in Section 14.4, the consequences of changing security for urban attractiveness and spatial behaviour are described. The main policy reactions from the cities involved are presented in Section 14.5. This paragragh also describes the specific issues related to the three themes (area-based safety problems, drugs and insecurity and youth crime and insecurity) and the policy approaches as presented in the different case studies. In Section 14.6 an urban typology which categorizes the cities involved in this study is presented. Finally, we finish in Sections 14.7 and 14.8 with some conclusions and recommendations for urban governments dealing with social safety issues.

14.2 Profile

14.2.1 Demography and Economy

The size of the cities involved in this comparative study ranges from approximately 100,000 citizens (Heerlen and Gera) to approximately one million (Prague and Birmingham). Except for the cities of Rotterdam, Helsinki, Leeds and Prague, population numbers have declined over the past decade or so. It must be noticed that these figures are related to the cities' administrative borders and not to their functional urban regions. Often, the population declined in the administrative region but increased in the neighbouring suburbs.

The economic situation in the cities varies as well (Table 14.1). Over the last few years most European countries have faced economic stagnation, although some cities have been more influenced by this than others. In Helsinki the economy appears to be flourishing with a gross domestic product (GDP) of more than €41,000 per capita in 2001 and moderate unemployment rates. Even though the GDP data do not consider differences in the purchasing power of European countries, it can be noticed that Bari and Prague perform less well with GDPs of €13,000 and €15,000 respectively. Bari also has the disadvantage of high unemployment: approximately 25 per cent of the labour force was unemployed in 2001. The Dutch cities seem to have a fortunate position as the GDPs are around average while the unemployment rates are low.

14.3 Actual and Perceived Security

This section starts by explaining the significance of security for urban development in general and then describes the situation and developments in both actual and perceived security in the involved cities. Finally, possible causes for the changing security perception and an often-increasing gap between actual and perceived safety are presented.

Table 14.1 Demographic and economic indicators

	Population number, 2001	Population development, past decade	GDP per capita, 2001, €	Unemployed, 2001, %
Rotterdam	595,255	+	29,000*	6
Antwerp	448,709	–	31,525	11
Glasgow	577,869	–	17,690**	11
The Hague	442,356	–	32,000*	3
Helsinki	559,718	+	40,972	6
Heerlen	95,149	–	23,000*	4
Leeds	715,399	+	16,072*	5
Bari	332,143	–	12,620	25
Birmingham	977,087	–	14,535**	10
Gera	107,413*	–	19,340	17
Prague	1,169,106	+	14,854	4

\+ increase
– decrease
* 2003
** 1996

Source: Eurostat, 2004; CBS, 2005; Thüringen Landesambt für Statistik, 2004.

14.3.1 Security and Urban (Economic) Development

In general, safety is one of the fundamental needs for human beings. In his 'hierarchy of human needs', Maslow (1943) describes that security needs are most important after the physiological needs such as water, food, and housing. Safety needs are about finding safe circumstances and stability, but also about job security and protection from fear and anxiety. This general theory applies to cities as well – when security is not guaranteed in urban areas, (well-off) people might change their spatial behaviour and move to a 'safer' place. In the long term, urban insecurity may imply an outflow of middle- and high-income groups from certain urban areas. This may cause a downward spiral for the district involved, but also an increasing segregation within the city which can be a source of social unrest.

The importance of security for urban areas is not new. In premodern cities the construction of urban walls was motivated both by fears for the physical safety of the inhabitants and by the desire to protect of profitability of economic activity in the city (Bannister and Fyfe, 2001). Later, in the mid-nineteenth century, Hausmann rebuilt Paris with the intention of reducing the threat posed by 'dangerous classes' (Ellin, 1997). More recent examples are the gentrified enclaves in modern cities, protected by gates, (private) surveillance systems, defence architecture, etc. However, all measures taken in order to protect the citizens also contribute to accentuating fear by increasing paranoia and distrust among people (Ellin, 1996).

Measures taken to improve urban security may imply less freedom for citizens, for example CCTV (camera control system) or gated communities. Decreasing freedom is a threat to urban attractiveness. An open and free urban environment is important for urban development as it stimulates urban diversity and therefore economic development. At the same time it is demonstrated that security is a vital need for human beings and thus for urban economic development. Openness and security are both essential and conflicting: more freedom means less security while more security means less openness (Crawford, 2002). For sustainable urban development it is therefore important to find a balance between security and openness.

Recently, political attention on security matters has grown in European cities. The foundation of the SecurCity network is one example of this growing interest in urban safety. One of the reasons for this rising attention is the observation of increasing fear of crime among the residents of many European cities. There appears to be a safety paradox: in many cities the actual security situation seems to be improving (with decreasing crime rates), while simultaneously perceptions of safety seem to be worsening. However, the gap between actual and perceived safety is not growing in all cities: a few cities show increasing crime rates over the past few years (for example, The Hague, Heerlen), which helps to explain the worsening safety perceptions and maintains the gap between actual and perceived security. Still, we can state that most cities in this study have safety perceptions that not reflect the actual security situation.

Another example reflecting the increasing interest in security matters in Europe is the presence of the issue of safety in the perception survey of the Urban Audit. The Urban Audit was launched in 1998 by the European Commission because of the increasing demand among policymakers for an assessment of the quality of life in Europe's cities. The Urban Audit provides the involved cities with comparable information on quality of life, of which safety perceptions are an indicator of (European Commission, 2005). The objective figures (e.g. crime rates) in the Urban Audit are provided by the national statistical institutions involved, the subjective figures (e.g. security perception) where collected by the Urban Audit team through public surveys. The following sections will describe the current situations and developments regarding actual and perceived safety.

14.3.2 Actual Security Situation

As described in the first chapter of this research there are different levels of security. Crawford (2002) draws the distinction between security at a micro level and at a macro level. Micro level security refers to 'everyday life' security or localized disorders, for example, graffiti, robberies, violence and theft. Macro level security refers to threats by (natural) disasters, terrorism or even war. This research focuses more on the micro level security (the localized disorders) than on macro level security.

Since World War II, the micro level security situation in European countries has generally deteriorated. Crime rates in the cities involved in this research have been increasing over the past decades. Obviously, there are differences between the cities, especially between the cities in Western and the former Eastern Europe countries. In the cities in the west of Europe, crime rates have been more or less continuously increasing. In the cities of the former Eastern bloc, crime rates were relatively low during communism, but after the fall of the Berlin Wall, crime rates took an upturn. Sadly, the social freedom gained in these societies also facilitated the progress of criminal behaviour.

Recent years appear to show a slow reversal in crime trends in the case study cities: in more than half of the cities, the micro level security situation seems to be improving. Table 14.2 presents the recent general crime developments in the different cities. This table also illustrates the actual crime figures per city in 2001 as known by Eurostat, the statistical office of the European Commission. However, it must be noticed that these figures were provided by the individual countries/cities and are therefore incommensurable.

Table 14.2 Crime records in the cities, 2001

	Recorded crime, 2001, #	Crime per 1,000 inhabitants, #	Development crime rate, 2000–2003
Rotterdam	81,065	136	–
Antwerp	52,255	116	–
Glasgow	85,165	147	–
The Hague	54,924	124	+
Helsinki	84,717	151	–
Heerlen	13,237	139	+
Leeds	46,756	65	–
Bari	20,415*	61	+
Birmingham	70,616	72	–
Gera	10,773*	100	–
Prague	99,966	86	–

\+ increase
– decrease
* 2003

Source: Eurostat, 2004; Veröffentlichungen BKA, LKA zur PKS, 2003.

Limited international comparability of crime rates

According to the figures in Table 14.2 it appears that Bari is the safest city in the Securcity network, with an annual record of 61 crimes per 1,000 inhabitants (crime rates from 2003 were related to the population number of 2001: as the population number is expected to be higher in 2003, the actual crime rate per 1,000 inhabitants in

2003 may even be lower). Surprisingly, the most unsafe city appears to be Helsinki, with 151 recorded crimes per 1,000 inhabitants in 2001. This result appears to be completely the opposite of the general perception: Helsinki is often regarded as one of the safest cities in Europe, while Bari appears to be competing with Naples for the questionable title of 'least safe city of Italy'.

The example of crime rates in the two cities taken above show that crime figures are not internationally comparable. There are two reasons for this. Firstly, the definition of 'crime' and the method of crime recording differ per country. Recordings of crime may therefore include more offences in a country with broader definitions of crime and/or with more means for registration (i.e., reporting with help of the internet). Another factor explaining large differences in crime rates between countries is the readiness of residents to report crime. In Helsinki, for example, the number of recorded crimes is believed to be close to the actual number of crimes. Here, people's willingness to report is high, as they need a report for their insurance claim. In Bari however, people's willingness to report seems to be lower. Local authorities here even state that the recorded crime would only cover 10 per cent of the actual total crime rate.

The willingness to report crime also influences crime figures within countries. For example, in Heerlen, the multi-agency project '*Operatie Hartslag*', aimed at diminishing drug-related nuisance in the city centre, stimulated residents to report drug nuisance to the police more often. The police themselves also reported observed drug nuisance in the city centre more often. As a result, the number of crime reports increased, although the actual number of incidents appears not to have increased. Obviously, the reverse is possible as well: a declining willingness to report may lead to lower recorded crime rates although actual crime remains unaffected.

Types of crime

Each city in the network has its own specific complexity of crime problems, but some generalizations can be made. The three British cities – Birmingham, Leeds, and Glasgow – for example, face problems related to the night-time economy. One of these problems is binge drinking, which is the habit of drinking as much alcohol as possible in a short period of time. Obviously this habit is a health risk for the person involved, but more problematic for society is the related violent and antisocial behaviour. There is also the problem of lack of sufficient transport: after the pubs and clubs close (around 2 a.m.), there is a large crowd trying to get home, but public transport is limited at that time of the day and the number of taxis is too small. Alcohol abuse in combination with large crowds of people in the streets around midnight having difficulty getting home is a source of safety problems in these cities.

In most of the cities involved the main recorded crime types are burglary from dwellings, violence against persons, violence against property and drug-related crime. The crime types most often mentioned by the involved cites as threats to safety perceptions are petty crime (theft, shoplifting, burglary, car crime, vandalism, etc.), violence (often in combination with alcohol or drug abuse), drugs and insecurity (drug use, nuisance, dealing, running, etc.) and youth crime (often involving petty crime). Other crime types may be severe problems for the police to solve as well, but may have a smaller influence on safety perceptions. Such crime types are, for example, organized crimes like trafficking of people or weapons and fraud.

Spatial differences in actual security

Similarities and differences between the cities in the SecurCity network have been identified. At a lower spatial level as well, differences in security problems may arise. Crime problems in the city centre appear to be different from the main crime problems in the suburbs: city centres are often characterized by a greater concentration of activities and people, which offers opportunities for bag snatchers and shoplifters, but which can also be a breeding ground for disorder and violence. As stated above, in the three British cities the night-time economy is a typical city centre problem. Other examples are Heerlen and Helsinki. Heerlen was characterized by a large concentration of drug-related problems in the city centre and especially around the central station. Here, drug users, dealers and runners are spatially concentrated, causing nuisance to passers-by. At a given time, people started to avoid the specific area in large numbers, especially during evening hours. In Helsinki, concentrations of crime appear around metro and railway stations. Because these means of transport have less frequent stops than, for example, the bus, there are relatively many people leaving and entering the premises. Especially during the evenings and nights, more people are under the influence of alcohol, which may easily lead to disorder. In the suburbs disorder and theft may be less of a problem than domestic violence, car crime and burglaries.

14.3.3 Security Perception

Measuring security perception

Figures of perceptions of security more difficult to come by than figures of actual crime rates and types. Some cities do have public surveys questioning residents' feelings of safety, but the reliability of these figures may sometimes be questionable. The response to questions about feelings of insecurity might make no reference to crime: not only real fear of crime but also broader aspects of quality of life will sometimes be seen as part of fear of crime (Simmons and Dodd, 2003; Bannister and Fyfe, 2001). Other aspects influencing security perception are, for example, maintenance of public space (graffiti, litter) quality of the built environment, people grouping together, etc.

The Urban Audit collected information on quality of life through perception surveys in a range of European cities. Feelings of safety are also part of this survey (see Figure 14.2). From this comparable study only the cities of Helsinki, Glasgow, Rotterdam and Antwerp are taken into the Urban Audit. Assuming Bari is in some way comparable with Naples (see Chapter 10), this figure confirms the statement that Helsinki is one of the safest cities and Bari is one of the least safe cities in the network, although objective crime rates appear to show the opposite.

Another attempt at measuring and comparing safety has been made in the city of Rotterdam. Here, the value of safety in the different neighbourhoods is measured with help of the safety index. This index combines the direct elements of security

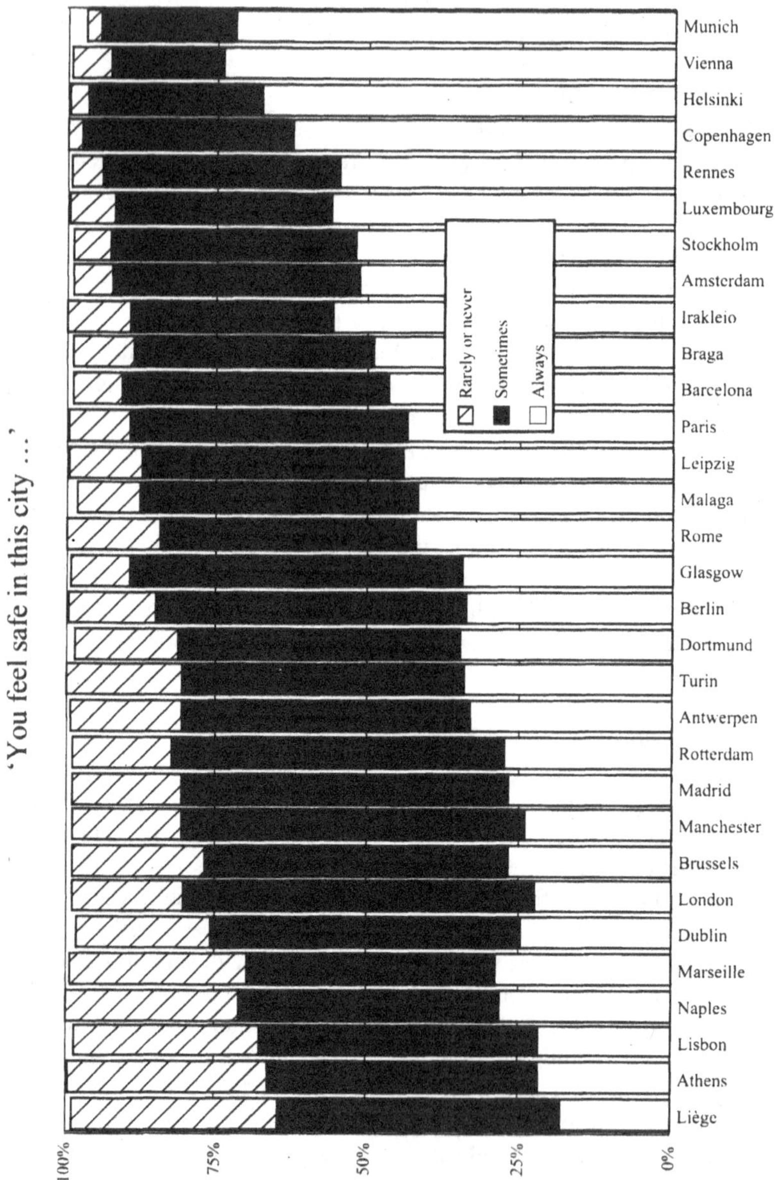

Figure 14.2 Security perceptions in European cities

Source: Urban Audit, 2004.

with elements of the environment/quality of life. The security-elements are measured with both objective and subjective figures of theft, drug nuisance, violence, burglary, etc. The environmental elements are believed to influence perceptions of security as well, for example, the number of people leaving the neighbourhood, the average life expectancy in the neighbourhood, the composition of the population, etc (Programmabureau Veilig, 2004). This safety index is a tool for the City to measure the security situation, to better understand the spatial differences and needs within the city, and to accurately follow the security developments.

Security perception in the cities

Data on perceptions of security were not available for all case studies. The available figures of the share of people feeling (un)safe are presented in Table 14.3. These figures are not suitable for (international) comparison – they originate from local public surveys and the questions behind these results may differ per survey. For the city itself, it is a useful tool for following the development of the security perception through time. To illustrate this, in The Netherlands the shares of people (sometimes) feeling unsafe in general have been monitored since 1999 (Table 14.4). In the first few years there was an increase of people (sometimes) feeling unsafe. The relatively strong decrease in safety perceptions between 2001 and 2002 may be influenced by the events of 9/11 or the assassination of Pim Fortuyn, the first political murder in the modern history of The Netherlands. However, there seems to have been an improvement since 2002.

Table 14.5 presents the general trends in security perception in the different cities over the past few years. Although figures are not available for some cities, they do sometimes present information on the development of security perception. It appears that in many European cities security perception has been deteriorating in the past few years.

Spatial differences in perceived security

Comparisons of perception figures between countries and even within countries are difficult: comparisons between cities may be complicated due to dissimilar questioning in public surveys. But within a survey area comparisons are indeed possible. In The Hague, for example, the share of people feeling unsafe in their own district was 28 per cent in 2003. However, there are large differences within the city; in the best district only 15 per cent stated feeling unsafe, while in the worst district up to 40 per cent felt unsafe. In Helsinki too there are large differences in perceptions. In the best districts, only 6 per cent of the population (sometimes) feel unsafe, while in some other districts up to 35 per cent of the population (sometimes) feel unsafe. Notwithstanding the fact that these variances may be due to several reasons, it is important for urban governments to be aware of the possible consequences of such segregation.

It os not only residents' perceptions of safety that are important for the general urban well-being and development. Safety perception of (possible) visitors is important too. Glasgow is an example of a city having difficulties with its image to outsiders: many people from the region, the country and even abroad perceive the city as tough

Table 14.3 Available figures on security perception

City	Feelings of insecurity	%	Year
Rotterdam	Population share (sometimes) feeling unsafe in city	43	2003
	Population share (sometimes) feeling unsafe in own district	20	2003
The Hague	Population share feeling unsafe in city	10	2002
	Population share feeling unsafe in district	28	2002
	Lowest and highest share	15–40	2002
Helsinki	Highest population share (sometimes) feeling unsafe in own district	6	2003
	Lowest population share (sometimes) feeling unsafe in own district	35	2003
Heerlen	Population share (sometimes) feeling unsafe in city	51	2003
	Population share (sometimes) feeling unsafe in own district	43	2003
	Residents (sometimes) feeling unsafe in city centre	80	2003
Leeds	Population share feeling fairly/very safe during the day	96	2004
	Population share feeling fairly/very safe during the night	51	2004
Birmingham	Population share feeling (very) safe in the area	90	2002

Table 14.4 Feelings of insecurity related to criminality in The Netherlands

Year	Population (sometimes) feeling unsafe, %
1999	21.9
2000	20.7
2001	22.4
2002	25.4
2003	23.6
2004	21.8

Source: CBS, 2005.

Table 14.5 General development of security perception

City	Development of safety perceptions, 2000–2003
Rotterdam	+
Antwerp	–
Glasgow	n.a.
The Hague	–
Helsinki	–
Heerlen	–
Leeds	–
Bari	n.a.
Birmingham	–
Gera	◊
Prague	n.a.

– deteriorating
\+ improving
n.a. not available
◊ stable

and unsafe. Obviously, this influences Glasgow's attractiveness as a tourist destination, but it may also deter people and companies from moving to Glasgow.

Safety paradox
The previous description of the actual and perceived security in the cases does partly confirm the generally assumed safety paradox of improving actual security with simultaneously more fear of crime. Actual security is improving in some cities but not in all. Figures on the development of safety perceptions are not available for all cities involved. Where they are available, it appears that the perceptions have been either stable or worsening over the past few years. It seems that in some cities the gap between actual and perceived safety is growing. However, in all cities, decreasing crime rates did not lead to improved safety perceptions (yet).

14.3.4 Causes for Changing Security Perception

Causes changing security perception
Throughout the case studies, several possible causes have been mentioned for the generally deteriorating security perception. The introductory chapter to this book has already drawn the distinction between endogenous and exogenous factors in explaining this trend. Endogenous factors relate to the elements within the urban system. Here, a distinction has been made between low quality of the built environment, an unbalanced socio-economic structure, disasters and actual crime rates. As stated, the crime types most often mentioned as influencing security perception are petty crime, youth crime, drugs and insecurity and violence. Exogenous factors relate to elements outside the urban system. These factors are therefore more difficult for urban government to influence. Three factors have been identified: immigration without integration, terrorist attacks and natural disasters. The first-mentioned factor was regularly mentioned in the different case studies. As well as endogenous and exogenous factors, personal factors were also mentioned as possible factors causing changing security perception. Vanderveen (2001) has stated that people increasingly try *to exclude* risks: they are unwilling to face any kind of risk and if there appears to be a risk they hold public institutions and the government responsible. This kind of behaviour is also called *riskism*.

Alongside the examples of endogenous and exogenous factors mentioned, three other elements arose from the case studies: political revolution, lack of economic perspectives and media attention. Firstly, a factor affecting security perception is extensive structural political changes. Cities in the former Eastern European countries underwent a political revolution in 1989 when communism gave way to democracy. Obviously the impact of this change on society has been, and remains, tremendous. The uncertainties accompanying such a shift cause social unrest and feelings of insecurity in the short term. But in the long term as well people have to adjust to a new system – a new reality. For example, official crime rates – for, for example, burglaries, violence and nuisance – were generally substantially lower during Communism than they are now. In those days, there was greater police repression, making residents feel that crime was under control. In addition, media attention on crime was less, keeping awareness of occurring crime low. Because of the freedom gained and the less repressive policing, crime rates could increase strongly. In combination with a growing (local) media attention on safety, this negatively influenced security perception in former Communist countries.

A second factor found in our study is a lack of economic prospects. In cities with high unemployment and bad economic growth prospects fear of crime appears to be high. This can be explained by people feeling less comfortable because of a lack of good prospects within that particular region. Furthermore, because of a decreasing number of inhabitants, urban areas can end up in negative vicious circles in which the fear of crime will increase. This perspective applies to two of our case studies: Gera and Heerlen.

A third factor regularly mentioned in the case studies is the increasing attention of (mainly local) media on criminal incidents. Sensational stories of robberies, burglaries or even murders appear to be commercially successful. However, such stories often give an irrational image of the actual risks people run in daily urban life. In addition, without realistic positive stories of, for example, decreasing crime rates or successful local projects that increase security perception, an unbalanced image of a highly unsafe society is easily created. The examples of Gera and Prague are characteristic in this respect. As stated, media attention on urban security increased after the fall of the Berlin Wall, strongly influencing people's perceptions of security. But in most other cities as well, media attention is mentioned as strongly influencing people's safety perceptions. Therefore, it is important that a city's local authority is aware of the impact of its safety strategy.

14.4 Urban Attractiveness and Spatial Behaviour: Three Domains

14.4.1 To Live and to Work

We have four observations regarding location behaviour of inhabitants related to urban attractiveness and/or perceived safety:

1. a strong growth of the number of residents in the city centre, contributing to perceived safety;
2. out-migration from outer-core areas, worsening the safety situation. In some cities observations 1 and 2 are simultaneously noticeable;
3. an outflow of people from certain cities to other regions. Within those cities from which people migrate most related safety problems occur in the least attractive places, which are the first to be deserted;
4. a more or less stable pattern. No large inflows or outflows of inhabitants are noticeable. Perceived insecurity hardly plays a role in location behaviour.

The *first observation*, the *growth of residents in the city centre*, is noticeable in Rotterdam, Glasgow, Birmingham and Leeds. Within these cities, on balance, more residents move into the city centre. This has contributed positively to the vitality of the city centres and also to the perceived safety. It is, however, a selective immigration trend. Most inhabitants have a rather high income. In general, the images of the city centres are better among insiders than among outsiders. The latter still often perceive the city centres as unattractive and unsafe. Urban images seem therefore to be quite persistent. This might result in some people avoiding the city because of their perceptions of it as an unattractive and unsafe place. Several city promotion projects have, however, contributed to a more positive city image. Moreover, city *centres* often determine status and image of an *entire* city. If a city centre is perceived as being unsafe the whole city might be perceived as such (by outsiders).

In Rotterdam, a clear correlation is noticeable between housing prices and safety – most areas that are perceived as unsafe show relatively low housing prices. An exception is the city centre, which is still considered as relatively unsafe (although the situation has clearly improved with respect to, say, 20 years ago) but also demonstrates relatively high housing prices. We expected such a discrepancy (see Chapter 2), because often the demand for houses and housing prices are high in city centres, as are insecurity rates. This is a normal pattern: residents in city centres expect and accept a certain level of insecurity. With further investments in the attractiveness, vitality and safety of the city centre, housing prices may increase.

The *second observation* is *out-migration from outer-core areas*. Within a number of cities a clear out-migration of residents is noticeable from outer-core areas towards suburbs. This out-migration is stimulated by decreasing attractiveness of the outer-core areas and often leads to a further deterioration and reduction of the perceived attractiveness and safety of the neighbourhoods concerned.

This phenomenon could be found in The Hague, Rotterdam and Antwerp. In outer-core areas of these cities, medium- and high-income people often out-migrate to suburbs, which are perceived as being more attractive and safe. In some outer-core areas, such as Rotterdam-Delfshaven, Antwerpen-Borgerhout and The Hague-Laak, 'phenomena of deprivation' have occurred, marked by external decay due to the convergence of economic depression, loss of employment, departure of tradesmen and the outflow of more affluent citizens. In such areas there are poor housing, empty buildings, inadequate social services and a relative poor quality of the living environment. The combination and concentration of problems in certain neighbourhoods can cause feelings of insecurity among the remaining residents. These often low-income inhabitants mostly live in social housing. A proportion of them does not care much about the physical conditions of their houses and their environment, and this does not contribute to an attractive neighbourhood. In addition, because of lack of purchasing power, quite a number of shops in these districts had to close. Another problem is that there are relatively many foreign and illegal inhabitants who contribute insufficiently to social coherence, whereas greater social cohesion is considered as desirable to improve the perceived safety.

The Hague has the three richest and the three poorest neighbourhoods of The Netherlands, in which there have been serious segregation problems. One of the poorest neighbourhoods is Laak, an outer-core area, which has been in a vicious circle of deterioration. In addition, Glasgow contains the three most deprived areas om the UK. These areas are characterized by unattractive tower blocks, high vacancy rates and high unemployment rates. Large welfare differences within an urban region are a threat to social cohesion: they may lead to a marked segregation of the population. A consequence of this can be a perception of decreasing security and – as a result – a decreasing attractiveness of the urban region.

The *third observation* is an outflow of people from certain cities to other regions. The urban competitiveness of the cities concerned is weak and there is a lack of economic prospects for part of the population. Unemployment is relatively high and the possibilities for jobseekers are small. Consequently, people move to other regions which offer better economic prospects. With a decreasing total number of residents, the least attractive places will naturally be the first to be deserted. In those places where there is a relatively large number of vacant houses people might feel unsafe. Examples from our empirical study are Gera and Heerlen.

Gera can be considered a city that has a double identity *spatially*. On the one hand, the city centre has a rich history; this is noticeable in the attractive historical inner city (although there is clearly a backlog in maintenance activities due to lack of financial means). On the other hand there are suburbs like Bieblach and Lusan with high-rise and drab apartment buildings which are generally not considered to be attractive. In these neighbourhoods, there are relatively high vacancy rates. The outflow of people from Bieblach and Lusan is directly related to Gera's general low economic performance. Inhabitants out-migrate to particularly western parts of Germany for better job prospects. Because of this migration there are areas within the neigbourhoods with empty houses and closed shops. This has led to lower safety perceptions and changed spatial behaviour: because of a lack of vibrancy, some people are afraid to go out during evening and night hours. Because of a lack of financial means, however, desirable reconstruction measures cannot be carried out for the time being.

Heerlen does not have a great attraction for new inhabitants and the city has a declining population. Explanations for this are the poor economic prospects and the city's perceived unattractiveness. As a result, there is insufficient basis for complementary facilities, such as daily shops and restaurants, which would enhance the city's attractiveness. The reducing number of inhabitants and the poor economic prospects have a negative influence on perceived security: people feel less comfortable in a declining region.

The *fourth observation* relates to those cities which show quite a stable pattern regarding location behaviour of inhabitants. Within their country or relevant economic region they are, and remain, economically very attractive. Therefore, no large changes of migration patterns take place and these regions more or less continuously attract residents. In these cities, insecurity appears to have no influence on location behaviour. Examples are Prague and Helsinki. In the former, hardly any evidence on location behaviour related to safety considerations could be found, but we assume that there have been no large changes, due to the considerable attractiveness of the city within the Czech Republic. In Helsinki, no signs of changed long-term spatial behaviour because of safety reasons could be found. Because of the well-known

Nordic welfare system, there appear to be hardly any social segregation problems. Moreover, the average quality and maintenance of the built environment is relatively high and because of the high demand for houses there are extremely low vacancy rates. Two neighbourhoods on the west side of the city, Mellunkylä and Myllypuro, are considered to be deprived areas by Finnish standards. Compared to the other cities investigated, however, no real signs of deprivation can be found there. Most of the housing is rented, but this hardly influenced the quality of the built environment. Also, vacancy rates are low in these areas.

In Chapter 2 we stated that people would be more sensitive to insecurity in the living than in the working domain. As a consequence, they were expected to take spatial decisions after discovering that their living domain remains unsafe. In our case studies, most of the evidence regarding spatial decisions linked to insecurity refers to housing areas. A safety problem more specifically related to the work environment can be found in Bari. In this Italian city, small and medium-sized companies are forced to pay money to criminal organizations. This is, of course, a threat to the safety perceptions of these companies. However, large companies appear not to be threatened by these forced payments. Moreover, no phenomenon of business relocation has been found in the region of Bari: neither large nor small or medium size businesses move due to safety matters.

14.4.2 To Visit

We have three observations regarding location behaviour of inhabitants related to urban attractiveness and/or perceived safety:

1 the impact of shopping function on an urban area. More shops means more vitality resulting in safer places. Closing shops, on the contrary, means less vitality resulting in less safe places;
2 if there is an imbalance of functions, centres can have relatively substantial different identities during the day and night. We found problems in this respect in British cities and Heerlen. In UK cities, the tide appears to turn with the inflow of more inhabitants;
3 tourists and insecurity. The attraction of tourists will often also attract petty criminals.

The first observation: impact of shopping function on an urban area

The creation of more shopping activities in a neighbourhood can be instrumental in improving the perceived safety. When these activities attract sufficient clientele it will lead to more vibrancy in an urban area, and hence often to greater perceived safety.

For instance, in the Rotterdam-Delfshaven district a prominent shopping centre – *Mathenesserplein* – functions as a catalyst for the attractiveness of the surrounding neighbourhood. By upgrading this centre the local authority hoped that more public and private investments could be attracted to the surroundings to further upgrade it and improve the perceived security. It appears that this is a successful strategy, because many new investments have indeed taken place in the *Mathenesserplein* surroundings.

Heerlen succeeded in the creation of new facilities for non-daily shops within the city centre, which resulted in the improvement of the vibrancy of the city during the day. It seems that this had positive consequences for people's safety perceptions during the daytime.

In the district The Hague-Laak, the closing of quite a number of shops was caused by an out-migration of inhabitants and the lack of purchasing power of the remaining and new residents. This led to a reduction in the attractiveness and perceived safety of the district. At the edge of the Laak district, a new mega-shopping centre has been developed. One of the expectations was that this would have a positive impact on the perceived attractiveness of Laak. However, hardly any signs of a relationship between this shopping centre and the Laak district could be found. They appear to function as two different spatial entities.

The second observation: different identities of city centres during day and night

Due to an imbalance of functions some city centres show considerably different identities during day and night. Though every city centre will show differences in vibrancy and the kind of people present during the day, in some cities these differences are relatively great. The main reason for this is often a lack of inhabitants in the city centre, together with a lack of complementary facilities, such as shops for daily necessities and schools.

In Heerlen, for instance, as already noted, the vibrancy during the day is relatively high. However, the number of activities during the evening is relatively low, as are the number of inhabitants in the city centre. Therefore, the vibrancy of the city centre during evening and night is quite low. As a consequence, a large part of the population appears to avoid certain central places because they perceive them as being unsafe.

These double identities seem to occur quite often in the UK where, during the 1960s and 1970s, many centres were in decline and where during the 1990s in quite a number of cities there was a new urban renaissance. As a result of these trends, the absolute number of inhabitants in UK centres is often still low. The UK city centres in our study are vibrant places during the day, filled with workers and shoppers; during the night, however, they are partially deserted and partly filled with visitors enjoying the night-life. During the day, city centres are being perceived as relatively safe because of the amount of activity in the area. At night, more people perceive the centres as unsafe, partly because of deserted places and partly because of occurences of antisocial behaviour related to the night economy. The absolute number of residents within these centres is small, though strongly increasing. Most of these residents are YUPs and students; families generally prefer to live in suburbs.

The impact of nightlife on safety and attractiveness can thus be two-sided: negative because of the nuisance generated (antisocial behaviour) and positive because of the attraction of more people, creation of more employment and local income and the creation of more vibrancy, and often the perception of greater social security.

The third observation: tourism often attracts (petty) criminals

Cities with a large attraction for tourists might also have an attraction for (petty) criminals. Tourists are often an easy and attractive target for pickpocketing, because they often carry a reasonable amount of money and attractive electronic devices and they pay more attention to urban attractions than to the possible hazards of the city.

With its architectural and cultural pomp and circumstance, Prague attracts many tourists. Related negative effects are overcrowded streets and the frequent occurrence of pickpocketing. However, tourists appear not to change their spatial behaviour as a consequence. The city appears to be so attractive that this sufficiently outweighs some degree of insecurity.

In Bari, the old city centre (Bari Vecchia) was considered to be seriously deprived. Only after dramatic redevelopments, financed by the European URBAN-I programme, did the attractiveness of the old city centre improve both for residents and tourists. Nowadays, Bari Vecchia is one of the most attractive places of the city for tourists to visit. Although the redevelopment has improved safety in this neighbourhood, groups of tourists are still accompanied by police officers. This measure has been taken in order to prevent petty crime negatively influencing the tourist image of the city.

14.4.3 To Move

We have two observations:

1 public transport can arrive in a negative vicious circle when it is considered to be unsafe and insufficient attractive;
2 the legally-determined closing hours of pubs and clubs in the UK leads regularly to major transport problems and related perceived insecurity.

First observation

When travelling by public transport is perceived as unsafe, the number of users will reduce, particularly during the evening and night. This might also reduce the city's attractiveness, because it will often lead to more people using cars and, consequently, more congestion and more pollution will occur. Moreover, the city will become less accessible, which might result in a reduced attractiveness for economic activities.

In some of the cities investigated we noticed that people were avoiding public transport because of perceived insecurity. In Gera, for instance, youth crime in public transport led to less occupation of public transport and in Helsinki during night hours some people avoided centres of public transport, particularly the central station and the metro stations.

In Rotterdam, the above-mentioned consequences of the reduction of the perceived safety on public transport appear to be acknowledged. Measures have indeed been taken to improve this perceived safety. To achieve this, modern technology such as CCTV and ticket gates are used and more conductors are present, in particularly on trams. Public transport is being transformed from an open to a closed system, which affords more control over the payment of fares and the type of passenger. The results are that more people feel safe on public transport and more paying passengers make use of public transport.

Second observation
In UK cities at night transport problems regularly appear after the pubs and clubs close at 2 a.m. Because most of them close at the same time, a huge demand for transport arises. However, during the night most public transport no longer operates. The night-life visitors are thus dependent on taxis, which are insufficiently available. As a consequence, unlicensed taxi drivers try to fill in this market gap. Even so, tensions and quarrels arise in these circumstances, often reducing the perceived safety.

14.5 Policy Reactions

14.5.1 Local Safety Policy

Even if safety is an important issue for most cities in Europe, it does not always have the same *priority in the local agenda.* Considering the 11 cities of this comparative research, safety is priority number one for the local authority in Birmingham, Leeds and Rotterdam, while in Antwerp, Bari, Gera, Glasgow, Heerlen and The Hague safety is important but does not represent the highest priority. Finally, in Helsinki and Prague safety has a modest role on the local political agenda.

The level of priority that safety has on the local agendas of cities depends on several factors. Sometimes the national policy on safety plays an important role: when the central government is firmly committed – both politically and financially – to tackling crime it is easier for the city to adopt urban safety as a high priority. This is the case for British cities (Leeds, Birmingham and Glasgow) where, with the 1998 Crime and Disorder Act, the national government has forced large cities to adopt a specific safety policy. In other cases the stimulus comes directly from the city itself. In this case, too, different factors can play a role. For example, Rotterdam decided to set safety as the highest priority in order to improve its image. For the cities of Gera and Heerlen, safety is considered an important tool in stimulating economic development.

The *main aim of the local safety policy* appears to be similar in most cities but it can be formulated in different ways (see Table 14.6). Sometimes it is very generic – 'to create a safer environment' (Glasgow) – and sometimes it is very specific – 'to achieve a 25 per cent reduction in crime and antisocial behaviour by 2006' (The Hague). Nevertheless three issues can be considered to be embedded in every urban safety policy: 1) the reduction in crime; 2) the reduction of fear of crime; and 3) the improvement of urban attractiveness. These three elements – crime, perception of safety and urban attractiveness – are interconnected (see Figure 14.3). A reduction in crime activities generates a safer living environment which makes the area more attractive: a more attractive environment can contribute to reducing crime (i.e. investments in an area can attract inhabitants and businesses and this can reduce criminal activity). Both of them, of course, have a direct influence in the perception of safety.

Table 14.6 Aim and priority of safety policy on the local agenda of the case studies

City	Aim of the safety policy	Priority on the local agenda
Antwerp	To enhance the feeling of safety	High
Bari	To simultaneously fight the highest levels and the basis of organized crime	High
Birmingham	To reduce crime and fear of crime	Highest
Gera	No official policy	High
Glasgow	To create a safer environment	High
Heerlen	To create a safer living environment and more social cohesion	High
Helsinki	No official policy	Modest
Leeds	To achieve sustainable reduction in crime and disorder and address the fear of crime	Highest
Prague	To enhance the feelings of safety in the city	Modest
Rotterdam	To enhance security in the neighbourhoods and in the city as a whole	Highest
The Hague	To achieve a 25% reduction in crime and antisocial behaviour by 2006	High

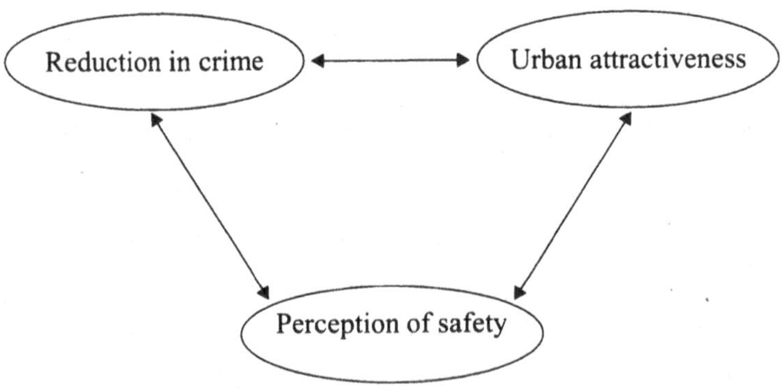

Figure 14.3 Main elements of the local safety policy

When talking about local safety policy an important issue concerns the *role of the national government* in designing urban safety. While the largest part of the preventive measures is usually elaborated at local level most of the repressive measures are decided – directly or indirectly – by the central state. In all cities presented in this comparative study the police force and the Public Prosecutor are under the umbrella of the national government. The sphere of influence of the national government can range from a very high to a very low level of intervention.

The country with the highest level of intervention of the national government is probably the United Kingdom, where cities must implement the policy decided at central level. This kind of strong influence from the central government has both positive and negative aspects. The fact that such political commitment is usually followed by a sound financial commitment must be positive since it leads to more resources being available for cities to invest in the implementation of the safety policy. Less positive is the fact that the specific local situation of each city cannot usually be properly addressed at the central level.

In The Netherlands the national government plays a less intensive role. Urban safety is, for the large part, decided by local authorities who select the approach to be used and the target to be met.

A comparison among the *financial resources* available for the urban safety policies in the 11 cities object of this study is not possible, mainly because many actors are involved in urban safety and it is therefore not possible to build one single budget for it. Even taking into consideration the city's administration in isolation, it is usually very difficult to determine the amount of financial resources dedicated to safety.

Communication plays a fundamental role in urban safety. In fact communication has a huge influence on people's perception of safety. In this context each city has to face the problem that 'bad news sell better than good news'. A city will rarely find help in the media to communicate the good results that a policy could have achieved: on the contrary, the media will often publish (and sometimes overrreact to) negative episodes concerning public safety. A consequence of this is that the impact of a single piece of negative news on people's perception of safety is far more important and long-lasting than the impact of good news.

In the research we noticed that cities have different communication strategies. The Hague, for example, put security matters high on the city's political priority list. However, they chose to give extra internal attention to the topic but little public attention. Their strategy is not to worry citizens unnecessarily by increasing public attention. On the other hand, the city of Rotterdam chose to give considerable public attention to the topic. Their strategy is to tell the citizens that the city council is working intensively on the topic.

Which communication strategy is chosen depends on the city council's safety policy objectives. In a city where security perception appears relatively good, much political attention for safety could accentuate the negative aspects of urban security and therefore have a negative impact on security perceptions of the residents. Conversely, in a city where security perception seems to be relatively bad, extra political attention could give the necessary signal that the problem is being tackled, presumably improving people's perceptions of safety. Alternatively, this policy could also have the perverse effect of worsening the perception of safety. In fact a great amount of political attention on safety can be perceived as a signal that the city must be very unsafe.

For local governments it is therefore important to be aware of the possible effects the degree of public attention given to safety policy.

14.5.2 Analysis of Local Safety Policies

As we stated in the theoretical chapter, there are endogenous and exogenous causes for urban insecurity. For the cities involved in this comparative study, examples of endogenous causes of insecurity are low quality of the built environment and unbalanced socio-economic structures. Immigration without integration, political revolution and terrorist attacks are typical exogenous causes of urban insecurity. Normally speaking, local authorities can intervene on endogenous causes, while exogenous causes are focus of national policies.

In order to tackle endogenous causes of urban insecurity local authorities can use three kinds of policies: repressive, preventive and proactive. *Repressive policies* are usually carried out by the police force in cooperation with the Public Prosecutor. They are usually meant to tackle the most urgent issues and therefore have a short-term orientation. For example, many British cities have problems of crime and disorder related to alcohol abuse and binge drinking. To face this problem, a specific measure known as 'Alcohol Restricted Area' (ARA), has been set up. Local police forces throughout the UK can apply for an area to be designated as an ARA if they believe this will help to prevent antisocial behaviour caused by alcohol. Inside an ARA the police have the power to require a person not to drink where they believe that this may lead to antisocial behaviour. The city of Birmingham, for example, has about 10 ARAs.

Local authorities are usually the main actors behind *preventive policies*. Preventive measures are meant to fight the root causes of urban crime and therefore have a long-term approach. The city of Bari faces the problem that many young people see organized crime as the socially winning model and this stimulates them to undertake a criminal career. To tackle this problem the city decided to intervene in the education system as early as primary school level. Members of the police and public prosecution are invited to primary schools to teach children that legality pays off better in the long-term than criminality does. Another example of preventive policy is the use of CCTV systems. For instance, in Glasgow there are more than 360 cameras located in the city centre and in some problematic suburbs. The CCTV system is used as a tool to help police prevent crime and disorder. Moreover, it is seen as a 'community resource' that helps to address wider social, economic, environmental and cultural issues. It is used, for example, to watch the behaviour of young children hanging around, to locate lost children in the city or as help point for citizens.

Proactive policies are meant to fight the causes of insecurity structurally and also have a long-term impact. Investments in the quality of the living environment, in education and in other socio-economic structures can reduce the probability of threats and crime occurring. Regeneration programmes aimed at the promotion of socio-economic redevelopment in deprived urban areas are examples of proactive policies. There are many examples of successful regeneration of deprived urban areas that led to a dramatic reduction in criminal activities: Bari Vecchia, Rotterdam Delfshaven, Heerlen and Helsinki show the potential effects of regeneration programmes – often (co)financed by the European Union – on urban safety.

Consequences of applying safety policies

Since safety has become a hot issue in many cities more political and financial attention is being given to the subject. This has led to a stricter *monitoring of safety policies*, especially when huge financial resources have been invested. The monitoring of safety policies is not easy and is very often based on data concerning objective safety. This stricter monitoring of safety policies can have two opposing effects. On the one hand it can lead to more efficiency. In fact the setting up of specific targets can help people involved in the implementation of the safety policy to operate more efficiently. On the other hand, since the monitoring is based on data about objective safety, the targets set can also mislead the work of the people involved since the objective data cannot (always) be trusted (see Section 14.3). Moreover, the monitoring system sometimes implies a certain level of bureaucracy that can be hard to 'digest' for people who have not had to deal with it before. In Leeds and The Hague some police officers complained about the fact that sometimes they have to spend more time writing reports than patrolling the streets.

A very important issue concerning the implementation of urban safety policies regards the risk of the '*dispersion effect*'. This is a typical consequence of some repressive measures with a strong spatial approach in particular. It consists of the fact that when crime and/or the root causes of it are tackled in one specific area and the action has proved to be successful, there is the possibility that crime has not disappeared but simply moved (totally or partially) to other areas. There are several examples of the dispersion effect. In Leeds the issue of rough sleepers suggests such a result: from 43 rough sleepers counted in the city centre in October 2002 only four were found in March 2004. Even if the policy adopted by the local authority can be considered successful, the possibility of the dispersal of rough sleepers to other areas of the city cannot be ignored. In Bari the huge regeneration programme undertaken with the URBAN Initiative transformed the old historical centre from one of the most dangerous areas of the city into an attractive and relatively safe one. Nevertheless, it has been noticed that the organized crime that was operating in the area is now operating in the neighbouring areas, which have become more dangerous than before. The hot-spot policy adopted by the city of The Hague – consisting in a special attention from the Police to specific delimitated areas – also carries the risk of dispersing criminal activity instead of fully eliminating it.

14.5.3 Actors Involved

There is a common trend in the implementation of urban safety policy in the cities which are the subjects of this study, namely the *multi-agency approach*. Cities have realized that safety is a very broad and multidisciplinary issue. In fact urban safety is no longer exclusively the concern of the police force and the Public Prosecutor: social organizations, educational institutions, the health sector and the private business community can all play an important role in the elaboration and implementation of the local safety policy. In some cities this multi-agency approach is institutionalized, as in British cities with the local Community Safety Partnerships. In other cities, such as

Bari and Helsinki, the multi-agency approach is still in its infancy. In these cases one or more authorities play the leading role. On the one hand this is necessary in order to promote such a multi-agency approach when the legal framework is missing; on the other hand, cooperation is not always smooth if one of the actors has a dominant position.

The role of the *private sector* in local safety is still relatively small. Normally speaking, safety has always been considered a public matter and therefore the public authority has always had the task of developing and implementing local safety policy. Nevertheless, it seems that the private sector can contribute to both the development and implementation of local safety policies. An example is the Business Improvement Districts in Birmingham, a partnership between the city and the private business sector whose aim is to create a cleaner and safer city centre. The Safer City Centre Initiative in Glasgow is another example. Its Radiolink project – a warning system that links more than 120 retailers in the city centre – is one of the urban safety projects in which the private sector is actively involved. The city of Antwerp has also adopted a similar scheme – the BIN (Buurt Informatie Netwerk, Neighbourhood Information Network) – to enhance security perception in some neighbourhoods. A BIN is a structural partnership between citizens and the local police in a specific area that aims to enhance the general security perception and to stimulate social control.

The framework of *organizing capacity* can be useful in the formulation and implementation of an urban safety policy. A clear vision has to be at the basis of the policy: sometimes this vision is translated into a very specific aim – as for The Hague, whose aim is to have a 25 per cent reduction in crime and antisocial behaviour by 2006 – and sometimes into a more general objective. The strategy that should implement the vision can have different forms ranging from very formal – as for British cities with the Crime and Disorder Reduction Strategy – to very informal – as for Bari where no official document can be found. In any case a clear and strong leadership is important for the implementation of the safety policy. The leadership is usually taken by the City Council (for Dutch cities) or by an ad hoc organization (such as the Community Safety Partnerships in UK). Sometimes a single person can have also a huge influence on urban safety policy, as is the case for Bari, where the newly-elected Mayor – a former judge – has completely changed the approach of the city towards tackling crime. It is usually relatively more easy to get political support for the safety policy – both from higher levels of government and from the business sector – rather than societal support. We have seen that communication plays a fundamental role in the relationsship with the local inhabitants, especially concerning the perception of safety. Finally the strong link between the socio-economic conditions of the city and the level of crime has to be highlighted. Normally speaking the level of crime is higher in deprived urban areas where the socio-economical problems are more acute.

14.5.4 Themes

Area-based safety problems (Rotterdam, The Hague, Glasgow, Helsinki, Antwerp)

Problems Within this research we have discussed two types of area-based policies:

within deprived areas (Rotterdam, The Hague, Helsinki and Antwerp) and within city centres (Glasgow). Regarding the deprived areas we can notice some similarities and differences. There was a clear accumulation of problems in the deprived – often post-war – areas of Rotterdam, The Hague and Antwerp. High percentages of unemployment, deterioration of the quality of the environment, illegal housing and slum landlords could be noticed there. Moreover, in these areas relatively many immigrants, young people and persons on social welfare could often be found. In these areas there appears to be very little social cohesion. In adition, we noticed that in these areas, many shops had had to close, often because of decreasing spending capacity. The main difference we found was the seriousness of the problems. In some areas the deterioration was clearly noticeable as, for instance, in Rotterdam-Spangen and The Hague-Laak; in others very few signs were noticeable, as in Helsinki Mellunkylä and Myllypuro. In Helsinki terms these areas can be considered deprived; in comparison with the other deprived European areas, however, this deprivation is hardly noticeable. Within city centres we noticed that there is often a strong accumulation of minor criminal activities. Because of the presence of many visitors and shoppers, these places are normally attractive 'markets' for petty criminals. Moreover, problems with drug trade and use are often concentrated within city centres.

Policy City centres are important in the determination of the image of an urban region. Thus when a city centre is considered as being unsafe, an entire urban region might be perceived as such. That is why several cities have paid considerable attention to limiting crime in the city centre. In almost all area-based policies we found physical restructuring processes. In some areas this is limited to renovation processes (for instance, in Helsinki Mellunkylä and Myllypuro), while in other urban neighbourhoods vast housing areas have been demolished and replaced with higher quality housing, often focused on middle- and high-income groups (for example, in The Hague-Laak). In quite a number of cases these restructuring processes were co-financed by European URBAN programmes (e.g. in Rotterdam, Antwerp and Helsinki). Rotterdam even has a pilot project for giving away houses, with the strict financial obligation to renovate their exteriors.

In some cities we noticed policies to reduce the nuisance of prostitution. In Antwerp the prostitution zone has been limited from a relatively large area to a few streets only and Rotterdam is closing its prostitution zone, which generated a lot of nuisance in the surrounding area.

Most of the case study cities use CCTV monitoring to assist the police particularly in their work to reduce (fear of) crime. Glasgow, for instance, has a vast network of cameras and inhabitants are very content with these devices. Residents even ask for CCTV monitoring in their environment, because it helps to reduce their fear of crime. Some cities set up a kind of zero tolerance policy in order to reduce high levels of crime. Rotterdam is a good example in this respect. This city combines zero tolerance with a person-oriented approach.

Drugs and insecurity (Heerlen, Leeds and partly Rotterdam)

Problems Problems related to drugs and insecurity are often spatially concentrated within a certain area, for example in the city centre (Leeds), around the central station (Heerlen), or specific parts of a district (Delfshaven in Rotterdam). Drug-related and safety problems come mainly in form of public use of drugs and trade in or trafficking of drugs. To what extent an addict causes nuisance also depends on the type of drugs being used. With the introduction of cocaine, for example, nuisance increased because of the highly aggressive reaction of users.

Drug use and trade also cause many side-effects. Drug addicts may group together in areas where drugs are sold or there may be drug premises causing nuisance and litter on the streets. Groups of people may be threatening to passers-by. As addicts need money for their daily 'fix', they start begging and stealing or breaking-in. Women may even end up in prostitution. Obviously, these side effects cause nuisance for the (local) residents and/or visitors. The consequences of these problems are a general deterioration in the quality of the neighbourhood and therefore a declining attractiveness of the area as a visiting or residential area. In addition, people's fear of crime is likely to increase and spatial behaviour may possibly be adapted. For example, in Heerlen the central station area and the adjacent city centre were being avoided by residents and visitors.

Policy Both the cities of Leeds and Heerlen have tried to tackle their drugs problems in partnerships between all organizations and institutions involved. Although Heerlen has more autonomy to formulate its own policy than Leeds does, they are both trying to combine repressive and preventive measures in order to diminish drug nuisance. In Leeds, two policing tools can be mentioned; the Drug Action Team (DAT) and the Drug Intervention Programme (formerly CJIP). The DAT is a multi-agency approach against drugs in specifically appointed (urban) areas. At first this method was focused on treatment of drug addicts. Recently, the emphasis changed more towards criminal justice. The Drug Intervention Programme is now more focused on 'stimulation' of drug addicts to get treatment. The approach is based on the well-known 'carrot-and-stick' method.

In Heerlen, Operatie Hartslag is considered to be successful in the fight against drug nuisance. This project is a multi-agency approach against drug nuisance as well. The aim was to 'diminish and be able to control drug nuisance in the city centre'. Measures taken were, among others, stronger repression by the police, further development of the supply of day- and night-care facilities for addicts and intensifying cooperation between local institutions.

Although the focus of Rotterdam was not on drugs and insecurity, this city has some approaches against drug nuisance worth mentioning. First, the *Alijda* approach: a collective action against drug dealers and runners. The police cooperate with the Tax Bureau, the Department of Social Affairs and Employment, the immigration authorities and the Building and Housing Supervision Department in order to address drug dealers and traffickers. In addition, the city decided to draw up a list of the 700 most troublesome drug users and dealers. This measure was taken as a consequence of the PGA (*Persoonsgebonden Aanpak* – person-oriented approach). A file is kept of every person on the list up listing all their offences, thus helping the police and public prosecution to carry out stricter repression.

Youth crime and insecurity (Bari, Birmingham and Gera)

Problems Some similarities and some differences emerge with regard to youth crime in the cities of Bari, Birmingham and Gera, where the issue is considered as top-priority in local safety policy.

A similar trend is that, compared to the past, youth crime is increasing, offenders are younger and the type of crimes committed is more serious. A second similarity concerns the strong relationship between school truancy and youth crime. It is clear that not being at school increases the opportunities to become involved with some kind of criminal activity. Finally it can be noticed that in most cases young people's involvement in crime is due to lack of alternatives. Whether because they do not have anywhere to go (i.e. to play) or because they have nothing else to do (i.e. a job) or just because there is no better social model than the one provided by crime, children begin to commit crime when they cannot find an alternative.

In Birmingham the problem of youth crime is not an area-based problem but it is spread all over the city. For the moment it is still a class problem: most of the young criminals belong to the poorest class of the population. Many young offenders are drug users and most of the crimes are committed against other young people. The phenomenon of bullying in particular is widespread in many of the city's schools. In Bari youth crime is a phenomenon that includes young people belonging to all social classes. In this city the biggest problem is the fact that organized crime is seen as the most attractive model; children are attracted by it and want to join. In addition the 'soft' legislation against young offenders plays a role in the use of young people for criminal activities: relatively they much less risk than adults do. In Gera youth crime represented 40 per cent of all crime in 2001: theft and criminal damage are the most committed by young people.

Policy While the characteristics of youth crime vary partially from one city to the other, the approach used by Bari, Birmingham and Gera to face this problem is quite similar. When dealing with youth crime the approach used is mostly based on preventive measures and work in partnership. The prevention of re-offending is especially central because it addresses the potential of young people who have committed a crime becoming persistent offenders.

Birmingham and Gera have set up specific ad hoc units focused on youth crime, the Youth Offending Service and the Youth Station respectively. Both have a partnership approach and involve the police force, the Public Prosecutor and other local authorities related to children operating in the fields of education, social services and health care. The main aim of these organizations is to prevent offending and re-offending by children and young people. This is pursued in several ways, but mainly by confronting young people with the consequences of their offending behaviour, by providing them new skills and opportunities and by giving help to their families.

These organizations seem to be quite effective: the only limit they have concerns the fact that they are only allowed to work with young people who have already committed a crime but cannot involve those children at risk of offending who have not yet done so.

Another important preventive measure is based on education, in which both Bari and Birmingham are investing. In Birmingham the most problematic schools have a permanent police officer (the Safer School Partnership Programme) who works in partnership with children, young people and school staff. The police officer has a proactive role and works with partners to reduce truancy and exclusion, victimization and antisocial behaviour within the school and its community. In Bari members of the police force and the Public Prosecutor's Office are invited to schools to spread the culture of legality and to help fighting the socially-winning model created by organized crime.

14.6 Urban Typology

Based on the general economic and demographic developments of the cities involved in this comparative study, we can distinguish four types of city. This characterization of the cities has been based on their most striking features and it is not an exclusive one. Cities could be part of more than one category. For our purposes, we chose to categorize the cases in only one of the four presented categories. We assume that, because of the particular dominant feature, some common statements can be made about the role of safety in such cities.

The four types of cities are (see Figure 14.4):

1 cities with reurbanizing centres: cities with strong and successful policies to catalyse the centre of the urban region (Birmingham, Leeds, Glasgow, Rotterdam);
2 declining cities: urban regions which are in decline because of a weak economic situation (Gera, Heerlen);
3 capital cities: cities with an accumulation of economic and administrative functions, attracting activities and inhabitants in a more or less natural way (Helsinki, Prague);
4 cities with strong internal welfare differences: cities that show wide welfare differences between urban parts – some flourish while others are confronted with a multitude of problems (Antwerp, Bari, The Hague)

14.6.1 Common Statements on the Urban Typology

Below we draw some general conclusions regarding the above-mentioned typology of cities. For each of the four city types distinguished we will make some general statements related to the three components of the SAP model presented in the theoretical framework: perceived **S**ecurity and the causes for insecurity, the urban

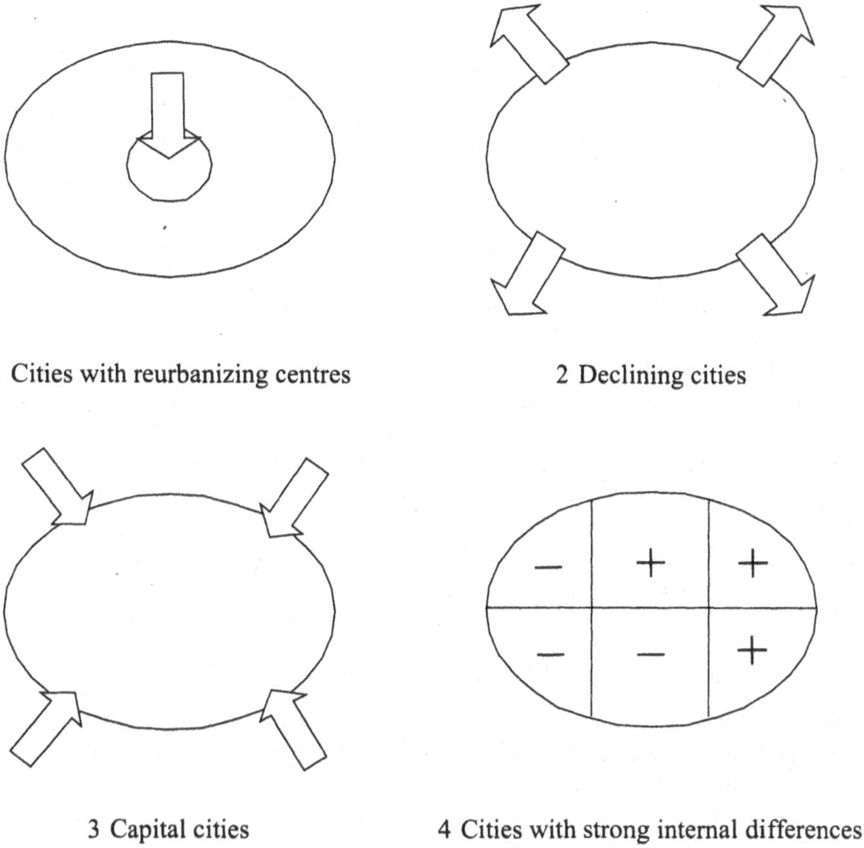

Figure 14.4 Urban typology

Attractiveness and spatial behaviour and the Policy reactions (see Figure 14.1). The statements are based on the outcomes of this comparative urban study and, therefore, particularly valid for the cases analysed. However, we expect them also to be useful for other European cities with similar characteristics.

Cities with reurbanizing centres

S In this kind of city, the city centres were perceived as being unsafe. Particularly around two decades ago, the outflow of activities and residents was clearly visible. There were relatively many vacated areas within the city centre and the number of residents was very low. Both actual and perceived safety has, however, improved simultaneously with the attraction of new economic activities and inhabitants. However, safety perceptions are sometimes negatively influenced because of rising tensions between some urban activities, particularly between housing and the night-time economy.

A New activities and residents have been attracted to the reurbanizing city centres. As a consequence, many more people can be found on the streets and the vibrancy of the city increases. An upward pattern can thus be noticed in these urban areas. Moreover, by mixing urban functions, the presence of people on the streets is spread over the day, which leads to safety being perceived as better during longer periods of the day. This can lead to the attraction of even more activities and residents.

P There are strong urban policies regarding the renaissance of the urban centre, accompanied by explicit policies to enhance perceived safety. The reurbanization was particularly stimulated by local investments in the attractiveness of the city centre. These investments were expected to contribute to attracting new activities and residents and to raising the competitiveness of the city centre in comparison with the suburbs. An important complementary policy aim is raising the perceived safety in the city centre. Two decades ago, the centres of these cities were (perceived as) unsafe. Things have changed for the better, but sometimes the bad image is quite persistent. Therefore relatively dramatic measures have sometimes to be taken to change this. Finally, because of, among other things, the rise of the shopping and tourist functions there is relatively much petty crime. Special policies have been developed to tackle this type of crime.

Declining cities

S Perceived insecurity in these cities is related to a lack of positive (economic) prospects. The economy of the cities involved is very weak and unemployment relatively high. For part of the population the prospects are bad; they probably will not find a job within the region. For some this lack of economic prospects will be mixed with feelings of increased insecurity. These feelings are also fed by the fact that people out-migrate to other cities, which leads to parts of the city becoming deserted. Such areas in particular will be perceived as being unsafe. In addition, some people without employment will begin informal activities to make a living. Such activities might also contribute to enhancing the feelings of insecurity.

A The fact that people leave the area might create a vicious circle. There will be less spending capacity and social cohesion will decrease. As a consequence, even more people will leave the neighbourhoods. Such areas might end up in a downward spiral. Shops have to close and economic and social structures deteriorate. Ultimately, entire social and economic fabrics might disappear.

P For the local authority, economic development is considered to be more important than investment in safety. The priority for the city is to attract new economic activities and to create more jobs, which will have a positive influence on attractiveness and safety perceptions as well. However, because of the bad economic local situation, there are often few funds available to develop a range of policies. Consequently, clear policy choices have to be made. Often there are no funds available for restructuring the least attractive areas. When no economic growth takes place, it appears that the tide can only be turned by support of non-local authorities.

Capital cities

S Although capital cities seem to be attractive for some types of (organized) crime, safety perceptions do not appear to be a major problem. An often-positive economic situation provides opportunities and prospects for most residents. On the one hand, the sound economic situation leads to fewer safety problems (most people have good economic prospects). There very few vacancies in houses and offices. Streets are busy with people and the fear of crime is relatively low. On the other hand, the relatively prosperous situation can lead to the attraction of people who also want to benefit in a more 'informal' way.

A The city is attractive for inhabitants and for economic activities. Perceived insecurity does not easily lead to changed location behaviour because of the relatively high economic attractiveness of the city. Thus, notwithstanding, the occurrence of some crime, most urban actors will not decide to move elsewhere.

P Safety policy does not have top priority because it is not perceived as being a large problem within the city in relation to changing spatial behaviour. There is more attention on setting up such a policy because of increasing competition between cities at the international level in attracting citizens and economic activities. An important point for attention within the safety policies of capital cities is tackling problems related to people operating in the informal sphere and to organized crime.

Cities with strong internal welfare differences

S There are large differences between neighbourhoods in many aspects: quality and maintenance of the built-up area, unemployment, education levels and skills, income and safety perceptions, etc. There is a high degree of perceived insecurity, particularly in the areas that are falling behind. This can lead to tensions, especially in border areas between high- and low-income areas. Because of the wide mutual differences it is difficult to come up with city-wide agreements on the seriousness of the safety problems. Consequently, predominantly in the low-income areas there will be a sense of urgency to tackle the safety problems. This will, however, be less the case in the high-income areas.

A There are large differences in general attractiveness. In the districts that have fallen behind, the maintenance of houses and public space, the supply of daily facilities, housing prices, etc. are lower. People who can afford to move will try to find a house within a more prosperous area. This might lead to segregation between people with low incomes and those with relatively high incomes. Moreover, it will imply a reduction of spending capacity within the declining districts with a consequent reduction in the number of shops and facilities. Such districts might thus end up in a vicious spiral.

P For the declining districts, tailor-made safety policies are necessary. Some areas need abundant attention regarding measures to tackle insecurity and some areas need them hardly at all. Often urban governments set up dramatic restructuring policies in the declining areas in order to attract more high-income inhabitants and stimulate gentrification processes. These processes should subsequently contribute to better safety perceptions.

14.7 Final Conclusions

Below we will explicitly answer the research questions of this study. This will ultimately lead to the answer to this research's central statement of the problem.

14.7.1 Can Statistics Reveal a (Significant) Change of Urban Safety and/or Urban Attractiveness?

Most cities do indeed show decreasing crime rates, thus it appears that safety situations are improving. However, the statistics are of very poor quality. It is not possible to compare the actual crime rate between European cities using the available data. According to this data, Helsinki should be the most unsafe city and Bari the safest one in this comparative study. This is clearly an implausible result and it can be confirmed by the Urban Audit whose data indicate that Helsinki is perceived as one of the safest European cities (see Figure 14.2).

What we noticed were changes regarding reported crime within cities. In the cities of Rotterdam, Antwerp, Glasgow, Leeds, Helsinki, Birmingham, Gera and Prague, actual crime has decreased in recent years, thus the actual safety had probably improved. These trend data are more reliable because, *inter alia*, the same crime definitions were used and no large differences in willingness to report were observed in the studied cities.

In addition, we observed striking differences between West and former East European cities. In the latter, before the fall of the Communist regimes crime rates were at a relatively low level, but they have increased relatively rapidly ever since.

14.7.2 Have Cities Become Less Safe (and Attractive) during the Last Few Decades, in the Perception of Citizens?

From the discussions held during our case study research, it appears that during the last decade in all cities of our study a larger proportion of the population feels unsafe. If cities are perceived as becoming less safe, this might lead to undesired spatial decisions for the cities involved. Some cities have figures on perceived safety from public surveys available – most show a worsening of safety perceptions. The enhanced fear of crime is thus an important factor for (local) governments to take into account.

14.7.3 Which Endogenous and Exogenous Factors with Respect to the Urban Region Involved Influence (the Changed Perception of) Urban Safety?

Important endogenous factors that influence security perceptions are actual crime, low maintenance and quality of the built environment, disasters, unbalanced socio-economic structures and lack of economic perspectives. People will perceive urban areas as unsafe more quickly when the quality of the built environment is relatively bad. When there is a lot of litter on the streets, broken windows, damaged cars, etc., people will feel less comfortable. Furthermore, people will be more inclined to add litter on the streets or to cause damage. Thus, processes of further deterioration can be expected in districts with a low quality of the built environment. This consequently will lead to a vicious circle and more feelings of insecurity.

In districts with unbalanced socio-economic structures there might be high welfare differences, high unemployment, vacant houses and closed shops. Some of the local inhabitants will be inclined to carry out informal activities to make a living. All such elements might contribute to more fear of crime.

In those cities with low economic growth prospects there will be relatively high unemployment. People will feel less comfortable if there are no reasonable possibilities of obtaining legal work. Again, some will develop informal activities.

Furthermore, fear of crime appears to be strongly influenced by the media (endogenous, sometimes exogenous). It is well known that bad news sells better than good news. But publishing only articles on safety-related incidents can generate a biased image of the real situation. Because of biased media attention, people might perceive some urban areas as relatively unsafe, while the reality might be different.

Exogenous factors which can lead to feelings of insecurity are immigration without integration, terrorist attacks, natural disasters and political revolutions. In some of the cities analysed there has been a large inflow of immigrants. When these immigrants do not speak the local language and/or are poorly educated, they will probably be badly integrated. This implies that they will not be able to find regular work, which often means that they have to work illegally. Moreover, they will not be able to communicate with a large part of the local population. This might contribute to more fear of crime among the rest of the local population, but also among these immigrants.

The occurrence of terrorist attacks in New York and Madrid has made other cities more alert to such hazards. Some cities might be earlier potential targets than others. This is particularly true for symbolic cities, such as capital cities or economically strong urban areas. Such cities, together with intelligence organizations, will have to develop adequate policies to anticipate possible incidents. In addition, it turns out that in the periods directly after terrorist incidents, there is more fear of crime among urban residents (in other cities as well). Thus it appears to be an important element to take into account in order to limit fear of crime.

Another exogenous factor for fear of crime appears to be political revolution. More concretely, the transition from communism to capitalism appeared to have a large influence on feelings of insecurity. In former Eastern European countries during the Communist era, police repression was more rigorous and there was hardly any media attention on crime. Both these elements changed during the 1990s: there was much less police repression and at the same time much more media attention on crime. Consequently, actual and perceived crime have risen dramatically in former Communist cities.

14.7.4 Which Factors Seem to Have the Largest Influence on Safety Perceptions?

Depending on the type of city, different factors might have a relatively large influence on fear of crime. Low quality of the built environment appears to play a role in all cities, but to a lesser extent in capital cities (they often are more able to invest in it continuously). Unbalanced socio-economic structures seem to be quite important in declining cities and cities with strong internal differences. Lack of economic prospects is particularly relevant for declining cities. Furthermore, terrorist attacks appear to be a particular threat for capital cities.

In general we can state that the quality and maintenance of the built environment and the media appear both to have a large influence on fear of crime in all cities. The quality of the built environment is a factor on which cities have large influence. But, of course, an important precondition is that cities have sufficient funds available to invest. This is, however, often an important bottleneck, particularly for cities in decline.

14.7.5 What are Economic, Social and Spatial Consequences of the Changed Perception of Urban Safety and Attractiveness?

Image and perception of safety appear to play a large role in location behaviour, because decisions taken by urban actors are rationally grounded (Simon, 1960). Perceived safety is more important than actual safety in this respect. If urban areas are *perceived* as unsafe and unattractive, this can have serious economic, social and spatial consequences, because fewer people and companies will be attracted to the districts involved. Moreover, such images seem to be quite persistent. When local situations change for the better, an image of unattractiveness and insecurity might remain. This implies that successful safety policies may need to be accompanied by sound communication policies.

There might be a correlation between safety perceptions and housing prices. This implies that worsening insecurity perceptions lead to lower housing prices and thus to a loss of welfare in the urban areas concerned. Moreover, complete economic and social infrastructures might disappear from certain areas when people start to out-migrate because of a lack of safety and/or attractiveness. The economic and social consequences of such a negative trend can thus be enormous.

It appears that when a city has a strong economic position within its relevant region, perceived insecurity will have less economic and social consequences. In such cases (for example, Prague or Bari), actors are not inclined to change their spatial behaviour, because of the strong economic attractiveness of the city involved and the lack of direct spatial alternatives. Contrarily, when there are several mutually competing cities within a certain region (for example, Rotterdam or The Hague), insecurity can have direct economic consequences. In such cases, actors have spatial-economic alternatives when they perceive certain areas as not being sufficiently safe. They might therefore decide to move their activities to areas which are perceived as being safer.

We have seen that following renovation activities some urban areas attract more tourists. Before these restructuring processes, the attractiveness and perceived insecurity were insufficient to attract visitors. These processes, which contributed to a decreased fear of crime, thus led to positive economic effects. We could also see that large tourist flows might attract petty criminals, which might be a nuisance, but (to a certain extent) not a reason for tourists to change their destination.

High fear of crime on public transport can imply a reduction in the number of users. Contrarily, improved perceived safety in public transport will normally lead to more users. This might subsequently have a relatively large impact on the economic well-being of cities, because it can contribute to less congestion, less pollution and better accessibility of city centres.

14.7.6 How Can the Changed Spatial Behaviour Affect Economic Development of Different Types of Urban Regions?

We have seen that there were clear reurbanization processes in some cities. In the centres of the reurbanizing cities, new (often higher-income) residents were attracted, which contributed to the economic vitality and to the perceived safety of these urban areas.

A clear outmigration of inhabitants was noticeable from some urban areas in the declining cities and the cities with strong internal differences. This frequently led to relatively high vacancy rates in the least attractive housing areas. Consequently, shops had to close down and general safety perceptions were decreasing.

We noticed that the location of new shops can play a positive role in the perceived safety of an urban area, because the more functioning shops there are, the more vibrant the areas involved will be. As a consequence, there will be more people on the street which often leads to less fear of crime. Moreover, vital shopping centres might lead to positive spread effects in the surroundings. New investments in these centres might stimulate private investors in the surroundings to invest in their buildings also. On the contrary, however, vacated shopping centres might have a negative effect on the vitality of an urban area. It might support a downward pattern in that neighbourhood.

The number of inhabitants appears to be quite important for the vitality of a city centre during evening and night hours. When this number is clearly insufficient, city centres might be perceived as quite unsafe during the evening and night and will show clearly differing identities during day and night. Thus a larger number of inhabitants will have a positive influence on the safety perceptions and – consequently – economic vitality of city centres (through, amongst other things, the attraction of complementary urban facilities).

We observed that night-life visitors to city centres have a double-edged effect. On the one hand, they will lead to more vibrancy during night hours, since more people on the city centre streets might lead to higher safety perceptions. On the other hand, some of the night-life visitors will generate nuisance, which can imply that some people will feel more unsafe.

14.7.7 What do Local Authorities do to Increase the Safety and Attractiveness within Urban Areas?

For three of the 11 cities in our research, fear of crime is considered to be so high that safety policies received top priority in local political agenda. Another six gave safety a high priority and another two a modest role within the local policy programme. Thus on average, safety policies played an important political role in our sample of cities.

In many cases the national government played an important stimulating role for local authorities to develop safety policies. In one case (Rotterdam), it was the city that had a relatively large influence on the national agenda for safety policies. Here, the local problems were perceived as beings so serious that new national laws were needed to tackle them appropriately.

In order to tackle safety problems in the city, local authorities have four different policy options: reactive or proactive and repressive or preventive policies. Usually the set of measures taken to tackle safety problems includes a combination of the above-mentioned options. Moreover, the implementation of these policies can have an approach that ranges between two extremes: the single-actor approach (police and judiciary only) and the multi-agency approach (i.e. the Community Safety Partnership in the British cities) (see Figure 14.5).

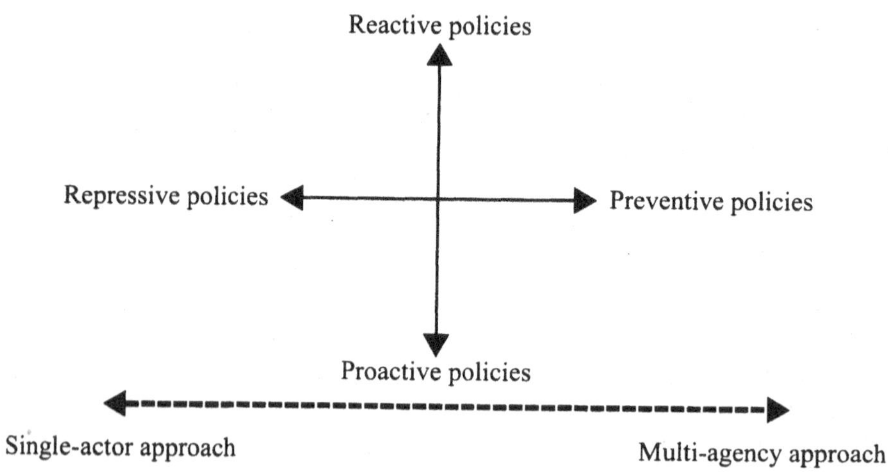

Figure 14.5 Policy options and approaches

It appears that *communication* plays a key role in safety policies. This is not very surprising after observing that fear of crime plays a more important role than actual crime in all investigated cities. Indeed, when the perception of the problem has more impact on the spatial behaviour of urban actors than the actual problem itself, sound communication can help to change this perception. A key question, of course, is what proper communication is. We observed that the media plays an important role by selecting predominantly bad news for publication. As a consequence, people receive a biased picture of the possible dangers of urban areas. In principle, local authorities cannot control the media. They have to set up smart strategies for disseminating safety-related news. Moreover, strategic choices have to be made about whether data on safety are to be published by public authorities. On the one hand, too much stress on safety data might lead to more fear of crime: on the other hand, too little attention on safety issues might lead to widespread feelings that the government does hardly anything for the better. The nature of good communication strategies thus depends on the specific local insecurity situations.

14.7.8 What Can be Learned from Successful Safety Projects in Cities?

This study aims to provide comparative material through which cities can learn from each other. It appears that there are many European cities with similar problems related to perceived insecurity. It is, however, of utmost importance to realize that the context under which these problems arise can differ. The distinction within city types can be considered as a categorization of different contexts. However, this is still a rough operation. Naturally, cities within a certain urban typology also show mutual differences, though these differences will be smaller than between cities of different types.

Though acknowledging contextual differences, cities can still learn much from each other. We should like to point particularly to the innovative safety policies discussed in which there is a multi-agency approach and in which a number of related policy fields are comprehensively involved. Some of them were discussed in this synthesis in the section on the three themes of the case studies (area-based approach, drugs and insecurity, youth crime and insecurity). In addition, we should like to point to the experiences of local crisis management in this study (Rotterdam and Prague). Furthermore, within each case study, several best practices of the cities involved in this study are discussed, which can be of particular interest for local authorities.

14.7.9 Our Central Problem Question Is: What is the Role of Security in Urban Development in the Twenty-first Century and What are the Local Policy Implications?

We noticed that in all cities fear of crime has increased, while in eight of the 11 cities analysed actual crime has decreased. Fear of crime is thus influenced by more factors than actual crime alone. Relevant factors in this respect are the role of the media, the quality and maintenance of the built environment, unbalanced socio-economic structures, disasters and terrorism. In many cities the role of the media and the quality and maintenance of the built environment appear to have a relatively large influence on the fear of crime.

In particular, for cities within polycentric regions (with more cities competing with each other), increasing fear of crime can lead to changed spatial behaviour of urban actors. A positive safety image appears to be important in this respect, especially because such an image can be quite persistent. Changing spatial behaviour can lead to serious economic consequences such as decreasing value of the built environment and the disappearance of economic and social infrastructures.

The quality and maintenance of the built environment can be influenced relatively easily by local authorities, although sometimes considerable financial funds are needed for the desired restructuring measures. For declining cities particularly it might be difficult to fund such measures. They therefore sometimes give priority to economic policies and are dependent on non-local authorities for additional funding. The role of the media is difficult to cope with. Cities need sophisticated communication strategies to limit the extensive influence of the media on fear of crime.

We could see that the more innovative safety policies are, the larger the number of actors involved and the broader the approach. With traditional safety policies, police and judiciary are the main agencies involved. The policies executed are particularly reactive. When safety policies become more innovative, they acquire a more proactive character. More agencies are involved and safety policies are embedded into wider policies that generally contribute to higher economic welfare and well-being. More innovative safety policies are thus embedded in such policies as education, employment, improving social cohesion, investing in quality of public space, etc.

Traditionally, national authorities have a large say in urban security matters, because police and judiciary are normally under the umbrella of the national government. National authorities can also stimulate a more innovative approach. They can demand that local authorities set up a multi-agency approach in exchange for allocating funds to the cities involved. Moreover, they can require a broad approach by demanding that safety policies are embedded within a larger range of related policies.

Local authorities can also influence national and even European policies. Local actors normally have abundant knowledge on specific problems and possible solutions for them. They can alone, or preferably together with other local authorities, try to influence national and even European legislation. We learned from the Rotterdam case within this research that specific local pressure on the national government can be effective in changing legislation in order to be able to execute innovative safety measures.

The more actors involved, the more complicated the organization of safety policies can become. A multi-agency approach therefore demands good organizing capacity from the local actors involved. In particular, an effective leadership is needed to achieve the aims envisaged. Lasting safety policies are normally embedded in such long-term policies as education and employment policies. However, there might be sometimes tensions between political short-term aims (to 'score within four years') and long-term needs (investing in social cohesion, education and employment). Within good and realistic strategies and subsequent safety policies, therefore, there is a good balance between short-term aims and the long-term needs of the city.

14.8 Recommendations

14.8.1 Focus on Fear of Crime

Fear of crime appears to have a larger influence on spatial behaviour than actual crime does. Fear of crime is influenced not only by actual crime but also by other factors such as the quality and maintenance of the built environment, fear of terrorism and the media. For governments it will be important to set up safety policies to reduce *fear* of crime. This implies that reducing *actual* crime alone will be insufficient – the use of more policy instruments will be necessary to achieve this aim. Locally, measures have to be taken to fight radicalism and terrorism. Furthermore, it will be crucial to continuously and structurally invest in the built environment, education, care, local economics, amongst other things. In short, *lasting* local safety policies always have to be embedded into broader policies which contribute to socio-economic welfare and well-being. Finally, it appears to be advisable to invest more in specific area-based programmes: several cases have showed good results with such a tailor-made approach.

14.8.2 Need for a Multi-agency Approach

It will be key to have a multi-agency approach for safety policies in order to achieve sustainable results. As stated, sustainable safety policies have to focus on a relatively broad range of policy topics varying from repressive and preventive actions, care, education and employment policies to physical restructuring policies. These and other policies already mentioned influence each other and are thus inter-related. Moreover, without supporting policies in education and employment, safety policies will probably not lead to lasting results. In order to carry out the above-mentioned policies, a relatively large number of actors has to be involved. In addition, further professionalization of crisis management at urban level is advisable, as risks of disasters and terrorism increase with, respectively, further densification of built-up areas and growth of extremism. Moreover, better crisis management might contribute to reducing the fear of crime and therefore enhance urban attractiveness. Furthermore, it will be increasingly important to involve residents in the design and implementation of safety policies. Their function to point out problems and their role in the maintenance and quality of the built environment are important in this respect. Another reason to involve residents is to increase their feelings of being able to contribute to safety and to influence the cities' policies, which is believed to have a positive effect on safety perceptions.

14.8.3 Need for a Good Balance between Repressive, Preventive and Proactive Policies

In some of the cities analysed, the safety problems are so serious that strong repressive policies are very urgent. These policies can substantially contribute to improving the fear of crime in the short term. In the middle term it will, however, be important to have good preventive policies, to avoid the occurrence of some of the actual crime. In the long term it will be key to set up strong proactive policies, to realize stronger and more vital urban districts with sufficient jobs available in the relevant region, with sufficient skilled and educated inhabitants and with an attractive and well-maintained built environment.

14.8.4 Need for Good Information and Statistics

In order to operate in an effective and efficient way, good information of urban districts is needed. It appears that there is a lack of specific knowledge about the actual problems in declining districts, such as the number and nature of problems related to illegal inhabitants, people with problems raising their children, residents with informal activities, etc. By connecting different available databases, better information becomes available to set up tailor-made policies. Moreover, it appears that statistics on security are not reliable. In particular, statistics on actual crime often do not reflect real situations. In addition, detailed figures on perceptions of residents regarding not only safety but also general aspects of living conditions are lacking in many cities as well. Improving these statistics is advisable in order to legitimate (new) safety policies more effectively.

The availability of facts and figures on crime rates and safety perceptions could improve not only at urban or national level but also at a European level. A first step has been made with the Urban Audit, but regarding crime records especially statistics are often not comparable. Improving this would help generate generalized knowledge of crime development in European cities. Moreover, it would help border regions to address crime collectively.

14.8.5 Need for Sound Communication Strategies

In order to reduce fear of crime in cities, sound communication strategies appear to be crucial. The contents of these strategies depend on the specific local circumstances. The most important element of these strategies will be how to communicate with the (local) media, because it turns out that the media has a large, often negative, influence on safety feelings. It will therefore be of utmost importance to set up sophisticated communication strategies contributing to less biased media information. Local authorities could also remind media organizations of their responsibility to deliver good, objective, and non-biased information to the population.

14.8.6 Future Research

This research has an explorative character. Much has been written on actual crime, fear of crime and spatial policies but comprehensive studies on the relationships between fear of crime, actual crime, spatial behaviour of urban actors and related urban policies were lacking. We have tried to fill in this gap. However, during the research process it became clear that many additional research questions should be addressed to compile a more complete picture on this topical subject. An example is the relation between fear of crime and spatial behaviour of urban actors. We could obtain some first clues, but more in-depth studies on this topic are needed to better understand this relationship and to better legitimate related urban policies. Furthermore, more research is advisable on how to improve the reliability and comparability of statistics on actual and perceived crime. Finally, it appears that there is a considerable need for more insight into the scale of the costs of insecurity in certain areas (for instance, not only the costs of police and judiciary, but also the costs of the disappearance of the economic and social fabric from urban districts) related to the cost and benefits of specific programmes to tackle (perceived) insecurity.

Note

1 URBACT is a Community Initiative Programme facilitating the networking between cities from all Member States. The efforts of URBACT concern mainly the cities and those areas, which are characterized by a raised level of unemployment, of delinquency and poverty and by the insufficient presence of public services (URBACT, 2005).

Discussion Partners

Rotterdam

2003

Ms B.M.P. van Bennekom, Commercial Director, RET (Municipal Public Transport)
Mr D. Berghuis, Commander of the Rotterdam Fire Brigade
Mr H.A. van Brummen, Public Prosecutor, Rotterdam
Ms R. De Faria, Alderman for Security Policy, City of Rotterdam
Mr T. Harreman, Chair, Daily Management, District of Delfshaven
Mr H. Hillenaar, Public Prosecution, Rotterdam
Mr M. de Langen, Director, Urban Renewal, Department of Urban Development and Housing (dS+V)
Mr L.P. Leijten, Director, Leijten and Partners, Project Developer
Mr A.J. Meijboom, Chief of Police, Rotterdam Rijnmond
Mr P. Mollema, Port of Rotterdam
Mr I. Opstelten, Mayor of Rotterdam
Mr T. Quadt, Security Programme Department, City of Rotterdam
Mr T. Reitsma, Security Programme Department, City of Rotterdam
Mr R. Sitton, Office Director, Woonbron Maasoevers, Delfshaven (Housing Corporation)
Mr H.C.G. Stam, Managing Director, City Development Corporation (OBR) Rotterdam
Mr P. Struijs, Executive Director, Vice-Chairman of the Executive Board, Port of Rotterdam
Mr R. Timmermans, Rotterdam Fire Brigade
Mr R. Ulrich, AEF, Andersson Effers Felix, Utrecht, Security Policy Consultant, City of Rotterdam
Mr E. In het Veld, Chief, Seaport Police Rotterdam
Mr S. de Vos, Chief, Department of Social Security, RET (Municipal Public Transport)
Mr A. van der Wal, Chair of Daily Management, Noord District, Chair of the United Rotterdam Districts

2005

Ms M. van den Anker, Alderman for Security Policy, City of Rotterdam
Mr C. Czyzewski, Director, Bouman GGZ

Mr R. Nagtegaal, Stadsmarinier (City Marine), District of Delfshaven
Mr T. Quadt, Director, Programmabureau Veilig
Mr P. Reehorst, Chief District Team Spangen, Police Rotterdam Rijnmond

Antwerp

Mr Lucien van Beylen, Chief of Police, Local Police Antwerp, Policy Support
Mr Wouter De Boever, Coordinator Project Line Spotting, Flemish public transport company De Lijn
Ms Karin Boden, Integration Department (DIA), City of Antwerp
Ms Anne-Mie van Cauwenberghe, Urban Consultation Drugs, Civil Affairs, City of Antwerp
Mr Dirk Grootjans, Alderman Integral Safety Care, City of Antwerp
Ms Kitty Haine, Urban Planner (involved in old prostitution zone), City of Antwerp
Mr Robert Janssens, Inspector, Local Police Antwerp (BIN networks)
Mr Sven Lommaert, Senior advisor staff, Local Police Antwerp
Mr T. Meeuws, Project Director Safety, City of Antwerp
Mr Mario van Poppel, Prevention Department, City of Antwerp
Ms Ineke Pycke, District Consultation (*Wijkoverleg*), City of Antwerp
Mr Gaspar Segers, Head Central Control and Premetro, Flemish public transport company 'De Lijn'
Mr Marc Smits, Chief staff Integral Safety Care, City of Antwerp
Mr Reinhard Stoop, Coordinator Urban Development Corporation Antwerp (SOMA)
Ms Prof. Ann Verhetsel, University Lecturer, Economic Geography, University of Antwerp
Mr Joris Wils, Prostitution Policy, Civil Affairs, City of Antwerp

Glasgow

Ms E. Borland, Director of Health Promotions, Greater Glasgow Health Board
Mr W. Caie, Inspector, Strathclyde Police
Mr J. Coleman, Councillor and Depute Leader, Glasgow City Council
Mr R. Dawson, City Centre Manager, Land Services
Ms A. Fehilly, Community Safety Initiative Officer, Development and Regeneration Services
Ms C.Higginson, Head of Primary Schools Education Services, Glasgow City Council
Mr W. Kean, Group Manager, Community Services, DRSA
Mr J. Kennedy, Manager, Clean Glasgow, Environmental Protective Services

Mr J. Legg, Head of Strategic, Planning and Management Services, Social Work Services
Mr B. Love, Principal Officer Community Safety, Community Services, DRS
Mr J. McLean, Assistant Chief Constable, Strathclyde Police
Mr P. Walker, Head of Service Community Services, Development and Regeneration Services
Mr R. Winter, Bailie, Chair of Community Safety Partnership Board

The Hague

Mr B. van Alphen, Municipal Councillor, City of The Hague
Mr B.J. Boelens, Municipal Councillor, City of The Hague
Mr W.J. Deetman, Mayor, City of The Hague
Mr H.P. van Essen, Director Haaglanden II, Haaglanden Police
Mr A. Hilhorst, Alderman Planning, Urban Development, and Housing, City of The Hague and District Alderman Laak
Ms C. Hofmans, Accountmanager Laak, City of The Hague
Mr M.J.J. van den Honert, Team Manager Haaglanden Zuid, Arrondissementsparket ('Court Region') The Hague, Public Proscecutor
Mr O. Hövel, Sectormanager, Urban Development Service (DSO)
Mr H. Jagersma, Managing Director, Urban Development Service (DSO)
Mr P.M. Jerphanion, Head District Team Noord, Haaglanden Police
Mr J.J. de Jong, District Coordinator Laak and Chairman Management Team Laak
Mr E. Kegge, Employee Social Management, Staedion Wonen (Housing Corporation)
Ms T. van Nimwegen, Municipal Councillor, City of The Hague
Mr L. Olffers, Chairman District Council Laak Centraal
Mr A.F. Oudt, Director General and Technical Services, The Hague University of Professional Education
Mr C. Rog, Urban Development Service (DSO)
Mr M. Vlaardingerbroek, Chairman Resident Platform Spoorwijk

Helsinki

Ms Chr. Huotari, Coordinator immigration affairs, Information Service for Immigrants
Ms P. Karkela-Aho, Public Prosecutor, Public Prosecution
Mr A. Khalil, Consultant, Information Service for Immigrants
Ms U. Korhonen-Wälmä, Project Manager, Lähio Projekti Helsinki
Mr M. Latvala, Emergency Planning Manager, City of Helsinki
Mr P. Lehtonen, Manager, Kontulan Kiinteistöt Oy (real estate company)
Ms A. Staffans, Chairman, Residents Association HELKA

Mr P. Tarvonen, District Officer, Eastern Police District Helsinki
Mr M. Tuominen, Researcher, City of Helsinki Urban Facts
Mr M. Virkamäki, Safety Consultant

Heerlen

Mr H. Don, Head Social Care, Salvation Army
Mr R. Kraaij, Coordinator Integral Safety, City of Heerlen
Mr W. Linssen, Unit Manager Interference Care (*bemoeizorg*), Mondriaan Zorggroep
Ms V. Malherbe, Project Leader *Operatie Hartslag*, City of Heerlen
Mr M. Mastenbroek, Head Public Order and Safety, City of Heerlen
Mr L. Noy, Chairman, Foundation for Citizens Council of City Centre Heerlen
Mr M. Roerink, District Chief Heerlen, Police Zuid-Limburg
Mr R. Schrijvers, Manager Addicts Care, Mondriaan Zorggroep
Mr W. Smits, Public Prosecutor, Public Prosecution Maastricht
Mr Z. Teunissen, Criminologist, City of Heerlen
Mr H. Theelen, City Centre Manager, Foundation for City Centre Management Heerlen

Leeds

Mr J. Bade, Director of Victoria Quarter Shopping Mall
Mr J. Birkenshaw, Crime Reduction Manager
Ms L. Hackett, Street Users Coordinator
Mr D. Henson, Police Inspector, CJIP Leeds
Mr K. Lawrance, Drug Action Team Leeds
Mr R. Matley, Leeds City Centre Management
Ms E. Minkin, Councillor, Leeds City Council
Mr P. Nicholson, Chief Superintendent West Yorkshire Police Authority
Ms S. Read, General Practioner
Ms S. Robinson, Chief Officer Leeds Community Safety
Mr K. Wakefield, Councillor and Chair of the City Council
Ms C. Young, Manager, Genesis

Bari

Mr Blonda, Prefect of Bari
Ms d'Elia, CRISI
Mr V. di Gennaro, Tecnopolis
Ms Lombardo, Substitute Public Prosecutor by the Court of Minors of Bari

Mr Magnini, Chief Superintendent
Ms Mazzei, Alderman for Social Services of Bari
Mr A. Pansini, City of Bari
Mr Scelsi, Public Prosecutor
Ms de Vanna, CRISI

Birmingham

Mr G. Butler, GOWM
Mr I. Coghill, Director Birmingham Community Safety Partnership
Mr G. Fletcher, Head of Birmingham Youth Offending Service
Ms N. Flyn, Safer School Partnership
Mr M. Kenwood, West Midlands Police
Mr K. Mitchell, Birmingham City Council
Mr N. Mushtaq, West Midlands Police
Ms J Olner, Team Manager West Youth Offending Team, Birmingham Youth Offending Service
Mr C. Spencer, Development and Prevention Manager, Birmingham Youth Offending Service
Ms Phyllis Walsh, Intensive Supervision and Surveillance Programme Manager

Gera

Ms Berthold, Head Kinderdorf SOS, Jugenhilfausschuss
Ms Engel, Social Worker/pedagogue, Frauen in Not
Mr Hein, Mayor, City of Gera
Mr Linsel, Police Officer, Youth Station
Mr Luckman, Netzwerk Courage
Mr Matz, Netzwerk Courage
Mr Quittenbaum, Chief Officer, Police District Gera-North
Ms Sauerbrei, District Manager Bieblach
Ms Scheel, Legal Youth Care Worker, Youth Station
Mr Schildt, Police Officer, Police District Gera
Mr Schneider, Weisser Ring
Mr Schulz, Public Prosecutor, Youth Station

Prague

Mr Petr Beran, Director Crisis Management Department
Ms Eva Brozova, Spokeswoman, Police of the Czech Republic

Ms Vilma Častová, Head of Public Relations Department, Metropolitan Police of the City of Prague

Mr Tomáš Čezník, Head of Prevention Department, Metropolitan Police of the City of Prague

Mr Jan Chodera, Councillor of Crime Prevention and Sports and physical Education

Ms Nina Janyšková, Head of the Drug Prevention Department, City of Prague

Mr Ludvík Klema, Deputy Commissioner, Metropolitan Police of the City of Prague

Mr Michal Kopecký, Assistant to the Mayor, City of Prague

Mr Vladimír Kotrouš, Chief Commissioner, Metropolitan Police of the City of Prague

Ms Alena Šindlerová, Head of the Crime Prevention Unit, City of Prague

Mr Jirí Šlapal, Head of Safety and Security System, Crisis Management Department

References

General

Bannister, J. and N. Fyfe (2001), 'Introduction: Fear and the City', *Urban Studies*. Vol. 38, Nos 5/6, pp. 807–14.

Becker, Gary S. (1968), 'Crime and Punishment: An Economic Approach', *Journal of Political Economy*, Vol. 76, pp. 169–217 (reprinted in Gary S. Becker and William M. Landes (eds) (1974), *Essays on the Economics of Crime and Punishment*, New York: NBER, pp. 1–54).

Body-Gendrot, S. (2001), 'The Politics of Urban Crime', *Urban Studies*, Vol. 38, Nos 5/6, pp. 915–28.

Castells, M. (1996), *The Rise of the Network Society. The Information Age: Economy, Society and Culture*, Vol. 1, Oxford: Blackwell Publishers.

CBS (2005), <http://www.cbs.nl>.

Cheshire, P.C. and D.G. Hay (1989), *Urban Problems in Western Europe*, London: Unwin Hyman.

Christopherson, S. (1994), 'Fortress City: Privatised Spaces, Consumer Citizenship', in A. Amin (ed.), *Post-Fordism: A Reader*, Oxford: Blackwell, pp. 409–27.

Crawford, A. (ed.) (2002), *Crime and Insecurity, The Governance of Safety in Europe*, Devon: Willan Publishing.

Cullen, J.B. and S.D. Levitt (1999), 'Crime, Urban Flight, and the Consequences for Cities', *Review of Economics and Statistics*, Vol. 81, No. 2, pp. 159–69.

Ehrlich, I. (1973), 'Participation in Illegitimate Activities: A Theoretical and Empirical Investigation', *Journal of Political Economy*, Vol. 81, No. 3, pp. 521–65.

Ellin, N. (1996), *Postmodern Urbanism*, Oxford: Blackwell.

Ellin, N. (1997), 'Shelter for the Storm of Form Follows Fear and Vice Versa', in N. Ellin (ed.), *Architecture of Fear*, New York: Princeton Architectural Press, pp. 15–45.

Ellin, N. (2001), 'Thresholds of Fear: Embracing the Urban Shadow', *Urban Studies*, Vol. 5, No. 6, pp. 869–84.

Engbersen, G. (1997), 'In de schaduw van morgen, Stedelijke marginaliteit in Nederland', Inaugural Lecture for the acceptance of the position of Professor in Social Sciences at Utrecht University, Amsterdam: Boom.

European Commission (2005), Urban Audit, <http://europa.eu.int/comm/regional_policy/urban2/urban/audit/src/getinv.html>, accessed April 2005.

Eurostat (2004), <http://europa.eu.int/comm/eurostat/>.

Financial Times, several articles.

Friedman, J. and G. Wolff (1982), 'World City Formation: An Agenda for Research and Action', *International Journal of Urban and Regional Research*, Vol. 6, pp. 309–44.

Hale, C. (1996), 'Fear of Crime: A Review of the Literature', *International Review of Victimology*,Vol. 4, pp. 79–150.

Kotler, P. (1984), *Marketing Management, Analysis, Planning and Control*, 5th edn, London: Prentice-Hall International.

Kragten, A.G. and M.H. Stekelenburg (2003), 'Kiezen voor Leefbaarheid', Report of a study tour to Philadelphia and New York, 17 April.

Leonard-Barton, D. (1982), *Swedish Entrepreneurs in Manufacturing and their Sources of Information*, MIT, Boston: Center for Policy Application.

Malmberg, A., O. Sölvell and I. Zander (1996), 'Spatial Clustering, Local Accumulation of Knowledge and Firm Competitiveness', *Geografiska Annaler 78b* (1992–2).

Maslow, A.H. (1943), 'A Theory of Human Motivation', *Psychological Review*, Vol. 50, pp. 370–96.

Meyer, David (1986), 'The World System of Cities: Relations between International Financial Metropolises and South American Cities', *Social Forces*, Vol. 64 (March), pp. 553–81.

Mitchell, W.J. (1999), 'Equitable Access to the Online World', in D.A. Schön, B. Sanyal, W.J. Mitchell (eds), *High Technology and Low-income Communities. Prospects for the Positive Use of Advanced Information Technology*, Cambridge, MA: MIT Press.

Myrdal, G. (1957), *Economic Theory and Underdeveloped Regions*, London: Duckworth.

O'Sullivan, A. (2000), *Urban Economics*, 4rth edn, Boston: McGraw Hill.

Oude Engberink, G. (2001), 'Excerpt: Urban Safety and Minorities: EX-O Project Contribution', Part II: Specific Themes.

Pain, R. (2001), 'Gender, Race, Age and Fear in the City', *Urban Studies*, Vol. 5, No. 6, pp. 899–914.

Pol, P.M.J. (2002), 'A Renaissance of Stations, Railways and Cities, Economic Effects, Development Strategies and Organisational Issues of European High-Speed-Train Stations', PhD dissertation, University of Delft.

Programmabureau Veilig (2004), 'Veiligheidsindex 2004. Meting van de veiligheid in Rotterdam', <http://www.rotterdam.nl/veilig>, accessed April 2005.

Prud'homme, R. (1994), *On the Economic Role of Cities: Cities and the New Global Economy*, Melbourne: Government of Australia and OECD.

Savitch, H. and G. Ardashev (2001), 'Does Terror Have an Urban Future?', *Urban Studies*, Vol. 38, No. 13, pp. 2515–33.

Savitch, H.V. (1996), 'Cities in the Global Era: A New Paradigm for the Next Millennium', in M.A. Cohen, A.B. Ruble, J.S. Tulchin and A.M. Garland (eds), *Preparing for the Urban Future: Global Pressures and Local Forces*, Washington DC: The Woodrow Wilson Center Press, pp. 39–65.

Schneider, R.H. and T. Kitchen (2002), *Planning For Crime Prevention, A Transatlantic Perspective*, London and New York: Routledge.

Simmons, J. and T. Dodd (2003), 'Crime in England and Wales 2002/03', Home Office Statistical Bulletin 07/03, London: Home Office.

Simon, H.A. (1960), *The New Science of Management Decision*, New York: Harper and Row.

Sociaal en Cultureel Planbureau (2002), *Zekere banden, Sociale Cohesie, leefbaarheid en veiligheid*, The Hague: Sociaal en Cultureel Planbureau.

Tatverdächtiger Stadt Gera (place and publisher unknown).

Thüringer Landesamt für Statistik (2004), <http://www.tls.thueringen.de> (accessed 26 April 2004).

URBACT (2005), 'Programme Initiative Communautaire', <http://www.urbact.org/srt/urbacten/flb/show?location.id:=1550>, accessed May 2005.

Urban Audit (2004), presentation Dijkstra at the Annual thematic meeting of Eurocities' Working Goup on Urban Research, Helsinki, 21 June.

Urban Audit (2004b), <http://www.urbanaudit.org>.

Van den Berg, L. (1987), *Urban Systems in a Dynamic Society*, Aldershot: Gower.

Van den Berg, L., E. Braun and J. van der Meer (1997), Metropolitan Organising Capacity, Experiences with Organising Major Projects in European Cities, Aldershot: Ashgate.

Van den Berg, L., E. Braun and A.H.J. Otgaar (2000), *City and Enterprise; Corporate Social Responsibility in European and US Cities*, Euricur Report (R2000–6).

Van den Berg, L., E. Braun and A.H.J. Otgaar (2002), *City and Enterprise: From Common Interests to Joint Initiatives*, Euricur Report.

Van den Berg, L., E. Braun and W. van Winden (2001), 'Growth Clusters in European Cities: An Integral Approach', *Urban Studies*, Vol. 38, No. 1, pp. 185–205.

Van den Berg, L., J. van der Meer and P.M.J. Pol (2003), *Social Challenges and Organising Capacity in Cities, Experiences in Eight European Cities*, Aldershot: Ashgate.

Vanderveen, G.N.G. (2001), 'Nederland vroeger veiliger?, De veranderde beleving van onveiligheid', *Justitiële Verkenningen*, Vol. 27, No. 1, 2001, pp. 34–48.

Van Velthoven, B. (1994), 'De economie van misdaad en straf, een overzicht en evaluatie van de literatuur', Research Memorandum 94–08, Rijks Universiteit Leiden.

Verhage, B. and W.H. Cunningham (1984), *Grondslagen van het Marketing Management*, Leiden/Antwerpen: Stenfert Kroese B.V.

Veröffentlichungen BKA, LKA zur PKS (2004), Altersstruktur junger.

Wilson, J.Q. and G.L. Kelling (1982), 'Broken Windows', *The Atlantic Monthly*, Vol. 211, March, pp. 29–38.

Rotterdam

CBS (2005), 'Statline', <http://statline.cbs.nl/StatWeb/start.asp?LA=nlandDM=SLNLandlp=Search/Search>, accessed April 2005.

COS (2005), 'Buurtinformatie Rotterdam Digitaal', <http://www.rotterdam.buurtmonitor.nl>, accessed April 2005.

DTZ (2005), 'Huurprijzen kantoren januari 2005', <http://www.dtz.nl>, accessed April 2005.

Ecorys Research and Consulting (2002), 'Ex-post evaluatie Urban-programma Rotterdam *Delfshaven*', Rotterdam, June.

Gemeente Rotterdam (2001a), 'Versterking veiligheid Rotterdam, Vijfjarenprogramma in samenwerking tussen stadsbestuur, deelgemeenten, stedelijke diensten, politie, justitie, bewoners, maatschappelijke organisaties en bedrijven', 18 October 2001 (behorend bij raadsstuk 2001–723).

Gemeente Rotterdam, Programma Veilig (2001b), Veiligheid in Rotterdam, Bouwstenen voor een vijfjarenprogramma (Verslag Conferentie Veiligheid en Veiligheidsbeleid Maart 2001.

Gemeente Rotterdam, Bestuursdienst (2002a), 'Veiligheidsindex Rotterdam, Voorjaar 2002', Rapportage Bevolkingsenquête januari 2002 en feitelijke criminaliteitsgegevens en stadsgegevens over 2001.

Gemeente Rotterdam, Bestuursdienst (2002b), 'Werken aan een veiliger Rotterdam, de aanpak, Het wijkveiligheidsactieprogramma', Rotterdam.

Gemeente Rotterdam (2002c), 'Collegeprogramma 2002–2006, Het nieuwe elan van Rotterdam … en zo gaan we het doen', Rotterdam.

Gemeente Rotterdam (2002d), 'Rotterdams Tij', No. 11, 5 December.

Gemeente Rotterdam (2002e), 'OBR en dS+V, 2002, Rotterdam', *Speciale uitgave Collegeprogramma 2002–2006*, Vol. 1, No. 3, November 2002.

Gemeente Rotterdam, Bestuurdsdienst Rotterdam (2004a), 'Persberichten veiligheid, <http://www.rotterdam.nl>, accessed April 2005.

Gemeente Rotterdam (2004b), *De staat van Rotterdam 2004*, Rotterdam: COS.

Gemeente Rotterdam (2005), 'Behaalde resultaten 2003', <http://www.rotterdam.nl>, accessed April 2005.

Havenbedrijf Rotterdam (2004), 'Haven in cijfers 2003', <http://www.portofrotterdam.com/abouttheport/images/29_56583.pdf>, accessed April 2005.

Kragten, A.G. and M.H. Stekelenburg (2003)), 'Kiezen voor Leefbaarheid', Report of a study tour to Philadelphia and New York, Rotterdam, 17 April 2003 and the accompanying letter of the Rotterdam participants dated 22 April 2003.

Littooij, A. et al. (1998), 'Victoria in Rotterdam', Artikel 174a, Gemeentewet in de Praktijk, Bestuursdienst Rotterdam, Rotterdam.

Ministerie van Justitie (2002), 'Criminaliteitsbeheersing, Investeren in een zichtbare overheid', <http://www.justitie.nl.

Politie Rotterdam-Rijnmond (2004), 'Algemeen Jaarverslag 2003', <http://www.politie-rijnmond.nl/Downloads/AlgemeenJaarverslag_2003.pdf>, accessed April 2005.

Programmabureau Veilig (2004), *Veiligheidsindex 2004. Meting van de veiligheid in Rotterdam*, Rotterdam: Programmabureau Veilig.

Programmabureau Veilig (2005), 'Veiligheidsindex 1999–2004', <http://www.rotterdamveilig.nl/Media/pdf/wijkanalyses/cijfers%202001-2004.pdf>, accessed May 2005.

SIDV, Steun en Informatiepunt Drugs en Veiligheid (2004), 'Drugshandel: Alijda-aanpak', <http://www.sidv.nl/roesmiddelen/lokaal_beleid/overlast/alijda.htm>, accessed April 2005.

Snippe, J., C. Hoogeveen and B. Bieleman (2000), *Drugshandel aangeslagen, Evaluatie Alijda-aanpak Rotterdam*, Rotterdam/Groningen: Stichting Intraval.

Van den Berg, L., J. van der Meer and P.M.J. Pol (2003), *Social Challenges and Organising Capacity in Cities, Experiences in Eight European Cities*, Aldershot: Ashgate.

Antwerp

Belgostat (2005), 'Belgostat Online', < http://www.nbb.be/belgostat>, accessed April 2005.

CDO (Centrum voor Duurzame Ontwikkeling, Universiteit Gent) and HABE (Departement Handelswetenschappen en Bestuurskunde, Hogeschool Gent) (2004), 'Stadsmonitor voor leefbare en duurzame Vlaamse steden. Editie Antwerpen', <http://www.thuisindestad.be/html/monitor/downloads2/rapporten/stadsmonitorantwerpen.pdf>, accessed May 2005.

CBO (Commissie Bestuurlijke Organisatie) (1997), *De organisatie van het Binnen-lands Bestuur in Vlaanderen*, Brussels: Ministerie van de Vlaamse Gemeenschap.

Danneels M. and K. Tuerlinckx (2002), 'De mening van premier Verhofstadt' (23 April 2002), <http://www.gva.be/dossiers/-c/crimiant.

de Brabander, G. (1998), 'National Urban Policies in Belgium', in L. van den Berg, E. Braun and J. van der Meer (eds), *National Urban Policies in the European Union, Responses to Urban Issues in the Fifteen Member States*, Aldershot: Ashgate.

de Brabander, G., L. Vervoort and F. Witlox (1996), *Metropolis, over mensen, steden en centen*, 3rd edn, Leuven: Kritak.

De Lijn (undated), *Voorstellingsnota Project Lijnspotting. Integrale aanpak van overlast op het openbaar vervoer in Antwerpen*, Antwerpen: Project Lijnspotting/Stad Antwerpen.

DSPA, databank sociale planning Antwerpen (2005), 'Toekomst in zicht', <http://www.dspa.be/new/#>, accessed April 2005.

European Commission (2000), *The Urban Audit 2000: Volumes 1 and 2*, Brussels: EC.

Kesteloot, C. (1996), 'Atlas van Achtergestelde Buurten in Vlaanderen en Brussel', Ministerie van de Vlaamse gemeenschap.

Lokale Politie Antwerpen (2004), in *Projecteenheid Veilig*, Stadsplan Veilig. Antwerpen: Stad Antwerpen.

Ministerie van de Vlaamse Gemeenschap (2000), 'Voortgangsrapport 1999', SIF-beleidsovereenkomst tussen de Vlaamse Gemeenschap en het gemeentebestuur en O.C.M.W. van Antwerpen.

Scoyer, C. (2002), 'Jaarrapport 2000–2001 Globaal Antwerpen', Bureau Misdaad-analyse, Dago-bestand 18 February 2002.

Stad Antwerpen, Burgerzaken en het Ontwikkelingsbedrijf (2000), 'Scheve stad in sterke positie', Sociaal-Economische Nota 2000.

Stad Antwerpen/OCMW Antwerpen (1999), 'Sociaal Impulsfonds Antwerpen', Evaluatierapport SIF 1997–1999, Antwerpen.

SODA (2004), *Beleidspland Drugs Antwerpen*, Antwerpen: Stad Antwerpen.

Van Baelen, J. (2002), 'Politiekorps presteert in moeilijke omstandigheden' (2 March 2002), <http://www.gva.be/dossiers/-c/crimiant.

Van den Berg, L. and P.M.J. Pol (1999), *The High-Speed-Train Station and Urban Revitalisation; A Comparative Analysis of Station Areas in the Cities of Amsterdam, Antwerp, Berlin, Cologne, Dortmund, Lille, Munich, Rotterdam and Utrecht*, Rotterdam: Euricur.

Van den Berg, L., E. Braun and J. van der Meer (1998), *National Urban Policies in the European Union, Responses to Urban Issues in the Fifteen Member States*, Aldershot: Ashgate.

Van den Berg, L., J. van der Meer and P.M.J. Pol (2003), *Social Challenges and Organising Capacity in Cities, Experiences in Eight European Cities*, Aldershot: Ashgate.

Van den Broeck, Tom (2002), 'Keeping Up Appearances?: A Community's Perspective on Community Policing and the Local Governance of Crime', *Policing: An International Journal of Police Strategies and Management*, Vol. 25 No. 1, pp. 169–89.

Van de Perre, P., A. Grobben and C. Matthijssens (2002), 'Alles wat u weten wil over de Antwerpse politie' (12 April 2002), <http://www.gva.be/dossiers/-c/crimiant.

Van Hove, E. and S. Nieuwinckel (1996), 'Het BOMboek, het verhaal van de buurtontwikkelingsmaatschappij Noordoost-Antwerpen', Offset Vandevelde.

Vzw Buurtinformatienetwerk (2003), *Het handboek voor de buurtinformatie-netwerken.*

Glasgow

BBC News (2002), 'UK's "Most Deprived" Areas Named', <http://news.bbc.co.uk/1/hi/uk/1826411.stm>, accessed 16 August 2004.

Community Services (undated(a)), *Community Safety Trends in Glasgow 2002–2003*, Glasgow: publisher unknown.

Community Services (undated(b)), *Action Progress to Date and Current Activity 2004–2005*, Glasgow; publisher unknown.

Community Services (undated(c)), *Glasgow Community Safety Partnership. Strategy 2004–2005. A Framework for Action*, Glasgow: publisher unknown.

Community Services (undated(d)), *Glasgow Restorative Justice Service. Summary of Practice*, Glasgow: publisher unknown.

Community Services (2004), *Briefing Note 2. Restorative Justice Service*, Glasgow: Community Services DRS.

Development and Regeneration Services (2004), 'Community Safety Structure' (not published).

General Register Office for Scotland (2004), Scotland's Census results, <http://www.scrol.gov.uk>, accessed on 24 May 2004.

Glasgow City Council (2001), 'CCTV and Monitoring Services within Glasgow City', Executive Summary. Service Review No. 96, Glasgow.

Glasgow City Council (2003), Draft Council Plan 2003–2007, Glasgow: Policy and Resources Committee.

Glasgow City Council (2004a), 'Regeneration – into a New Millennium', <http://www.glasgow.gov.uk/en/AboutGlasgow/History/Regeneration.htm>, accessed 9 August 2004.

Glasgow City Council (2004b), 'Post-war Housing', <http://www.glasgow.gov.uk/en/AboutGlasgow/History/Post+War+Housing.htm>, accessed 9 August 2004.

Glasgow City Council (2004c), 'Glasgow City Council', <http://www.glasgow.gov.uk/en/YourCouncil/>, accessed 9 August 2004.

Glasgow City Council (2004d), 'Cultural renaissance: the 1980s and 1990s ', <http://www.glasgow.gov.uk/en/AboutGlasgow/History/Cultural+Renaissance.htm>, accessed 16 August 2004.

Glasgow City Council (2004e), 'Community Safety Partnership', <http://www.glasgow.gov.uk/en/Residents/YourCommunity/CommunityServices/communitysafetypartnership.htm>, accessed June 2004.

Jacobs, J. (1961), *The Death and Life of Great American Cities*, New York: Vintage Books.

MORI (2003), 'Glasgow Panel Survey Autumn 2003', research study conducted for Glasgow City Council.

Pacione, M. (1995), *Glasgow. The Social-spatial Development of the City*, Chichester: Wiley.

Safer City Centre Initiative (2004), *Annual Report 2003/2004*, Glasgow: Safer City Centre Initiative.

Scottish Enterprise Glasgow (2002), 'Labour Market Profile', autumn/winter 2002/2003, place of publication unknown: Futureskills Scotland, <http://www.scottish-enterprise.com/publications/se_glasgow_profile.pdf>, accessed August 2004.

Scottish Enterprise Glasgow (2004a), <http://www.scottish-enterprise.com/glasgow>, accessed 24 May 2004.

Scottish Enterprise Glasgow (2004b), *Glasgow Economic Monitor*, Spring 2004, <http://www.glasgoweconomicfacts.com/documents/Spring2004EconomicMonitor.pdf>.

Scottish Executive (2003), 'News: Making City Centres Safer', <http://www.scotland.gov.uk>, accessed 25 April 2004.

Scottish Executive (2004), 'Scottish Indices of Deprivation 2003', <http://www.scotland.gov.uk/library5/social/soiddata.xls>, accessed 11 November 2004.

Strathclyde Police Authority (2004), *Public Performance Report 2003/2004*, Glasgow: Strathclyde Police Authority Administration Department.

The Hague

Andes-Tensing (2004), <http://www.kaart.nl/kaartnl/index.html>, accessed March 2004.

Buurtmonitor (2004), <http://www.buurtmonitor.nl>, accessed February 2004.

CBS (Centraal Bureau voor de Statistiek) (2004), 'Statline', <http://www.cbs.nl>, accessed February 2004.

Den Haag (1999), 'De Kracht van Den Haag', Haags plan GroteStedenBeleid, Periode 2000–2003/4.

Den Haag (2002a), *Stadsenquete Den Haag 2002*, Den Haag: facilitaire dienst/multimedia.

Den Haag (2002b), *Leefbaarheidsmonitor Den Haag 2002*, Gemeente Den Haag.

Den Haag (2002c), *Beleidsakkoord 2002–2006*, Gemeente Den Haag.

Den Haag (2002d), *Concept. Een veilig Den Haag. Een opdracht aan alle Hagenaar: een kwestie van aanpakken en doorzetten*, Gemeente Den Haag.

Den Haag (2003a), *Concept Stadsdeelplan Laak 2004–2005*, Gemeente Den Haag.

Den Haag (2003b), *Concept Werkplannen 2003. Wijkbureaus Gemeente Den Haag, Politie Haaglanden*, Gemeente Den Haag.

Den Haag (2004), <http://foto.denhaag.org/images/laakkwartier/laakkwartier-nu/index.htm>, accessed March 2004.

DSO (Dienst Stedelijke Ontwikkeling) (2003), *De Staat van Den Haag*, Gemeente Den Haag/Ecorys.

European Commission (2004), <http://europa.eu.int/abc/maps/index_nl.htm>, accessed March 2003.

Politie Haaglanden (1999), *Zinloos geweld, beter bekeken*, Den Haag.

Stadsgewest Haaglanden (2002), *Monitor Werkgelegenheid Haaglanden 2002*, The Hague.

Stadgewest Haaglanden (2004), <http://www.haaglanden.nl>, accessed March 2004.

Van den Berg, L. and A.P. Russo (2003), *The Student City*, Rotterdam: Euricur.

Van den Berg, L., A. Otgaar and E. Braun (2004), *Op weg naar een geïntegreerde aanpak van citymarketing*, Rotterdam: Euricur.

Helsinki

City of Helsinki (2002), 'The General Safety Strategy of the City of Helsinki', City Office of Helsinki, series of publications A 13/2002.

City of Helsinki (2003), *Helsingin kaupungin tilastollinen vuosikirja 2003* (*Statistical Yearbook of the City of Helsinki*) (in Finnish, partly translated), Helsinki: Urban Facts.

City of Helsinki (2004a), 'How Helsinki is governed', <http://www.hel.fi/english/decision/index.html>, accessed November 2004.

City of Helsinki (2004b), *City of Helsinki. Annual Report 2003*, Helsinki: F.G. Lönnberg Oy.

City of Helsinki (2004c), *Helsingin kaupungin tilastollinen vuosikirja 2003* (Statistical Yearbook of the City of Helsinki), Helsinki: Urban Facts.

Eronen, A., J. Luomala, E. Paju (2002), *Metron tuomat. Itähelsinkiläisten kokemuksia hyvinvoinnistaan* (in Finnish, partly translated), Helsinki: Sosiaali-jaterveysturvan keskusliitto ry.

GeoHive (2004), 'Map of Finland', <http://212.204.253.230/cd/link.php?xml=fiandxsl=xs4m>, accessed November 2004.

Haapanen, A. (2004), Vähemmän häätöjä, Helsingin kaupungin tietokeskus,Tutkim uskatsauksia (English summary).

Helsinki Lähiöprojekti (undated), 'Brochure of the Neighbourhood Project 2000–2003', <http://www.hel.fi/lahioprojekti/pdf/project2000-03.pdf>, accessed December 2004.

Helsinki Lähiöprojekti (2003), *Lähiöprojektin toimintakertormus 2002*, Helsinki: Lähiö Projekti.

Helsinki Lähiöprojekti (2004), *Lähiöprojektin toimintakertornus 2003*, Helsinki: Lähiö Projekti.

Heiskanen, M., O. Roivainen and M. Tuominen (2004), 'The Security of Helsinki Residents Under Study' (English translation), *Urban Facts*, 2/04, pp. 41–6.

Holstila, E. (2004), 'Finland: Towards Urban Innovation Policies', in L. van den Berg, E. Braun and J. van de Meer (eds), *National Urban Policies in the European Union*, Rotterdam: Euricur.

Mercer (2004), 'Overall Quality of Life Ranking', in *2003 Quality of Living Survey*, <http://www.mercerhr.com/summary.jhtml/dynamic/idContent/1128060>, accessed November 2004.

Schulman, H. and P. Bäcklund (2003), 'Summary and Conclusions Regarding the Neighbourhood Project', in Urban Facts, *Evaluation of the Neighbouring Project*, City of Helsinki Urban Facts Research Series 2003:4

Transport Plus (2004), 'Map of Helsinki Region', <http://www.isis-it.com/transplus/doc/images/helsinki_map.gif>, accessed November 2004.

Tuominen, M. (1999), 'Turvallinen Helsinki. Pahoinpitelyrikollisuus Helsingissä', in City of Helsinki Urban Research Series 1999:10, Helsinki: City of Helsinki Urban Facts.

Urban Facts (undated), *Helsinki 2003. Facts about Helsinki*, Helsinki: City of Helsinki Urban Facts.

Urban Facts (2003), *Statistical Yearbook of the City of Helsinki*, Jyväskylä: City of Helsinki Urban Facts.

Urban Facts (2004), *Helsinki Region Trends 2004*, Helsinki: City of Helsinki Urban Facts.

Urban Facts (2004a), 'The Regional Economy of Helsinki from a European Perspective', Helsinki City Urban Facts Office: Webpublications 2004/31.

Urban Facts (2004b), *Statistical Yearbook of the City of Helsinki 2003*, Helsinki City Urban Facts Office: Webpublications 2004/10.

Urban Helsinki-Vantaa (2003), 'Information Urban I and II Helsinki-Vantaa', <http://www.urbanfinland.info/Resource.phx/urban-eng/mainpage.htx>, accessed December 2004.

URBAN (undated), 'URBAN Community Initiative Programmes in Finland 1995–1999', <http://urban.decode.fi/dman/Document.phx/~public/Julkaisut/Urban+1+englanti?folderId=%7Epublic%2FJulkaisutandcmd=download>, accessed December 2004.

Van den Berg, L., E. Braun and J. van de Meer (1997), *Metropolitan Organising Capacity, Experiences with Organising Major Projects in European Cities*, Aldershot: Ashgate.

Van den Berg, L. and A. Russo (2004), 'The Case of Helsinki', in *The Student City. Strategic Planning for Student Communities in EU Cities*, Aldershot: Ashgate.

Van der Meer, L., W. van Winden and P. Woets (2004), 'E-Governance in Finland: the national context', in L. van der Meer, W. van Winden and P. Woets, *Social and Economic Impacts of ICTs on Selected Cities in North-Western Europe (MUTEIS)*, Rotterdam: Euricur.

Heerlen

Bureau Onderzoek en Statistiek (1997), 'Gemeente Heerlen', Indeling in stadsbuurten en subbuurten, volgens collegebesluit No. 02.34/1367, 2 september (bewerkt).

Bureau Onderzoek en Statistiek (2004a), 'Monitor Parkstad Limburg', <http://www.parkstad-limburg.nl/monitor>, accessed November 2004.

Bureau Onderzoek en Statistiek (2004b), *Centrummonitor Heerlen 2003*, Heerlen: gemeente Heerlen.

Bureau Onderzoek en Statistiek (2004c), *Kerncijfers Heerlen 2004*, Heerlen: gemeente Heerlen.

CBS (2004), 'Statline', <http://statline.cbs.nl>, accessed November 2004.

Clark, A.E. and A.J. Oswald (1994), 'Unhappiness and Unemployment', *Economic Journal*, Vol. 104, No. 424, pp. 648–59.

European Commission (2004), <http://europa.eu.int/abc/maps/index_nl.htm>, accessed March 2003.

Gemeente Heerlen (2001), *Operatie Hartslag. Naar een veilige en beheersbare binnenstad*, Heerlen: Gemeente Heerlen

Gemeente Heerlen (2002), *Meerjarig Bestuurlijk Programma 2002–2006. De kansen benut*, Heerlen: gemeente Heerlen.

Gemeente Heerlen (2004a), 'Heerlen nu', <http://www.heerlen.nl/Smartsite.dws?id=3201>, accessed November 2004.

Gemeente Heerlen (2004b), *Meerjaren OntwikkelingsProgramma GroteStedenBeleid Heerlen 2005–2009. 'Geloof in eigen kracht'*, Heerlen: Gemeente Heerlen.

Jacobs, J. (1961), *The Death and Life of Great American Cities*, New York: Vintage Books.

Parkstad Limburg (2004), <http://www.eurorue.net/parkstad-limburg/index.html>, accessed November 2004.

Parkstad Limburg (undated), *Beleidsplan 2004 Parkstad Limburg*, place of publication and publisher unknown.

Leeds

Chesterton (2003), 'Leeds Evening and Night-time Economy Study – Final report', October.

City Centre Leeds (2003), *The 5th Leeds City Centre Audit*.

Home Office (2004), *Home Office Departmental Annual Report 2004*, <http://www.homeoffice.gov.uk/documents/annual-report-0405/>.

Home Office Drugs Strategy Directorate (2002), *Updated Drug Strategy 2002*, Crown Copyright 2002.

Home Office Drugs Strategy Directorate (2003), 'Factsheet – Breaking the Link between Drugs and Crime', August, Crown Copyright 2003.

Home Office Statistical Bulletin (2003), *Crime in England and Wales 02/03*, London: Home Office Statistical Bulletin.

Leeds City Council (2003a), Census 2001: Local Base Statistics, Chapeltown Police Division.

Leeds City Council (2003b), 'Leeds Community Safety. Best Value Review Part 2 of: Community Safety (Burglary)', <http://www.leeds.gov.uk/council>.

Leeds City Council (2003c), Leeds Economy Handbook 2003, <http://www.leeds.gov.uk/council>.

Leeds Community Safety (undated), 'Trends in Several Crime Types in Leeds', unpublished.

Leeds Community Safety (2002), 'Leeds Crime and Disorder Audit 2001', available via <http://www.leedsinitiative.org/default.asp?initiativeIdentifier=200299_8388699.

Leeds Initiative (2003), 'Census 2001: Leeds – The Big Picture', available via <http://www.leedsinitiative.org/default.asp?metaPageTitle=Leeds+Initiative+Documents>.

Leeds Initiative (2004), <http://www.leedsinitiative.org>, accessed April 2004.

Leeds Initiative (undated), 'Leeds Community Safety Strategy 2002–2005', available via <http://www.leedsinitiative.org/default.asp?metaPageTitle=Leeds+Initiative+Documents>.

Leeds Initiative (undated (b)), 'Local Partnerships Making Things Happen', available via <http://www.leedsinitiative.org/default.asp?metaPageTitle=Leeds+Initiative+Documents>.

Lewis, M. (undated), 'The Urban Geography of Leeds', <http://www.brixworth.demon.co.uk/leeds/leeds3.htm>, accessed March 2004.

The Economist (2004), 'Britain: The New Blacks; Students and Cities', 22 May.
West Yorkshire Police Authority (2003), Policing Plan 2003–2004, < http://www.westyorkshire.police.uk/section-item.asp?sid=14&iid=342>.

Bari

DATAR (1989), *Les villes européennes*, Montpellier-Paris: La documentation française.
DATAR (2003), *Les villes européennes. Analyse comparative*, Montpellier-Paris: La documentation française.
Emmanuel, C. and F. Governa (1997), 'Il milieu urbano come fattore di differenziazione e di sviluppo', in G. de Matteis and P. Bonavero (eds), *Il sistema urbano italiano nello spazio unificato europeo*, Bologna: Il Mulino.
Equipe Paris – N. Cattan, D. Pumain, C. Rozenblat and T. Saint-Julien (1994), *Le système des villes européenne*, Paris: Antropos.
Il Sole 24 Ore (2004), 'Qualita' della vita – Dossier sull'Italia del 2004', 20 December.
Legambiente (2001), *Ecosistema Urbano 2001. Ottavo rapporto sulla Qualita' Ambientale dei Comuni Capoluogo.*
Occhiogrosso, F. (2002), *Il Malessere del Benessere*, Bari.
Palma, E. (2003), 'Dalla citta' competitiva alla citta' visionaria. Bari: un palcoscenico di eventi senza direzione strategica', doctoral thesis, University of Bari.
Palma, E., A.P. Russo and L. Scandale (2003), 'Il ruolo della cultura nella creazione di un milieu innovativo: il caso di Bari', in *Atti della XXIV Conferenza dell'Associazione Italiana di Scienze Regionali*, Perugia, 8–10 October.
URBAN I Initiative (2004), <http://www.europa.eu.int/comm/regional_policy/urban2/urban/initiative/programmes/bari.html>, accessed February 2004.
Van der Meer, A., W. van Winden and P. Woets (2004), *Urban ICT clusters and E-governance Policies in France, Germany, Italy and Spain*, Rotterdam: Euricur/MUTEIS.

Birmingham

Baber, A. (2001), 'The ICC, Birmingham: A Catalyst for Urban Renaissance', The University of Birmingham, Centre for Urban and Regional Studies.
Bhabra, S., E. Hill and D. Ghate (2004), 'Safer School Partnerships – National Evaluation of the Safer School Partnerships Programme', Youth Justice Board for England and Wales.
Birmingham City Centre Partnership (2004), 'BIDstalk', Business Improvement Districts Information Newsletter, May, Birmingham.
Birmingham City Council (2003), 'The 2001 Census of Population – General Report', Birmingham.

Birmingham Community Safety Partnership (2005), 'Crime and Disorder Audit – Summary for Consultation', Birmingham.

Birmingham Community Safety Partnership (2002a), 'Birmingham's Crime and Disorder Reduction Strategy 2002–2005', Birmingham.

Birmingham Community Safety Partnership (2002b), 'Birmingham's Crime and Disorder Audit 2002', Birmingham.

Birmingham Community Safety Partnership (2002c), 'A Review of Birmingham's Crime and Disorder Reduction Strategy 1999–2001', Birmingham.

Birmingham Community Safety Partnership (undated)', <http://www.birmingham-csp.org.uk>, accessed January and February 2005.

Birmingham Youth Offending Service (2004a), 'Birmingham Youth Offending Service Review 2003', Birmingham.

Birmingham Youth Offending Service (2004b), 'Birmingham Youth Offending Justice Plan', Birmingham.

Braun, E., A. Otgaar and L. van den Berg (2004), *Op weg naar een geïntegreerde aanpak van citymarketing*, Rotterdam: Euricur.

Home Office Statistical Bulletin (2003), *Crime in England and Wales 02/03*, London: Home Office Statistical Bulletin.

Moore, R. et al. (2004), 'ISSP – The Initial Report', Probation Studies Unit, Centre for Criminological Research, University of Oxford.

Gera

Auswertung Jugendstation Gera 2001–2002, publisher unknown.

Gera Stadt (2004), <http://www.gera.de>, accessed April 2004.

Landesamt Thüringen Polizeidirektion Gera (2004), 'Polizeiliche Kriminalstatistik 2003. Presseinformation', place of publication and publisher unknown.

Mayer, N. and P. Perrineau (1986), *Le front national à decouvert*, Paris: Presses de la foundation nationale de sciences politiques.

Polizei Direction Gera (2001), 'Modellprojekt Jugendstation', place of publication and publisher unknown.

Thüringer Landesamt für Statistik (2004), <http://www.tls.thueringen.de>, accessed April 2004.

Van den Berg, L., H. Arjen van Klink and J. van der Meer (1993), *Governing Metropolitan Regions*, Aldershot: Averbury.

Veröffentlichungen BKA, LKA zur PKS (2004), 'Haüfigkeitszahlen ausgewählter Städte', place of publication and publisher unknown.

Veröffentlichungen BKA, LKA zur PKS (2004), 'Altersstruktur junger Tatverdächtiger Stadt Gera', place of publication and publisher unknown.

Prague

City of Prague (2002), *Policy Statement of the Prague City Council for the 2002–2006 Term in Office*, Prague: City of Prague.

City of Prague (2003), 'Prague Facts and Figures', Prague: City of Prague.

City of Prague (2004), <http://www.praha-mesto.cz/fsts.aspx?l=2>, accessed December 2004.

City of Prague (undated(a)), 'Conception of Crime Prevention Prague during the Period 2005–2008', Working version, Draft #4.

City of Prague (undated(b)), Strategic Plan for Anti-Drug Policies City of Prague For the Period 2002–2006. Prague: City of Prague.

City of Prague (undated(c)), power-point presentation from the City of Prague.

CNB (2005), 'ARAD data series system', <http://wdb.cnb.cz/cnbeng/docs/ARADY/HTML/index_en>, accessed December 2004.

International Business and Research Services s.r.o. (1999), 'Hlavní město Praha. Analýza pocitu bezpečí – výtah' ('The Capital of Prague. Analysis of the Perceptions of Safety – abstract'), Prague: International Business and Research Services s.r.o.

International Cooperation = Šindlerová, A. (2004), 'International Cooperation', document related to international cooperation regarding crime prevention and security policies priorities of Czech Republic.

Landenweb (2004)', <http://www.landenweb.com/economic.cfm?LandID=162andTSJECHIË>, accessed December 2004.

Law §31, Parents' responsibility as set of rights and obligations (translated into English).

Meeting of the Working Group of Consultants (25 March 2003), Congress of Local Authorities of Europe. Local Policing in Europe, Worksheet crime statistics 2000/2001 collected by Police of the Czech Republic.

Městká Policie HL.M. Prahy (undated), *Metodické programy útvaru prevence* (*Methodical Programmes of the Department of Prevention*) (translated into English), Prague: Municipal Police of the City of Prague.

Neubacher, F., M. Walter, H. Válková and K. Krajewski (1999), 'Juvenile Delinquency in Central European Cities: A Comparison of Registration and Processing Structures in the 1990s', *European Journal on Criminal Policy and Research*, Vol. 7, pp. 533–58.

OECD (2004), 'OECD in figures 2004 edition. Statistics on the member countries', <http://213.253.134.29/oecd/pdfs/browseit/0104071E.PDF>, accessed December 2004.

Prague Information Service (2004), <http://www.pis.cz/a/page.php?menu_item=1100andpage_id=1255>, accessed December 2004.

Šindlerová, A. (2004), 'Zamyšlení nad statistickými čísly na konci r. 2004' (translated into English), *Ǻlánek – Strážník-statistika*.

Sykora, L. and Z. Cermak (1998), 'City Growth and Migration Patterns in the Context of 'Communist' and 'Transitory' Periods in Prague's Urban Development', *Espace, Populations, Societes 1998–3*, pp. 405–16.

Worldbank (2004), Gender Statistics Czech Republic, <http://devdata.worldbank.org/genderstats/genderRpt.asp?rpt=prfileandcte=CZE,Czech%20Republicandhm=home2>, accessed December 2004.

Index